What people are

Love Unle

Love Unleashed is unlike any other book I've read in the genre of transformation and spirituality. Beautifully written, it offers lived, profound wisdom teachings and grounded practices woven together with remarkable true and inspiring stories. Nicola Amadora is a modern-day mystic who's walked the path of liberation through extreme ups and downs, and she shares her depth and vulnerability. Her transmission blazes like a fire through the pages, making this book alive and captivating. An exceptional and essential read about how to turn around the tide in our lives and this shaken world by unleashing embodied love.
Marci Schimoff, #1 New York Times best-selling author of *Happy for No Reason*, and featured teacher in *The Secret*

Reading this book is an initiation, a way to wake up to both the challenges and the miracles that are on our path — not to smooth things, but to instill this deep love for our human existence. Nicola Amadora offers us a raw, radical, and at the same time beautiful and brilliant way of living on this planet. Read it and become part of the spiritual warriors so needed in this time of transition.
Ton van der Kroon, author of *The Return of the King*, and founder of Connecting the Dots

A passionate flame of love shines through stories and truths that uplift and offer direction for a life fulfilled. Her epic journey is deeply moving and inspiring. The book is a feast — a powerful transmission of love, fostering courage and compassion in a time when we need it the most.
Joy Taylor, best-selling author of *Inspired*, founder of A Soul Inspired Life

Our planet is on fire and we are caught between the flames that seek to consume us. Not unlike Nicola's real-life story of riding her horse and suddenly being surrounded by a forest fire on all sides with no break in sight, we are on a hero's and heroine's journey. This is a book for our times, written by a true master of the heart. In it, we are given the full compliment of her deep wisdom and courage to inspire and guide us through our own perilous journeys. She calls us to awaken and into action with the only tool for survival that we need: love unleashed.

Yamini Redewill, award-winning author of *The Joy of Uber Driving: A Wild Ride to Self-Love* and *The Natural Goddess*

This is a book from a wise woman, drawn from the depths of her life, calling those who read it to meet the love within their being. Nicola helps us to turn courageously towards all that arises in times of crisis and discover the truth that as old structures die, we can be reborn into love itself.

Sally Kempton, author of *Meditation for the Love of It* and *Awakening Shakti*

Nicola Amadora's marvelous book offers not only her lived experience but also the hard-won wisdom she has woven from that. Her voice is unique and real, grounded in and transmitted through the female body. The truths and practices in this book are exactly what the world needs right now, as we undergo the huge shift we are in the middle of. Nicola's work is essential for creating the new, where all people thrive and the earth is restored. The combination of personal narrative and transformational practices makes this book both an inspiration and an exceptional guide for all who are seeking to grow and contribute their own gifts.

Nancy Swischer, MA, MFA, author of *The Life That Woke Me Up Was My Own*, and founder of the Women's Club

Love Unleashed arrives as a much-needed guide from the deep heart to gracefully navigate through the storms we face in this turbulent time in our world. Through captivating stories, embodiment practices, and wisdom born of her own inner work and decades of clinical experience, Nicola offers us a trustworthy and deeply compassionate helping hand to live spiritual depth in our own homes, relationships, and in the streets of this world. Shimmering with the transmission we all need most, this book is a rare gem.

Miranda Macpherson, author of *The Way of Grace: The Transforming Power of Ego Relaxation* and *Boundless Love*

Love Unleashed

How to Rise in a World on the Edge

Love Unleashed

How to Rise in a World on the Edge

Nicola Amadora, PhD

BOOKS

Winchester, UK
Washington, USA

JOHN HUNT PUBLISHING

First published by O-Books, 2023
O-Books is an imprint of John Hunt Publishing Ltd., 3 East St., Alresford,
Hampshire SO24 9EE, UK
office@jhpbooks.com
www.johnhuntpublishing.com
www.o-books.com

For distributor details and how to order please visit the 'Ordering' section on our website.

ISBN: 978 1 80341 180 4
978 1 80341 181 1 (ebook)
Library of Congress Control Number: 2022933221

A CIP catalogue record for this book is available from the British Library.

Design: Lapiz Digital Services

Printed and bound by CPI Group (UK) Ltd, Croydon, CR0 4YY
Printed in North America by CPI GPS partners

The author of this book does not dispense medical advice or
prescribe the use of any technique as a form of treatment for
physical, emotional, or medical problems without the advice of a
physician, either directly or indirectly. The intent of the author
is only to offer information of a general nature to help you in
your quest for emotional and spiritual well-being. In the event
you use any of the information in this book for yourself, which is
your constitutional right, the author and the publisher assume no
responsibility for your actions.

We operate a distinctive and ethical publishing philosophy in
all areas of our business, from our global network of authors to
production and worldwide distribution.

Contents

Also by this Author

Nothing but Love: Poetry
ISBN: 978-1494382292

Prologue

I was sitting alone, silently, in the dark. In the stillness of a campsite at the base of Mt. Shasta, I watched the silver moon slowly rising in the starlit sky. In prayer I asked: "How can I be of greater service, given what is going on in our world?"

The soft summer wind was rustling through the branches of the large fir trees surrounding me. I was taken into a vibrant communion with the earth. Suddenly, I heard steps nearby, human or animal? I could not tell, until it was a few feet away. Only then did I recognize the beauty of a grown stag standing before me, looking deeply with his brown eyes into mine. Mesmerized we both gazed, it seemed for eternity. In that moment, I heard clear words: "Write for love and all of life." As if to confirm the message I had received, the stag approached and touched my shoulder with his soft snout. Then slowly he turned around and walked back into the woods. I reached for my shoulder, indeed I wasn't dreaming, the spot was moist. He had given me inspiration to write this book and a blessing, one, which I will never forget.

What makes such a timeless, natural connection possible?

What motivates people to wake up, to care for the environment, to put their lives on the line for those whose human rights don't even exist, to create works of magnificence and beauty, to heal the deepest wounds, to reach a hand across the chasm of different worlds to truly connect with another, and kiss this life as it is in wild abandon? Love. Here. In each of us, and alive between the stars.

At the core of each person I've met or worked with is a profound yearning for unconditional love. To feel alive, connected and present. To awaken and make a difference, especially now. The deepest pain is this agonizing disconnect from our innate nature, which leads to personal miseries and horrifying deeds in our world.

Do you experience yourself as a force of love and have the capacity to weather any kind of storm? Few do. We are all searching to find fulfillment, peace, happiness and liberation. But, we see suffering and wonder what in the world is going on, why the longing in the heart hasn't been answered. We continue to ravage the earth, practice racism and wage wars without end. Many people are deeply traumatized and cannot turn around. We have reached the edge.

How do we rise together in such a time as this? How do we sail through the tumultuous rapids and deal with all the issues at hand? What offers us wise solutions to turn our ship toward new shores, personally and globally?

Love's power certainly helped me; it is my beacon and refuge no matter what happens. It took me on an epic journey throughout my own life, a fire, which consumes me to this day. On this heartbreaking and wondrous path, I have discovered this fierce, tender love in the darkest trenches of human suffering, in relationships, in the company of animals, while walking with saints on mountaintops, and in the stillness, beyond duality, of my being.

I know firsthand that love's presence does turn lives around, and what is possible for our planet through its brilliance. Love is an answer for hungry people and a world on the edge.

I mean a love that's big enough to embrace your own excruciating pain and wild joy, your neighbor next door, the cat on the street. It is an unshakeable presence among the crashing waves, unleashing power in us to make a stand amidst adversity in our world, to courageously show up, even when challenging. And it is real love, which meets you in deep, murky waters and lifts you beyond the horizon of heaven to discover new possibilities and ways to live in kinship with nature and each other. Often we experience it with a warm touch, a kind word, the taste of chocolate, and a smile.

I am still amazed each day as the sun rises and sets across the ocean where I live. Standing in the shaft of light that pierces through the darkest clouds and sorrows, my soul meets yours across this page right now. True love leaves nothing and no one out. Not even you. It calls us all home and invites us to cultivate our soil for real love to grow. Spreading far and wide, inspiring lives and changing the world. One heart, one flame at a time.

This is the gift I am honored to share with you.

And what is in this book?

This book has come into your hands for a reason, and you might discover it while reading. Parts of the book will speak to you, some not. Take what resonates for you. Most importantly, let yourself experience what is alive, touching or inspiring for you. Often, when writing in front of my window overlooking the ocean, I got out of the way to allow love's own voice to speak through my hand.

I did not so much want to talk about presence and love in a philosophical or conceptual manner, as this has been done many times over, but rather write directly from flesh and blood experience by including true stories in each chapter. Most of the practices in the love in action sections have evolved and been applied during thirty years of working intimately with thousands of people from around the world. I have been deeply immersed in many spiritual traditions, and this book offers the red thread that underlies and unites them at the core. Therefore, feel free to replace "love" with any word that most closely reflects "the One with many and no names" for you.

The book is based on a nondual approach, where transcendence meets immanence in real life. It is about awakening, down-to-earth embodiment and actively engaging in the world, unleashing love's power right in this moment where we are. Fresh from the river of life it speaks in the voice of the feminine, weaving from the intimately personal, to consciously relating with each other, to nature, and the universal. I wanted this book to be a living expression from the source of wholeness, like a symphony with many parts and instruments, which, when played together, lifts the spirit, touches home and offers practical ways to turn our ship in real life action.

Because a living transmission flows through this book, it is written in a less common structure and each chapter stands on its own. Therefore I encourage you to directly experience and engage with it in your own way.

I am grateful for all the voices of people who have contributed to the making of this book. I can't count how many hands and hearts are present here, each woven into its very fabric. I wish to thank my faithful friends who stood beside me and endured me reading to them over and over. Thank you to each person who has contributed to the making of this book, without you it would never have come into fruition. I send a blessing to all the animals, the ocean and trees, for without you, this book would not be. I am especially thankful for my teachers who walk their talk. I bow to all of you. And my deepest surrender is toward the dharma, Her and the mystery, which cannot be put into words, but lives in all of us.

I invite you to dive in; the door is wide open. You are the long-awaited, welcomed, and honored guest at this feast of love.

May this book ignite the fire in our hearts and grow our capacity to rise in a world on the edge. May it touch, guide, lift and bless you. Maybe one day we will meet in person—or have we already? I am sure life will surprise us. Until then, ride the waves in life with unabashed love. Thank you for reading *Love Unleashed* and passing on the flame.

The magical story of this book

My friends often wondered where I had disappeared to for a whole year. During that time, I was living in a little beach rental in Santa Cruz, California, with paper, fountain pens and an old laptop computer. I talked on the street with folks from every kind of background and nationality and meditated often alone in nature. All for a book that I did not plan to write. Actually, it pushed itself quite ruthlessly into my life on a stormy winter solstice night, when I heard from within: "Write the book you have lived." I had been given that message before, but dismissed it since I had no time for such luxuries. But the pressure was on now. I could not argue anymore with such clear guidance from life.

Despite the doubts that tagged along of course, I committed myself wholeheartedly, to give my all without knowing the outcome. I felt as if I was walking barefoot faith on a shoestring across a chasm, when I did not focus on making a good income with my work, but instead turned toward writing. But love gave me the strength, forbearance and inspiration to take the leap.

It's not always easy to take a risk, to step into the unknown, but it is worthwhile when serving a greater cause than oneself.

At first, the book and I had a wondrous and innocent love affair (you know those?). I was filled with intense passion and could not speak about anything else, nor could I stop writing. I felt inspired and on fire, as if the book was starting a revolution and I had the honor to be the bearer of the flame. I listened intently to life, which was showing me which chapters to write and how. I was on a magical adventure, filled with energy and unstoppable enthusiasm. Then the book, without asking me, moved in and literally took over "my" entire life. The apartment was soon filled with recycled paper everywhere, lights got turned off well past midnight, and I was awakened somewhere between three and four in the morning with yet another important piece to write. Who was in charge here? Ridiculous you think? Oh, it only got worse.

I remember, when I stopped my car at a red light, and the words came rushing in unexpectedly, so I took a pen to write them on my arm and hand. And the cars behind me were honking. Soon enough I was writing on napkins, receipts, and business cards. Wherever I went, I found scraps of paper—even when it meant that I was writing on toilet paper.

Hey, what do you do, when it is urgent and the sound of truth is speaking to you?

At some point, I just had enough and needed a break. This was like a twenty-four-hour job of raising a baby. As if you can ever turn off the pulse of life (we can, but that is a surefire way to create suffering). Several times, I walked away. Shortly after, I would meet a friend who asked the question I did not want to answer: "How is the book coming along?" Next, I would run into my neighbor who started talking: "Hey, guess what happened..." Of course, it was exactly the message I needed for the chapter I was stuck on. The same day, the two-man crew who cleaned the beach every day waved me over only to say that they would like to buy the book once it was finished. Odd? No, encounters like these happened all the time. I just could not get away unnoticed. As if the universe wasn't clear enough, after several days of not writing, I actually got depressed, but could not deny the incessant howling from the pages piling up under the bed anymore: "Get me out. Write on."

As in any relationship, no matter how much you love one another, sometimes you just can't stand each other.

I would argue that I should focus on more important matters and that no one would read this book anyway. Books on instant success, money and sex have a bigger appeal for most folks. Who wants real love, when it can get uncomfortable and under your skin? When love teaches us to meet the pain and not run away, when it invites us to open in ways we have not previously and discover what wonders are before our eyes? When it asks us to center in our hearts, to become stewards of the earth and act for social change? My opinions did not matter, because love has its own agenda. What could I do, but to surrender? So, I picked up this spirited book again and galloped on, and magic was happening without any charms and manifestation spells. I was happy when the writing rolled and flowed. I had no idea where in the world I was going, what I would encounter, and when this would end. If ever!

After most of the book was written, I launched a fundraising campaign to be able to pay for publishing it. I felt awkward asking people for help. But, what to do? Could I stop with all the pages in my hands? During a meditation, I realized that I was not raising funds for me, but for a project that could benefit others. The book's voice spoke clearly: "I want other hearts involved. It's about love after all." It takes a village to raise a child, many hands to publish a book and all of us to turn the tide in our world. Receiving this message changed my attitude and gave me courage. My notorious independence and fear of rejection had been my companion throughout my life, but commitment gave me strength to move ahead anyway.

Love always pushes us to grow beyond our comfort zones. A solid commitment helps us to take chances and leap through fear.

Days after I had launched the campaign, I attended a birthday celebration. I was sitting at the table filled with cakes, sharing with a friend that I wasn't sure if I should continue on. One person overheard the story and inquired about my enterprise. Suddenly he placed several hundred dollars into my hands with words that hit me to the core: "I believe in you and want to support this book. It's important for others and the world too." He did not know me, had not seen the manuscript and did not do it to get anything. His genuine generosity gave me

7

a boost; and grateful, I ran with this precious miracle. We all need a hand at times, especially when we are down. And his act showed an important message of this book: Real love begins when we expect nothing in return.

Now, I am sitting here with all these pages into which I have poured my love. A baby is born with this book you are holding in your hands. With you the movement of love continues to grow. I feel inspired, passionate and vulnerable with my heart on my sleeve. It's like going naked into the world. But real love tends to bring us to the edge, and it always takes courage to jump off a cliff. Do I have a choice? Not really. This book is not mine, but life's own, written as an offering in benefit for all.

Love simply offers, and open hands receive the gift.
Enjoy your magical journey with this book.

I. For Life

1. The Power of Love

How to define what doesn't fit into a box?

Be still and let the noise of this world drop away. Lean into peace. The world spins fast, but no one is going anywhere. What humanity is seeking in frantic despair cannot be found on the wheel of time and changing form. Let the mind surrender into this moment now, don't visit yesterday or stray into tomorrow. Rest, for love is here. The answers you are seeking can only be found in silence below the waves. We meet where time stands still and peace is for eternity.

It is so simple, when the veils of illusion fall away, only truth remains. Come home, dear one, come home. You have wandered far away and feel lost in the jungle of this world and your own creation. Your pain of separation ends in love's embrace and in the presence that you are. The layers of conditioning are like thick fog, which make it hard for humans to see what is real. These delusions are acted upon by the way the earth is used and abused and in how people destroy each other.

Often, in the last hour, when the world is on the edge, humanity calls upon God, Goddess, consciousness, wisdom or love… it does not matter what name is used… to intervene, to help, to save, and to restore what is broken and lost. Yes, know this: we are here and aid you always. But to fully turn the tide in one's life and in the world, each human being is called to awaken from the trance of separation, to return to love and live from it. Only then the suffering of each being will truly come to an end and life will thrive for all of us.

— From an Angel at Castle Lake at Mt. Shasta, California

A wake-up bell is sounding across the world, urging us to rise up in response to our current situation. Environmental pollution, challenging social issues, corrupt politics, failing economic systems, a pandemic, relationship breakdowns, major psychological problems and traumas affect each of us. After all we are interconnected in the great web of life. How then do we unleash the power of love and turn the tide in our own lives and this world? How do we face what is going on and not get stuck in the ditches of denial and despair, or succumb to fear, but rather stand in unshakeable presence, speak power to truth, and live from love? What does it take to show up for real when a hurricane or fire takes our town, or when scared people turn toward hatred and shoot a gun?

What would happen if you and I stepped into the dawning of a new story for humanity, our earth and ourselves? We have the power, and in my eyes, it is as simple as it is profound.

We are called to turn toward what we are longing for and fear the most—love's tender and fierce power, residing within and all around us; pulsating in our very own hearts right now, alive in the purity of a spring gushing forth, the roar of the lioness, and in every human walking upon this earth. Love is our very nature, uniting us in the web of life. We may realize the truth, yes; indeed beyond all conditioning and duality is this vibrant presence, this river of love urging to be lived for real, through our steps and actions in life.

This is the labor then, to cultivate the soil for love to flourish, and to grow the capacity to show up awake, embodied and engaged in a world on the edge.

The voice of the feminine is rising at this time, as we have worshipped a transcended god far too long, a paradigm, which disregards form—our humanity and nature—and this has pushed us toward a dangerous, precarious edge. To turn the tide, we need to recognize that the sacred is immanent, alive as much in the cat, as in a budding flower, and in our friend. We are called to live and relate in ways that honor this simple truth of interconnectedness.

But, sometimes we don't feel love and connected, because love is not a changing emotion, it isn't created or made. It is the very ground of being, life itself. And through our action love becomes embodied here on earth.

It's easy to talk the talk, but it takes daring and wisdom to act. If we care about nature we stop using harmful toxins in our homes and tend to her. Similarly, if we cherish our mate, we may need to speak more kindly or listen more deeply. Love lived is a whole different shoe than love felt, conceptualized, or realized. It is made real through the way we treat our child, mate, the waitress in a café, the trees and animals, and ourselves. Ideas, knowledge and concepts about love can keep us stuck in the mind. We might have a nicely-drawn map of the dharma in our hand, but if we do not walk the actual journey through the mountains and valleys, then realization isn't actualized.

We do not know how bread is baked, until we learn the craft. We don't know how grape juice tastes, until we drink it. We can say that there is nothing to fear, but when you lose everything you hold dear, how do you walk through the shock and root in faith then? For love to be unleashed, we need to awaken to what's real, to embody it and learn to traverse any terrain in life, so we can offer the life-giving elixir for parched lands and hearts. And it is love itself, which guides us into deep connection and moves us into powerful, liberating action, for all hands on deck are needed now.

Often, when I awake in the mornings and look outside my window, I see sunlight piercing through the clouds, illuminating a golden pathway across the ocean. I hear the constant rhythm of the waves, seals barking, children laughing and playing at the beach; the doves sit happily at my windowsill. I can't help but smile in joy for the sheer beauty and gift of this precious life. Then I turn to the news of girls who are brutally used through sex trafficking, and people who go hungry in an affluent country. On the main beach where I usually collect trash, I meet

13

a pelican who cannot lift into flight across the blue sky, because oil covers its feathers. The pain pours like rain.

Can we allow our hearts to break open, be as wide as the world in answer to this? Are we willing to make a stand and let love take and live us, amidst the sheer beauty and horror, the pain and the joy, that exist in our world? Are you ready to turn and open to the gift you have inside, to let it unleash and actualize it step-by-step, for the sake of all?

Torch bearers and way showers in our world

So many people, you included, have been and are living love in the best way we know how. Ancient teachings of loving kindness and the way of the dharma from the Buddha, which the Dalai Lama embodies today, continue on in an unbroken lineage. "Love your neighbor as yourself," the message of Christ, is held in the hearts of millions after more than two thousand years. Mary Magdalene is rising from the ashes of the oppressed, liberating women into power and true life. Ammachi has meanwhile embraced about 40 million people from all over the world. Mother Teresa began with one penny in her pocket, and in the course of her life, fed thousands in need. Gandhi moved a whole nation to free itself from the shackles of oppression. Rosa Parks, an African-American woman, took a seat on a bus where only white people were allowed to sit. By this very act, she ignited a change that led toward ending segregation. Jane Goodall dedicated her efforts to understanding the chimpanzee and saved valuable wildlife habitat. My Native American friend and elder leads sweat lodges with great heart and respect. Walking Eagle has taken many young men under his wing, who follow his example to end addiction and to walk the "Beauty Way" instead. Bruno Groening lived in Germany during the time of war and by his mere presence he healed thousands who were severely wounded, including those who were lame and had lost their sight. Dedicated to love, his circle of friends has spread quietly around the world and to this day miraculous healings are reported every day. Greta Thunberg, the Swedish teenage climate change activist, sat every Friday alone in front of her school. At first they laughed at her and thought her weird, but then more and more children joined her. After six months children in over 100 countries went to the streets for an international school strike to wake us up to this urgent cause. I know a lovely elderly woman in Santa Cruz, who converted her laundry room into a shelter for rehabilitating hurt wild animals, simply because she cares. Seemingly small acts done from love have left a great impact. We may not notice, but they are happening every day. We have many unsung heroes and heroines in our world, who courageously live their love with their hands in small and big ways, making a difference for each of us. One newspaper couldn't cover all the stories, but it could inspire people to read one story each day.

What moves us to love?

Such an immense power love is, flowing through all cultures, rich or poor, educated or not, old or young, through all traditions and religions, from one hand to another, among the animals wild and tame alike, through the tiniest grain of sand to the magnificent redwood trees, from rivers to the ocean— love connects us as an endless stream. It breaks through any conditioning, as grass makes its way through cement. How could a tiny seedling under rock-hard asphalt sprout through concrete, with just a tender leaf, and grow into a mighty tree, whose roots upheave the entire sidewalk, turning into a nesting place for many creatures? What magnificent power love is— untamable, unstoppable, and uncontrollable—that grows even the tiniest flower through a wall.

What moves people to make a stand for the environment, for social justice, or to raise healthy children? What inspires one person to practice compassion, and another to act out with violence? What ignites one person to awaken and another to sleepwalk in ignorance through life?

I have met many inspirational people all around the world, who are not known in the hall of fame, but they have this in common—they are motivated by their hearts and a deeper calling. Willing to face their troubles and injustice in the world, they care and feel connected with the web of life. I have also encountered the worst expressions of humankind. What did they share? A disconnect from life, their own humanity and soul. I have seen and experienced tremendous suffering, when the most precious gift of life is buried, denied, violated, or dismissed, through the ways we relate and live.

It's never black and white, I know, we are all a mixed bag, but some dare to make a clear stand for love and others hide out. My grandfather stood up to the Nazis when they told him he wasn't allowed to feed the Jewish people in his restaurant. He fed them anyway. He was a mensch and inspired me. I had the good fortune to learn from those true teachers like Thich Nhat Hahn, who walk their talk, not perfectly, but sincerely and with integrity. They supported me to awaken, to be present and to live love more and more in my body, right smack in this world. I yearned for nothing else than that and it took me on a profoundly challenging and wonder-filled journey. I wanted to be part of the solution, when I realized the level of insanity and unnecessary suffering we had created on our planet and in our very own psyche. I found a deeper truth on this path, not just in myself, but everywhere.

The spark of benevolence is inherent in all humans, because love always makes a comeback, even in the face of horrendous evil, such as Hitler. We would have destroyed ourselves already entirely, if it weren't for this eternal flame shining in everyone. Even if buried, it is in every human. When kindled and strengthened it rises up and becomes a glorious fire illuminating the world.

The same genius and urge to love and be loved pulsates through every heart, in plants and animals, emanating through the body of every living being. It is through the intelligence of the heart that life communicates—natural, simple and true. If we are present and open we begin to understand, hear and speak a universal language, which is known deep down by all beings. No matter whom I have engaged with, whether with monks in the Himalayas, the indigenous people in the Amazon, people in the dark streets of Paris, or those who own expensive homes in California—each person has the same yearning and knowing inside. Everywhere is the one flame at the core of all creation, uniquely shining, unbroken in our being. Always here and present amidst the ever-changing tide of impermanence is Love itself.

I've experienced what is possible through love's ravishing power; my own life is one testimonial among many (read "The Choice" chapter). I know firsthand that love can heal what seems incurable, overcome insurmountable challenges, break chains of ignorance, reveal the truth no matter how uncomfortable, and bring forth transformation for good. You may have experienced how love shows up in times of disaster, how people gather, bridge the gap of cultural divisions and help one another. By accessing the source and engaging in the ways of love, I have witnessed how rifts and conflicts in relationships mend and people became more authentic and kinder, and how intense grief and trauma was healed by its balm. Even in our worst moments we are held in its hand. Love's brilliance creates awe-inspiring works of art, such as those of the Italian masters, timeless monuments to beauty. There are those stunning moments in sports, when the whole team is in the zone, playing in perfect union together. And when we are present, we might be captured in awe by seeing a butterfly, as if for the first time.

Love is alive. Its power breathes life into the womb, and if we align with it we birth forth new ways to contribute to the flourishing of all beings, whether through science, medicine, nature conservation, education, psychology, or a multitude of arenas. Love can ignite greatness in a person with such a unique expression as never seen before. What is most natural in all of life has unprecedented intelligence and power beyond comprehension.

As we turn to be present with our human experience and tap into the source to unleash its force, we are rising and turning the tide in our world, personally and globally. What story will emerge then through our hands and hearts, written by the ancient power of love itself? Can you imagine?

Cutting through delusion and rising in love

Yet, to this day, whilst we have flown to the moon, developed the most sophisticated technology and Internet connections, we know so very little about love's power and how to live in kinship with all of life. Love and power are the most used, misused and misunderstood words in our world. We feel afraid of raw power and love's embrace. Why? Because, they are greater than each of us, get under our skin and destroy our made-up delusions. But, can a wave turn away from the ocean? Only we do, and then, of course, we suffer.

We have hang-ups around power, which has been mistaken as exerting control, like the slave owners who used brute force to threaten people into submission by torturing and killing them. Just like love, true power is not driven by fear. Rather, it is rising directly from the very pulse of life. But, we clogged the pipes and stuffed up the river. We have heaped a mountain of conditions, concepts and projections upon the power of love. How many stories have you heard and do you carry around?

Usually, love solely relates to an intimate relationship. The Western world in particular is captured by this myth— Hollywood films promote the perfect romantic relationship, which is being chased as a way to ultimate happiness. As I am writing, I am listening to music from around the world. Funny, the songs about love have usually to do with one other person: either you have fallen in love and are high as a kite, or you have fallen out of it and are in a pit. That pretty much sums it up. And few know why you fall in and out of love. Plenty of roller coaster rides are taken in the name of so-called love. No wonder many people have confusion around intimate relationships and are at a loss of how to connect in healthy ways, whilst repeating old patterns passed down from generations before.

Love has become a popular word in the field of spirituality and sometimes gets confused with "woo-woo wishy-washy love and light," which serve to bypass, to cover up what is uncomfortable to face, leaving out what's dark, and using it as a convenient escape from the whole enchilada of life. However, love beholds everything, the good and the bad, nothing is left out. Sometimes love is lifted onto a holy throne of high ideals, which nobody can ever reach. With expectations of perfection, life then turns into an endless string of disappointments and everyone falls continuously short. The reality is that no one loves unconditionally all the time on this human plane. And love is not something outside of us to get. Can we let the world off the hook?

The veils before our eyes cause us to feel separate. We block love with all sorts of stuff from our vast collection of accumulated hurts, fears and judgment; hiding our gift, we live like the dead. Some people close off altogether, because they experienced hurt when being vulnerable. Love then appears as dangerous, to be avoided, manipulated and held at bay. Sometimes, we do not want anything to do with life and relationships anymore, or only a little bit (as long as we think we control it). We move to the sidelines, shut down, and feel isolated. If we think love is the culprit for our misery, we create barriers against our own light, to others and toward life itself. We build asphalt around our bodies, feelings and souls, some more sophisticated than others. And we wonder, where did happiness and connection go? We argue about how the world should be. Trying to fix others, ourselves and everything else, including life.

The problem is not life, is not the mud or the flower

It is a deep-seated sense of separation, and how we relate to our human conditioning and unhealed wounds. And through our actions we may perpetuate and accumulate more suffering. We cling to false beliefs and ignorance; each one of us has a different version. What is your favorite one?

Some people have given up on this "love thing" altogether, since life can be better controlled and no tears are shed anymore. But there is no laughter either. Most go bargain shopping to somehow get more love from somewhere or somebody; nobody knows where. Often we get stuck with the pretty wrappings that appear as if it's love, offering a "grand" promise and looking so very tempting, as an answer to satisfy all our hunger and thirst. As soon as you think you've got a taste securely in your pocket though, poof, it is gone. If we find a little, we want to keep it safe. But love cannot be contained, for the mystery is far too great to capture in a box. There is intense searching to find happiness and freedom from suffering, and a lot of fingers point in thousands of directions. It's easy to get lost in that. The messages we have received about what love supposedly is, where to find it and how to live it, are endless and can lead into a maze of delusion filled with ever increasing suffering.

What arises in you, as you read this word: Love? Resistance, agitation, a sense of bittersweet, fear, confusion, longing, curiosity...? What do you experience in your body, when you sense into what love is for you, beyond the preconceived ideas, stories, beliefs and opinions? Warmth, fear, hunger, a smile... Just be curious. What happens, when you become aware of your defenses and follow your yearning deeper into the heart?

What awaits you here? And how does love move you to act right where you are in this moment now?

Maybe the pressure of our situation on the planet, a personal crisis, a breakdown open us most acutely to what we have forgotten along the way. We don't need to suffer endlessly, we are capable of remembering what is true and who we really are, vaster than the made-up and false identifications. *It is you.* This flame in us yearns to shine, to live, to connect with others and to be of benefit in the world. Sometimes it emerges in little moments, when our heart is touched by a story, a beautiful sunrise. We fall into love's embrace, when we open amidst loss and grief, if we don't use suppression as an escape. It rises as we courageously cut through the lies and deceit. We experience genuine loving, when we are giving someone a hand or nurture an animal. We find it in the middle of a conflict, when we remember our shared humanity and shift toward vulnerability and understanding. We abide in love as we refrain from betraying a friend or ourselves. We see it when disaster strikes and folks help each other. Breathing our breath in this moment now. Here our loving presence emerges, shining through a crack in our minds, rising through us, in connection with each another.

Unleashing love from the ties that bind

We experience love in that place beyond time and space, where past, present and future are united in the now. How does love show up for you in this second? Even in the emptiness something is alive. Or, as you receive a wink from a person in the subway or hear the song of a bird as you walk by. Or sense the stream of life flowing through you, as you are breathing in and out. Let concepts pass by and discover anew, feel what you are feeling, tend to a hurt, experience the raw life energy of fury and let love touch, fill and move you. Let it unleash you in a way as never known before.

Love wants to ravish you, yes, the whole of you! Gentle and fierce, it pulls us inward toward our being, and then moves us out to act fresh and undefended, making a difference in our world. Take the tiniest step; it does not need to be a leap. Like reaching out to a stranger to bridge the gap of isolation; to share what's in your heart, whether joy or pain. Or roar truth as loudly as you like. Surprise yourself. And maybe love whispers into your ears tonight: "Sweetheart, I love you as you are." Maybe you feel stirred to get up and plant a tree, learn communication skills, meditate, dance ecstatically, stand up for what is just in your work, or go toward fulfilling a dream, buried far too long. If you listen, you know what is calling to be unleashed in you.

For love wants to be lived—passionately, deeply and utterly—no matter how imperfect it looks. Moment by precious moment we create the string of pearls on our walk in life. Every drop and kiss of true love matters. It ripples further than any of us might see and has a greater impact than we might realize. Just like drops of water cause the dam to break and unleash the river of life to flow free again.

Love braves us to break out from our prisons, to get into the muck of things. To not always conform to the status quo, to boldly take a stand in what is true. Stop trying to fit in, you are not made for a box. Let your arms wiggle out, then your feet, step out and leave the box of convenient familiarity behind. Stir the pot in our world, oh let love roam free. For all of our sakes, come forth.

Even if stuck in the deepest suffering, when all seems lost, a light reaches for you, maybe through a friend, or a spark ignites out of nowhere in your soul. Love's intelligence is far greater than our little minds can comprehend and forges a way we could not see previously. It moves us to step beyond the old story—into life itself. Unleashing us from the shackles and delusions into wild liberation. To live in kinship with all of life.

It only takes a yes. To connect with wild aliveness and this timeless moment now. To wholly immerse in love, between the good and the bad, as we allow our minds, bodies and hearts to soften and open. Just like the way a rosebud naturally surrenders into the warming light of sunshine and blossoms, we discover love is who we are.

The pathless path of love is not for the fainthearted though. We need grit as we will be humbled to the ground and raised up into more that we can be, over and over again. If you walk this road in life it takes everything and then some more; only to unleash the true gold, far greater than any riches of this world, residing at the root of the human spirit—in our own heart and pulsing vibrantly between you and me.

Be assured, love's power leads from the shore of suffering to liberation and knows the way, even through the most impossible situations. There is no savior this time. It is up to each of us. In this crucial time I believe it matters more than ever that we wake up, cultivate our abilities and unshackle our gift to the world, as if it is our final day. Do you hear the sound of the rising tide? This tidal wave cannot be stopped and is growing everyday with each person who jumps in. A power is unleashing and turning our lives and the world, in this extraordinary moment and these unprecedented times. Love. Here. Alive, in you and all of us right now.

Rising us into a new dawn to live the greatest love story ever told.

2. Voices of People and Saints

Hope for desperate times

If we want our species to survive, if we are to find the meaning of life, if we want to save the world and every sentient being that inhabits it, love is the one and only answer.
—Albert Einstein

It wasn't the popular kid on the block, or the woman who had the perfect looks and show. It wasn't the guy on top of the ladder. Nope, none of them lifted a finger, when it came down to the wire. It was Joe the clerk in a tiny supermarket, who stopped Martin from taking his life. It was the shy girl with the long black braids, who stood up for Barti, a young boy bullied daily for his missing arm. They beat her up and still she spoke up. I met beautiful Anne who cares for her disabled children and helps women in India to make a decent wage. And then there is Randi who plants trees for no gain other than for his love of the earth... These voices and stories of everyday heroines and heroes usually don't make it into the news. But I hear and see them in all sorts of places and people almost every single day. These are stories of human greatness, inspired actions, from a heart that beats in all of us.

Maybe that's what living awake and love is really about?

During the pregnancy of this book I engaged in interesting conversations with tech guys, a Harvard student, post office clerks, a wise homeless guy under the bridge, mothers and children, saints and strangers I met in different cities. First, I connected casually and then asked: "Does unconditional love matter to you? Do you believe it would help us in these crazy times?" Or, "What motivates you to care about the environment or social justice issues...?" Most people would reply eagerly, reveal stories and gems of truth in response. I felt like an undercover agent for love.

I've collected a long list of fascinating wisdom pearls from everyday folks you meet on the street, in a coffee shop or grocery store. A few of these I share here to inspire you. May these voices spark your flame and ignite hope. Hey, and next time you ride the underground train or walk into the office, remember there is more in people's hearts than the eyes behold. Just gotta dig a bit deeper, connect and open the magic door. Go find out for yourself!

Voices of Everyday People

Every time I saw Kakua, an elderly woman from Hawaii, who works as a cashier in an organic grocery store, she was singing. One day when it was my turn to be checked out, I asked her if she thought love mattered and why? Her spontaneous reply was this:

"True love can overcome everything. I know this from my own life. I could be bitter, given all the betrayals and horrors that happened for me. But instead I could heal, forgive, let go; and now I sing all day long at the checkout counter. It makes people smile, gives them a little joy on their way. So yeah, I know for sure that the power of love is the greatest. I am living proof of that!" She laughed and handed me my bill.

***

I met a group of women, social activists, full of energy and joy. They collect food and clothing for the homeless who sleep under the bridge, they created an emergency support system for the Muslim families, who are threatened by the latest wave of racism in the neighborhood, they walk into the streets at night to stop sex trafficking of young girls and they support each other. These diverse women have become best friends over the years and formed an unbreakable bond. What motivates them? All agreed when I asked: "The love for each other and our common cause is what unites and inspires us. It gives us a sense of power that we can change things, and a lot of energy even in the bleakest times."

***

Robert, a young manager of a large tech company, was angry when he came to his leadership session in my office. He shared passionately: "I am done with this sick greed approach, where employees are used like disposable objects. It's disgusting. I must do something!" He changed the workings in his company to a more relational and caring approach. What moved him to take action? He said: "I care. It's in my heart and I just got to act or else it drives me nuts." He made steady progress to change an inhumane system so commonly seen these days.

***

She has been involved in protecting wildlife habitat and endangered animals most of her adult life. For years she has been dealing with disappointments, challenges and hard-won but small victories, given the scope of destruction of the last remaining wilderness in our world. But, Anne has an infectious enthusiasm; she doesn't give up despite all odds. What keeps her going? She grins: "I love the wild and I will stand for it until my last breath." I am not surprised that she ignites a whole room of people when she walks in.

***

Doreen, a mother of two and counselor, said, "For me there is no greater task than learning to keep my heart open, not to become hardened with all that life throws at you and instead show up with love. This, in my eyes, is the greatest victory a human being can ever achieve. And I have a long way to go. But I am dedicated to that and I want to help others to open their hearts to love!" Her eyes sparkled as she spoke.

***

Alvin, a software engineer and entrepreneur, exuded passion that was inspiring: "I have this incredible solution developed, once it is up and running, it will make a fortune and change lives."

"What drives you, Alvin, to do this?" I looked at him curiously. "What gets me to work day and night is not the prospect of wealth, but my vision of what I can do with this money to lift up and support people who have fallen into the ditch. That's inspiring to me. I was once down in the pit myself and someone cared enough to give me a hand. I want to pass that forward to as many people as I possibly can." I have no doubt he is doing just that already.

***

Riding my bike along the footpath every day next to the bridge I kept seeing an elderly man living in his tent. One day I walked up to him to offer warm food and to ask what he thought about love. Given he was living in this miserable condition, thrown out into the streets in Oakland, California, just because he could no longer work and earn his keep, I expected he would brush me off. Instead he sincerely replied:

"My belief—and I do not mean religion—in a love greater than all this misery, holds me, even where I am. It keeps me alive and helps me not jump from the bridge over there." He smiled and thanked me for the food. After I walked away, he called out loudly, "Hey, lady, that act you did is the love I am speaking off. You see, it literally keeps me alive." He lifted a spoon with the veggies I had given him to his mouth and we laughed in mutual understanding and joy.

***

Michael is a friend and an activist for the ocean. He sailed on his little boat all the way from San Francisco to Tokyo, to raise awareness and to halt the ongoing brutal slaughter and drive-fishery capture of dolphins at the Cove. He has labored for years to protect the dolphins and whales from slaughter, imprisonment and cruelty. He formed a group and goes to marches, writes petitions and acts on behalf of many beings that have no voice in our world. Why has he given himself to a cause that is fraught with so many challenges and disappointments? He says: "It's my love for them. It's my heart and I will act on that until I die." A true Bodhisattva who inspires many.

***

Herman who lives in the Congo, one of the most troubled and darkest places in Africa, is an inspiration. My friends call him a saint. How does he do it, to help orphaned children who live on the streets, women who have been raped as a weapon of war and people who are starving? He and his family have endured many atrocities. But despite what he has gone through and the horrors he faces every day, Herman shows up inspired, kind, optimistic and keeps helping wherever his feet touch the ground. What gives him this strength? He says he believes in God and in a love that is greater than all the hardships. This is what offers him sustenance to shine a light, even in the worst hell.

The same Congolese man, Herman, came into the life of my friend Clare. She learned of his compassionate efforts to help the needy in his community. The fact that almost 6 million people had died and still do as a direct result of war and ongoing conflict for over twenty years, and that so few people knew or appeared to even care, broke Clare's heart and moved her into action. My friend said, "I couldn't know about all of this suffering and turn my back." Herman sent her a picture of deprived children, who were being held hostage by a hospital, that would not release them until their bills were paid by a family member. But by being poor, they could not pay. What would happen to the kids? Death. They could not rescue all of them, but one sweet child's face touched Clare, and she asked Herman to find Ishara's parents in the refugee camp. The family was incapable of taking care of their little boy. What to do? Clare and Herman decided to rent a house. And this is how Ishara House was born and it is now the happy home for many children, bursting at the seams, ready to expand. Gladly, Clare continues to give her heart, time, money and energy on a daily basis to this worthwhile labor of love. (You can find out more about Ishara House in the "Welcome Humanity" chapter.)

***

I couldn't help but ask John, who sat next to me on in a cramped airplane, after we had chatted for a bit, what matters to him most in life. Eagerly he replied: "It has changed over the years. I used to be pretty selfish and felt empty in life. I tried to get the hotter girl, the better car, the higher paying job, and the bigger muscles—all in an attempt to find satisfaction and happiness. I did not find it that way. But, ever since I am a father, I just care much more; I want my boys to be happy. And it may sound cliché, but I feel happy because I love. So, to love well is what matters for me more than anything now."

***

She was cheerfully folding laundry, and I asked Debbie, who works at a local laundromat in Santa Cruz, California, if she could transfer mine from the washer into the dryer when done. She replied that she would be happy to do it, but she had to keep an important appointment with a dog. "A dog?" I asked. "Yes, you see," she went on, "my other job is taking care of several dogs for people who do not have much time. And this particular dog is in a crate; he can't wait to get out, so I have to hurry and fetch him. My house is one big place for dogs; I tell them to be nice to each other when they come to me. For some reason the big and little doggies get the message and they get along with each other just fine. And I just love being with them."

She smiled with her sweet crinkled face and added, "You might think I am nuts, but for me dogs can feel, and hurt just as we do, and I believe they deserve the same respect and kindness as every living being does."

I knew her story would be included in this book, because I got the truth bumps (goose bumps on the skin) again. I asked her what was so special for her about taking care of dogs? She eagerly replied: "Their love is unconditional, their eyes and manners reflect it. They teach me everything about love. I give them food, water, affection and they completely love me up. I can just be myself with them. Then I go to the laundromat and shower people with it. Some people are very unhappy you see, stressed and angry when they have to wash their laundry here, so I don't react, but give them a treat of kindness instead. It usually works and they are lighter and cleaner, when they leave. I mean, loving is an everyday practice, and sure, it's not always easy for me. But it's important to walk the talk and not just talk it. The dogs keep me on the right trail."

Debbie added, "You know, Dog is God spelled backwards... I believe the animals are helping us to know what true love is." A human angel, who loves dogs and people, while working in a laundry shop. Who would have thought?

***

I was buying stamps in a rundown building of the postal service in Berkeley, California, and I asked Jessica, an African-American woman, employed as a post office clerk, "What is most important to you?" The dark-haired lady glanced up from her large pile of documents and letters to stamp, and although she looked surprised, she replied eagerly:

"I believe unconditional love is the most important thing in the world. If we had more we would not create all the wars and insane problems we are having now. So anything that helps us find and live it, I am all in!" she said with a big grin. Wisdom of the sages can be found in a local post office too. The clerks, who sat near to her, stopped their work for a few moments and engaged in a lively discussion with a long line of customers who also had important views on the matter to share. After all, it was close to Hanukkah and Christmas time, what better subject to explore!

***

I was stranded at the airport in France... I could not get the car I had rented; actually I couldn't get any car, because I had forgotten my passport at the house where I was staying. It was in the boonies—unreachable by public transportation and at least an hour away. I had no idea what to do, so I whispered a prayer, "Help!"

I'm sure I looked like a lost sheep, and Zak a guy who worked at the airport car rental place in Marseille approached me. He told me, "I have been stranded too in the past and people helped me. How about you take my own car and bring it back tomorrow?" Still speechless, I accepted his car keys and we exchanged phone numbers. This good man from Morocco did not know me, did not want anything from me, he only wanted to help. It was a fancy car too!

When I returned the next day we talked. I was so curious to find out what motivated him to hand his car to a stranger with such trust, and he replied, as if it was no big deal at all—that his prayer is to have the opportunity to help someone every day. He sure did. I guess two prayers were a match and divinely orchestrated in an airport parking lot. Thank you, Zak!

***

She was eighteen and we were completing therapy when she said, "I got horribly depressed, because my heart was shut down. I can't imagine anything more important than connecting to my spark. Because, honestly this is what healed me and brought me back to life! I am so grateful; I can't even put it into words you know. So of course, love matters, actually in my case—it saved my life."

***

Jennifer, a university professor from Massachusetts, and I, met as strangers on a bench at the pier near Big Sur. I had a hunch to talk with her and asked if she would like to hear the cover letter that I had written for the publisher of my book. Amazing how synchronicity works... She teaches writing and literature, and gave me helpful feedback about my writing. In the end she said that she really hoped that this book will reach many people and requested to buy it herself. She clearly was inspired, so I asked her, "Why do you feel that real love is important?"

"Because nothing is more valuable than that. Most people long to know love and their greatest regret is that they have not experienced and lived it. I have had moments and hold them like jewels in my heart. I want more of it!"

***

When I was camping on Mt. Shasta I met a lovely couple; they looked like they were madly in love and had just recently met. Turns out they had been married for eighteen years and they told me—when they saw the look of surprise on my face—that they were even more in love with each other now, than in the beginning. "That's unusual and beautiful," I remarked, curious about their story. After they invited me to use their warm solar shower in the woods (quite a treat after a week of camping), I asked them to share around the campfire. They could not stop talking, while I tried to keep up, writing with pen and paper in the darkness:

"In the beginning we recognized we had an undeniable soul connection. It was incredibly deep, like we are from the same planet. We understood each other in ways we can't even explain. When we were together all things felt possible for us. But we also encountered a time, when we could not stand each other. We fought and argued. A lot. But we could not for the world walk away from each other. We tried, but it was as if our souls were in agony then. Love's message was clear: we belong together and we had to just burn through the fire.

We had to let go of our expectations, to really get to know one another, break old habits and ways of being in relationship that did not serve, release codependency, become more authentic with each other. And we had to learn new ways of communicating. We committed to doing the work; we changed and learned a lot throughout the process. This labor was not easy, but so worth it. There is nothing more important, than to learn what it takes to truly relate and to love.

We both know that we are responsible for how much love we get to experience in our lives. And we have a lot to share these days." I could confirm that just by sitting next to this shining couple.

***

I was stuck with my car in the mountains on a side road. Landslides made it impossible to drive further, nor could I go back as a huge tree had fallen. I parked behind a long line of trapped cars and decided to take a walk, where I met people gathered together, laughing and talking. Cell phones didn't work, we did not know if we ever would get out to drive on. But we, the contractor, a sweet schoolgirl, the Google tech guy, a grandma and many others, made wonderful connections. After hours of waiting, my belly was loudly growling. Suddenly, a voice from a car called out to us, "Anyone hungry? I have plenty of vegetarian burritos to share!"

Maria, a Mexican lady with the biggest smile I have ever seen, had made them to sell to a restaurant, but wouldn't get there in time to deliver them. So she fed a whole crowd for free. What a gift—love in action. I was curious and wanted to hear what love meant to her. Her reply was immediate:

"You see, for me it's straightforward: If I love I am very happy and contented. Without it, I cannot see what's good and then I am miserable. Sharing the burritos made me happy. It's just sharing love. I think that is why we are here in the world. We just sometimes forget."

She was cleaning houses and making burritos to sell for a living, but I admit, this lady was happier than most I have met, and for all I know Maria inspired everyone she fed on that mountain road.

***

I love collecting real life stories of human kindness. I believe these acts change the world and maybe one day they will change corrupt governments too. And there are many more beings who have pearls to share with us.

Voices of the land, animals and saints

People are not the only ones love matters to and who will communicate it in their own voice, if we are willing to lend an ear. Often I sit down in silence at a creek, a tree, or in another holy place (such as temples or shrines), and listen to the voice of life itself. Once in the redwoods while the fires were burning up miles upon miles of forest and towns in California, I wondered why this power in nature does not help us with our environmental crisis? The answer arrived from the deva of the mountain landscape: *"If we shift it for humanity, you would learn nothing. You would create the same situation again and again. We are more than ready to work together with you, because through love we shift the tide."*

When I spend time alone in the wilderness animals come and speak to me. The dolphins, the mountain lioness and the last wild horses I met, all are alarmed about what we have created on the planet, and they suffer. Some are brave to come close to humans to help us wake up and change course. Like the whale mother who carried her dead baby for two weeks on her back, signaling in her grief that this baby could not live because the whales are starving to death due to overfishing and pollution of the oceans. Her picture went viral and people were moved to speak up and act. (In the "Loving Wild Earth" chapter are plenty of stories about communicating with plants and animals.)

The Voice of Mt. Shasta:

"The mere survival of humankind depends on realizing love. That which connects us, which breathes life through you and is alive in all forms of creation, is love. Without it humans cannot live and will go insane. Caught in delusions they create suffering. But when you remember whence you came from and who you truly are, peace and freedom are at hand and you create what is most beneficial for all. You live in harmony with life. There is no greater happiness found than in love itself."

35

The Voice of a Spring:

"Love is a life-giving pure stream — just like my waters that flow to nourish the meadows and animals that come here to drink. When you scoop my crystal clear water and drink, I fill every cell of yours with fresh, pure life. It is love that gives, and it is love, which moves this river. Only humans can forget the source and poison a river. Love itself is pure. Let this purity and joy fill you!"

I have had the good fortune to learn from great masters and had many encounters with saints in form or appearing as a strong, light-filled presence. You yourself may have experienced those moments, when you felt you were not alone, but were surrounded by a loving being walking beside you. Maybe you did not hear a voice, but received a sense, an insight or an image then. I happen to hear words, see and feel their presence. A few of these voices I share with you here. There are more who were keen to jump onto this page, but I'll leave room for you to add your own.

The Dalai Lama said: *"Without love and compassion humanity cannot survive."*

Thich Nhat Hahn, the great Zen master, speaks simply: *"We need to cultivate mindfulness and understanding for true love to grow."*

Amma, whose religion is love, and who tirelessly serves those who suffer, speaks this simple message over and over again: *"Love is your true nature. Within you there is a wellspring of love. Tap that source in the right way and it will fill your life. Love makes everything alive and conscious. Love is the answer to all sorrows in life."*

Babaji, an ancient master of the Himalayans who is known to have attained enlightenment and who after his transition still appears to people in sacred places at will, unexpectedly appeared on the mountain to me and spoke: *"I am everywhere and nowhere. For those of pure heart I appear. You ask about love.*

The question has only one answer: Open and surrender and you experience it, you are lifted into nirvana. Some call it the pure land, others heaven. The name is not what matters, but only by love for the divine, the sacred, and living in purity through thought and action, can a person attain the highest goal in life. It is the devotion and surrender that allows anyone to come home into the love that is always here, which exists beyond time and space and creates all life."

Bruno Groening, the famous healer, whispered into my ear when I was down: *"Don't give up, with love all things are possible."*

Hazrat Inayat Khan, a Sufi master spoke: *"We do not necessarily survive on food. Our soul lives on love, the love we give and receive. The absence of this is our unhappiness, and the presence of it is all we need."*

Christ's voice sounded through the little chapel where I was sitting in France: *"Love wants you as much as you want it. God wants her sons and daughters to return to where all hunger and thirst is quenched. The fountain is awaiting everyone without exception. But many wander lost in a desert crying out for love. Come home to the heart, enter and we are here to lead you to the fountain of eternal life."* Beautiful, but I had a bone to pick with him. Too many were killed and raped in his name. Just look at the bloody inquisition. *"So, what do you say to that?"* His reply was straightforward: *"Not all who use my name, live by what I am."* Made sense to me.

Once I asked Mary Magdalene, "Where are you? I have not felt you for awhile." No answer came at first, until I drove on the same day along a small road in the Berkeley hills and suddenly the car just stopped. My head turned to the side of the road. Before me was a human-sized, ancient painting of her. Here she was—the gorgeous red one in full regalia. The picture leaned against an electric pole (funny the synchronicity). I got out of the car, touched it to make sure it was for real and then heard her voice: *"You find me in the streets of humankind. You find me among the rich and poor and you find me in nature among the wild. I am in this world—always, always loving each as my own."*

Just then a man stepped toward me who must have seen my mesmerized stares and asked, "You want the painting? If you do, it's yours." I gleefully nodded and he loaded her into my car. She did not fit in, half of her hung out of my trunk. I laughed. Like love itself, she doesn't fit into any mold. She will speak and appear to you in her own way. You will sense and recognize when she does—her intense loving and wild, untethered and alive energy is unmistakable. So, yes invite her and love to your kitchen table and enjoy the feast!

***

I immersed myself deeply in many spiritual traditions. I was digging for the red thread that unites them in the core. The expressions and flavors of the traditions are different, but we find the message of love woven through all religions and spiritual paths. In Buddhism, cultivating loving kindness is one of the main practices. In Sufism the lover and beloved unite as one. Christianity teaches the path of charity and love that Jesus has shown. In Hinduism you discover deities who guide humanity to realize the bountiful aspects of love. Paganism worships the earth with love. The feminine wisdom path is strongly centered on fierce love and connection. In the Advaita nondual teachings we discover through inquiry that in presence and stillness love just is. It is you.

So, whatever path you feel drawn to, make sure to follow the red living thread that unites, and most of all, listen to the voice of your own heart. It knows.

Love in Action
Your story and voice matter

Your voice is as important as the voice of everyday people, of saints and animals and the land. Open to your own well of wisdom, allow your unique soul voice sound into our world. No one has a message that is the same as yours, and your love story is essential in the orchestra of life.

- What do you know is true? Write it down, share it with others and of course—live it.
- Is there a story in your life when you experienced love most strongly? What helped you in times of greatest pain and despair or when you were lost? What got you through? Share this. We need stories of healing, of inspiration and truth, more than ever now.
- What ignites you to experience aliveness and warmth in your heart? Nurture that.
- How is love moving and speaking through and as you right now? Discover freshly now.
- What does love speak to you, if it had a voice? Lean in and listen below all the concepts you have ever heard. Lean into what life is speaking to you right now. Maybe you hear a voice, get an image, or you sense wildness or stillness. Give thanks and keep engaging.
- Let your voice speak, even if it feels awkward and you are afraid. It does not need to sound like wisdom, nor does it need to be polished and perfect; let it arise from what feels juicy, fresh right now. Sometimes we preach and lecture others, but by doing so, we drive everyone away. You may feel afraid to say your piece of truth, because it feels vulnerable. We fear being rejected, ridiculed, or dismissed. This often happens when we speak the voice of our soul, which doesn't fit the "nice and normal way." Feel your feelings and do it anyway. Speak that true voice of yours. Go ahead, step to the edge and jump.
- And listen to the soul voice of your partner, friends, and colleagues, and speak from your soul to them and watch what happens then.

- You don't need to channel someone. Let your own voice be the message of love, the one that only you can speak and sing.

3. Wisdom for Crazy Times

A wild ride into the eye of the hurricane

A whiff of smoke entered my nose, was it just a campfire? I was galloping on my spirited, white Arabian horse "Magic" upwards a mountain in California. But when I turned around I saw: A wildfire was burning its way rapidly through dry brush from behind me. I wasn't too worried, as I could easily find a way down from the other side. Or, so I thought. When we arrived at the top with a sweeping view across the valley, to my utter dismay, I realized that a ring of fire below the mountain surrounded us. We surely only had minutes before we would be consumed by raging flames. It seemed there was no way out. My horse was shaking and rearing up in panic. I froze in shock. My heart pounded as loud as church bells in my chest. Fear grabbed a hold of me and I almost fell from my horse. What to do? I did not want to burn up alive, at least not in this life. Suddenly, I remembered my powerful initiation with the anaconda snake in the Amazon jungle, which taught me what to do in terrifying moments such as this one (read this story in "Foundation Stones").

It arose from within: "Get present. Connect, root in love and you will find a way." Easier said than done.

Hey, I had no choice left, we were out of time. I couldn't turn off the fear, so I acknowledged it, felt the sensation for a second and gave it breath. I centered into my larger presence by landing in my body, and with my breath I connected down to my belly, my horse, and the earth all in one go. Magic calmed down, he felt the shift. There was one more thing that had to happen. Awareness just isn't enough, I had to tap into love. Not easy when under pressure. I connected into my heart through feeling love for my daughter and let it expand to include the ring of fire as well. Surprisingly, I dropped below duality, into the eye of the hurricane, into stillness, and experienced oneness in my whole being with all creation.

My fear dissipated, and I knew what I had to do. Magic and I were in unspoken resonance, he trusted me to guide us through. Slowly we rode directly toward the heat and flames. It seemed insane. But I felt I was guided by an invisible hand and had complete faith in this pure intelligence of life. I found the small openings where the fire had not yet reached. We wove our way step-by-step through this humongous fire down the hill, not knowing if we would hit a wall of flames around the next corner. But somehow we never did. Drenched in sweat, we finally reached the river and there was only one thing to do: jump in. Tears of relief washed through me as Magic dunked his overheated body in the cooling water and shook himself like a wet dog. We walked home through the lifesaving river. After that I knew in my very flesh and bones that love's presence is the way, even during the craziest and most frightening of times.

***

As I am writing this chapter we are standing at a precarious edge in our world. Our house, this earth is on fire. The old structures of the patriarchy and how we have lived on our planet aren't working, much is falling apart and crumbling to dust. The new has not emerged yet. It is scary and exciting to experience this intense unraveling and purging, the urgency and unknown, whilst preparing to welcome a birth. How do we kindle hope in times of sheer despair? How do we tend wisely to what is arising within and around us in the midst of chaos? How do we break the chains of our rather insane history, which is built upon mountains of lies, ignorance, abuse of power, women's and racial injustice, and destruction of our environment? How do we deal with collective and personal trauma? And how do we rise up from the ashes in our hands and lands?

Because I am working with people around the world, I heard many different stories of the recent global quarantine time. One man from India told me how the poorest in his neighborhood had nowhere to go after the police demolished their little cardboard box homes in the slums. He used to bring them food. But during the shutdown he wasn't allowed to go out onto streets because of the government regulations. What happens to people without the privilege to shelter in a cozy home? What happens when they can neither work nor find food?

Some experienced this COVID quarantine as a welcomed stop from the rat race. They practiced yoga online, planted in the garden and discovered how beautiful life is, when walking a little bit slower. Others felt isolated or imprisoned. Many didn't know how to pay the rent and feed their families. Some folks in Germany got well taken care of by their government. Italians sang from their balconies, but do we know what's going on in their homes and hearts?

We share diverse colors of this human experience, but none is exactly the same. It's not just the internal; it's the external, our society, culture and environment that influence each of us as well. If we live in privileged countries with kind folks surrounding us, a quarantine is far easier to live through. And if you sit on the street, it's tough, very tough.

Often we generalize and project our own experience unto others. But for compassion to flower it is helpful to look deeply, and as the Native Americans say: "to walk in each other's shoes." Because oneness is not sameness. This situation invites us to get to know each other across the borders and skin color, beyond our preconceived ideas, to reach through to the heart, even if we have to do it online. To do this simple human thing from time to time and ask: "How are you? How is this situation really for you?" creates a bridge and makes a drop of difference.

How do we unite in the darkest hour of humanity and rise to unleash the greatest love the world has ever known? It is upon us to navigate this difficult transition, to be facilitators and midwives of awakening, change and transformation in these unprecedented times. A task assigned for each on a soul level.

The great passages from one way of life to another, like transitions of death and birth, and this apocalypse on our planet are usually marked by intensity, chaos, and fear. We are thrown into turbulent, uncharted waters and don't know if and how we will make it through. Or what will happen next. Issues that have been covered over for centuries are busting through society's carpet of denial. Truth is not comfortable, it always reveals what is hidden. Some truth is hard to digest, such as the destructive effects of patriarchy, power misuse and climate change. But during a crisis, a breakdown when nothing works anymore as it used to, with an honest reckoning, a new way can be forged.

Kali appears on many altars and on the streets to end our crimes against life. With her unrelenting compassion she destroys delusion and shreds the veils of denial. People are stepping out from their closets to voice traumas and injustices instead of keeping the "messy and ugly" under a cover of shame. Before we can birth a healthier, more soul-attuned life, the destructive and false must be seen and purged. **Because we cannot build a new world on a rotten foundation.** During this pandemic we were forced to a standstill and had to face what is. Will we awaken and turn now? It's not a given. It depends on each of us.

But help is always available and opportunity is found in the pressure cooker of adversity

You know this. For such a time as this, foretold by ancient prophecies and anticipated by those with eyes to see and ears to hear, when our survival is hanging by a mere thread and we are at the edge of a new dawning, you—*yes, you*—have been born. Otherwise you would not be here. I honor you for that. Many of us had a foreboding a long time ago of what is unfolding now. We have been preparing throughout our whole lives, walked through hell and back, to be able to show up for these times. To stand in the eye of this mighty hurricane, so we can be a refuge and a lighthouse, to guide and blaze a trail through the darkest hours of human history. To help in the great turning. Together, not alone.

Because none of us can do this on our own and no one is exempt. What befalls the rivers, the trees, and people across the world, is affecting each person without exception. In this world of duality, good and evil always dance back and forth, now even more extreme. And for sure, our bodies will die one way or another. Basic truths of life. Despite this knowing, fear arises; it is so very human to feel shaken in the face of uncertainty. You are not alone if you experience confusion, disorientation, terror, anger, pain and shock, and a sense that the rug has been pulled out from under you, throwing you into a whirlwind of emotions and relentless thoughts of worry. You might wonder what is true in the midst of conflicting messages that are being shouted through the media channels. You may feel overwhelmed, lost as your ship is being tossed mercilessly in this hurricane. Many do not know how to navigate intense storms when the shores of familiarity and normality are nowhere in sight.

Relentlessly tumbled in the waves of change and apparent insanity playing out on a grand scale, we must find deeper ground and anchor in what truly holds. Do not follow the sheep, and do not succumb to control in order to feel safe. Do not reach for the familiar; how things used to be in order to feel safe. As tempting as it may be, it is only a temporary soothing fix, like drinking from the same cup every morning, but it will not help you when your ship has crashed and you have to find a way to survive and thrive, not just for your own sake, but for all of life here on earth.

Seek not the fleeting safety of this world, my friend, but take refuge in the only safety there is: your heart. The truth itself or call it love.

What else helps in times of turbulence and crisis? Spiritual practice, nature, friends, emotional resilience, healthy food, strong navigation and life skills, courageous action, and a good dose of love. Every day. But, please do not tell others or yourself not to panic. It only makes it worse. We don't need to act from fear or build a shrine to it. But we do need to grow resilience by learning how to navigate challenging times, to feel our fears and meet them instead of living from our basic survival brain— to fight, freeze, fawn or flee. Resilience grows when we do not grab onto nor reject any experience, which is what the Buddha taught already ages ago. We practice radically welcoming it all. Resisting what is, denial or disassociating never helps. And c'mon, don't follow the panicked mind around. Rather, walk this direct way home.

Use this liberating approach:
Face what is here through the eyes of presence. Acknowledge the situation in the world and within you. Say radically *yes* to what is here and what you are experiencing, whether you like it or not. Acknowledge what you feel, be it fear, anger or a tight belly. Land in your body, feel the emotion in the pulsation, sense it as a physical sensation. Stay with that. Let the body shake; allow it to move, to dance, to sound. Keep touching the constriction with your breath; embrace the one who is scared with kindness. Whether it is your friend, a neighbor or the kid inside of you. Offer presence, breath and most of all the hand of love. (See more in the practice section on how to take good care of your fear.)

You want to liberate the energy that is contracted and held in fear, harness the fire inside your captured fury, free the kid in the dungeon, and fiercely stop the bully from destroying lives.

This liberating approach requires that we root in what is alive right now, what is unshaken, beyond duality, below the surface and the dance of samsara.

For that you will need to anchor your ship in love with your commitment and intention again and again. I mean a love that doesn't shy away from the tough places, a love that holds you now and forever, it reaches into the pit and meets you right where you are and what is going on in our world.

Here, freedom is found, not from anything, but being free to be able to respond from loving presence instead of reacting from ingrained patterns and conditioning. It frees you to stand and speak up, no matter if you are attacked or celebrated. Can you imagine what is possible when we root and live in that to bridge the gap of isolation between each other? This is how we heal the traumas of centuries and blaze a new trail. This is how we turn this human ship among the relentlessly pounding waves, as the world we have known is ending and a new world is being born.

The way of the great Passage:

In a deeper approach, we can liken what is happening in the world and in us to a passage that all mystics, shamans, bodhisattvas and those who walk the path of heart must undergo. Will we come through to birth forth a new way of living, far more conscious and aligned than before? Will we be able to heal our trauma and wake up? Will we be able to change the course of things, before total destruction takes what we value and care about, like our human rights and the health of our environment? I don't know. It is not an easy one. Because it calls each of us to walk into the unknown, to sail bravely through the hurricane.

How then do we travel through this death and birth passage to light the way for others and ourselves too?

We can't make this initiation on our own; it is life taking us through this passage, if we are willing and give permission to let love do us through the timeless stages of this life-altering journey.

In order to travel from one stage of life or consciousness to another we must leave behind our old clothes. We enter the phase of death, a dying before death takes you, which can be extremely challenging and unpleasant for most of us. We are creatures of habit, we like "same and safe." Our most important step on this passage is to look death squarely in the eye, to face what is behind the façade, the clothes we have covered ourselves with. To start stripping down. And to turn toward the hidden, to feel our fears, pains and ecstasy courageously. The stuff we usually avoid. What terrifies you the most? Sit with that and see what arises from the depth of your being.

If you are ready, offer unto the altar all the things and roles you have identified with. Give over your ideas, the stories you cling to, your beliefs—whether they are nice or awful—your status, the people you are attached to and a way of living that you call normal. Hand it over, take off your clothes, not just mentally, but emotionally, spiritually, and even physically. Let yourself be stripped naked by love's grace.

Use this powerful inquiry question for the stripping stage:

What is left when all else fails?

What remains when everything radically disappears? Do not answer this with your mind. But stay there tonight in silent prayer, beloved, let your mind empty. Open beyond concepts into your direct experience, to raw feeling, being just present with what is emerging. You might experience your broken heart, how ancient grief wells up in you, or the surge of fury or angst. Let it move through the body. You might realize you never had any control and it isn't needed even. Rather, feel into how love is doing you. Surrender into that which always holds you, the earth, and what is alive, breathing your body and beautiful heart. Give into this unraveling, from what you have been hiding, even if it is only for a night. Release the grip you hold on life, even for a moment let "thy will be done."

After the disillusionment, the dying phase, we enter into the threshold stage. With nothing to hold onto we walk emptied out into the tomb. Here we lay down on the altar and rest in stillness, in the unknown of the great mystery.

No one to be, nothing to do and nowhere to go.

You don't know who you are anymore and what was before is no more. You might feel shattered; the world as you have known it has crumbled to dust. Give it your *yes*. For here, in this sacred ground between time and space, silence wraps you and love unfolds you. Allow yourself to rest here for a while.

Fall into the shining darkness. Steep in that. Abide in this peace beyond death and birth. Sense, and feel into it. Savor and allow yourself to be merged with creation itself. Beloved and Lover are uniting in this sacred tomb, something new is being conceived and created from the deep dark. It is pure, breathing you, without a name, snaking and winding through your spine. Lean in, trust that life force, which has no ending and no beginning. Love wants the whole of you. Let it ravish you all the way.

Stay close, a profound mystery is unfurling, which knows and flows between the crevices of your heart and the great song of life.

We are emerging into the third stage called the birthing. You may experience a quivering, a shaking, and a waking. A stirring and rising from within. Pulsing red blood and the living waters are filling your vessel anew. You are being resurrected into life. Like a newborn child your eyes open gently into the wee morning light. A dawning into a world you had forgotten, but it was painted, written, edged into your soul so long ago. You breathe new life, rejoicing in simply being here in this precious life. You only ever had this moment. Now, more fully alive than before.

You sense, taste and feel this: Love is being unleashed, set free in you. As you rise up, you know in your blood and bones that no matter what happens you can meet it, even the terrible, even when you are shaking in your boots, you know to love your way through. For love shines and lives as and through you in benefit to all. And it always finds a way!

In the fourth stage of this passage you discover your true life's calling and gather the down-to-earth skills to be of service in the world. You free your voice to speak up. You go forth with many others to be a living bridge between the worlds, between the lost and found, between the me and other, you shine forth your gift, that unshakeable light, into the community and our world to be of benefit. Every step emerges from the unknown, new. You are not merely rewriting history, it is life truly living as you.

This sacred passage can be taken over a lifetime or it happens within a moment. You can consciously undertake this journey like the ancient passages for three holy days and nights. However, to emerge all the way through we cannot skip any part of this sacred passage. And usually we need a seasoned guide, a wise person to support us on each stage. This transition is not a neatly packaged, streamlined path that can be forced or created. This living resurrection passage is deeper than that, profoundly powerful, and surprisingly, utterly alive and true.

You are needed now. And you are not alone; we truly are together in this. You find hard-won wisdom and many helpful practical ways to navigate through this turmoil and unleash love throughout this book. Let's raise our torches and sail this crazy, beautiful human ship bravely right through the eye of the hurricane into a new dawning for the sake of all beings.

On this holy journey life is the greatest teacher and love is the ultimate guide through the great passage of our times. Let it take you through hell and heaven, through crisis and emergence, all the way home.

May we rise and unleash love, come what may, as if our life depends on it. It does.

Love in Action

Tending to Fear:
Fear is a normal and healthy response to actual danger. But often we are not used to being with intense feelings, so we become even afraid of fear. We may try to bypass the emotions, but this is a trap; or we may act it out, which only makes things worse, and we get stuck in an unhealthy rut. When fear is running unchecked it gains momentum and affects everything. The nervous system is not only ringing the alarm once or twice, but now you are pressing the alarm button nonstop. Therefore you feel constantly under threat and in danger. The mind runs 500 miles an hour, worries and races to find a way to get away from the fear, the danger. We may disassociate, numb out, lash out, react... the body is tense and tight; the breath is shallow to preserve oxygen. The little kid in you is terrified and isolated. You feel disconnected, out of touch with nature, each other, and most of all—your presence. And love, the living spirit seems nowhere in sight. You can interrupt this cycle by tending to fear.

Practical ways:
This is not a step-by-step program. Use what you find helpful in different moments.

First acknowledge: there is fear. Bring your awareness to what is actually here and happening. Do not analyze or try to change anything.

Connect to a resource: Look around the room you are in and notice one thing that feels safe (plant, animal, a book, etc.). Rest your awareness there and notice what you feel.

Sit on the earth. Feel the solidity underneath you. Let your weight drop into the ground. Notice how you are held and supported from below, by life, even when you feel shaken. This helps the emotional body a lot and you can more easily feel that love holds you, even when all falls apart or you do not know what will happen next.

Take conscious deep breaths. Breathe in through the nose while counting till four. Hold the breath while counting till four. Exhale through the mouth, counting to four. Keep that rhythm up for several rounds and breathe into the belly. It is a quick way to settle the nervous system.

Go to the sensation in the body. Is the fear in the belly? Notice the sensations, the fluttering or tightening.

Offer your breath. Flood the area with strong and soft breath. Long out-breath.

Say an inward yes to this. "Yes" to feeling discomfort for one minute for now (the mind needs an end point to feel a bit safer).

Shaking is an efficient way to complete the cycle of fear. Daily shaking is powerful stress relief; it supports your kidneys and lymphatic system. Think of it as emotional hygiene.

When you feel overly worried, turn it into a practice. Each part of this practice lasts 3-5 minutes. Begin with frantically pacing back and forth, thinking about everything you worry about. Exaggerate, play a little theater. It's fun! After that, shake the body and/or dance. End with holding and stroking your body gently.

Feel that little kid inside of you and give it a hand. Speak to him or her from your heart and presence: "I am here with you. I got you." This is very helpful.

Please do not tell others to calm down or not to panic. Nor tell anyone that everything will be OK. It doesn't really help and can actually make things worse. You want to give a hand, be a bigger person who isn't afraid of their fear and who can hold them. "Yes, I understand that you feel really afraid. And I am here with you." Simple connecting statements ease the panic in another. There is more you can offer of course, but that's the basis for love to unfold.

Terror, pain or anger may emerge below the fear. Tend to these feelings wisely (read more on how to befriend emotions in the chapter "This Human House"). In this process trauma can surface, please seek professional help then (read more in the "Healing Wounds of Life" chapter).

Essential Practices for Turbulent Times:

Commitment: What are you living for? What are you standing for? Inquire deeply into that question. And once the answer from your being emerges, commit yourself to that on a daily basis. Use it as your anchor. If you are dedicated to something greater than yourself, you will have more strength and confidence, even if you are shaking in your boots.

Grounding: If you are floundering, feel overwhelmed and lost at sea; use a basic grounding practice to root yourself into what always holds you. Touch the earth, feel the chair you are sitting on. Let your body weight drop into it. Breathe down and notice how the chair right now holds you, how the earth always holds you. Take refuge in that. (There are more grounding practices throughout the book.)

Connect with others: Share what you are experiencing with like-minded people. Do not isolate yourself, but reach out and engage with others, grow a circle of community. Especially when the going gets tough mutual support is essential. (Read more in the "Connected or Living Dead?" and "Connecting for Real" chapters.)

Spiritual Practice:
A daily meditation practice is helpful when your world is rocked. (Read more in "The Kiss and Gold" and the "Foundation Stones" chapters.)

Awareness Practice:
Notice what colors you can see in your room. Notice the sounds you can hear. Notice the smells. Turn toward the situation or difficulty and become present to it through seeing, sensing, hearing, feeling what is here. (See more in the "Foundation Stones" chapter.)

Presence Sanskrit Mantra:
Sohum: I AM. It also means: I am here now. "So" with the in-breath and "hum" with the out-breath. Repeat it for several rounds or minutes with one hand on the heart and one on the belly. Feel your feet on the ground and breathe into your belly.

Heart Sutra:
Whisper to yourself again and again, like a silent mantra: "Love is here." Look around in your environment and notice what you see and hear, whilst repeating softly: "Love is here." Use your senses as an entry gate. Sense into the field of love that is here, even amidst turmoil.

Heart Connection and Activation:
An easy way to connect and activate your heart is to remember a person, place or animal that you love. Bring one to your mind. Feel the appreciation and love you have for this one. Allow this warmth, this love, to fill your body and let it flood you all the way. Bask in that and fill your cup.

Cultivate Emotional Resiliency:
To be able to navigate internal and external pressure and intensity it is essential to cultivate resiliency, to learn to acknowledge and feel your emotions with ease. (See more on this in the "This Human House" chapter.)

Anchor in Ahimsa (Nonviolence):
You will be attacked sometimes, you will feel triggered and you will experience pain as well as joy in this life. How do we stop

our usual reaction habits of flight, fight and freeze? Here is a simple mantra for you to anchor in nonviolence: "May I refrain from reacting. May I refrain from causing harm." Acknowledge and feel your feelings, no matter what they are. Redirect and anchor yourself: "May I root in truth (use your own intention) right now." You will find many helpful approaches and practices throughout this book.

Benevolence and Service Practice:

Serve Love itself. Ask frequently: "Show me how to be of benefit in this situation/with this person." Listen and follow the guidance in action. If you are hurting or experiencing difficulty it helps sometimes to expand it beyond yourself: "There are many beings, who, like me, are experiencing pain." Reflect on how you feel as you include others. Then send a wish out: "May all those who are suffering find ease." Or help someone in action. A simple blessing to offer daily, for any situation or person: "May you be happy, at ease..." use your own words and silently bless the people, animals and plants you meet on your path. Notice how you feel when you do that. Engage in actions to make an actual difference in the lives of others. (See more in the "Service Rocks the World" and "Welcome Humanity" chapters.)

Bowing to Life:

I still use this practice I learnt in the Himalayas and my deep dive with death (read the story in the following chapter: "The Kiss and Gold"). Try using it for a day or for the rest of your life and see what happens for you. Bow inwardly from your heart to trees, flowers and any animal you meet. Bow silently to people, whether they are behaving nicely or not. Remember, you are bowing to their divine spark, to the essence of their being, to their Buddha nature. And here is the challenging part: bow to any feelings that arise for you—anger, sorrow, joy—and any experiences you encounter, whether they are good or bad. And then bow to your whole life. Even to the parts you do not like and don't want to have. Maybe you do not enjoy your job, or an illness is tough. Bow to the suffering, and bow to the dislike and unhappiness as much as you bow to the things that make you smile. What does it feels like and what opens up in you when you bow to both equally?

This is strong medicine, leading to freedom beyond judgment and our endless struggle with life. From that space it's easier to find a way through difficulties. And the beauty is, that bowing to your life may just open your heart to deeper love and connection with yourself and all beings.

A Spiritual Warrior Fire Practice:

This is a spiritual practice to harness power, clarity, truth, and bravery from the energy of anger. Turn away from the story and the blame to directly face your fury. Feel it fully and stay present. Notice where the sensation is most alive in your body. It often is found in your belly or solar plexus. Give your "yes" to it. Breathe with the anger; feel the fire, let it move through your body. You might feel strong sensations, burning; just stay present, and allow it to move. At some point allow a sound to arise and be expressed. Let the anger energy express itself through your voice and sound. Don't try to force it, nor diminish the power. Let it fully arise and move. As this energy is liberated you will feel power surging through your body. Don't collapse, stay with its fierceness, as if a lioness or lion is waking up in you.

Once you feel this raw power then let words come from the deeper truth. Let yourself be surprised, these words might not be familiar to you. It is life itself speaking through you. Maybe there is a roar: "Enough. The line is here." Just feel this, allow this, and hear this. And then lean in, rest right into this life-giving power. It is the power of love, of life itself. At some point it will move you into action naturally. You will know what to say or do in the world, and you will have the strength and wisdom to carry it out. This power has nothing to do with control, nor with hate or vengeance, blame or any story the mind may play. It just cuts through the BS and delusion with an open heart; it shoots an arrow of truth and hits the mark. It frees you to take inspired action in the world and your life.

Release Spiritual Misconceptions and step into Freedom:

Certain popular spiritual teachings cause more confusion and harm. If your heart feels shattered by what is happening in the world, you feel afraid, experience loss or fall on financial hard times, please do yourself a favor and don't subscribe to half-truths. There is nothing wrong with you if you experience any of the above. It is not because you are stuck in victim consciousness, are not aware or enlightened enough, think in a low vibration, aren't doing enough affirmations or have faulty beliefs. Or, if you were fully rooted in love, you would get a pass from being human on this earth.

During a crisis of this magnitude, everyone experiences to some degree survival angst, anger, confusion, etc. It is a normal human reaction to an "out of hand" situation. We are interconnected and therefore we are affected by what is happening in our world. You are not the sole creator of this turmoil; far more people and greater forces are involved. You cannot control other people or disasters, but remember that your main power lies in loving presence and how you relate and respond to what is occurring. This is your ticket to freedom. Ask yourself: "What is the calling for me in the midst of the biggest challenge for human kind?" Listen and then act on that as if all life depends on it.

This is how you unleash love, step-by-step, breath-by-breath, without knowing the outcome even during the darkest and craziest of times.

Lean In

Lean in closer, much closer.
Lean into a tree, or dazzling sunlight
And your beloved's skin at night.

Lean into heartbreaking grief and delirious joy
Leave nothing out.
Ruthlessly, lean in all the way.
Oh yes, fear too.
Feel its gripping, pulsing, shaking in the core.

Lean into exquisite surrender,
This holy moment, nothing to gain, nothing to lose.
What has been is gone and what you imagined would be, is
not here.

As you loosen the grip, you slip into recognition:
When you lean in all the way you fall
Into the deep unknown beckoning you since before time.
With nothing to hold unto,
Arms wide open and a mind without control,
You are falling into the only thing that is true.

Something utterly alive is capturing you
When nothing seems to hold...
Oh yes fall, dear, fall closer into truth,
This flame that remains after all else has been blown away.
Dare to fall through comfy layers of delusions
And the hardened armor around a tender heart.
In this holy instance, when all is gone and nothing seems to
happen,
In this moment between the old and new, death and birth,
Breathe.

Something is taking you… is finally overtaking you.
Ahhh… yes, Lean into that.
You are falling into love.
Embracing you. All the way, as you are.
Lean in.

4. The Kiss and Gold

A field guide home

One drop of love can cure a lifetime of pain, one touch can uplift, one kiss can awaken us from the slumber of forgetfulness — and one moment of love is eternity taking us home.

When I was nineteen years old I attended an intensive retreat in a Tibetan monastery in the Himalayas. I was bursting with life, eager to learn from the ancient masters. I knew nobody who had done this, for I grew up in a time and place where Buddhism was almost nonexistent. On arriving, I felt I was stepping into a magical world. The monastery was surrounded by snowcapped mountains and colorful prayer flags encircled the rooftop of the orange-red painted buildings, carrying the message into the wind: "May all beings be free from suffering. May all beings be happy."

I sat in the temple together with ten other retreatants, facing a large statue of the Buddha and many fascinating objects on the altar — a feast for my eyes. We were given our own hard cushion, and after an hour sitting cross-legged, my leg fell asleep, and I wanted to itch my mosquito bites nonstop. I figured we'd soon eat or walk in the lovely courtyard, or do something else. I had been meditating daily already for years, and thought I was prepared for this. I had no idea we'd meditate on death for ten hours straight for weeks on end.

After the first day, I thought these highly respected Tibetan Lamas were plain nuts. But I hoped the second day would be better. Did they have a resurrection maybe? No, just more about death instead. We had to visualize in detail that everyone we knew was dead, our father and mother, friends and animals. The mind really has no shame, and it occurred to me that it would be quite nice for my mum to be dead (not very compassionate, I know), but this was a rather pleasant meditation. I wept for hours for all the others, though. Now I was going nuts too after this exhausting day, for nobody actually had died, as far as I knew. I was clear I would not do such a death-trip again. I would just meditate on life and ignore their instructions. My mind was arguing the case and protesting loudly. I mean really, the Christians had Christ hanging on the cross, Islam had a thing about killing yourself for a holy cause, and now the Tibetans were worshipping death too. What was wrong with these self-destructive religions? Maybe *The Tibetan Book of the Dead* was written by a dying old cracker? Forgive me, but ten hours a day can really do you in.

I couldn't wait to fall asleep on the hard ground, with only a blanket to wrap around me. Bells awakened us, before the sun had risen and while birds were still napping cozily. We splashed ice-cold mountain water into our faces, stretched our half-frozen bodies, then off into the temple again. The monks were chanting in deep voices, and I was sure these beautiful prayers reached far and wide. Since I did not understand a word, I just hummed along. My tummy was growling; I couldn't wait for the silent breakfast, disgusting yak milk tea and some gruel, which at least was warm. We held our clay mugs with wool gloves, as the Himalayan air, pure and often hot during the day, was freezing at night.

After breakfast, again back to the temple. The full body prostrations were a good workout; they made me feel humble and I began to really mean my prayer. Panting and sweating, I could not think of anything else anyway. It was a little much for a novice; the monks had stronger muscles. But I didn't want to be the only one who collapsed in a heap, so I bit my tongue and kept going with German determination.

The third day was the worst of all. Now I was told to imagine that I was decaying under the earth, my flesh eaten by worms.

Feeling it as if this was happening for real was disgusting, I admit. What was I wasting my time with? I had more important things to do in this world while alive. After all I was young, eager to discover a whole new world out there. I thought these beaming kind monks and nuns must be out of their minds; this was the reason why they were smiling happily all day long. Well, it was a close guess, but I didn't know about that yet.

I decided I was done with this death camp and hiked resolutely down the hill on a dusty path toward a nearby village. On the way I saw a group of red-robed Tibetans chanting around a little mound. I was curious. As I came closer, I saw that these smiling monks were picking up little things from the road. What was it? Ants! Ever so gently they held the ants in their hands and chanted to them, saving their lives. Yes, everyone could be our mother from another life, they said.

These monks were hard at work to build a road, but decided not to build it through the area where the ants had set up home. They moved the road further away, adding at least two weeks more labor for them. I sat for a long time with one wise monk who taught me the words "Om Mani Padme Hum" to bless the busy hardworking little creatures.

Mesmerized, I sang this mantra for hours and was picking up ants too. It was here I awoke into the reality that not only are we interconnected with all of life, but all forms of life are sacred and deserve to be honored. I gained such respect for these people, that I turned around and walked the windy path up to the monastery to sit with them again at four o'clock in the morning before the sun had risen. They had found what matters and were humbly living it.

OK, I get it, even if it needs to be through dying before death takes me, so be it.

What is left when all else is gone? What remains? This was my daily bread and inquiry. It can't be answered by the intellect; instead I was being stripped empty. At first, it felt so good to release the heavy burdens of beliefs, karmic entanglements and conditioning. Like, ragged clothes with big holes falling off. But then it felt like being skinned alive in my mind and body alike. Utterly excruciating. Until I had no clue what was true and who I was anymore. The only thing that made any sense: get on my knees.

At last, after the cycles of decaying and disappearing into nothing, a pure light pierced through, powerfully blasting and illuminating everything. No words are adequate to express what happened when the veils had fallen, when I was nobody and nothing. The next days were timeless; the gates had opened for me to what is beyond the cycle of birth and death. The priceless gift was revealed. The fear of death most of us have, dissolved. I left with a clear mind, a heart full of compassion, and gratitude for the teachings and those who practice them in daily life. From there the journey unfolded — with many kisses and challenges — leading home to the gold in the heart and learning to live from this boundless love, step-by-step, one act at a time in the marketplace of this world.

***

Do you remember the juiciest, most passionate and loving kiss you've ever shared in the arms of a beloved? Far greater is the taste of a kiss with the divine in its fierce tenderness. If you abandon every shred of control you hold and throw caution to the wind, you might be waking to beauty beyond your wildest dreams. Intense longing arises, never leaving us alone, until we fully come home.

What seemed since ancient times to be reserved only for saints, mystics and enlightened ones, is now emerging for people everywhere. Realization of the transcendent and immanent, what is beyond and also found in all forms of life, is what many are seeking. It is the answer to the great questions: *Who am I?*

What is this life for? Why am I born? What is this all about? In the vast nature of reality, far beyond our made-up constructs, beliefs, and all knowledge, lives the vast mystery that all sages point to, the sacred that exists within a tiny mustard seed and is alive in all beings. To be free from suffering ultimately means realizing truth, the undying, unborn, unchanging nature at the heart of all. It beckons us to enter into true happiness, peace and compassion, into a freedom unbounded by conditioning, circumstances, appearances and false identifications. It calls us to live awake on the carousel of our world. A cordial invitation is written in the universe with your name on it, to come to the cliff, to fall with arms wide open into the unknown, into source, where true love is catching you all the way.

Yet, most of humanity is living in a faraway land of separation. Have you ever gone to a costume party? Welcome! We are all dancing in the grand masquerade ball of this world, feverishly playing hide and seek, forgetting and remembering. Some of us are dressed as kings and queens, others as villains, or CEO's...

Unfortunately we tend to forget to take off our costumes at the end of the performance. We remain thoroughly identified with our chosen character, while who we truly are stays tragically hidden behind the façade. At some point the game just isn't fun anymore, and we look for a hidden treasure we sense exists somewhere. We may have glimpsed it outside the show, when a door opened into the garden, as the moon was rising in the silent midnight hour. Maybe you were captured in rapture and left the grand ball there and then. Maybe the starlit night kissed you, waking you to a far greater reality than the one you previously knew.

For many of us, suffering surfaces at some point in the midst of the mad dance. We find ourselves in broad daylight in yet another nightmare, stuck in a repetitive script that we did not write, or so it seems. Every avenue we take to leave the show leads to nowhere, until we are so exhausted, we cannot resist anymore, and we hit rock bottom. Reality might just reach you there and then and get under your skin so deep; you will never forget its exquisite touch.

One kiss of true love can end your world, as you have known it. The kiss of love is like a fire, burning everything that is untrue, without escape. In the final surrender, as nothing is left, the deepest yearning is fulfilled. You are the living flame.

Awakening has dawned and there is longing for so much more

The endless tale of forgetting has become as old as a worn-out shoe. You can't raise your glass one more time to nonsense and insanity. The show carries less and less thrill, the dramas are not as interesting, the whole thing feels shallow, like a lie; and you might be tired of faking it too. Wherever you go an ache limps along. Terribly thirsty for the water of life, hunger for the real bread is at the tip of your tongue now, as you look for what you have longed for your whole life.

And so we begin to search... digging for gold. There are many paths that lead home. The journey is different for everyone; one size does not fit all. Some have found treasures of wisdom, valuable insights, and a sense of the sacred along the way; others have already discovered who they are. Maybe you've been in a labyrinth, circling madly around yourself, seeking desperately to find the exit. Now as you turn to an open window between the relentless streams of thoughts, a glimmer of knowing shows the way.

Our journey might take us through deep, dark valleys, steep mountains, dry desert, or jungles; we may encounter terrible and beautiful experiences, sights and sounds. We will find interesting characters on the road; some deceive and others help. We meet challenges, demons and dragons, or receive guidance from magnificent beings of light who have travelled the path before us. In Life's forest, signs in the right direction and signs in the wrong direction create confusion, until we learn to listen with the ears of the heart.

Lean into what resides below the surface of the play; see with the eyes of the soul, dedicate your whole attention to being present and to a love that is always here. Even in a simple moment, as you cross the street, walking toward the laundromat, the sky may open and a touch of light pours through.

Kisses of love and waking come as gifts; honor them but don't make a philosophy of them, for they go deeper every time, just as you are breathing into your belly and feet.

Know though, if you walk the journey in real life, not just in concepts of the mind, the fiery kiss of grace and waking can be dangerous, shattering all that you've constructed, taking everything—including your house, the pretty paintings, and all the things you held dear and imagined as true. Even what you thought love is. The fire will radically burn an entire make-believe world you held on to so tightly or tried to improve. When we dare to go all the way through the dark night of the soul, being stripped, and stand naked in utter surrender, what is given then is beyond any words to express or thoughts to comprehend; for it is all we ever yearned for and so much more:

The gold. Who you truly are, and all that is.

***

I felt I was blind, when I walked through Satya Sai Baba's ashram in southern India. A dark, grey film covered my eyes and I barely saw the people sitting in rows, chanting mantras. In desperation, I climbed up the little hill with the shrine on top and devoted myself to staying awake throughout the night, sitting in prayer silently on a rock. The stars shone brightly as I wept, wrestled with my internal darkness, and then surrendered. My eyes opened at dawn, as a gentle glow of sunlight poured across the valley bathing all in light. I listened to the first song of a bird sitting on a branch of the only tree nearby. And then I heard the words so clearly: *"Be still and know I AM."* Rapture and bliss captured me, filling every cell of my being. The spiderweb of delusion had been cleared from my sight and mind. I gazed across the valley and could only see beauty and love permeating all. On that same day Sai Baba came to me in person, offering sacred ash from the palm of his hand into mine. He touched my forehead with the ash and I opened, seeing as if for the first time what is eternal and true. What a blessing, still alive today.

***

In stillness I am looking across the ocean to the horizon, and then further, beyond time and space, beyond all the made-up worlds, and there is nothing but love here. Or one can say, nothing but truth, light, emptiness; where "I" as a separate entity disappear into nonexistence, being one with all. And then I land on the ground of form, rooted deeply in the earth, dark, red blood rushing through my veins, my senses awakened to sights, smells, and sounds. I am turned on by raw life, breathing the fullness of love. It is the end and it is the beginning. Standing in the center of birth and death, at the threshold of a true life emerging.

Love always asks for embodiment where daily life becomes the temple shrine

Awakening is half the coin; the other is embodiment, for this is where the rubber meets the road. No matter where we are on our journey, no matter whether we've experienced the fullness or small moments of awakening or discovered pearls of wisdom along the road and found a deeper sense of compassion, it is actualized only by living it day by day, step by step. Meaning, we take our meditation cushion and what we know and live it in the world. Waiting for enlightenment to happen, before engaging fully with life and being of service, is as much a mistaken notion, as acting in busyness with worldly delusions. Being and acting, silence and movement are important, like two wings lifting into flight. Returning home over and over, to the ground of what is true, to this moment now.

Love isn't real until we act from it in this world. It lives in the way we touch a child's hand or a rock, how we relate to our mate and coworker, how we respond and get our hands dirty with humanity, our earth and the suffering we've created. Often we need to kiss the dirt to be able to embody love in this world. This implies that we meet and compassionately embrace our own humanity, our sorrow, hurts, anger and fear and the many guests we entertain in our house. If our room is filled with a mountain of boxes, we need to deal with it and clear out the clutter so the light can shine through and reveal who and what else is here.

Allowing the masks and lies to fall off like old leaves, we walk more freely. Everything we dare to face, embrace and work through turns to compost; I promise you, even lead can be turned to gold. By healing our wounds our gifts can fully emerge. This transmutation takes courage and a solid commitment to offer love where there might be only darkness and utter despair.

A great sculptor chisels away all our covering, until one day, the face of a beautiful one is revealed in the market square for all to see. You are the body, a sacred vessel through which love is expressed and lived. Form is as divine as the formless. There is no difference between divine and human. The sense of separation is yet another delusion, for God is everywhere and in everyone. Compassion is in the monasteries among the monks and nuns, as it is found on the streets among the homeless too.

Love becomes real through us by living it moment by moment fresh, without flinching from whatever we might encounter — whether joy or pain, the trash can that needs emptying, diapers to change, a business meeting to attend, to heal a conflict with a mate, or colorful flowers being offered into your beautiful hands.

As you engage in the marketplace of the world, let yourself feel the connection to your heart and what is vaster than all of the appearances, and is right here, when you relate with another. To dare to ask for help when lost, to rest in the quiet peace amidst the buzz, to feel the presence in your body and keep breathing; this is your ticket home.

As veils are shed, we experience life engaging with us through this world. Whether we are talking or listening to life, life is continually speaking to us in varied ways. You briefly come across a stranger in a coffeehouse, who tells you the answer to an urgent question. You walk by a river and hear wisdom guiding you in an important decision. Your mailbox contains an unexpected check, just in the nick of time, when you needed it the most. You lose your job, and instead of spiraling into despair, you open to possibility; and someone offers you work you never would have considered, maybe better than imagined. A door opens as another closes; synchronicity becomes normal then.

More and more the mystery reveals itself to you through every being and event, guiding and loving you. Life is in love with life. Love is revealed as you, loving all. May you dance with the natural movement in life with both feet on the ground of this earth, your head high in the vast sky and your heart right here with all of us, simply sharing love. Keep drinking and receiving from the well, it has no limits and is free of charge. May you be filled until your cup runneth over with the most wondrous dark red wine of life. If you are still searching for the fountain, do not drink from pits that only make you sick. Let your longing take you home. Even if you only have a few drops of water to share, pass it on to another. Every drop matters in this world.

***

I had been in silence for two weeks, camping alone in the wilderness. I never felt isolated among the wild animals, the ancient redwood trees and the clear springs gushing from the holy mountain. When I was drinking with my cupped hands from the spring one morning I heard her speak, "Fill your cup, receive this nourishment. You will need it for what's coming now."

Kissed by pure, fresh water I felt revived and made my journey to the top of the mountain. Once I reached the plateau I bowed, captured by the majestic magnificence of its snow-covered peak. Just stillness enveloped me. And then, without further ado, I was pushed by a force greater than my own, and I could not help but surrender all the way down to the ground. "Thy will be done," I called out loud. In that moment, as if the gates of grace had opened, I was illumined from head to toe, every cell drenched in an immense golden river of love. Sacredness was filling and surrounding me, so real and divine, just one. Being transfigured by this power, this grace, I felt so happy and alive... "Love All," I was told. Simple, without trumpets and fanfare.

And then the people came; one by one they arrived on the mountaintop out of nowhere, lining up to receive help, a word or a blessing. How did they find me? I had no clue. But I knew what to say, and at times a simple touch or a look sufficed to bring about a healing, or wisdom for life, an opening of the heart, or a profound awakening and sweet connection. It went on for hours... and when I left the mountain, the stream of people continued, finding me wherever I went to guide them home. Sounds grand, but honestly I feel more down to earth and humanly vulnerable than ever. The journey from the mountain back into the world called me to engage from this love in everyday life amidst the challenges, and it continues to evolve through relating with all of life.

Love is showing us a new way of being and living together — so urgently needed now.

Love in Action

The cornerstones for the spiritual path

I touched the four cornerstones, which St. Francis had used to restore a fallen apart church in Assisi, Italy. These rocks are strong, solid and still standing after hundreds of years. And while he built the house of God by his own hands in the cold, snowy winter's time, he sang the song: *"If you want your dream to be, build it slow and surely. Small beginnings, greater ends, heartfelt work grows purely. If you want to live life free, take your time go slowly. Do few things but do them well, simple joys are holy. Day by day, stone by stone. Day by day, you'll grow too, you'll know heaven's glory..."*

These cornerstones below, found in all ancient wisdom traditions, provide the foundation for the journey to build your temple. For a more in depth approach and essential key practices please read the chapters: "Foundation Stones" and "This Human House." Maybe one day you arrive where all roads and practices end and the mystery takes hold of you. No matter where you are, be true to yourself, listen to your inmost teacher and let love live you all the way through. Day by day, stone by stone...

A Spiritual Practice:

Since I was 14 years old I have been meditating without missing a day. I can attest the enormous benefits I received from having a consistent spiritual practice. There are several forms of spiritual practice; those found in ancient traditions are prayer and meditation. The practice of meditation bears many fruits and is essential. It is a window into what is larger than the limited self. The more often you open this window, the more you become aware, find peace, and hear the inner voice of wisdom. Meditation is a door to freedom, compassion and other pearls, including equanimity. It cultivates the soil of real love. An ongoing practice is like putting logs into the fire of the heart, until one day it is a flaming torch. Avoid "spiritual practice hopping," picking from the buffet in the spiritual marketplace. It keeps you on a superficial level and will never give you the satisfaction that only comes from going deep with one.

In the beginning you might explore Buddhism, Christianity, or another path that calls to you. When you find one that is right for you, stay with it and practice regularly. Whether you practice meditation for ten minutes or for one hour a day is less important than doing it every day. Your consistency has an effect on your whole life and on others as well. Meditation is a skill, like any art, for which basic instruction is needed. Find someone who can teach you well, practice alone and in a group. If you have been meditating for a while and feel stuck, find a guide to give you a nudge. Maybe your practice needs to change.

Anchoring in what's true and alive every day is the surefire highway home.

A Teacher, Mentor or Guide:

Certain journeys need to be undertaken with an experienced guide, one who is an expert in the field, who has authentically awakened, who walks the talk, and offers a transmission that cannot be received through mere book learning and knowledge. We may have one root teacher or learn from different ones. Nobody is perfect, neither are guides and teachers. Consider if the person has integrity, sincerity and knows the spiritual and human world well. Avoid those who decorate themselves with glamour; there are many false prophets out there. Make sure the teacher doesn't exploit his/her position for sex, money, prestige or personal benefit.

Most true teachers tend to be rather simple, real and ordinary. Some live hidden from the public eye; some are on the main stage of this world. A relationship with a teacher can help, for with a supporting hand and a strong light you won't get lost so easily. Authentic spiritual teachers won't put themselves on a pedestal, but will always point you back to yourself, to your innate wisdom. They will be with you and give you a hand when you need it, they will challenge you where you're stuck, uplift you by recognizing your highest potential, and hold you to your deepest aspiration, value and commitment in your soul.

A teacher is a fire that ignites yours.

A Sangha/Community/Spiritual friends:

A sangha is a circle of people committed to awakening and practicing together. It can be difficult to keep up a spiritual practice alone, but when you do it together it is much easier to follow through. Find a spiritual community of people who support and uplift each other to awaken to the highest potential, who hold each other to this commitment, and give a hand when one falls. Such a group can be a strong vehicle where the learning, growth and awakening are accelerated for everyone.

A sangha is not an exclusive club with uptight regulations. Even one friend dedicated to the truth can be a crucial source of support, helping you both on the way. Since we're not all blind in the same spot, we can compassionately illuminate one another's areas of blindness, which might otherwise keep us stuck for years. At its best a dedicated group provides a safe, kind and truthful container where tremendous growth can occur. Such a circle of spiritual friends can create a field that uplifts and deepens us naturally.

We need times of aloneness, but a group of dedicated spiritual friends makes possible what we are unable to accomplish by ourselves.

Healing and Integration of the Personality:

Therapy isn't included in the ancient teachings as it did not yet exist, but it is essential for those of us who live in the contemporary world. A certain myth is perpetuated, that with mere spiritual practice, awakening experiences and wisdom teachings, the personality and our shadow material can be transcended or that a healer can wave all our troubles away. There might have been rare occasions, when this occurred.

But the vasanas, karmas, traumas, shadow aspects and energetic knots arise, especially after an opening or a realization. As you open the door to the light, what was stored in the closet can finally be seen. You cannot meditate the shadow away. No matter how much you try to escape or rise above, it is still here when you "come down" and follows you around like a faithful old dog. Our psyche needs to be met and tended to in a different way. And it is often necessary to find help from a skilled person to address unhealed issues and wounds we carry from relationships and life.

These days, different healing modalities and many kinds of therapists are available. Choose the one that resonates with you, and a person who has sufficient skill and experience. It doesn't matter if the therapist has the same spiritual approach as you; what matters more is that they understand, know how to relate and emanate a field for healing, respect and trust.

To love being human with all our vulnerabilities and fragilities and to embody presence, truth and love into the field of relating, and into the marketplace, is what it is about. If the work of integration isn't done, a person may have great mystical experiences, awakenings and insights, but emotionally be stuck as a four-year-old unable to relate with their mate or be responsible in life. There are spiritual masters who can't function in the world, or who exploit women in the guise of tantric initiations. This indicates a personality that is undeveloped. When the personality is treated as the enemy or the thing we must get rid of and the preparation of the human vessel has not been undertaken, or is only partially completed, spiritual embodiment does not occur. It is also important for the nervous system to be sufficiently aligned so a greater energy can flow freely through, instead of creating havoc or blockages due to our unresolved issues.

It is a labor of love to refine the human instrument so that it can play masterfully to its highest capacity in harmony with the grand symphony of life.

Service:

To serve in action something greater than ourselves is an important element. My daughter went one day to her volunteer project at the homeless garden. She left grumpy and in a lousy teenage mood. Later she returned on her bike with flowers in her hand and a big smile on her face: "Mum, this was just wonderful to help out. I feel so much better now. It's much more meaningful than school."

The service we offer without expecting a return connects us with our nature and what matters in life. Service is a spiritual practice, often undervalued, but is a profound way to let go of selfishness. When we give fully and serve a greater cause, we grow too. To feed another who is less fortunate, feeds us too. This can happen through helping in a soup kitchen, at an animal shelter, by giving someone a hand, fixing a flat tire, going shopping for a sick neighbor, and more deeds that inspire and set the heart on fire. (Read more in the chapter: "Service Rocks the World.")

Selfless service opens the heart and unleashes love.

Awake relating and engaging in the world:

The path of enlightenment meant in the past to leave the world. You would enter a monastery, live in a cave or ashram to practice undisturbed with one-pointed attention. This certainly is helpful for a while. However, sitting on the meditation cushion is one side, the other is to embody love in the world. Meditation and action is one flow. Realization is not complete until you engage from that here on earth. As a mother or father you can approach parenting as your spiritual practice ground. You might experience deep states of peace in your meditation, but when your kid is screaming at the top of her lungs, how do you respond then? From peace or agitation?

Our relationships with people reveal where our triggers are, thereby providing fuel for our awakening—if we see it as such. Often in relating with another we are brought to our edge; this shows exactly where work and healing are needed. How you dance in relating gives you a reality check, where you are truly at, and what is calling to be tended to in and between the two of you (read more in "Resonance Communication for Every Season").

And then there is the wider world, the fabric to which we are intrinsically connected with. We may know conceptually that we are related to every human whom we meet on a busy street or café. But how do we relate in a way that affirms our interconnectedness and creates a society where each person is respected and cared about? We may enjoy and love nature, yet how do we commune with plants and animals, and protect our environment? In this time of great turmoil we take our meditation cushion into the streets of this world for inspired, empowered and wise action—in benefit for all beings we turn the wheel (read more about it in the "Welcome Humanity" and "Loving Wild Earth" chapters in the book).

We meditate to access and abide in the truth, and we venture into this messy and beautiful world to act from that, no matter what. This makes the circle whole and love real.

5. Foundation Stones

The two wings approach

Spirituality, like everything else, can be used as an escape from life, each other and ourselves. From the world with all the beauty and horror. From the pain that aches in the heart, deep down. From the joy knocking at your door, unexpectedly. From the consequences of our actions and those pesky relationship troubles.

Actually, spirituality calls and leads into life—as it is. Inviting us to show up present for the whole human experience—real, heartbroken sometimes, getting our hands dirty, navigating both difficulties and glorious moments with wholeheartedness—and letting love live us no matter what. But we feel this strong urge to escape, especially when s*** hits the fan and the fire is on. It's OK and so very human to want to run, to hide, or to rise above to get away. Then it helps to remember why you have come. What beats in your heart that's bigger than the survival fear. What holds you right now—the earth, God/Goddess, the dharma, your own loving presence or the hand of your friend. And maybe, just maybe, turn around and walk right toward what is calling out your name since forever long.

This is the bread and butter chapter for unleashing love in our life and this world. It provides a solid foundation to stand upon for the journey of awakening so that we do not build our lives on shifting sand, while offering essential cornerstones for those who guide and help people. It enables us to turn toward what is calling our name. The "Two Wings" approach aligns with any spiritual path you may have, or if you wish to simply experience more love and happiness in life, these are the most important ingredients you will need for baking life-sustaining bread to share with the world.

Throughout the book, and in the retreats and trainings I offer, you will find more magical ways for living present, wholehearted and connected—no matter where you are at and what your circumstances are. They can move us from a mere conceptual understanding of loving presence into walking our talk, navigating storms and challenges wisely, and responding, rather than reacting to life. The field of love is always here, but this approach and these practices help to return home when we feel lost, to reconnect in the midst of turmoil or fear, and to live from this alive presence to rise in a world on the edge. Be assured, these foundation stones, if applied, will transform lives, relationships, our work and the world at large—positively, constructively and often miraculously, into the presence of love that is already always and forever here.

***

Years ago, when spiritual tourism didn't yet exist in the Amazon, I had the good fortune to train with a powerful, wise shaman woman and lived with the indigenous tribe in the heart of the jungle. I slept on bare earth in a tiny hut and learnt to be in communion with nature.

Much happened in the many months of rigorous training, and one auspicious day, my crinkled old medicine woman, motioned me to follow. Curiously, I walked barefoot with some men and women from the tribe beneath the vibrant, humongous trees and thick roots until we reached an opening where the sun pierced through. It was so hot, I was dripping wet. She told me that this was my initiation and if I succumbed to fear I would definitely die. Then she asked in a serious, fierce tone, if I am ready. Well, if I died here it would be alright, or so I thought. (I didn't have a child yet.) There is little that scared me, except big hairy spiders, and I encountered plenty of these here, even in my bed. So I motioned, unperturbed, with no clue what awaited me: *Sure, ready for anything.*

She covered my eyes with a worn cloth and began chanting and drumming. I dropped into stillness, while heavy barefoot steps approached. Suddenly from behind, an enormous weight was laid upon my shoulders. Immediately I sank to my knees and ripped off the scarf from my eyes. Shock jolts surged through my entire body. This was a full-grown anaconda snake hanging on me! *Holy Mother*. My teacher laughed through her brownish teeth, and declared that the snake hadn't eaten. So if I freak-out she would strangle me and could not be loosened. Was she joking? I realized quickly, unfortunately not. Slowly, but surely the snake's head moved straight toward my face, with her tongue sticking out, hissing at me.

No fear? I was terrified out of my wits and shaking like a leaf. To make matters worse, with focused motion, she was slithering closer and closer toward my wet, soft neck. Instinctively I had put my hands there. Naïve, for that would make no difference whatsoever now.

What do you do, when you can't stop fear and it will surely lead to what you fear the most?

Will it be life or death? I had only seconds. Sweat was dripping from my forehead. This was the test for real, without drugs or crutches. Would years of spiritual practice and her training get me through? Luckily, I remembered to breathe and breathe again into my belly, then, into my feet. I leaned my weight into the ground, to root down to earth. I acknowledged the fear and turned toward presence, widened my awareness, seeing lush green leaves and hearing the monkey haulers laughing. Breathing deeper, and consciously relaxing in the midst of terror. Seemed counterintuitive, but it calmed my shaken nerves, and helped me to be to fully present. She responded, stopping midair. But it's not enough, without love. How to connect with this enormous, hungry anaconda? I opened my heart a bit, by seeing her beauty, and a flicker of love sparked between her and me. To my astonishment exactly in that moment, she slowly dropped her head lower and lower. As I merged with this primal force of life that unites us, she rested her head gently against my belly, wrapping her body around mine. Awed I squatted down and lo and behold, she fell asleep peacefully in my lap. I felt her intimately as I stroked her shimmering skin. What an awesome life power this snake embodied, utterly sensual, and wild. We spent an unforgettable hour together, until she slithered gracefully away to find another prey.

My crazy teacher grinned from one ear to another; apparently I'd passed my shamanic initiation. Something irreversibly changed in me. I was not the same person who entered the jungle several months ago— silent presence had taken over and the feminine power had awoken in me. Like the snake, this pulsing and rich life power, surges untamed through all creation. It's not to be feared. I can only surrender into that and let it live me how it wants, all the way.

***

Loving Presence
The Two Wings of Awareness and Embrace

Awareness and embrace are our two wings, which support us to awaken into our natural loving presence and to unleash its power untethered and skillfully in the world. We need both wings to fly, flourish and serve. Awareness, or mindfulness, helps us to show up present in this moment as it is, to cut through delusions and transcend our limitations. But, awareness alone can lead to cold detachment; dry and disconnected from our heart and humanity. Embracing is the other wing. It opens us to love, to experience warmth, empathy, connection and compassion. On its own it can lead to codependence in relationships, and the loss of our discernment and will.

We turn on the light of awareness to see what is in our house and environment with a clear lens. And it is lovingness, which fills the home with warmth, food and flowers at the table. As awareness is the empty sheet of the canvas, the way of embrace offers the colors, filling space with life's wonder. It is through the sword of insight that we can end an abusive relationship, and it is through loving embrace that we recognize the innate goodness in each, even if buried, so we do not cast the person out from our heart and grow hate. Through presence we can lead people in a brilliant way, and through our human heart we generate the field of profound connectedness. It is through awareness that we come to understand the nature of suffering and take steps to end the cycle of ignorance. And it is through compassionate embrace we include and hold all in our love, without exception, pouring kindness into life and standing with bold fierceness on earth.

We need to unite the earth—the feminine, and the sky—the masculine, within us. To realize that human and divine are one. And when the two wings of awareness and loving are joined the bird flies home, benefiting our lives and this world. Like a fledging bird we practice using our wings in everyday life. This frees us from suffering and to embody love in this eternal moment now.

The Wing of Presence—Awareness and Mindfulness
Ascending to cultivate the masculine principle: the sword, insight and clarity, spaciousness, non-attachment.

Who is here in the now?
We know about the Buddha, who taught the path of the dharma, which applies today, just as it did thousands of years ago. There are many great masters: Shiva, who cut through all delusion to be free for eternity; Babaji, who still appears to followers in the remote mountains; and Yogananda, who brought yoga and

united timeless teachings from East to West. Others are devoted to Christ, the master healer, who showed the path of love by his way of life; or Pir Vilayat Khan, a beautiful Sufi teacher who took many souls home before he departed the earth. You may have met Thich Nhat Hahn, the Buddhist monk who paved the way for mindfulness to flourish in the Western world. There are other awake ones—maybe your father, grandfather or a mentor who guides you on the path. Each teaches in their unique way the importance of seeing through the delusions to discover freedom, showing us a clear path through the mire of impermanence and samsara (the wheel of ignorance and suffering) to guide us to the brilliant light of truth and wisdom, which is available to each of us in the now.

Transcendence has been the way from ancient times, practiced to ascend beyond form and the drama of the world, to rise above the delusions and the ignorance of our minds. Here we learn to use the sword of insight and discernment to cut through the endless mountain of baggage we have accumulated and shoot our arrow straight into what is true. When Buddha sat under the Bodhi tree and illusions assailed him, one-pointedly he focused on truth and was enlightened in that moment.

The practice of awareness takes us to the recognition that our human body is limited, that life is impermanent, and that who we are is far vaster than our daily worries and desires and who we believe we are. Being present is like standing on the mountaintop and expanding our view. Here, we can find a path through our attachments and deceptions. When we step back from our familiar movie to gain a larger perspective, we breathe fresh air and face things as they are, without identifying so closely with the images on the projection screen. What is true becomes far more interesting then.

Our minds often look through a magnifying glass at a problem; the little spider becomes a monstrous creature then.

We do not see reality and our perspective tends to be distorted. We may argue with someone that the leg of the spider is an elephant's trunk, while they claim it to be a tree trunk. Both views are limited; thereby we do not understand each other. Confusion arises, we argue from our different perceptions, we get into a mess, and, soon enough, reality is dismissed. It is almost funny, but it is sad too how we create rifts. When we wear rose-colored glasses over our eyes, we project our imaginations—and we usually think we are right—onto the world and other people as well. This is the cause of the divisions and tensions between this person and that person, this group and that group.

Cultivating awareness breaks the grip of our "trips" to discover the light. Without awareness we just repeat patterns and scripts that usually have nothing to do with life or love. With awareness your internal space becomes larger, we see more then what the usual eye beholds.

A mindfulness practice helps to find clarity, ungluing us from the television screen of projections, assumptions, and old stories; allowing the struggle with life and other people to cease. We are able to face reality as it is; walking freely and relating with others authentically. A natural sense of acceptance arises toward what is here and we find ease in meeting it, rather than stressing about what should and shouldn't be there. Whether the dinner with your family is pleasant or unpleasant, you learn to notice what is happening inside of you and in your surroundings. It is how it is right now. When we talk to one member in the family our shoulders and belly might tighten up and we are ready to jump to attack. What breaks the spell of the reaction chain is to shine the lamp of awareness: "I notice tension and defensiveness in me."

Through the mere act of noticing what is happening in the moment, exactly as it is, you are able to step back from the habitual reactions, take a vaster view, or just rest in peacefulness, because you don't need to defend yourself anymore. The view on politics from Uncle Joe can be here, as well as the worries of Auntie Jane and your own upset—is OK, too. You might even laugh, free to play in the whole charade.

But, how often we argue and struggle with life instead. The mind tends to fight with reality and tries hard to control, and the odd thing is it doesn't change life as it is. However, if we turn on the light of awareness we get unstuck, we see another perspective and can step out of the trance. You may observe, "Ah, yes, I notice I feel entangled in my all-too-familiar movie script." If we refrain from judging, we can ask, "What is here and what is true?" Then we actually have a choice not to perpetuate suffering and respond wisely, or ignite change for the better and act from love. You might just walk out of the old movie there and then.

Awareness leads us beyond our attachments, the past and future obsessions into powerful presence, for in the now we are free to be, and anything is possible then. If you are a leader of a group, it is crucial to access awareness and center yourself in presence. Only then can you easily include all the different personalities and brilliantly guide the group toward a greater vision and wise action. Being present helps us to actively listen to what is of benefit now, without internal interference of our own opinions and thoughts, and guides us to find a way, even in the most challenging situations.

A client came to me who was fuming with fury. I supported him to fully feel the anger, to stay present with his experience, meaning not to go into the past story or a future scenario, but to be with what is happening now and trust the flow. To breathe, to feel the anger in the body and let it move in its own way. And I was present with him, not trying to change or fix him, looking into his eyes and meeting the anger straight on. He felt safe to feel it then, and his fury burst like a volcano; his power was set free and a deeper truth was revealed. He sobbed in utter relief.

Unhappy, he had carried this burden for a lifetime, and now much more alive, he skipped like a happy, young child.

When we are neither caught in the past nor chasing a distant future, we abide in the eternal present. And it only works one magical moment at a time to return to here and now.

The Wing of Loving—Embrace and Heartfulness
Descending to cultivate the feminine principle: the grail, devotion compassion, juiciness, connectedness.

What is longing to be embraced?
The great mother, the feminine face of the One, is revered in many countries, and she also has been hidden, degraded and disregarded for centuries. Yet she rises again and again, especially in times of great turmoil in our world. She is the Black Madonna, who lifts up the lost and fallen ones in the dark streets of cities and forgotten villages. She is Tara, with eyes in her hands and feet, who swiftly takes those in fear to the shore of peace. She shows up as Kwan Yin, the great compassionate one, and the Shekinah and Sophia, who infuse us with wisdom. She is Mary Magdalene, gentle as a dove and fierce as the lioness, known also as the beloved of Christ, who embodies the deep way of love. She is Kali who devours the demons and burns through delusions to nirvana. And she is Mary, whom people call upon, often when in utter despair. She is the earth, the great Pachamama, who feeds, restores and sustains us always. She might appear as your grandmother, your mother, or a mentor who takes your hand to lead you across the bridge from suffering to loving. In this time we need the feminine, she who restores and revives dry lands and hardened hearts, she who connects us with the soft, wild earth and each other with a love that radically embraces everything and everyone, without exception, into her wide, open arms. And through her fierceness she makes

a bold stand for justice, truth and love. She is unleashing herself through you and me.

She is rising up from the deep dark

The wisdom teachings of the feminine are as old as creation itself, usually passed on orally from one generation to another. Her way is to descend into the body, the rich ground of life. Her juice is the power of creation itself, feared as the snake, which rises up in our spine. In her fierceness she roars like a lioness to make a stand for life. And she is gentle like a dove, soothing you like a tender mother at night. Her love weaves through our relationships and the intimate connection with all beings. She goes down and in, unafraid to meet what she finds, to return all her children home. And it is through her boundless heart that she embraces the divine spark in all forms and expression on earth. She is alive in the wind, the laughter and tears of a child, the eyes of your mate and the tiger hunting his prey. That is why she loves and honors all as her own.

The way of the feminine is about embracing all life, no one and nothing is left out of her infinite warmth of love and compassion. A baby is cradled and lovers hold each other in sweet embrace. Remember when you were lying in soft grass, how you felt nourished and supported by the earth? Resting in the welcoming arms of a friend, we sigh and relax. When we are received just as we are, we feel safe, accepted and at ease. We have tasted this warmth and nourishment somewhere and have offered empathy and kindness to others too. It feels natural and good when we do.

The feminine, her immense life force is one of the strongest expressions of love. As mothers, if healthy, we embrace our baby unconditionally, whether it cries, poops or smiles. A mama receives her little one, unquestioned and meets the baby's need by offering all of herself. It's an act of sheer devotion and surrender toward love, which catapults us out of familiar limitations and selfishness, into experiencing pure aliveness and joy.

I remember when my daughter learned to ride her red bike. Beaming, she rode happily with her long blond hair flying behind her. She lifted her hands in excitement to wave to me; so proud she was that she had made the first round. Oh, it was painful to see, when she fell and scraped her legs bloody, tears streaming down her face. I ran and scooped her up, held her in my arms, until tears ebbed into hiccups and then subsided. I offered what was needed for her—a comforting embrace, and, of course, a colorful plaster for the scraped knee. And soon she smiled again. "Want to have another go?" I nudged. I walked beside her and told her to keep her fingers on the handlebars. I cheered her on with every turn she made and picked her up each time she fell. Soon enough she mastered riding the bike and was off with the wind.

We rise up and fall down in life. When we are loved in our glories and failures, with our joys and pains, we develop confidence and courage; we feel accepted as we are. Remember how good it felt when you were down and out and a friend held you, sobbing into her shirt, in a simple embrace? Or when you opened without restraint to joyously embrace your beloved or friend? Or, when a person simply listened, did not try to fix you, but understood you, and expressed validation and compassion? This is the ability of empathy, emotional intelligence, which allows us to experience connection. And of course we feel happier too.

The capacity to embrace others and ourselves with genuine empathy emanates from a tenderized and open heart. And through acceptance we receive people, situations, our partners, the world and even our human self: the sweat on our bodies and our messy hair, the joys and sorrows, the embarrassment and shame, our hardness and beauty. Allowing the luminosity of every being to touch us, to receive each into our heart, leaving out nothing and no one. She is everything after all; how then could anyone be left out in the cold, separated from existence itself? And yet, this is often how we feel. Offer this sense of isolation, the orphaned feelings, the worthlessness into the mother's lap. Rather than rejecting, welcome the shame and exuberance in others and yourself.

Embracing is not being codependently enmeshed, or merged in an infantile manner, nor is it expressed through smothering. Rather, we practice receiving into our hearts the reality we encounter, we give permission for the raw force of life to surge through us, letting shadows to be seen, and allowing our resistance to melt. We offer our love by understanding and meeting another exactly as they are. How have you felt when a person genuinely embraced you? Accepted, loved maybe? And what do you leave out and resist in the world or in yourself?

Wrap your arms around the suffering and what you fear the most.

Embracing is a lifelong practice, which leads to greater compassion and connection

It's not an easy path, because it means to face our inner hells, barriers, judgments and fears. But our capacity for love grows each time we nudge closer toward what we wish to keep out in the world and in ourselves. The shadow is her cauldron and it's calling for your liberation. And yes, it's a wild ride to uncover her and there is caring in the midst of it. Not the girl like "niceness" but real kindness, which is a courageous act. It's cultivated by applying it in everyday situations, such as relating to the trash collector with the same respect and friendliness as with the vice president of our company; whether we like or know them is beside the point. And let there be kindness for you as well as you drop the veils.

She is awaiting you, lean into Her and let her feed you the fruits of life. Lean into love, like floating on a river, you are carried. Just like the earth, who supports us, she invites you to experience being held by letting go into her. It is an act of surrender to fall into her grace, a way of softening the hard edges into what is greater than our little self. This allows us to feel safe, nourished and held. Being in love is the ultimate and complete embrace; the yearning for such union is edged deep in the soul.

By allowing ourselves to lean in, a fierce, tender feminine power emerges, the one who cradles us gently and sets fire under our sweet butt. For, she is the one who dares to make a stand for justice, the one who raises her voice to speak truth to power, who honors and protects what is precious, vulnerable in life — regardless of the consequence and cost.

She is the One we need now in these troubled times. Walk through your fear and meet her, she is ready to be unleashed in you for the sake of all!

Embodying Loving Presence

The invitation for being here on this earth is: Realize who you are and embody it in the here and now, in the muck and beauty and in the way you live and act.

Who we are is greater than any obstacles we face in our lives and the world. When we spread our wings and fly home, our deepest longing is fulfilled and true happiness abides, independent of circumstances and conditions. We feel alive, experience pain and joy more vividly, we might feel raw, vulnerable and yet, so strong too. We are falling in love with life as it is — beautiful and terrible. The more we connect and embody, the more unprecedented intelligence and power flows through us to create, and love takes up full-time residence. And so, we practice to walk our talk and live with integrity more and more, even when we fall unto the ground many a time. Like a tree, as we grow in maturity, others will find refuge in the loving arms of our presence; at times they will be ignited and wisely guided to make a difference in their lives, relationships and our world. Thank you for being you and for stepping into the power of love now.

Love in Action

These are ancient and modern East-West practices to fly with both wings into the heavens and walk with both feet on the ground of this earth.

The Feminine Wing – Elements of the embracing practice:

I am here with you: Whatever arises within or around us, it helps to speak: "I am here with you." It's the hand we need when we feel scared.

Grounding: Centering into the earth and our body is crucial, or else we tend to loop around in our mind or disassociate and experience anxiety and stress. Wiggle the feet. Shake your body or dance. Let the movement come from your body; let your wild animal move as it wants. Lie on the ground and feel how the earth or the chair holds you. Let the weight of your body drop down. Feel the support from below and how safely held you are. Stay in touch with the natural rhythm of your breath and enjoy.

Sensing and inhabiting the body: Let yourself enter your body and experience all sensations. Open into the sense of aliveness. (Read more about relating to the body in the chapter: "This Human House.")

Feeling: The ability to feel freely is crucial for empathy and compassion to develop and essential for our relationships. Let yourself feel without rejecting, dramatizing or making up a story. Allow feelings to arise, to move through you and flood them with breath. (For more on how to relate wisely to feelings see the chapter, "This Human House.")

One Taste Pleasure: A tantric practice to take pleasure in the one taste to experience fulfillment. Take pleasure in one bite of fruit, let it linger in your mouth, taste the flavor, texture, take delight in that. Take pleasure in one touch. Receive in full. This practice undermines the craving for more. Taking pleasure in one taste is a practice you can apply for your whole life.

Receiving Nourishment: Bring your attention toward what is good and nourishing in your environment in this present moment. This could be a tree, a cat, a friendly person, a beautiful picture, a favorite poem, a bird's song, or delicious food... breathe it in. Allow yourself be touched, revel in the good and be nourished by it. This feeds you, and it also helps in times of distress. For women a beautiful practice to destress and connect with the nourishing breath of oxytocin: breathe in through the nose, breathe out a sound of pleasure through your mouth. Let the sound of pleasure travel into your belly, then into your solar plexus and into your heart. It works miracles!

Welcoming Intention: Put your hand on your heart and say to yourself: "May I receive these tender feelings (situation, experience) into my heart. May I be kind and compassionate toward what I experience. May I receive you... (name of the person) into my heart."

Softening and Opening: Open and soften toward what is joyful or painful. Use your breath. Stay in your body. Feel while opening to it. Let the contraction in your body and psyche melt.

Say Yes: To your experience as it is in this moment and embrace yourself as a good mother or father would.

Cradling: Receive your own and another person's vulnerability with gentleness and utmost care. Cradle the tender, fragile places with your heart; infuse them with your love.

Answering the need: Ask yourself or a friend: "What do you need?" Sometimes it means just simply being there; at other times it is a word of comfort, a touch, or a helping hand. You may need a warm bath, a hug, healthy food... ask for what you need without expectation from others, and take good care of yourself too.

Allowing and Acceptance: What is here as it is, whether we want it or not. When you allow what is here, such as a certain feeling or situation, you open and can respond fresh. You are at peace with life on its own terms, including yourself. Allowing yourself to just be as you are, not trying to change or work on something, relaxes and restores. Allowing is giving permission for what wants to happen naturally; then we move in alignment with what is good for all involved.

Radical Embrace: Hold the world in your arms, just like a great mother would. Embrace what is showing up in your hands. Slowly lift it toward your heart. When you encounter resistance receive this too. Breathe in the discomfort, breathe out and offer friendliness toward it.

Meet and tend to what is here: Let yourself feel all the feels, without trying to change them. With loving kindness tend to the pain, let warmth fill you and reach a hand to the part in you that feels alone. Softly speak, *"I am here with you."* Or: *"May I take good care of my fear."* This offers safety and a sense of being held. Sometimes we are so lost and confused that we cannot access our kindness, and then it helps to take refuge in what is bigger than us, like noticing how the earth is holding you right now. Let yourself relax into that. Don't try to be different or more enlightened, but rather attend to your experience like a friend. Allow the love to move through you and like a good mother or father to touch and love it all.

Boundaries: Embracing doesn't mean we have no healthy boundaries and invite everyone into our home or give all our money away. We can love everyone, but we don't invite everyone to sleep in our bed, or put up with abuse. Discernment helps us to make wise choices. The temple of a human being needs protection; as does a child, an elderly or vulnerable person.

First the tree sapling needs a high fence to keep the deer from eating it, and later when grown mature and strong no fence is needed, and the deer join to rest under its shade.

Devotion: This is a way to open the heart and be filled by unconditional love. We give ourselves over to Truth, the mystery, the dharma; what we love deeply, be it nature, the mother in all, or our own essence. We worship and honor Her in all forms through offering our attention, cherishing acts, and by the way we walk and live. "I offer the fruits of my actions unto Thee."

Receptive Listening and Being: Sitting in silence under a tree and being receptive to what the tree may tell us, or just feeling the peaceful energy, is nourishing and connects us. Being receptive is an ability we can cultivate, by turning to life and our heart, listening to what it tells us. We might be moved to sing a song, stretch the body or just to rest, being in stillness, with nothing to do.

Opening the Heart and Vulnerability: Is the golden key to loving and happiness. We may believe our heart is open, yet we all have barriers to block out the light. Most of us are afraid to be vulnerable, as we have experienced hurt before. Read the chapter "A Heart Wide Open" for more about this.

Fierceness: It can be scary to meet the fire of a lioness who roars: *"Enough. No more. Not with me." "You will not destroy this earth, the line is here. You have no right to abuse and violate what is sacred..."* Connecting to your authentic power and voice is essential to bring forth change. Fierceness is not hard and aggressive or self-righteous, but rather arises from a profound love, willing to do whatever it takes to stand for justice and what's true. This power rises from deep within your belly and womb; if you allow, she will speak and act through you.

Shadow Work: The presence of love, by its very nature, brings up everything unhealed in us and shines the light into our knots, attachments, fears, judgments, etc. for only one purpose:

to set us free. In order to live an integrated and healthy life, to not create harm, and be able to walk our talk and benefit others it is important that we face our stuff, instead of bypassing it or sweeping it under the rug. For more on Shadow work, see the following chapters: "Healing Wounds of Life," "Loving You," and "The Kiss and Gold."

Flow of Aliveness: Take a step back and open to sense the aliveness in your body; stay present and allow it to flow. Notice how and where the natural flow of life moves you. Listen deeply and follow it. When we lead a group or work with clients, we need a structure and our professional tools in place. And we want to move with the natural unfolding of the group as well. This requires a deep connection with ourselves, others, and a felt sense of how the intelligent flow of life wants to move in the most beneficial and efficient way. (Read more in the chapter, "Follow the Red Thread.")

Forgiveness: We are set free when we are willing to forgive, but this doesn't mean to condone a grievous act done by us or another person. Premature forgiving does not work; at most it is a superficial bandage that covers an infected wound. When touched it will hurt again and again. We have to do the labor of moving through our pain, the anger, the grief, and then forgiveness emerges naturally, like nectar flowing from a flower. How do we move toward forgiveness? (Read more in the "Healing Wounds of Life" chapter.)

Gratitude: As a family we always spoke this before a meal: "Thank you for this meal and the bounty of our earth. May all beings be fed as well as we." We can practice gratitude by saying "thank-you" for everything we receive; this opens our heart and helps us to see the glass half full, instead of half empty. You can create a gratitude practice by naming three things or people or experiences you are grateful for. For example, write or say, "I am grateful for the soft wind touching my body. I am grateful for my friend and his care. I am grateful for a healthy body."

Choose simple, everyday things, and notice how you feel when you practice being grateful. Gratitude for even small things offers nourishment, and we become more open to receive and give love.

Savoring Nectar: This is soothing and nourishing for your whole being. It fills your empty cup with love. Find it in the practice section of the "Love's Sense" chapter.

Surrender: The deeper we surrender to love's way, to the truth, the freer and more aligned we live and breathe. Surrender is not just a one-time affair. It goes deeper each time we bow our head in service to the heart. It is a deep surrender to the divine will, to truth, or the intelligence of life. This can catapult us through anything, if it comes from sincerity. With our whole heart we can say, "Thy will be done." Watch what happens then.

Service: Letting love serve through us. Offering our gifts, talents, resources and love in service to the world allows us to step out from our little shell; it benefits others and us too. For more on service see the practice sections in the chapter "The Kiss and Gold" or the chapter "Service Rocks the World."

Meditation for Loving Embrace:

Sit upright and allow your face to relax and your shoulders to soften. Let your weight drop into the chair or ground, breathing gently into your belly. Lean into the support from below, feel how the earth is holding you and give yourself permission to simply be as you are right now.

Gaze with your eyes open into your surroundings and see or hear something that is good, it can be the view from your window, a picture, a song, or your pet. Breathe in that goodness; let it nourish you in every cell of your body. Notice how it feels. Relax, open and revel in it, as if you are taking a bath in beauty and allow yourself to be filled by a moment of simple nourishment. Feel how you are nourished and held by life in this moment now, no matter what else is going on. Just be, nothing to do. Stay with that for a few minutes.

And then begin breathing into your heart. Thank your heart for keeping you alive and working so hard for you. Let the area in your chest soften a bit, allowing the breath to flood you. Then place your hands on your lap. Imagine you are holding in your hands someone, or a part of you that needs your love and care. See it as a child. Don't try to fix or change it, but rather connect with the mother in you, with the wise one, the grown one who is capable of receiving a baby or a friend with kindness. Receive this one by lifting your hands slowly unto your heart. Let your hands rest there and feel that you are the mother, embracing a lost or frightened child with infinite compassion. Reside here for a while and notice what you feel and what happens in you when you say these words: "May I embrace what is hungry and aching for a drop of love." Allow that drop or stream from your heart to embrace and fill this little one. Enjoy what arises, maybe a sense of warmth, a tickle, an opening and gentle surrendering, giving into the arms of love.

The Masculine Wing—Awareness Practices:

Mindfulness is a practice, which you can use all day long. You notice you spaced out for ten hours. Simply noticing this fact, without judging, you are returned to the present moment. If we wish to resolve an issue, we can use awareness to find new solutions, instead of travelling the common road taken: trying to figure it out with a frantic mind. Step back, breathe, let go for a moment into spaciousness, as if you are standing on a mountain with a vast view, and expand to see the bigger picture. You can use the following techniques to help you in your practice:

Concentration: Return your attention over and over to the breath or a mantra. Bring conscious attention to the task at hand, such as noticing that you are typing at the computer. Do whatever you are doing deliberately slower, mindfully with your full concentration, as if nothing else exists. It helps the mind to return to the present and reduces stress.

Three Senses Practice: This is a straightforward and simple practice I developed for people who need a quick and easy way to return to presence. It helps to relieve anxiety, lessens stress and other dilemmas:

Notice three colors you are seeing in your environment. Notice two sounds you are hearing. Become aware of one smell or taste. Notice your breath and the rising and falling of your belly. Become aware of the ground or chair holding you. Let your body weight drop into the support from below. Ask, *What else is present in this moment?*

What am I experiencing in this moment? Ask this question frequently. Bring mindful attentiveness toward body sensations, feelings, and thoughts, without trying to change them. Just notice and lean into your experience as it is. Moment by moment stay with what is happening now, even when it is uncomfortable. I promise, you will not only survive, but also become more alive and experience greater love.

Awareness: Ask, *What am I aware of in my environment?* Engage all your senses: see, hear, smell, taste, and touch. For each sense perception choose three outer objects to focus on that are here now. For example: I *see* a bird flying. I *hear* the hooting of a car. I *smell* jasmine.

Witnessing: Observing what is going on. Paying attention to this moment. Notice the environment, other people, actions, and our internal landscape with its sensations, thoughts, and feelings, without grasping or rejecting. Become aware of what is actually happening. It is irrelevant if we think a car's horn should not be honking. It is honking and it isn't personal. Simply notice your discontent. It's OK; it is what is here for now. And then it changes again.

Being curious and meeting what is here: Curiosity allows us to perceive with an open mind and discover the world with fresh and new eyes. Let yourself be curious like a child. What else is here that you can explore? Apply curiosity to your own experience: "Interesting that I feel fear, I wonder what is going on?"

Mind: Getting to know the workings of our mind and taming the bull of our mind is important for gaining clarity and awareness. (For more help with this, read the section on relating to the mind in the chapter "This Human House.")

Widening Focus: Use a soft and inclusive gaze: *I see the flower and the sky is here too. I notice my agitation and the sun shines too.* There is more than this particular circumstance or experience. This helps you to get unstuck.

Acknowledge what is here: Greet what is showing up like a guest. Look with clarity, face the situation directly. No analyzing, fixing, changing, but seeing it nakedly as it is. For example, "I acknowledge my boss is coming and I feel like running." Acknowledge your experience as it is, but don't react to it.

Validate and accept: "I accept judgment is making a case in my mind. I honor that I feel sorrow beneath it." It is OK. No labeling "good" or "bad," judging it as "right" or "wrong." Validation and acceptance does not mean we like or agree with what is showing up—the rain, a bill to pay, an angry person. It simply means that you are not struggling against what already is happening. Only then do we actually have space and freedom to choose and act beyond our usual conditioning.

Insight Questions: Asking open-ended questions can undo the knots in our mind. You do not ask the question in order to get an answer; rather the question is an exploration that opens the door to our presence. An insight question can be: "Who is here?" "What is true here?" or: "What would happen in me, if I knew that I am loved?" or "What occurs if I trust life?" Then you allow whatever comes in response to arise. Keep asking the same question. It unravels hardened mind formations and will take you deeper each time.

Plans and Detachment: We make better plans when present. Imagine you are on top of a mountain and look from above at your ideas and thoughts. Release the need to control for a moment, and ask, what is the best path here? Then listen and survey the land. If you get an insight, follow through and act. Release attachments toward what you think the outcome should be. It is easier that way. Often plans need to be adjusted, depending on the changing nature of life.

The Sword: Recognize what is here, observe the sounds and sights around you. Become aware of your feelings and your body. Be mindful—of what is here in your environment and with another—in this moment, without trying to change or judge it. Take the sword and cut through the mire of delusion by asking: "What is true here?"

Letting it be: Allow everything to be as it is, because it already is. The fear, the turmoil in the world is already present, no use pretending that it isn't. This basic acceptance includes your resistance to what is currently happening within you or in the world. Accepting what is does not mean agreeing or doing nothing. It implies that you stop fighting with what is, first, then can you respond wisely. Letting things be as they are allows us to relax even in the midst of challenge and then you can find a way through. Speak a silent YES to what is here, whether this is your sadness, your enthusiasm or your fury and see how it feels for you. This can end the war against life and ourselves. (Read more about the way of mindfulness and awareness in the "Presence" part of this chapter.)

Responsibility and Authenticity: Taking responsibility for our own issues, what we want, our intentions, our needs and our actions, is essential for love to flower and to keep the field clear and open. Being open and honest about our own affairs and showing up authentically in the world makes us far more real. For this to occur, of course, we need to turn on the light of awareness, which helps us to see what is going on, without blaming anything or anyone. By taking responsibility for ourselves, it's easier to "fess" up, if we mess up and set it right in the best way we can.

Integrity and Sincerity: Without honesty we won't get anywhere. We lie a lot to ourselves, but with sincerity and a dash of humility we can face truth. By walking our talk with integrity we embody spirituality. We become real and therefore trustworthy.

Awareness Meditation:

Relax into your body for a moment, take a breath. Sit back and become aware of what else is here, right where you are. Engage your senses. What do you see around you? What sounds do you hear? Feel the warmth or cold of the air. Let it all be as it is, without judging, trying to fix or changing anything. Just breathe and allow your belly to soften, letting the breath find its natural rhythm again. If the mind keeps taking over the reins, bring it back to the present moment like calling back a mischievous puppy. Pay attention to this breath and simply acknowledge what is here and arising in the present moment. Notice the sensations in your body. Become aware of any tension. Is there heat or cold in your body, a pain or tingling? How is your left toe doing and your little pinky finger? Let it all be as it is. Just become aware, say hello to the house you live in. Then bring your awareness to survey the landscape of your mind. Is the train speeding fast with lots of whirling thoughts, or is there space? Just notice and refrain from trying to stop the train. Neither reject nor cling to any thoughts. Let them move through like clouds in the sky, let judgment and confusion pass by. Then gently turn your attention toward what you are feeling. Allow any emotion that is arising, like joy or sadness; feel it, and then you might notice a natural shift. For this practice, do not get lost in a story, especially when raw emotions emerge. We tend to escape the experience by talking ourselves out of it, thinking about the story and disconnecting with what is happening in this moment. Just acknowledging the feeling, like a guest in our home, helps to end the wars within us. Let your awareness expand beyond your own self. Notice what happens when you let the mind open into vast sky and spaciousness. Realize you are the witness, and then allow yourself to let go, expanding into pure awareness. Drop into stillness and reside here.

Love and Presence soaring as One:

Become aware of your direct experience and what else is here, then all the different arising phenomena. There is the sky, the earth, the silence of your being, the love in your heart... Rest into that, take refuge. Surrender into the force of life. Let yourself feel the aliveness pulsating through your body, the joy of just being here. Take refuge in your true nature over and over again. (Read more about this throughout the book.)

What is your life for? Inquire deeply, honestly. It matters. If you stand for love, know, you will be tested. All conditioning will arise. It is not for the fainthearted to meet the demons and the turmoil. But there is nothing more worthwhile than to stand for and as love in this world.

Embody your Nature in Action: Love becomes real as we live it, is the mantra throughout this book. But how do we liberate and live that power in the midst of losses, sorrows and joys? You do not need formulas, but rather to be in touch with the alive presence and love and act from there. Let your intentions and words match your deeds. It sounds simple and it is, but it's not easy, as we all have accumulated conditioning. Yet, with our sincere dedication, practice, some skillful means, a dash of curiosity and willingness to engage, we step into freedom and live in a whole new way and in our relationships. And thereby we are turning the tide in our world. (Read more about this throughout the book.)

A practice for everyday life:

Breathing in and out let yourself settle in your body. Notice the sensations, your feelings, mind state and your environment. Don't get busy with it all, don't completely identify with it and don't reject anything. Let it all just simply be. Turn on your curiosity to discover: *What else is there?* Allow yourself to widen and to discover with an open mind.

Then speak to yourself this dedication: "I take refuge in presence and love now." What happens in you? Just notice. Speak it again: "I take refuge in love now, regardless of what is going on." This is your anchor when the sun shines and when the storms rage. Deepen into this practice. Feel how it affects your body. How would your body seat itself or walk, if you knew you are a king or a queen? Notice what happens if you allow your body to show the way.

If you like, take this further into your daily life. Ask yourself with the same curiosity and openness: *"How would I speak if I remember that I am love's presence?"* Or: *"How does the king or queen in me relate to this tricky situation in my life? How is love wanting to relate to my partner right now?"* Discover this fresh moment by moment and then actually act on it. Ask yourself from time to time: "How do I live out of integrity in my actions?" Then align yourself and your behavior again and again with the love and the truth you have dedicated your life to. (Read more about this in the "Walking the Talk" chapter.)

Because it is the living of who you truly are moment to moment in everyday life, no matter what is going on, which leads into spiritual embodiment.

You are the living water and wine. As you allow the source to move you unabashedly, a wave of love unleashes with a liberating, benevolent impact for your life and this world.

6. Touch of Grace and Grit

Miracles on the soles of our feet

Yesterday, in the dark and rain, I saw an old man lying crumpled up on the side of a business building in San Francisco. His only shelter was a small rim from the roof that kept him barely out of the cold rain. He laid there in a shabby sweatshirt and thin pants. I went to my car, got a thick blanket from the backseat, approached him and asked, "Sir, would you like me to cover you with a blanket?"

He looked up, he wasn't ill, drunk or on drugs, and replied: "I apologize, if I am in the way."

I kneeled down so he could hear me: "May I put a warm blanket around you?"

He nodded and then looked up bewildered: "Is this for real, or am I now going to heaven?"

I replied, "It's both, it's called human kindness. Sorry, sir, sometimes we forget that on the earth. Thanks for being in the way so I could pass some to you. Sweet dreams and good night."

He smiled happily. Wrapping him in a warm blanket was such a simple thing to do; it not only warmed his body, but both of our hearts.

A miracle, so easy to miss on the streets of this world.

***

After I had taught a spiritual retreat for a group of 50 people, tired, but pleased with the day, I sat down on our cozy red couch with four cats purring beside me. Outside a storm was howling and rain poured down in sheets, matching the wild array of feelings arising in me. Loneliness and sadness joined with my cup of tea. Our living room with its high ceilings seemed far too large after everyone had left… I had a difficult reality to digest: I had ended my marriage a few days ago. I experienced relief and grief. The dam broke, a flood came gushing, and I sobbed into the night. With a lit candle I hiccupped a prayer: "All I want is a bucket for my tears and flowers for my heart."

The next morning, I went to one of my favorite spots to walk along the ocean cliffs. When I looked toward the worn-out wooden bench, I rubbed my eyes at first. Was I imagining this? At the edge of the cliff, next to the bench, stood a forlorn big white bucket (the kind contractors use) and from it peeked a colorful bouquet of flowers. I put my nose in; the flowers smelled fresh, the lilies and roses were exquisite. Surely, they belonged to another lucky woman, so I strolled away.

Today was Valentine's Day; it used to be special, but now it just sucked. I mumbled, too bad that the universe can't write a card or send me flowers. I heard a loving voice inside of me speak, "Look over the cliff, your card awaits you." I gazed to the beach down below and laughed out loud. In large letters written in the sand were the words, "*I love you.*" Life is the best and most faithful lover ever.

After my walk, I returned back to the bench to enjoy the view of sunlight dancing across the horizon. This mysterious bucket with my favorite kind of flowers was still there. From the same loving voice I heard, "This is for you." *No, this couldn't possibly be, someone must have left them and will come back.* I stood glaring at those flowers; I really wanted them. Well, if they are truly for me, then please make it clear, I asked.

Only minutes later an older man came to the bench to sit down, and turned to me with a broad smile. "You received quite a gift there, hmm? Enjoy and happy Valentine's to you."

Was he an angel? Could be; they are not just floating around in a faraway heaven, but walk among us, if we have eyes to see and ears to hear. I did not wait any longer, but happily wrapped my arms around the bucket and flowers to take them home. And I gladly shared the Valentine's card in the sand with others, who too needed a wink from the universe to know that they too are loved.

***

Who orchestrated such a marvelous, ingenious display?

An apple seed grows into a tree. A baby is born. Nature paints the canvas of the sky never the same as the day before. The sun rises every morning. It feels as if you have known a new friend from another time. Just when you are in the ditch, a stranger speaks words that offer solace to your soul, or someone's hand points to a path and opens a door for you. Synchronicity is the natural expression of being in the flow of life, and love.

Miracles appear as everyday treasures on the road and some fall out of the ordinary; the hand and voice of grace are everywhere if we are willing to see beyond our usual ways. Miracles become obvious, when we are open to love and ready to be surprised.

We do not need to believe, but acknowledge what is already here. What we call miracles is natural—we experience them when we are present and available to the innate wonders in ordinary life. A birdsong from afar reaches your ears. The breath breathing you right now. None of this is of your own making. You did not create the dance of waves in the sea; you can't control the movement of the clouds.

Stop in the midst of busyness to look around and notice life's hand and movement. Allow yourself to open to what else is here other than the stories of your mind and the colors of emotions. One miracle is already occurring, and you have the honor and pleasure to recognize it. What is it? It can be a smile from a shopkeeper, a friendly wave of a hand, the wind, the moon rising... relish and enjoy. Then you will realize more and more those infinite touches of grace in everyday life and can respond more graciously and bravely toward anything that comes your way.

And there are those miracles that are beyond our comprehension, leaving us speechless, in awe. A woman whose one leg was shorter than the other, limping all her life, and after a deep healing meditation and prayer, with tears of joy she got up and walked straight for the first time. She threw away her crutch and never looked back. The boy, who hadn't spoken for two years after the accident and his father's death, uttered his first words into the ears of a horse, after I showed him how to talk with his new friend; and from then on he engaged with people again. The family who had been growing ice between each other, who lived for years in daily conflict, stoic silence and misery; after two hours of working with them, the animosity began to melt and a bridge into connection and communication was made. They came together and related with each other again.

We often say it's a miracle, when despite all odds a person regains their health, or when challenges seem insurmountable and a way appears out of nowhere for you, just when you threw in the towel. Situations that are out of our control can open the mind and heart and reach beyond our usual ways and perception of reality.

***

One beautiful autumn afternoon I rode my horse through the redwood forest and up into the mountains. The air was crisp, but still warm and we galloped in sheer joy along a steep, sandy trail, which we both knew well. Suddenly Magic my sure-footed horse faltered, stumbled and fell. Just in the nick of time I jumped off to save my little butt. With his body shaking all over, he was stuck, unable to get up. The last rains had made an unseen tunnel under the sandy trail and he had broken through.

His one leg was inside of a hole, and to my dismay I watched how his knee swelled up like a balloon. Bad news. Had he broken his leg? That would be the worst, as he would need to be lifted out by a helicopter or shot on the spot.

What to do now? I was alone, he was trembling in pain, unable to walk and the sunlight was fading fast. I did not even have a cell phone with me. But who could help with this anyway? Only a miracle would save him now. I put my hands around his throbbing, thickly swollen knee. I humbly asked for the power of life to flood through my hands and heal him, if possible.

Maybe it was because there was no other way, maybe because I was pushed to the edge and loved my horse... who knows. What matters is, in that moment, I could feel the tingling and rising of a strong, cooling energy flowing through my hands. A surge moved through me and into his knee. Within seconds the swelling had dissipated entirely; Magic shook himself vigorously as if he had woken from a bad dream, then looked at me, as if to say, "Hey, ready to go?" I could not believe my eyes. And that smart horse clambered out of the hole and walked cheerfully beside me without limping down the trail, toward home.

***

In the blazing heat and high winds the wildfire ravaged trees, brush and houses at lightning speed. It was scary for everyone involved—the families who resided in the area, the cows, the wild deer, and the critters. All ran for their lives. Some were left behind.

Two days later Joe came back to his land, where ashes covered the ground like snow. He searched, with no hope to find his dog alive. Suddenly, he heard a soft whimpering from a crevice in between the mountain. As Joe crawled into the tiny cave to see what was there, he was rendered speechless: a deer and a sheep were resting closely with his Irish shepherd dog. Their fur was singed from the heat, some flesh was raw and burned, and they were slowly dying of thirst. His brave dog had guided them into the cave and was licking their wounds. What a miracle that they survived! After receiving good care they healed and one day they walked together across the field like three best and most unlikely friends.

***

A brilliant idea to boycott bananas took off across Europe. Several countries united due to the pressure of the people to stop importing bananas. This helped end apartheid in South Africa. How did such a movement spread? From one spark to another.

One tiny seed sprouted in our high school, when I invited Greenpeace to educate us on how we could change the sad reality that the rivers were polluted and forests were dying in Germany. The director of this Bavarian conservative school, who had been completely opposed to these facts, after connecting with us, changed his mind overnight. We rallied other schools to transform the course of things. A movement grew, the rivers are revived and trees are growing healthy again. What caused the turn? People cared, and this mysterious force we call grace had a hand in it too.

***

Touches of grace have nothing to do with manifestation spells, beliefs, wishful thinking or because you deserve it. It is a way of being, seeing, hearing and most of all—connecting—to the stream of love. Miracles are already there, they are happening all the time. The question is only this: Are you aware of them or not? If the latter is your answer, then explore what it is like

109.

to get out of your own way and open to the magic of life. If your mind insists on reality being a certain way, acknowledge this view, but do yourself a favor and don't get stuck there. Consider the mystery is far greater than you or I can ever know. Then be curious and discover...

***

Have you ever dreamt of something that seemed impossible, and then it not only came true, but surpassed by far what you could imagine?

Such was my love story with a wild Bottlenose dolphin. I was twenty-five years old and had moved to Scotland to work as an educator at the Findhorn Foundation. One day as I walked along the wild sea, I felt this strong longing arise to swim with a dolphin. I had not heard of people who had done it, nor was I sure where or if it was even possible. But I spoke a prayer out loud to the ocean and the sky, "If there is a way, let it be fulfilled." I heard the wild geese honking as they travelled by.

It was not long after, when I overheard a guest speaking about a lonesome Bottlenose dolphin (they usually are in groups) in Newcastle-Amble, who was staying for an unusually long period of time. Immediately upon hearing the news, I dropped everything and ran to pack a few things into my duffel bag to take the journey by train along the coast. My heart seemed to beat at double speed. Could this actually be happening?

I arrived at the harbor the same day. Dark clouds covered the sky; it was freezing cold and stormy. I did not care; nothing could stop me now, not even this grizzly weather. An old fisherman kindly brought me out into the sea in his little boat to an area where he had last seen the dolphin. All I longed for was to meet him. Whatever it would take, I would do. And that meant entering the icy cold ocean in a bikini. Luckily, I am rather hot-blooded and had been swimming in the Atlantic

6. Touch of Grace and Grit

during the winter every day. The fisherman, in his yellow oilskin and covered up with a thick beard to keep the cold away from his weather-beaten face, told me that he would pick me up sometime later and wished me good luck. Then he returned to the harbor.

I was left behind, alone in the sea, calling with my heart for this dolphin. I wasn't sure if he would come, nor did I know about communicating with animals then, or why I was so nuts about swimming with a dolphin. When a powerful urge of the soul calls, you don't ask questions—you just follow and live it. And that is what I did.

It seemed forever long that nothing happened, other than the relentless waves crashing into my face. I would not give up, not now that I was so close. I became very quiet, paddling just enough to keep afloat and waited, although freezing, in anticipation. Suddenly, I experienced an immense love welling up, and in that moment skin touched my skin. Soft, like silk. Belly to belly. A huge being touched me from below the waves. Shocked and shivering, I realized that he was here. The dolphin was far bigger than I had imagined. He was there, completely still next to me, his body pressed against mine. Ever so slowly, I caressed his skin with my hands with utmost tenderness. He moved even closer in, and then he turned toward me. I could not believe it. Was I dreaming, or was this for real? It still brings tears to my eyes and makes me smile, as I am writing this.

He lifted slightly out of the water and looked into my eyes. He put his face and snout into my open hands. I was met with such pure love, it burst my heart open. I wept and laughed with delirious joy. We looked into each other's eyes for the longest time and communicated in ways that were of the highest intelligence. I just understood him; I do not know how. I got connected to the universal language of the heart of all beings. That was one of the many gifts he gave me, and it has never left me since.

After a while, he gently nudged me. I wasn't sure what he wanted until I got it—play! Dolphins live and learn by play. And so we frolicked, wild and free in utter delight and bliss. I would hold onto his fin, and he pulled me through the water. Such fun it was, when he went under me and then shot out. I dove after him, but of course he was faster. We played hide and seek—he had the easy part for I could never disappear from him, and was always slower in my clumsy, human moves. He was so incredibly sensual; I admit he was the best lover I had ever met (sorry, gentlemen). His love—pure; his joy—infectious; we shared in ecstatic beauty. He showed me what it is like to be and dance in complete union.

Well, what can I say? I was in love. Utterly and madly. With a dolphin. It was truly unfortunate that I couldn't live with him in the ocean. I wished I could transform into a dolphin myself. Instead, I went every weekend over a period of six weeks and swam with him until my hands and feet turned blue. Some others heard of him and came to see, and a few were brave enough to venture into the icy sea—of course with fins and wetsuits. I preferred to touch skin-to-skin, to be able to fully feel him. Only when I went back to the usual rainy shore did he let some other people come near. I must have been special to him; he certainly was for me.

When we were together, we danced in perfect love as one being. I don't know how else to attempt to describe it. Here words end and the mystery—life itself—speaks. Only poetry can even come close to it. Or as the Sufis express it: It is the moment when lover and beloved are one. The longing, when departed, seemed endless, only to lead into greater love when we joined again. It was as if he, too, was in love with me.

The fisherman once said: "I don't know what this is with the two of you. I have never seen Freddie (so the folks in Amble named him) do that or be like that with anyone else around here. I wonder why he is still here. Very unusual..." he would mutter in his heavy Scottish brogue.

One Sunday morning, I woke up in the nearby bed and breakfast and knew that this would be our last time to be together. He allowed me to put my arms around him and kiss him everywhere, while he nudged me affectionately. We both knew and deeply savored our last delicious and intimate touch. The old man picked me up. It was definitely the moment of our good-bye. I climbed on board and knew we would not meet again. My beloved dolphin did something highly unusual: he literally jumped across the boat, above my head. Three times. Back and forth. The fisherman was in awe and I was sobbing buckets of tears. My precious friend was saying good-bye to me in his own way. I called out loudly, "I love you!" He is always and forever in my heart. He had shared with me the gift of pure love. A dream had come true.

***

I have experienced so many miracles in my life that I could fill books with endless stories. Some people call those experiences extraordinary, but it's natural to be in intimate relationship with the whole of life. It feels abnormal, when I am out of touch; then even magic is nowhere to be found. I suffer, when I am out of sync for one reason or another. The swifter I reconnect, am present, shift my perception and open, the less stuck and the more grace can flow through. Honestly, how can anyone be happy, if cut off to a lesser or greater degree?

We may expect grace to arrive in pink colors and with soft textures. We imagine miracles to be glorious: you strike a gold mine, become famous overnight, or meet your forever soul mate. This is a surface perception and frequent delusion. Don't get hung up there. Grace has little to do with our fictions. It is the force of life's intelligence in action. The more we open, and become available to be touched and moved by this pure and mighty stream, the more it flows as and through us. It takes grit, as grace can be ruthless and fierce; it has its own agenda, especially if you sincerely want to awaken all the way.

***

We never know how our prayers are answered.

Many years ago I came to her trembling, I could feel something big was about to happen. With my hands in her chocolate brown hands, those who had lifted up so many people, I said, "Take me all the way through. The fastest way." I burst forth with words straight from my soul, not comprehending the meaning or implications. Ammachi laughed out loud and then smacked my forehead.

I received Shaktipat. Lightning struck, as if 1,000 volts ripped through my body. The sheer power of it threw me onto the floor. I lay on the ground, shaking for hours, sobbing and laughing, an intense energy surging through my spine, and I felt a flood of divine beings entering me. Her touch of grace had opened me and activated a tremendous power. Kundalini had awoken and was rising up.

After I went home I knew life had changed forever. For the better or worse I didn't know. A power, raw and sacred, was unleashed in me that both thrilled and frightened me. I felt waves upon waves moving through me (like having an orgasm all the time). Gee, I couldn't tell this to anyone, only when people touched me they felt the burning, as if I was on fire; I was. It was wonderful and dreadful. That fire burnt through me, every delusion and lie surfaced and was shattered, every wound came up to be healed, every action had instant feedback—both good and bad. And I was utterly in love with life. I experienced those mystical states saints have described, and entered into non-duality or what they call nirvana land. I had no mental context or concept for this, nor did I know a person who had gone through this. Yes, I had tastes and glimpses before, but this was beyond anything I knew. Was I going mad? It did not feel so; actually I felt saner than ever before. Connected, alive, and awake—as if I had just entered through the gates into truth itself. The "me" I had identified with seemed gone. I was bathed in grace, miracles happened naturally.

I had to meditate in the nights for hours; sometimes in sheer devotion I was taken into rapturous ecstasy, at other times I was using cooling mindfulness and awareness practice, watching all sorts of phenomena arising and passing by. I had found quickly what helped and what did not so my circuits wouldn't blow. And I went into therapy again; so much trauma and stuff was arising from the dungeons of my consciousness. During the day I showed up for people, the land, animals, work demands, for public appearances and teaching. I practiced living in this unified field of connection through my actions and communications. It was like learning a whole new way of living in radical intimacy, for which I had no preset script. Life itself became my greatest teacher.

But, it grilled me in the oven with no break and no way out. Resistance and struggle made everything worse, yet being present and opening to what was happening allowed me to breathe freer and freer. I was the bread, this was not just about self-realization—this was about embodiment in real life—and I would bake until done. If ever.

Was it glory and bliss forever? Oh no, so wrong. Destruction set in on a massive scale (find more specifics in the "Turning Challenges into Victories" chapter). True awakening will take everything and have you all the way. Grace, when it arrives in the form of disappointment, rejection, failure and loss, can seem like a cruel teacher. The fire of love literally burnt up my entire life and probably a lot of karma as well. My marriage, work and everything else too. I had to let go of all I was identified with, what defined who I believed I was. Every spiritual concept flew out the window, and I learnt to curse like a sailor when the stripping reached bare bone.

I remember sitting alone on a rock in the ocean, tears falling for grief at all that was lost. Being grateful for what is given is easy, but to be grateful for what is taken is a labor of love. Is this it? I asked, disappointed and entirely disillusioned. *What's left?* All I could feel and know was love, my soul free and illumined, but what kind of life was I living so emptied out? *What now?* I saw the bones of a dead bird lying on the ground. I picked up one and threw it far into the ocean with a shout, "Here have the rest of me." I was finished. For good.

The ocean had been calm, but in that moment it changed. Out of the blue, one enormous wave rose up and swept me off the little rock I was sitting on, tumbling me mercilessly into the sea. I went under. Finally, I released the struggle and then was lifted with tremendous force, thrown right back onto the beach. In a pretty dress, soaked, covered with seaweed, sputtering water, I must have looked to people as if I had come from a mythical land. I did. I returned from this journey different than the person I had been. Fierce grace had stripped me empty of everything I had held onto and took me home. And that was just the beginning...

***

Don't worry it won't get that intense for everyone, as each journey and calling is different. But if you are sincere, grace has an easier time to get through and you experience miracles on the soles of your shoes every moment, every day.

Love in Action

Grace is a way of being and miracles occur as we make ourselves available to live in the natural flow of life. You'll find many practices throughout the book to support you. Following are a few pointers you can apply:

- Turn toward your heart and ask, "Help me to see what is real." Feel the pulse of aliveness in your body. What are you experiencing? Expand your consciousness and curiously discover what else is there, besides your personality. What is alive in your immediate environment or with another person? And then explore what is arising in the space between the sounds, sights, and words right now.

- When disillusionment and hopelessness arrive at your door, consider it as the grit of grace. Inquire with this question: "What is left when I give in?" A sincere prayer may lift you through the veils of limited perception; ask, "Show me life's way, help me open to grace." Humbly lay down your own ideas, thoughts and expectations. Pay attention to the hand of grace showing up throughout your day.

- If you are shopping, for fun ask to be guided where you would find that cool sweater or the pants that fit you. Be open, though it may just come through another person, who hands the clothing to you. Let go of ideas of how grace should show up. You can't manipulate or control that. Rather, add to your intent, "Show me what's for the highest good, in the perfect way and the right timing." This affirms that you are willing to trust the greater intelligence of life, within and all around.

- And sometimes it is as simple as turning your sight toward the miracles appearing in ordinary life. You have a meaningful encounter with another person, or you experience peace when walking along a busy, crowded street. A ray of grace touches you whilst you gaze into the sky and your heart swings open unexpectedly...

May you soar home on wings of grace. For this ordinary moment is already holy, drenched in eternal grace.

7. This Human House

Who gets fed and where does your rascal hide?

Whoever made this up? That peace is bland and has no spine, that tolerance means you must agree all the time, that spirituality is eternal bliss, that you have to be so strong as to never wail or fail, that compassion means you cannot roar like a lioness, that being conscious implies you live in the head and ignore your gut, and that holiness is floating in transcendence of our humanness...? Whoever made it up must have been terrified of the whole of life in its full splendor and horror.

A master musician knows how to play all the tunes of a violin. Only then will this exquisite song of grace, as never heard before, pour through to touch and pierce the heart, making you feel so utterly alive and madly in love with all of life.

The room was stuffy. I was facilitating a group of transformational leaders to find common ground and take the next step for their project. At first, each spoke their important opinions in a polite manner and tried to listen to each other. But soon enough, as it became apparent that some did not agree with the vision, I could feel emotional intensity building. I leaned back to let it play out until a crescendo was reached. The different faces of humanity showed up: Carl tried to take over and assert his power by raising his voice and intimidating the rest, the woman in the corner got quiet and shut her mouth. The lady in the stylish black suit did not succumb; she was ready for the kill, fighting with all her might to get her way. Joe, the Indian guy, on the other hand was keen on smoothing things over to establish harmony. I could tell by his tense face, that he was uncomfortable with conflicts and tried to avoid them at any cost, but to no avail—no one listened to him anyway. Barney, however, was clearly savvy in the fine art of manipulation and won several approving looks when he spoke. Meanwhile, people had lost their cool, heavily engaging in an outright war, and I was glad no guns or baseball bats were in sight.

Who would win the game? It was time for me to step in. I asked the group, "How are you all feeling? Angry? Stressed? Hurt or pressured? Let's take a few breaths." I had to open the windows to let some air in, before I continued. "Ladies and gentlemen, what is happening in this group occurs in each person internally and it is playing out in the world—to our detriment. As you can tell we are going nowhere, other than creating unhappy faces, stress and anger. Would you like to go on the same road?" Someone mumbled a no. "If we can turn the tide in this meeting, we can do it for ourselves, in our relationships, at work and in the world. Would it be OK with you, if we approach these pressing issues in a different way?" Nodding heads. Apparently, they had exhausted their old style of relating, ready to learn something new.

"What do you really want?" After a while, every single person's desire came down to this: to be heard and acknowledged, to connect and create something of value together. Finally, we had dropped down to our common human ground and then I was able to demonstrate how to communicate in an effective and empathic way that connected them. We practiced voice dialogue, deep listening and had fun. The vision and approach for the project changed in the process to something far more brilliant because each brought their insight to the table, and in the end everyone was glad to be on board. The ship turned as each person felt included and heard, and the group rose up to create what could not have been done by one person alone.

***

As human beings we fall into the lowest valleys and rise up to reach the stars. We all have experienced our cup filled with joy on a warm summer day and hours later we find ourselves in the land of despair. We wander happy-go-lucky through the world and then get lost in a forest of confusion. We want to kill at times, or bless each person we meet. Our psyche contains every seed and character, all living under one roof: our human house.

In most spiritual or religious traditions our human nature is seen as something to go beyond, to disregard or to overcome. Some call the spirit the higher self and what's human, the lower self, ego or even sinful. This creates a split, a war inside and further separation. In my experience, human and divine are one, there is no difference when we have come home. We discover that the spark of life is as much in human form as it is in the beyond. **Our human vulnerability is the gateway home.** See our humanity as a mandala, a vessel through which our innate nature—love—shines through and gets embodied. As imperfect as our chalice appears, it is the house of our soul and infinite potential.

You are the home in which the dark and light is arising through.

But the question is: who is the landlady or landlord of our home? Who is in charge? Your essence? Or is it the different, disjointed characters that roam through? And who resides in your house? We find judgments, delights, and fears in hiding, enjoyable or horrible thoughts, tightness and peace flowing as a silent river beneath the house. A whole array of voices, feelings, sensations and thoughts move through us, and some take center stage and create nothing but misery.

Most of us have an inner bully running the show and we lock up the littlest, most vulnerable one in the closet or cellar. This dynamic usually plays out in our own life and on the world stage as well. The bully tries hard not to have you ever experience pain again and its stance is: If you don't feel or show your human vulnerability, all is well. And so the bully pushes the little one down, dismisses and judges the part of you that is tender, who feels joy and pain intimately, and who holds the key to your heart and love. The bully is the guard dog who barks at every visitor. The bully per se isn't bad; he/she tries their best to help you to survive and protect you from harm, to keep you safe, but unfortunately in a way that often causes more suffering instead. We usually do what was done to us when we were young and pass it on. We see it happening in how vulnerable beings—the elderly, children and animals—are treated in the world. This travesty can end with us for good.

What do we do instead? Turn on the light of awareness, get to know who camps out in your house and relate to our internal companions in a friendly way. Let your true nature, that CEO or queen or king, or your sane grown-up, take the main seat and reign in the house. That allows us to relate with genuine kindness and to embrace our whole personality, life story, follies and victories, our longings, cultural conditioning and talents. And then of course it's easier to relate with everyone else in the world, as we discover that all the characters reside in us as well, each in its own odd and weird way wanting to come home and be touched by love.

***

Have you ever talked to yourself out loud? One beautiful, sunny day, when walking along the pier, I was upset. I didn't like the sun—it shone too bright and I rather would have liked a stormy day to match my mood. I was mad as hell at the man who had attacked my friend's daughter and I felt I could burst. So I let the angry voice rant out loud. Luckily, people thought I was talking on my cell phone; otherwise I would have been publicly condemned as a raving lunatic. It felt freeing to allow this voice to have a go, to acknowledge it, to fully feel and be present with rage surging through my body. Soon enough another voice chimed in and shared pain. This one too was welcomed and I allowed the tears to freely flow. Finally, the entire inner team showed up and had something to say about the matter. I sat down at a table and offered each a place to be heard. It felt good, my heart opened and peace was restored in my house. From rage, fierce love emerged and I knew what action to take to make a stand.

***

Gathering at the table of love

All the characters and parts in us need to be honored; each wants to be heard, seen and met and longs to come home. The ancient and radical practice of love is this: **"Nothing and no one is left out."** (Of course, this does not mean we go to bed with everyone.) How about inviting the mischievous rascal in us to the table, giving Miss Doubt a place to relax, offer a seat to the shabby homeless one, as well as the bossy and pushy guy? It's fun to be with the whole gang and feed them a meal, which consists of this:

"How are you?" we ask and listen to each. We let our guest know, *"I am here with you. I honor you. I hear and see you. You have a place and right to be here. But you do not get to run my life or take over, nor do you need to hide in the cellar anymore."* We bring every character to the table of love and interact with each in a consistently kind and sometimes firm manner. We won't need to resort to repressing what is uncomfortable. Violence, oppression, and judgments don't take hold of our home or act out; and interestingly it just won't occur anymore, because you know your gang and show up present to love each part of you.

The more aware and friendly we relate toward our own humanity, which includes our mind, emotions and body, the more love fills the table.

However, if worshipping, decorating, fixing and improving the house—our personality—is our primary occupation we get stuck in the survival and improvement lane. We may try to become more successful, gain more capacities and positive attitudes, and this certainly can improve the appearance of the house and lead to a better life. But when we only focus on our personality by changing the color on our walls and keep shifting the furniture, life becomes driven, stressful, empty and fearful, without meaning and depth. It's good to remember that you are not your house; who you are is not the fears, likes, dislikes and appearances. Who we are is far greater than that.

You are the house in which all comes to rest and is fed at the table.

On the other hand, if we use spirituality and pretend we are above all things human, then a neglected and deserted house cannot embody wisdom in this world and at some point just falls apart. If we try to get to a higher self and leave our lower nature in the dust, guess what, it will catch up with you and a split is created (with various undesirable side effects) which isn't a pretty sight or a good life.

Being truly human simply means to be whole and at ease in your own skin.

So, let's discover more of our own home

Are you at home with yourself? What does your inner house feel like? Warm, friendly and welcoming? Cold and sterile? Is your internal home cluttered and filled to the brim with stuff? Are you at ease within your own body? Are you mainly living upstairs in the attic of the mind? Or are you emotionally homeless, departed from yourself? Do you live in your home full- or part-time maybe?

The mansion of our human psyche has many rooms. Some are well lit and lived in and others we have locked up, too scared to face what we might discover in the unknown and darkness. Such rooms are usually marked with a sign: "Dangerous. Forbidden for anyone to enter here." Certain rooms are forgotten, like an area of the house that is dead, numb like a cut-off limb. Often this is where trauma or a fragment of your soul is hidden. We like to close the door to the cellar, where our scary memories live. But by doing so, we become less and shrink, we shut off from all that we are.

Rejected and denied parts of us will always call out to be freed from suffering. Neglected people who are left in dungeons need to be comforted at a warm fire and fed at a well-lit kitchen table. You might have stuffed up your undigested past and stored away the hurts. But we will hear the ghosts roaming through the house at night and the people closest to us will experience the nastiness or control issues that we have been trying to hide.

A foundation built on lies, deceit, and inauthenticity is a structure built on shifting sand. It will collapse one day. If our sacrum is locked up, we stand on shaky ground, accompanied with a sense of insecurity and anxiety; and an earthquake may shake it loose unexpectedly. But, when the base of our house is rooted deep into the earth, we experience the natural support and juicy power of life.

And if our mind is in charge and busy all the time, due to overcrowding issues upstairs, rays of light and insight have no space to pour through the ceiling of our home. When our wires are crossed, the natural flow of life gets either blocked, stuck or we experience an overload that causes rather unpleasant jolts. Time to rewire the house!

We often hide our greatest treasures in one of the forgotten cabinets and rooms, and live in a dimly-lit house, too afraid of our own light, beauty, and power. Don't worry, the soul has its own agenda, and all our secrets will be revealed one day. Get curious and discover what wonders you carry inside, the wisdom, the joy... it will be the turning of the tide in your own house. And don't be afraid of all the other creeps and demons, you can learn to deal with them and one day—without further ado—sit down with them for tea.

As we get to know our own humanity, we can reclaim what is lost. As we bring loving awareness to every part in us we reconnect to what we originally were born to be.

On this path we feel our feels all the way through. We touch our sadness with tender care, we regain a true sense of power by meeting our worst fear, and discover gifts even in pain. We learn that resistance can be met with curiosity. And forgiveness emerges naturally as we are present with our anger. As we digest our life experiences, rich bread is made and gold is spun from straw.

When you walk through your house, peek into closets with a sense of curiosity and adventure. You may gather the hidden gifts you did not even know you had. There is reason to celebrate! For every room and part you are reclaiming, every piece of treasure you uncover, there is life unleashing more abundantly.

Love then isn't a mere concept, but feels real and embodied in our home and walk in life.

By opening our rooms to the light, we reject and judge others and ourselves less, because there is nothing in our house to defend against anymore. As we end the wars inside we don't project them out into the world. By befriending our own humanness we naturally grow friendlier with other people too. We discover that our heart is big enough to include all sorts of characters on the streets of this world, because we feel safe inside. We find more ease to speak truth and set boundaries from a connected place. By welcoming our own humanity, we realize that each person is part of us, for there is no difference between inside and outside, and the concept "we are one" turns into a living reality.

Discover your internal house, but do not get too wrapped up or lost in your psyche, or else you might overlook the world around and the love that is always here. Let yourself be simply human with all you are and dare to meet what and whoever you encounter; shining your light into the vast human house we share. How we relate to our humanity either creates more suffering or allows for more love to be lived. It's up to you.

Love in Action
Tending wisely to this human house—body, mind and emotions.

Relating to the Mind
Is your mind racing in circles, charged with a lot of energy or is it in an open, spacious, creative state? Just be curiously aware. Thank your mind for working so hard for you, without any overtime pay.

Often we are lost in the mirages, fabricated by our mind. It's like walking in the desert and imagining all sorts of delicious or awful things, whilst being parched and desperate for the water that quenches our thirst. The stream of thoughts is not a problem, unless we keep following them around or take them for truth. Then we end up chasing one mirage after another, but never find the source where our thirst is satisfied. Just let thoughts come and go, like a river with fallen leaves, watch them swirl and disappear. Don't reject a thought, nor cling to another. They are all just leaves with a different shape and color. Watch the dance of the mind. You are not your thoughts.

Do not try to stop the mind from thinking. It's a lost battle from the start. Step back internally and watch the mind with fascination, as if you are watching a movie. Don't jump into the movie, get lost in the drama and believe the entire show. It's a theater, remember? Make sure you leave the cinema afterward and don't camp out there. Some movies are so captivating and thrilling that we get stuck in them and without realizing we've pressed the replay button for the hundredth time and then wonder why we are feeling like a nervous wreck. If your particular movie is pretty nice you may just stay stuck and wonder why it's "Groundhog Day" every day of your life. It's your mind's show, but it isn't life.

Let's not mistake a tool for truth. The rational mind it is not equipped to lead our life, to know love, nor can it relate to others in a fulfilling way. It is a great tool for planning, making structures and to-do lists, for reading maps and useful for many practical matters. It becomes brilliant, if surrendered and infused by truth. It can turn into a fantastic servant for love.

The mind is doing the best it can with what it knows, trying to help us to survive. Our mind is not a problem, as long as we don't let it drive us around. Let it sit in the back seat, not be the main driver, for thoughts can never show you reality and may lead you far astray. Give your mind a job; for example use it to repeat a mantra, think about what is meaningful or pay attention to the silence between the thoughts. Otherwise, do not get lost in the stream of thoughts and don't believe everything your mind tells you. If you find yourself spinning or looping around, instead of trying to figure it out and running into the same old wall for the hundredth time, just stop. Breathe and feel your body. It might be that beneath the ruckus upstairs are feelings screaming or begging for your attention to be met.

Essential pointers on how to befriend the mind:

- Observe the thoughts: Allow yourself to have them, but know you are not your thoughts.
- No fight: Do not battle your mind. Accept the river of thoughts as it is. Become aware of the state the mind is in: Is it contracted, racing, slow, or quiet?
- Stand by the river: Notice when you resist or cling to a thought. It is just a thought, not the entire truth. Release and step back.
- Bring the puppy mind back to its master: If the mind gets busy and takes over, notice what is happening and return

your focus to the present moment or use your breath or a mantra as your anchor.

- Look for the open window: The gap between the thoughts, the silence in between the talk. Pay attention to that. Open into spaciousness: Let go and move through the window into vastness.
- A beautiful practice is: "I surrender my mind to love in this moment now."
- Say: "Dear mind, thank you for your service, for your labor... I honor you."

Relating to Feelings

What are you feeling in this moment? Just acknowledge and allow the emotion and its movement. Thank your feelings for being there.

Feelings are the colors of life, constantly in motion they offer us a gateway into Love. They connect us with our heart. In touch with our emotions we are alive. Feelings are natural in every human being; we are endowed with a wide range of emotions such as joy, anger, fear, and delight... As feelings arise, welcome them with awareness and kindness. Allow yourself to directly experience your emotions, allow them to be here at the table, each is a bearer with a gift. Tend to the recurring ones with curiosity. A healing might be needed or a message of truth is pushing to come forth. Get familiar with your feelings, for no matter what you try, you have them, and can learn to relate to them.

Some emotions are comfortable; with others we experience intense discomfort. The more we allow them to be exactly as they are though, the more connected, open and at ease we feel. Yet, we have learnt early in life to contract around uncomfortable emotions. The mind has sophisticated strategies to pull us away from experiencing what potentially could be painful or uncomfortable. The alarm signal from the mind is useful, when crossing a street and a truck is coming head-on. But a big emotion is often registered as a truck, and this is where the problem begins. We fear that this truck feeling, i.e. rage, could take us over and destroy us. Feelings have never killed anyone, but the contraction around them can cause coldness, dissociation, drive people insane, and lead us into decisions and actions we might regret one day.

It only gets overwhelming to the extent we try to get away from any experience. When we close off from what we feel, the mind turns into a spinning wheel, the body gets tense and breathing becomes shallow then. The more we try to escape, the more we become disconnected and ungrounded. We leave our body and therefore we are more anxious. A common reaction to unpleasant emotions, such as fear, is to shut down and numb out, which only leads to a sense of deadness. If we suppress and push our feelings down, it leads to depression in time. All these methods sap life energy, because it takes effort to keep your feelings controlled and held tight in a box. Over time they only grow bigger; if not dealt with, we experience constant struggle and unhappiness. Love cannot flow, because we are blocking the stream with all that is unresolved in us.

We tend to label and judge our feelings as good or bad, negative or positive, OK or unacceptable. We try to improve them, cut them out, fix, and reason with them, working hard to figure our feelings out. We ask, "Why am I feeling this? You should not feel this..." Have you noticed that it only makes you more tense, when you try to change a feeling? The guest who wants to have your attention, if rejected, will persist and will only get louder, grab, nag, lament, eventually grows into a mighty monster, lurking at the corner, coming at you when you have your guard down, and finally capturing you in misery. It just gets worse. We do not need to walk this suffering road.

Feelings are not the enemy, nor a problem. So, how do we relate to them in a healthy way?

Be the gracious host at your table, the landlady or landlord in your house, who can afford to offer attentiveness and a bowl of love. With that you will be able to take good care of your pain. Relate from the wise woman or man in you, from a good mother or father, or from a simple kind presence to a feeling. Find what resonates for you most and address your emotions from this place, giving what was missing before. Sometimes we might feel like a frightened seven-year-old. Well, how would you relate to a child, if you were a kind parent? What does she or he need? When a little child is scared he needs a grown-up to give him a hand, to hold him, and say the words, "I am here for you." This will truly help.

If we stuff emotions we get stuck and stuffed up. If we act them out, it may cause damages we may regret. And this behavior repeats, getting worse with every day. But if we befriend our feelings, we find wholeness and liberation.

Just notice what you feel in this moment. Acknowledge what emotion is present: "I am aware of anger churning in me." Accept what is in your emotional landscape. Without any explanation or story, turn kind attention and curiosity to the feeling. Let it be there, because it already is. Locate where the emotion lives in the body and flood it with breath. Know what you are feeling right now is alright, and that you are more than this emotion. Fully feel the whole nine yards, without fixing or manipulating the anger, the joy... into something different. You may drop into a deeper layer, and deeper still. Stay. An emotion completely felt often lasts no longer than a minute. As far as I know no one has died from feeling too much and we can learn to ride big waves by staying present.

Many more treasures are revealed when we engage graciously with our feelings and offer love where there was none, and presence where nobody was home. Such a relationship is empowering. It becomes a means to grow into more of who we are, enabling us to relate, instead of reacting to what is happening in us and in the world. We are freed, to live with far more ease, as we learn to accept, meet and treat our emotions like friends in our house. Some we like, others we rather do not want to meet, even in broad daylight. Whoever is showing up, welcome all the guests in your house with friendliness and presence, as they are messengers from beyond.

Essential pointers on how to befriend your feelings:

- Curiosity: What is here? What am I feeling?
- Aware: Turn on the light of mindfulness and become present to what you experience. Where in your body is the feeling held?
- Acknowledge: Just name it. Hello sadness, fear...
- Allow: Do not fight it, or try to change or fix it. Open up to what you are feeling with acceptance.
- Give permission: Say *Yes* to what you are feeling, even if you do not like the emotion.
- Locate in the body: Notice the feeling as a sensation in your body.
- Breathe: Meet the emotion and flood it with breath.
- Relax into it: Soften and open, instead of contracting.
- Feel what you feel all the way and move with it: You might cry, laugh... allow the fullness of its expression without story, restraint or drama.
- Embrace: Receive what you are feeling with love, with care and kindness!
- Nourishment: Offer what is needed, for example it might be comfort or encouragement, receiving, a hand in the aloneness.
- Follow natural flow: Let the emotion flow through and be expressed.
- Say: "Dear feelings, thank you for giving me aliveness, for all the colors of experiences... I cherish you."

Relating to the Body

Do you feel alive in your body or do you feel distant from your body?

Do you enjoy living in your body or do you use it like a machine? Is it in pain? Just notice, without judgment. Thank your body for all that it is doing for you. After all you are alive and can breathe.

Love and enlightenment are lived through the body, otherwise we are stuck in a conceptual realm. Our relationship to our bodies, however, is usually a dysfunctional one, as we have grown up in a society which feeds us images of how a body should look to be valuable and beautiful. We overfeed or underfeed in an attempt to change the vessel in order to be loved. Few people enjoy inhabiting their bodies fully. But, wisdom lives in our body and love flows through it, if our body is open and at ease. Every cell contains higher intelligence and is aligned when healthy and attuned with the stream of life. Our bodies help us to be grounded, centered and to embody what we wish to live. There are so many good reasons to be friendly toward our bodies, so let's begin with a simple practice:

Notice your breath, the inflow and outflow. Your little left toe, is it warm or cold? Is your belly tense or relaxed, hungry for lunch? Are you holding the world on your shoulders, or are they relaxed? Notice if you feel numb and armored in certain parts of the body. Don't make changes, unless they happen organically. Just discover with a sense of curiosity how the state of affairs is in your body in this moment. Then flood your body with breath. Smile to it, touch your belly and thank it for digesting the food so you can live. Thank your feet for carrying you around all these years. Continue with other parts of the body that could use kind attentiveness. Then ask your body animal what it needs. Maybe it wants to move, go for a walk or drink some water.

Give your body respect by feeding it with what it really needs: healthy food, good sleep, movement and basic care. We often use our body like an object until it breaks down. We accumulate tension, as more and more traumas get stored. This inhibits the flow of life and our energy becomes low, if we do not release those patterns and knotty knots. Grow a relationship with your body temple, listen and tend to it. Your body is a friend, even in its imperfection, a gift in its unique shape, different from anyone else. May you treat your body with the care it deserves and it reveals to you the wonder of life.

Essential pointers for being at home in your body:

- Practice mindfulness of body, sensations and breath.
- Engage your senses to be present in your body: What do you see, hear, smell, taste in your environment at this moment? Use the three senses practice: Identify three things you see, two things you hear and one taste or fragrance.
- Grounding: Put both feet on the ground and notice the connection with the earth, the floor beneath your feet and how the earth supports you from below. Let your body weight drop into the seat or ground that holds you from below. Shake your body from time to time and rub the places that may feel numb, which gets the blood and circulation going.
- Belly touch: Put your hand on the belly and let it soften.
- Centering: Put one hand on your heart and one on the belly. Breathe in through the nose and out through your mouth. For each breath, count for four beats so that the in- and out-breath is even. Do this for several rounds.
- Breathe into your hips and allow the space to widen.
- Ask your body: What do you need right now, dear? Act on it if you can.

- Follow aliveness: What is tense and what is alive in your body? Be aware of the slightest sense of aliveness and open into it and follow it.
- Let it move: The body has a natural way of moving, when allowed it frees itself from all the energetic knots. Follow its movement without impeding, forcing or directing it. It may feel awkward at first, but generates a whole lot of pleasure if you give permission.
- Say: "Dear body, thank you for being my vessel, thank you for... I love you."

And we are so much more than our human house:

There is a magical door in everyone's house, a gateway that leads to our greatest treasure: the love that we are. Sometimes we bury that passageway with a lot of stuff, boxes of past memories, our assumptions, judgments, fears, hurts... and cover up the entrance with paintings of tempting delusions. Then we can't find or even forget the way to the most important and magical door in our house. Gotta do a little digging then to find your way through.

Once found, we realize the door was always open, inviting us into a world that takes us far beyond our little house into the field of peace—presence—our radiant being. It does not matter where you are, just heed the whisper, the glimpse. Let the longing for your true home lead you toward that magical door, swing it wide open and walk right through. If a friend, a guide, a teacher comes along to take you by the hand, one who already lives there and knows the way, take the hand.

Welcome home, my friend! Bring your pots and pans and put up camp.

8. Connected or Living Dead?

Crossing the bridge from suffering to loving

I entered a café yesterday. Dead silence. Has something happened? I looked around curiously. The tables were occupied by people of different ages, each staring intently at a computer or phone screen. Not one engaged with another. The clattering from the barista was a relief to hear, she turned on music to fill the deadness in the room. Did I just walk into a sci-fi film? Nope. This is the modern world I was told.

Later that week I went out for the evening in San Francisco and came upon one of the oldest cafés and bookstores. The smell of well-read books mixed with coffee and pastries was an invitation to taste the richness of life in the room. People sipped tea and actually talked with each other. A couple snuggled on a worn couch, their kisses delicious and wild. Two students argued heatedly, the topic sounded like politics to me. A grey-haired woman was softly playing guitar as a stylish gentleman wrote his screenplay. Aliveness and creativity were flowing naturally here.

This reminded me of when I was on a boat to meet whales on the coast of Hawaii. Suddenly, as we travelled beneath the clear, blue sky two humpbacks rose from the water only a few feet away and a school of dolphins joined and joyously played in the waves nearby. The faces of the people on the boat lifted into smiles and cheers. Best facelift ever! We all know these moments. When we feel connected and in sync with life, we experience happiness.

***

But, when we feel disconnected to a lesser or greater degree from life, each other, and ourselves we suffer. This misery and its symptoms are known by most who have not entirely numbed out. A common "solution" is to disassociate from our bodies, from the ground of the earth, from each other, and to escape into our head, which only disconnects us further. We may go back and forth between feeling connected and then being off kilter. We may be at peace at one moment, and in the next we are stressed, for instance, when we hit an unexpected traffic jam on our way to work. For some, this sense of disconnection is experienced as a constant nagging discontent, anxiety or depression. Out of touch, we feel isolated and lost, wondering where the flow and magic we experienced as children and in times of connection have gone. And so, we simply practice the art of reconnecting—again and again. But, for many people it isn't that easy to return, because of trauma or having caught the bug of a silent disease.

The "living dead" gang is growing at an alarming rate these days, and actions taken from disconnection always spread the infection of suffering and turmoil in our world.

***

When I met him in my office, there was no spark in his eyes and he could not sense the warmth in his hands. He was intelligent and accomplished in his early thirties with a high-paying job as the CEO of a well-known company, impacting many people he was leading. He was married and could afford a holiday to Hawaii in a fancy hotel. On the outside he looked healthy, no one could see this unrecognized disease that made him feel so unhappy: he did not feel care for anyone. This condition is unfortunately common, quietly spreading across the Western world, taking more and more people down.

A young lady entered after him, twenty years old; she suffered from numbness, depression and the loss of her soul. She functioned normally, just like the businessman, and was an honors graduate from Stanford. She told me that she didn't want to live anymore and that psychiatrists wanted to medicate her. A serious case with a ten-year history. She had no interest in anything, having lost her joy, creativity and ideas. For hours she would stare into empty space or cry without end. Uptight and with shallow breathing, I could see, she was barely here. Nobody knew what's going on inside of her—it's too weird to tell, she said. She felt isolated, her relationships were superficial, even though she had many. When I asked her to describe her feelings as if they were a landscape, she said, "It's like an unnamed disease that spread across the land, where no one is really alive and a grey cloud has taken over everything, sucking out my blood. I call it 'the empty nothing.' I am walking dead, while alive. I hate my life." A never-ending void had taken her in, turning her, just like the successful gentleman, into a zombie, unable to feel with a heart turned to stone.

***

Drugs do not help what this man, the young woman and millions more suffer from. Disconnection from source, separation from love, loss of soul is much harder to cure than the poverty of people who need food in Africa. It's hidden behind the masks of everyday people, who appear to be just fine. This sense of disconnection creeps in slowly, leaving each empty, feeling nothing, only random thoughts passing by. Life has no meaning, spirit is a concept, the heart barely feels, the body becomes an object to feed, and in relationships there is no sense of love. Disassociated and disconnected, we are not really here on this earth, but vegetate in some strange inner-outer space, craving for what we cannot name, but what is more essential than money and fame—that which fills us a with sense of aliveness, joy, creativity and zest for life. Love. A living connection with the flame inside of us.

Children whine for parents to connect with them, to be here and engage from presence and heart. They need it more than anything to thrive. Lovers get tangled into complex knots and have no words for a strange emotional distance, which cannot be bridged with clever advice from the latest Internet formula. Isolation is so much worse than a broken leg, and feeling disconnected from people when walking through a crowded street can be plain agony. Numbed out to avoid the pain, care for other beings is forced, becoming a "should" and is eventually forgotten. When we are in separation, suffering arrives in its many disguises, if given food to grow it worsens, and deadness spreads out on the living room floor.

***

"What's so difficult about being alive, just feeling and engaging with each other?" asked an Italian guy I recently met. He couldn't understand this deadness he saw in people's eyes. It's no "problema" for him, I could tell by the twinkle in his eyes. I had spent quite some time exploring this phenomena and tried my best to explain it in the simplest way.

"Well, certain experiences and emotions are uncomfortable or terrifying and they are hard to face for folks, so some check out and disassociate. Many people have grown up in a culture, or home which sterilizes our shared humanity and our feelings, it teaches people to avoid the challenging parts of life and commodifies love. But, deeper than that, people are afraid of experiencing pain, they close off and therefore can't connect with their soul and heart."

Still, my feeble attempts to explain this did not make sense to my charming Italian friend with his gorgeous looks, who wore his heart on his sleeve and talked at the same time as I did. He had not tasted the poison yet, and hopefully he never will. But many who live in this culture have taken a sip or more. What's the cure for this?

***

Recently, a large group of Germans gathered in Hamburg for a political protest. To show how disengaged many people are, they covered themselves in grey mud and walked in orderly rows like the living dead. No emotion showed in their drooping, stoic faces, but apathy and numbness expressed the level of detachment from life and what is happening in the world. And then suddenly, the whole group came to a halt. Ever so slowly, one man took off the grey coat and revealed his colorful shirt below. Some began to move their bodies in dance, others made funny faces, looked up at the sky, at each other, and one by one the crowd came back to life.

***

How do we recover, live connected more and more? What's the ingredient that will get us back on track to experience untethered aliveness once again? Pasta and vino? A trip to Florence? When we have found and then lost the golden thread, maybe a workshop for a weekend will give us a temporary high? Yeah, for a little while it may work, but it's short-lived. What helps us to open the door into life again, to be present and connect with each other? And what enables us to meet challenges with courage and celebrate life with gusto, regardless what comes our way?

***

"I am here with you," I said while looking straight from my heart into her eyes. Something flickered in her, and then she avoided my eyes. But I stayed present with her, listening with my whole being, and feeling into her world to let her experience that I am here with her. I met the Stanford girl in her parched land, the empty nothing, where she had disappeared due to emotionally unavailable parents who couldn't be there for this sensitive girl who felt completely alone. She had closed down to the pain and therefore also to her spark inside. I reached through her deadness and offered my hand, and it was this moment of real connection with another human being, this being met and not alone in the pain, that glimmer of love that touched and stirred her awake. From there, step-by-step we walked the journey back to the river of life and revived her flame.

She learnt to connect with her body, to allow the whole range of her emotions to freely move again and heal the wounds that kept her stuck. She followed her longing into her heart and returned to what's vibrantly alive. And by uncovering her soul she began to thrive. It did not take long before her spark was ignited again, and she was galloping into the horizon with new ideas and a zest for life. The grey nothing could not take hold of her anymore, for she was too strong and connected now.

The successful business leader dared to feel, became more present, connected to his humanity and learned to communicate in an authentic, more vulnerable way with others. He paid attention to what truly mattered to him in his heart and was able to transform his life. After waking from the dead he quit his seventy-hour-a-week job, invented a new model for computers that would help people, and as far as I know he is happy. How did it turn? By being connected with his spark.

***

There are many ways to feed that spark and flame of connection.

Cultivating awareness helps us to recognize to what degree we have shut ourselves off from the river of life. Awareness is an important first step. Acknowledge what's going on for you, be honest about where you are at. If you feel numb or out of touch, acknowledge that. Don't fight, nor succumb. Rather, offer your presence, drench the experience with breath and touch it with kindness. It eases the way home.

What's the next step? It's that willingness to directly experience, to feel it all, consciously—the numbness, the anger, fear, exuberance... the entire range of emotion without suppressing or dramatizing and acting out. Instead allow the emotions to flow through you, dance and move with them. But how often have we been told not to feel anger, or cry... how often do we reason ourselves away from certain emotions and experiences? It requires an unlearning from our cultural and parental conditioning. And if unresolved trauma is at the root of disconnect, then it's time to tend to healing it with skilled help, and not alone.

Landing in our body is part of the journey: to sense, touch and taste the whole garment of this living being. Stopping the train of busyness, to listen and feel into our nature, helps us to fall in love with who we are and life as it is. Whether we smell the garbage on the side of the road or the scent of the lilies in a garden as we walk by, we commit to being in touch and alive, leaving nothing out. Stroking the soft fur of a cat, touching the warm skin of a hand with all our senses, is a gateway home. (Read more about this in the next chapter "Love's Sense.")

There are a myriad of ways to reconnect to source, to the flame in your being, to that juicy aliveness, the sense that the birds are not just singing outside on a tree but inside your chest, the felt intimacy in the gaze between two people who just met today...

Connecting isn't so difficult. We get the knack of it; if we are willing to be uncomfortable at times, we'll experience the richness of life. Especially, if we want to enjoy meaningful relationships we need the basics for connecting. (Read more about that in the "Connecting for Real" chapter.) Or, if we are confronted with a natural disaster like a fire or flood, we need to be present to make choices that can have life-changing impact.

First connect then act is a good motto to use when under pressure

It helps us find the right path. We turn toward connection by rooting into the ground and presence, when the fire is on at work, in relating or our larger world. This enables us to get centered, tap into our knowing and make a brilliant move, even when all looks bleak.

It takes a bit to show up for what life throws our way, instead of going into our head, to experience all and feel. Even when we are shaking in our boots with fear, we root into the ground that holds. We connect with source and then act. Connected we grow courage to step beyond our comfort zones, to take a risk, even if it means being rejected by someone we declared our affection to. We come alive when we allow ourselves to have a good belly laugh, cry torrents if we need to, and share words and deeds out of love. We experience richer connection by daring to be authentic and vulnerable, even if we fall flat on our face many times. (Read more in the "Vulnerability—Friend or Foe?" chapter.) It's not easy to do, but it's worthwhile to keep turning toward the present and alive, felt-sense experience moment by moment in our life.

Sometimes, wild aliveness surges through us, we feel connected with everything quite naturally. For other times, it definitely helps when I sit down with myself, feel the feels, sense the life pulse in my body and drop into my heart, listening to wisdom and acting on it. Sure, it's a practice to keep connecting ever more deeply. We will weave in and out of being connected in a visceral way, but the more frequently we stop, breathe and take the road back home, the more aligned and in love we live, right in this spot where you are now.

Slowly the connection with our nature, the divine spark is restored and experienced directly, beyond the usual concepts and surface appearance. Life begins to arise lusciously, like a wellspring to nourish the lands and everyone else, including ourselves. In such connectedness we feel most happy and alive, know truth, and love fills and moves through us into this world, offering the food that people hunger for.

At some point, joining the living dead is just too high of a price to pay.

Love in Action

This chart provides basic markers to use as a way to recognize whether you are connected or not. Use your own discretion; often you might be in-between. If you are in a serious and/or long-term condition such as depression, please seek professional help.

	Connected	**Disconnected**
Body	sense of flow, alive	tense, out of touch
Feeling	feeling the whole range of emotions, an open heart, empathy	limited experience of emotions, numb, anxious, depressed
Mind	quiet, clear, creative	rapid thinking, spaced out, constant overwhelm
Seeing	depth, multidimensional	flat, distant object
Sensing	alive and rich	plain, limited
Behavior	wide range of responses, unique	controlled, tense, reactionary
Relationships	depth, width, rich, we are in this together	superficial, masked, separate, isolated islands
Living	fully engaged in life	in the mind
Spirit/Soul	inspired, present	buried, hidden, closed off

Creativity	in every way, original	nothing original, frequent boredom
Pace	natural, in rhythm	always in a hurry
Word	Alive. Human.	Dead. Zombie. Vampire.

Practices that help us to come back and connect:
Emergency for stress:

Breathe through nose all the way into belly, count to five.

Hold breath, count to five.

Release breath through the mouth, count to five.

Repeat three times.

Connect with your body:

Wiggle your toes; are they cold or warm? Tense the body with the in-breath and release the hold with the out-breath. Repeat three times. Shake your booties and hips. Make a sound. Feel what you feel. Touch the dirt, a tree, hug someone, taste food. No matter how bad things might appear—you are alive.

Returning to presence: The three senses gateway

What are three objects in the environment you see?

What are two sounds you can hear?

What smell stands out?

First connect, then act:

If you have a difficult decision to make, are stuck in a rut with your mate, or need to find a way—connect first before you act. When you do, it will make a major difference in your life, work and relationships. The way in is best through the body and grounding into the earth, so you can feel safe and present. Acknowledge your feelings, and then simply ask your heart or wisdom, "What is alive and is for the highest good right now?" Sense and listen—the knowing for the right action will emerge.

Fallen off the wagon?

Sometimes life throws us a curve ball and we get knocked over. It's OK, it happens to all of us. Don't try and process why you fell, first get up and reconnect. Feel your feet ground into the earth; breathe into your belly several times. If you are afraid or hurting, connect with something greater holding you, like the earth beneath you and comforting you. You can pray like this: "Please help me to feel held and to know that I am supported in this moment." Notice what you experience. Maybe imagine being held in the arms of someone you trust and love. It helps to feel safe and to regain a sense that you are not alone.

What if?

The *what if* question helps us to explore, and puts us into a state of curiosity, instead of living from fear and resistance. "What if I connect now, what might happen then?" or "What if I connect with this person instead of talking from my mind, how might it be?" Use your own questions and see what happens if you apply it in any situation.

Follow your longing:

What do you yearn for? What do you truly desire, when it comes down to the wire? What arises in this moment for you, when you ask that question? Sadness? Joy? Feel and follow this opening.

What are you grateful for?

Use what is most obvious and simple. Such as, "I am grateful for food in my tummy." Really feel this gratitude. Notice the drop of warmth when you feel gratitude, because it can melt the ice inside of you.

What inspires you?

Follow spontaneous bursts of aliveness and ideas. What ignites your heart? What sparks your interest, even a little bit in this moment? Go for that.

Give and receive:

I know it sounds old-fashioned, but it works. Offer something for free, without expectations for a return. A smile, helping someone out, giving a hand to someone who carries a heavy load, or simply appreciating another, can get us out of our own cell, to help us feel connected again. Receive the smile, the compliment, and a kindness given to you by acknowledging it. Notice whether you feel more or less connected.

Curiosity:

Discover the world and whatever arises with a sense of curiosity. It defeats fear, helps you to step beyond the wall of judgment, it grows connection and gets you in touch with what is here. Approach people, your experience and life with a sense of adventure: "What is happening? What can I discover or learn? What is going on in me?" When something uncomfortable shows up, instead of rejecting or clinging you can respond, "How interesting."

Follow aliveness:

Tune into your body and curiously notice where you feel most alive. It can be your breath, the pulsation or warmth of your hands, or energy moving through your body. Give it attentiveness. Soften and open into the felt sense of aliveness, breathe into it and revel in it. It will get stronger if you stay with it and rest into this vibrant field of life.

9. Love's Sense

How does life taste?

He asked if he might smell the white lilies I carried in my hands. We were standing next to each other as strangers, listening to a violinist at a busy street corner. Surprised I offered, he put his nose deep into the bouquet. I never had encountered a man rejoicing in the scent of flowers like that. He was refreshingly alive and related directly, that's what spoke volumes for me.

We talked about how we feel more alive when in touch with our senses and he tickled mine awake. I could smell my favorite kind of lilies now as well, and suddenly everything around became intoxicating, vibrant. The old ruddy dog, the sparkling Christmas lights on the tree in town; I heard people talking nearby, and felt the connectedness with each other, as we tasted the sound of words we shared. Life, love right here. Where had I been? Being out of touch is always miserable, depending on the severity of disconnect. The senses brought me back. I was grateful we had met out of the blue. Even if our meeting lasted only for a brief intimate moment in the grand wheel of life, suddenly my world was lit up; basic sanity arrived, my heart opened and all made sense again.

***

Love can remain a dry concept, or be experienced like a field of wildflowers, an aliveness tickling the senses, when we are present and open. Touching, tasting, hearing, seeing, smelling, feeling, as well as the sixth sense are the gateway into life and connection.

How does love taste for you? Like fresh air, or honey, bread or fruit maybe? Or bitter? Where do you see love when you look around? In the trees, faces of people, a smile, or a limping cat? How would love touch pain? Kind, like a mother holds a child, offering soothing words...

And how does your hand want to reach out to your mate tonight? With a gentle or passionate touch, or a surprise meal? Oh and what's the sound of love for you? She plays many instruments, if ears listen from inside. Pay attention to the felt sense and soon enough you enter, voila—into the land of the living again, where love actually makes common sense and serves as medicine for the ailments and dilemmas we carry around.

What I speak here so lightly of is in fact a profound matter. Scientists used to believe that only empty space existed in between molecules, people, plants and the elements. But now they have come around to admitting, that this emptiness is filled with an unlimited intelligent living essence. I call it Love; others name it a benevolent force, or another name... As all ancient traditions tell us, it is found within and all around us. When we experience it, our thinking is clear, contentment is here, and things make sense because we are able to see with the eyes of the heart, have access to brilliance and feel at home in love.

However, we often hang out in disturbing and disassociated states, when the mind races and is confused, when emotions are deadened or in turmoil. Sometimes we feel plain numb. And nothing makes sense to us anymore—everything appears as chaotic or awful. Then we act it out and our relationships and world turn usually into a mess.

We either reject or cling to praise and blame, to gain and loss, to pleasure and sorrow and thereby we circle around helplessly on the endless wheel of samsara. We forget that none of our attachments offer us lasting happiness nor do they lead to the end of suffering. We know this, deep down. But, when we lose touch with the "real" and awareness has gone out the window, we are stuck in a strange rut. Our world reflects so many forms of our insane states; people killing and torturing each other is just one of the extreme versions. We each have our own personal ways that we lose touch with common sense.

Now how do we get back to basic sanity and the refreshing wellspring of love?

Remember it hasn't gone anywhere, the ocean is always here, and you as the wave may have simply forgotten you are part of her. Luckily, our senses help us to reconnect. They provide a gateway to return to life, by which you experience the ocean and the unique wave you are, as one love.

It is the ancient tantric way, a savoring, a surrendering into bittersweet love, where you feed on tears and laughter alike, when every taste and sound is realized as the divine nectar. Found in the beautiful and the horrible too. Then life is experienced and lived in a fuller, richer way. You feel sane. OK. Enough now of these mental explanations, it's so easy to stay up in the head talking about it. Far better to actually experience and live it.

How about we jump into the water together, or at least put our toes in warm sand, or wiggle our tiny left toe right now, stretch our back like a cat, smell the air? And what are you tasting in this moment? Sing out loud your friend's name in a high and then low tune. You might think this silly, but give it a try and have fun. And then notice how YOU FEEL, allow the emotions, the sensations and acknowledge that ache, that pulsating, the joy... What happens when you breathe with what is arising within and around you? When you refrain from judging, denying, rejecting or grasping? When you are simply feeling, sensing and being present with what is here, even if it tastes not so nice? Do you experience more aliveness then? If so, welcome back to the green valley, fields of flowers and pure rivers, where only love makes sense.

And then it's no problem to touch with unconditional love what's out of touch, what feels separate or nuts within and around us. It's the only act that makes sense anyway.

Love in Action

You are alive:

Take a breath. And another. Just pay attention to breathing without changing anything. Notice your environment and become aware of what you see. Notice the colors, shapes and forms. Listen closely to all the sounds you can hear. Sniff and smell the air. Become aware of any other sensation, be curious what you discover. Do you feel more or less connected now?

Pay attention to what is alive in and around you. Move from thinking and mental noting to actually feeling. Involve all your senses. For example: You hear a child laughing. You notice a smile on your face and a tingle of joy arises. Savor this one taste of joy, savor it as if you are tasting it the first and last time in your life, let it spread into your whole body and your actions.

Be present to the sounds, smells and what you see, whether pleasant or unpleasant, without judging, and dive into the experience, as if it's God, the mystery, the dharma or life communing with you.

Touching the Mystery:

Dive into the senses even further and see the ocean is God/the Goddess, is the great mystery. Your hands touch water, you are touching the divine. You are breathing air, life is breathing you. You are stroking a cat, thereby stroking all creation. Your partner is holding you, the whole of life is embracing you.

This too is Sacred:

For a whole day explore this: Whatever you see, hear, or taste, name for yourself: *This too is sacred.* Even, if it is the garbage on the side of the street or an uncomfortable emotion such as fear. It is a practice that can take you home into connection and love itself. But, you might rightly ask: what about all the horrors in our world, to call it sacred is ridiculous and crazy. You are right. In this practice, however, we are not judging right from wrong, but we are connecting to the love that is alive and deeper than all situations and appearances—horrific or beautiful.

Savoring Nectar:

Feel as if your hips and sacrum form a pot with honey in it. Breathe into this area. Feel the golden honey, sense its texture and taste the liquid. Stay in the body. Allow it to pour down your legs and up through your belly, back, and arms. Let the liquid pour through your brain and face. Feel the sweetness and warmth. Do not just imagine but taste the nectar in your mouth. Let it pour into your heart and the areas that are in pain. Let it soothe your nervous system and nourish every part of you. Drench in honey. Become a honey cake.

Love's ruthless Kiss:

Sense your experience, be it awful or pleasant. Taste and feel it in its fullness. Offer your breath. Do not try to change it, but savor it—whether it is the sensation of pain, the tears of a heartbreak, the fury fire in the belly or quivering joy. Kiss whatever is here with a radical *yes*, through your presence and love. This practice will take you deep and welcomes your whole human experience as the divine tasting itself.

Love's Sense in Action:

Most of the time we make choices based on our knowledge, and what is familiar to our mind. That is certainly useful at times. But in order to step beyond the usual trodden roads into life itself we can ask ourselves: "What would make sense in the eyes of love? What action makes sense to take, if I see this situation with the eyes of love?" Be present and with your whole being sense and feel your way into the answer.

II. For You

1. The Choice

Where is love in hell?

Choices have power. Decisions emerging from our deepest nature can have an earth-shattering impact and can turn our own lives and this world around.

Both wonderful and terrible things happen in everyone's life. We cannot always choose our circumstances, and we certainly won't be able to control how people behave, nor prevent natural disasters. But it is empowering to know that we can choose *how* we walk through the highs and lows, how we relate and respond to people and situations.

I have had the honor to be in the presence of true saints, and I've also encountered cruel people who had seriously forgotten their light. Heaven and Hell do exist in the world and in our own minds. Goodness and evil are seeds in each of us, and we get to choose what we grow and act upon. We have the capacity to go in either direction—and all shades in-between. How we live is up to us, no matter what appears along the road. But usually we are unconscious, driven around relentlessly by conditioning. The key is to remember that love is always present, inviting us to follow its wild beckoning home. Then every step and choice leads into true life.

When it comes to making almost any decision we have endless possibilities in the Western world—so much so that it can be overwhelming at times. We have the freedom to decide which clothes we wear, the kind of partner we want to be with, and the work we want to do. Have you driven yourself nuts trying to figure out what is the best road to take? Yet, these decisions are not as relevant as this one: Do you choose to be present and turn to love in this moment, over and over again, no matter what? Even if we turn away, may we love ourselves with that.

But what does it mean to turn to our loving presence, when we are in the middle of a fight with a family member—when it seems so much easier to attack and defend when we feel wronged? What does it take to show up and connect while your child has a meltdown—when it's easier to walk the old wacky road of reacting instead of responding? Do you engage in an authentic way with colleagues at work, or do you hide behind a wall of pretense to be liked? Do we bend down to pick up a plastic bag on the beach, or is it too much effort? Do you have the nerve to call the person you can't stop thinking about and say what you really feel—even at the risk of being rejected?

In every second it is possible to turn toward what is true and alive in our hearts. It's a matter of tiny choices.

Life can be lived in different ways—it is our intention and commitment, which gives us direction. One small decision leads to expansion, while another keeps our world seemingly safe, but actually causes us to contract and lose out on life. Every tiny pebble choice we throw in the direction of love leads us closer home. How we walk the rocky road is up to us. But each step we take for sure has an impact on all of us.

People ask me, "What makes us move to higher ground, to live our innate goodness and face our stuff? And what causes us to fall below our basic humanity in the way we behave?" I can only say that, despite popular belief, the way we were brought up as children is not the entire reason. The following story is proof.

This true story is a testimony to Love's power, leading to freedom where there was none. Hitler and the girl in this story had similar upbringings, but each made different choices. One kept turning to the heart; the other did not. One life led to suffering, the other to benefit. But both had big consequences, since each life impacted many people.

This is the power residing in each of us.

***

A Little Girl's Choice

Once upon a time in a faraway land, not so long ago, there was a little girl. With a tear-stained face she sat at the windowsill, looking out through her blue eyes into the vast dark sky, waiting for the first snowflakes to fall. All was silent when she opened the window into the icy cold night and reached with her tiny hand for magic, which she knew existed somewhere in this forsaken land.

Almost blue at the fingertips, for she would not give up, the long-awaited moment arrived. From high above—lo and behold—the wonder of the first big flakes fell into her open hand, smelling pure, born from another world, tasting like utter delight. It was like catching a fallen star, upon which she made a wish. In this timeless moment, she made one of the most important decisions in her life; it changed the course of this precious life for good.

This little one had been born into a home you could name in one word: hell. The child's mother truly acted like an evil witch. You know those creepy stories—except this one was real; it wasn't just made up in the pages of a book that could be closed and put away on the shelf when you'd had enough.

This mother hated having children, especially this girl. She often failed to feed her, and beat her daily with sticks and rods, screaming a constant stream of curses and cruel words at her. She locked her up in a cold cellar and used other ways of torture to inflict pain. She treated her as less than human and never held or loved her. As is the case with many children who are being abused, even today, this woman seemed intent on destroying the child slowly, surely. "Break her" was her mission.

Why did she hate this lively, skinny angel? One could only assume that when light touches a closed heart, it hurts. Light always illumines one's own hidden darkness. Of course the mother did not want to face her shadow, so in her insanity, it made sense for her to keep pursuing the path of maliciousness and to destroy what she mistakenly perceived to be the cause of her suffering: her own baby.

This is true for all of us: When we aren't willing to face the demons inside we cause suffering—and it really will make the mind insane. The suffering may appear in manifold expressions, some more extreme than others, but the result is always the same: We inflict pain upon all of life through our own projections.

Perhaps, if the mother had taken a different path, it would have led her back to her own deeply buried heart, which was aching to be healed and released. Ultimately, it might have enabled her to answer her locked-up natural longing simply to love her child. Yet, like so many, she had forgotten her own flame a long time ago. The more vicious she acted, the more insane she became. When the little one lay once again crumpled on the floor, barely breathing and unable to move anymore, the mother felt a surge of power. The greater the young girl's pain, the more pleasure she gained. Hers was not a smile of joy, but one of sick satisfaction. So great was her insanity that it made her act blindly. This is what creates child abuse, in every country, among the rich and poor, the educated, the illiterate— it is a poison that has spread everywhere.

The girl's papa was working hard, to provide for their family, yet he disappeared so much into his work that he was barely home. And unfortunately, he lived in a faraway land called denial. A thick blanket covered his eyes, and he did not see the horrors that happened in his very own home. Although good-hearted, he didn't have what it took to face what was right in front of his nose, to protect and make a stand.

One might forgive him, for it is fear, which walks hand in hand with denial. You may have experienced this too: There is an elephant in the room, but everybody pretends there is none. "The china did not fall and nobody heard it break." The bruises, the wounds, and the lonely sobbing were overlooked. Yet, so much more was shattered; a broken heart was by far the greater crime.

Now, some say it is karma, where and to whom you are born; some call it a mistake or luck; but it doesn't matter, really. What matters in the end is what she made of it. And how did our girl fare in all this? Did she survive the constant neglect, abuse, and deprivation? When children, especially those at a very young age, do not get affection and healthy attachment in any way, not even from one person, however little it might be, they do not die for lack of food—they literally die from a lack of love. Few survive such an ordeal; if they do, then it is with heavy costs to their sanity.

Did our girl remember who she was or did she too forget? That's the question for all of us, isn't it? And where was love in such a forsaken land anyway? What was her choice then, when she had no power over the circumstances and people in her life?

Her choice came on the special night we began this story. As the beautiful snowflake gently melted in her hand, this love-starved seven-year-old girl made the choice that surely the stars and angels heard: *I will always keep my heart open and I will find love, no matter what it takes.* Where does such a choice come from, if not from the wisdom of a soul far older than the body it is housed in? The little girl did not want to become like her mother, and in the depth of her being, she knew what she had to do. Children are still much closer to their inner light, for it is less covered over with all the experiences and beliefs we accumulate throughout our lives. She did not comprehend what this choice would entail, nor what it meant. She just knew the flame and voice in her heart. That is what she held onto for dear life. And this indeed was her saving grace.

Did the situation get any better at home? Did the beatings stop; did the constant emotional tearing down end; along with the other abuses that caused so much pain? Was she ever held once? Did someone take her tiny hand to guide or praise her when she learned to ride a bike? Did she hear a kind word ever? Was she encouraged when she lost confidence, or asked what she needed or wished for? Was she listened to when she told stories, or comforted when hurt? Was she ever seen—God forbid—she wasn't supposed to even exist!

Oh no. None of that was given to her. Such simple acts of love did not occur in the house of hell.

Of course, over time she did what all children do when they are completely deprived of the most essential need. The agonizing question that they ask, "Why am I not loved?" demands an answer. She had to make sense of this, because parents cannot be wrong, for they are like gods to us, when we are very young.

So she concluded, that she must be the cause of this nightmare. She began to believe that she was not worthy, that she was no good, that something was wrong with her, that she didn't deserve to be loved, that she had no right to exist, that she had to be perfect and please everyone to survive, and that she was not wanted (which she clearly wasn't). She believed that she was trash—this must have been the reason she was treated the way she was. This at least made sense to her little mind.

That she too was valuable, just like the cat in her arms or the flowers that blossomed in spring, never occurred to her. This is what happens to all children who internalize cruelty when something happens in life that is far too difficult to understand, and when no one is there to help them through. And often they won't tell another single soul about what is going on at home, for the shame is too great, and they believe it is their own fault anyway.

So where was love in our story then?

Despite the beliefs she formed about herself and life, there was one red thread that led her through everything. For whatever reason, she never let go of the one thing she knew was true: the light in her heart. She literally had nothing else; here she found a glimpse of love. And her choice in the winter's night, when the first snowflake fell, made her know and feel it even more. A whole new world opened up to her. She found refuge in that light, when days and nights were filled with suffering far too great to bear. She felt that little light in times of deepest despair and when she went alone into nature among the animals and trees, where she was truly at home.

Because of that light, which one could see shining through her big blue eyes, she could still laugh and enjoy an innocence that no one could take away or destroy. There was power in it, and a newfound strength grew in her; one that nothing and no one from that day on could break. It gave her the courage to go on, even when it would have been easier to jump into a lake and drown (which she considered at times, when things were especially extreme).

It made her creative too, as you see often with kids who grow up in slums, on the streets, or in homes of neglect, abuse, or poverty. Out of pure survival, they can take anything and make something out of it. For the child, trash became toys, trees became the ones that listened, wild animals became best friends, food was found in dumpsters, times imprisoned became occasions for making up magical stories, and beatings turned into a marathon of how long she could endure without a scream.

As years passed by, this intense suffering caused her to turn more and more toward this light. She discovered its voice, deep inside—not the one in the head that is running noisily around, but one that came when she quietly listened to a well of love within her. She let that guide her, because it was the only thing in the hell-house that felt sane. Of course she cried many tears, which after many years would become a great river of suffering. Yet, it was this love and flame in her own heart that kept her alive, when all else failed. She had nothing to hold onto but that.

You know how young children are curious and ready to try out anything. Remember when you were little and went on explorations yourself? When you looked in forbidden rooms for what you might find or when you explored the drawers in your parents' bedroom or tasted your first worm (we all did it— admit it). Children discover and learn most through curiosity and play.

One day, two big fat warts appeared on her hand, and the evil one wanted to burn them away. The girl was scared of the burning and talked to her warts, saying, "If you do not want to get burnt up, you just need to disappear now." She let the light from her heart flow to the warts to help them along. With all sincerity she believed that the next day the warts would be gone—and sure enough, they were. That's how she discovered what we call magic.

This became a favorite adventure, an endless wonderland. Was it mere fantasy or a reality that most do not acknowledge? Our little girl certainly had found what many are searching for these days. Wonder and magic are natural in life, in this very moment— if the heart is open and one can look with innocent eyes.

By the age of fourteen, the girl was physically strong. One day, when her mother tried to beat her, as usual for no reason, the girl, who had always been terrified of the evil one, finally stood up, grabbed her mother's hands, and held her in a locked position. Strong power surged through her like a thunderstorm, as she looked straight into her mother's eyes. She was ready to rip her apart, like a lioness, if need be. She shouted out loud, "Never ever will you hurt me again. It ends now, for good!"

With that, she broke the chains of a lifetime. The old one backed down, for she had no more power over this young girl, who until then had desperately hoped that her mother would just love her, if only for a moment. A drop would have been good enough for her. But it had never come. And on this day, hope died and she let go.

The mother made one last attempt to kill her daughter, as punishment. The girl was severely sick from fish poisoning and her mother would not give her any water. On the third day, the girl fell unconscious. It seemed like a near death experience what happened then. She left her body and felt herself floating upward into a great tunnel, pulled toward a distant light. Incredible joy began to awaken, and all burdens dropped from her, like leaves falling from a tree in the autumn winds. As she flew toward a golden and immense light, it felt as if she was truly coming home. Such freedom!

But just before she could fully immerse herself in this light, a voice stopped her. A luminous being appeared, asking her to return. She was told that her mission was yet to be fulfilled and her time to leave the Earth plane had not come. She felt conflicted. More than anything, she wanted to merge with this enormous love. What was holding her in this cruel world, really? In this moment of yet another crossroad, a choice needed to be made. She was reminded of why she had come to Earth. She hesitated, for the longing for the light was overwhelmingly strong. But the profound wish to fulfill her calling caused her to return once again. The little angel did not depart to the other side, despite her brush with death.

Her mother had failed at her last attempt to destroy this brave girl. Only fifteen years old, she packed her bags and left the house of hell to find her own way. She moved toward a different life, and a whole new story unfolded then. And on her journey she not only found what she longed for the most, but turned the poison she was raised with into gold.

One day, after many arduous years of healing the bloody wounds of abuse through tears, fury and sweat, and deep spiritual practice, she chose to visit her mother in the mental institution in Germany. Upon seeing her, she did not need her to change, nor did she expect this drop of love anymore. The denial, the hope, the anger and pain, all of it was gone. From deep stillness, she could embrace her sick mother exactly as she was, be present with her and genuinely say from an open, unfettered heart: "Mama, I love you." Tears streamed down her face, she knew this was her final good-bye to her mother and toughest teacher of her life, who died soon afterward. As she walked out onto the street on that auspicious day in the hospital, she felt how the burdens of a lifetime had released, a sense of liberation swept her up and she experienced in every cell of her being the victory of true love. And this became her gift for our world.

With a twinkle and a smile to you, from a once-upon-a-time seven-year-old girl, the one who has written the book you are holding in your hands right now.

Love in Action

Making Choices, Setting Intentions:
Maybe you already have done so, or are you discovering the most important choice and commitment you want to base your life on? For some it is truth, justice, and peace, and for others it is love. It does not matter what you call it, only that you feel how this higher intention feels true and inspires you.

Once you know your deepest intent, dedicate yourself wholeheartedly, arrange your life around it, and align your actions with that. Let this choice guide, illumine and teach you. It becomes our greatest learning and gift.

The inquiry to apply is: "What would love do or say in this moment now?" Each step we take reaffirms our commitment to walk in love. It does not mean we do this perfectly. By all means, don't attempt perfection. It just implies that we set the general course and live it to the best of our ability. You will continue to grow, and sooner than later, it will be so natural to walk in love that you won't even think about it anymore.

The choice to live with integrity, to be accountable and follow through, to speak honestly and refrain from harming any living being entails effort, practice and some discomfort. What's the reward? How do you feel when you live with dignity and bravery? What legacy do you want to leave behind?

The choices we make about how we relate and the actions we take determine the kind of impact we have in our life and the world. If we are waiting in line in the grocery store ask: "How does love want to move through me and act right now?" Or, "How can I be loving right now? Show me who to serve, what to say and what to do." You will be guided: an insight, a nudge, a sense will arise. Suddenly you turn to the person in front of you and engage in a conversation that will help both of you. Or you receive a clear message about your next step from the neighbor next door.

Much is possible when you make the choice—second by second—to show up from love. Synchronicities happen when our choices, thoughts, emotions and actions align. There is a power at play in our lives far greater than any ignorance can control or destroy. Never give up, no matter how difficult the situation is. If the little girl could do it, you can too. Trust, grace and a loving hand (seen or unseen) help us through even the greatest troubles, just like the little girl who was guided home.

Taking actions toward ending abuse in our world:
To be able to love, we need to open our eyes and heart and meet the world as it is. Here are some actions to make love real, and to help end the vicious cycle of abuse in this world.

- If you witness child abuse in any way, speak up and act. Silence is not an answer to violence. Abused children usually will not tell anyone, as they want to protect the parent she or he depends on. Contact your local center or the police, if you suspect abuse.

- If you have been abused, seek out help from skilled professionals. Trauma has lasting lifetime impact and requires healing. With help it can be healed. For now, know this: What happened to you is not your fault and there is nothing wrong with you. You are worthy and deserve to be treated with respect and kindness, as all of us do.
- Those who are vulnerable—children, the elderly, and animals—often experience abuse in our world, and it usually happens behind closed doors. They need our protection, care, and voice. Please look out for them.
- Child labor and sweatshops are tragically common in the world. End this crime and don't buy clothes made in sweatshops.
- Sex trafficking is currently the fastest growing business in the world. It affects children as young as six years of age. It doesn't just happen in Asia, but is rampant in every city in the Western world. What can be done? Gain awareness and speak out to protect girls. Educate men not to patronize brothels that exploit underage children. For more information on sex trafficking visit the international human trafficking websites.
- Offer support to a child in need. With the hand of a bigger friend, he or she will be able to heal and recover. None of us should have to walk alone through pain.

Greatness of soul is often born in the hardest moments of our life when we turn to love anyway.

2. The Calling

From the river of life

Do you sense the whisper, a stirring when life emerges in spring as the first daffodil, when tiny chirpings of birds tickle you to smile, or the moment, when all is still, and suddenly shattering thunder and lightning pierce the sky?

What is urging us to rise up and what moves us to turn the tide? Do you hear the roar, the song from deep inside, in the middle of the night, when you are alone, twisting and turning with restlessness that nothing seems to satisfy, no matter how hard you have tried to tie it down? Or looking out across the ocean to the horizon, a longing arises and a fire ignites. An ancient knowing is awakening in us.

No matter how much we do or achieve, how busy we keep ourselves, how many dramas we may be entangled with, something keeps calling. You know what I'm talking about. Sometimes it arrives as a whisper, carried by gentle winds and landing softly in our ears. Sometimes it knocks fiercely on the door, plans fly out the window and we are thrown onto the ground, with nothing left to do but to hear.

It may arrive through an unexpected event—the loss of a loved one or being fired from a job. In the shock and grief our walls may tumble, we are more open to what else is here. Or it wakes us up by facing our climate crisis. Or through a chance meeting with another person we are touched. A journey into new lands may bring a dawning vision; standing on a mountaintop with vast views there is space to see what's most worthy of our attention. The divine slap can happen anywhere, perhaps in the grocery store, when you've forgotten everything on your list, the mind is blank; there in the gap you receive a revelation of your life.

The beckoning from the soul, spirit, our wise heart, from a greatness beyond the usual is a call from life, reminding us why we are here on earth, and what our path and unique gift is. A radical invitation to a life that can only be fulfilled through you. If you allow and follow, it will guide you every step along the way home.

Pay attention to the urging from the unknown. Listen closely to the pulse of destiny, and answer, for it is the most important invitation of your life—giving you the power to rise and light up the world. It only takes a breath into silence to listen to the heart. What is being revealed right now, beckoning to be lived?

***

Finding Love with Mother Teresa in the Slums of Calcutta

I just had turned eighteen and freedom knocked my door wide open. Remember this moment? I heard my calling and answered with an excited *yes*. I was hungry to discover and know true love.

The day after high school was finally finished I kicked off for the ride that would change my life for good. I had enough money saved up for the cheapest airplane ticket, taking me to a place where no one I knew had travelled before. I had no idea what was awaiting me there. I packed a toothbrush, a few shirts, underwear, pants, and a passport—my bag was light. The Russian aircraft was shabby, but never mind, I was on an adventure. It was not surprising that we had an emergency landing; we ended up in freezing Moscow. I spent the night on a bench with several others, swapping stories from our homes and towns; some I did not even recognize from my geography lessons in school. Finally, at sunrise, we took off toward warmer weather. Yes, we actually got there and landed with applause in a country buzzing with life: India.

I blinked; the sun was so bright and hot, within half an hour my white shirt was drenched with sweat. No wonder heads were turning as I tried to cover my breasts from stealing looks. And then I stepped out of the airport and almost buckled over onto my knees. I saw children looking like sticks and bones, gaunt with hunger, begging with outstretched hands. Old people with a missing leg or arm sat half-naked in the dirt between cow dung and blaring stinking trucks. Shocked and shaken amidst the noise and squalor, I sobbed. The intensity of suffering and poverty hit me hard like a hammer. I handed out rupees like bread; I couldn't help it. Money ran fast through my hands for food for those who lived trapped in the streets with no way out.

Exhausted on my first night, I buried myself in a blanket and fell asleep in a cheap hotel room; one barren bed and a toilet that consisted of a hole in the floor. Welcome to India.

A month later, after a life-changing stay in an ashram, I boarded a crowded train to Calcutta. There were no benches in third class, only a small corner on the floor was left. I crouched, crammed together with the local Indian people, pigs, chickens and bags piled between us. The Westerners had advised me to take first class for this two-day journey along the coast, warning that I would regret a different choice. I was stubborn and ignored their well-meaning advice. I wanted to experience how the majority of people in India were living. After ten hours of sitting squashed between the locals and animals on the floor of the rattling train, I did wonder if this was such a good idea after all. My whole body ached so badly I could barely move my arms and legs. But I was determined to go the whole way, for you really get to know a culture or a person when you walk in their shoes.

I took this quite literally I guess, but I did get to know the world of India more intimately than I had bargained for. We rubbed not only shoulders, but shared fleas hopping around on us, and meals so spicy I thought I would burn up from the inside. Animals littered everywhere and the stink was intense, but after a while I got used to the smells. Some of us were chanting and praying; this is not a secret affair in India, but as normal as drinking sugar chai, ten times a day or more.

Having just spent a month in a Hindu ashram it was a perfect place to practice all I had learned and repeat my mantra. After awhile I was able to accept things as they were, and the ordeal turned into a rather meditative experience. What else was there to do? It was too hot to get worked up about anything. And after all, I was thirsty to discover what real spirituality meant, how one could love humanity and make a difference that touches hearts and feeds the people.

For many years I had wanted to work with Mother Teresa in the slums of India. I was impressed with this remarkable woman, who started without a penny to serve the poorest of the poor, and had dedicated her whole life uncompromisingly to God and humankind. Now I was on my way to meet her. If the train ride was already extreme by European standards, it prepared me little for what I encountered, when I arrived in the city of Joy and Hell: Calcutta.

At four a.m. I walked toward the nunnery. The sun was just rising over the city. What I saw shook me once again, to the core. On the side of the filthy streets, next to colorful temples, people lay sleeping, covered only with ragged loincloths. Some were washing themselves in muddy rain puddles. Many were skinny, some were severely crippled, and some were taking their last breath. The poor literally had nothing—or so it seemed.

I entered the nunnery with my heart pounding. I went up the stairs toward the prayer chapel and met a small woman in a blue and white nun's habit. I asked her where I could find Mother Teresa. She reached out her hands to me, with a warm smile, and said, "Welcome. It's me." Her obvious love, simplicity and purity touched me deeply, and tears streamed down my sunburnt cheeks. For several months I had the honor to work alongside Mother Teresa and her joyous nuns. Every day we went together to the slums to offer food and medicine to the poorest of the poor.

I saw that though these people had nothing, they shared their little bit of rice with each other. They were there for one another and many had a deep faith. The hunger and illnesses had left hallowing marks on their faces and bodies, yet frequently their eyes shone with an inexplicable joy. "Who really is poor?" I wondered. "People in the West with our excessive wealth, isolation from each other, and loss of soul; or they?" We have a different kind of poverty that may be harder to heal than the one in India.

A little five-year-old girl in the orphanage offered Mother Teresa her only toy to take to the children in the slums. I could see how precious this ragged doll was to her, yet how happy she looked to be able to offer her gift. Mother Teresa did not want people to give leftovers from their abundance, what they did not need. What matters, she always said, is how much love we put into the giving. That is where true joy is found. She lived what she spoke; I saw it in her eyes and in the way she held the hand of the old thin man, who was dying in peace.

When I entered the house of the dying, I too felt enveloped in a real sense of peace. The sisters tended so kindly and respectfully to the ones close to death. The elderly felt loved, maybe for the first time in their lives. In the beginning it was hard for me to wash the stinking, oozing wounds and face all this agony. How could the sisters bear to live and serve amidst the worst of human suffering? What was it that made them capable to do this work daily, with such apparent joy and dedication? I remember, while praying beside Mother Teresa in her small chapel, as if answering my unspoken question she said, "My love is Christ and he is in everyone. In serving the poor we love, feed, wash, and clothe him. In giving love we are loved. Treat everyone like you would treat Christ."

There was a faded handwritten paper pinned on the wall of the chapel, which read: "When I was homeless you opened your doors. When I was naked you gave me your coat. When I was in prison, you came to my cell. When I was lonely, you gave me your love. Searching for kindness you held out your hand. When I was happy, you shared your joy." Every person, often the ones closest to us, is offering a gift—a chance for us to love. We do not have to be Christian, Buddhist or of any religion to make a difference. This humble and strong woman certainly had changed my life. Mother Teresa was more than a saint. The way she acted and lived showed me what real love is. I am grateful for her, as many are whose lives she has touched.

Listening to the whisper of my soul set me on my path and led me into the greatest calling of life: True Love. May you hear and answer the call from your soul. May you enjoy your journey, the one you will never regret and which fulfills what you were born for on this earth.

Love in Action

A simple practice is to say: "I choose Love's power in this moment now and act from that." No need to do it right or to always know what that will look like. We simply give permission for the natural knowing to emerge and thereby live it more and more.

Meditation is a sound way to listen into the deeper wisdom river. Regular meditation practice attunes us to our own nature and calling. (Go to the "Foundation Stones" chapter and to the "Love in Action" section of "The Kiss and Gold" if you wish to read more.)

Practice being present in daily life. The more aware you are, the more you walk in alignment. And a genuine prayer from our heart offers access to our greater intelligence. Ask, "Help me face what is here and see it through the eyes of love." Or,

"Show me the next step to help others and myself." Take time to be in nature or in quiet places. Feel into the earth, listen to the sound of water, and drop deeper. Wisdom speaks through all of creation. Relax and give yourself space for your deeper knowing to unfold. Do not try to figure things out; the rational mind does not know the route of the soul.

Usually your soul's path and calling emerges step-by-step. The whole picture may not be revealed at once. Take one step in soul direction. (You can read more about this in "Igniting the Fire.") Trust your intuition and act on it. The more you do, the clearer it becomes. If you are not sure about guidance, ask, "Is this beneficial in any way?" If not, do not go ahead. If yes, you have nothing to lose. If unsure, let your pot simmer on the stove, give it time. If something sounds too complicated and complex, it's your mind holding the reins. (Read more in the next chapter, "Follow the Red Thread.") If something keeps calling your name over and over again, value this. Answer your heart by following it.

With the inner eyes to see and ears to hear, life is the messenger in every way.

3. Follow the Red Thread

The still small voice and the blade of truth

When I first learned about the still small voice inside of me I practiced listening rigorously, with intense passion, much to the dismay of my girlfriend who was hitchhiking with me through Ireland. We were two teenagers with vastly differing worlds and ideas. I drove her nuts when I sat down and closed my eyes at every crossroad to ask which direction to take. There are many crossroads in this green hilly country and it rains quite frequently. But only when I received a clear answer would I get up again. That usually took awhile, whilst my friend was swearing in the cold wind, waiting for my "holy divine" guidance among the cows and sheep that foraged along these old Irish roads. I was determined, for better or worse.

But my inner guidance did lead us to horses we could ride, to friendly Irish folk, a dolphin to swim with, a magical island, and other marvelous adventures. It even helped us to discover hidden guns and got us safely out of a dangerous terrorist house in Belfast. It was an unforgettable journey, and the voice of intuition became my best ally and guide; even my travelling companion began to listen in from time to time, especially when she needed to decide which of the good-looking Irishmen to go out with.

***

One foggy day, I walked along a soft, sandy beach in Santa Cruz to clear my mind. I was under a deadline and had to find a rental fast. Nothing seemed to be available anywhere, other than ridiculously overpriced little shacks. I heard the voice inside of me ask, "What would you love?" To which I replied, "I don't have time for this. I need to find a solution immediately."

Again the insistent voice knocked on my door, "What would you love?" Reason snapped back—"It doesn't matter. What I would love won't happen anyway." Back to my important thinking about what other avenues I could take. Once again I heard the voice louder this time, "What would you love?"

This was annoying now. Only to silence this voice, I replied, "Well, if you want to know, what I would love is to live right next to the beach, to hear the waves at night and the seals bark and have windows that face the sea, with a price I can afford. And this is an outlandish wish that won't be possible, especially in this overcrowded town." But just the image of it made me feel lighter and relaxed, my heart had opened up and spoken.

Three days later exactly such a place was offered to me, with an easy affordable rate. I lived there for a year. Every day I crossed the road to the beach and listened to the waves and seals barking at night. The incredible view from my home was inspiring, the perfect place for writing. Through the large windows I watched plenty of sunrises and sunsets across the ocean, light piercing through the clouds and dancing upon the water, and I saw the stars, while living in a town. This was a miracle and my rational mind remained silent, blown away... at least for a little while.

***

Our intuitive sense guides us on the path of love, and it even helps us to find what we have lost along the road.

It's sometimes good to lose your stuff... but not necessarily if it's a cell phone or favorite sweater, gifted by a friend. I took a lovely walk at night on the beach, and upon returning to my car, I realized that my phone had fallen out of my pocket. I wandered around on this long beach under the stars, so glorious, if it wasn't for having to hunt down a tiny thing that had my most important information in it. Like searching for a needle in the haystack... how in the world would I find it? And the tide was rising. At some point I stopped this hopeless endeavor and decided to release it. But then, before I left, I remembered something far more important than finding stuff: get still, attune, and ask to be shown. I let myself be guided, and as if an invisible hand was directing me, within minutes, I lifted my cell phone, which was half buried in the sand, into my hands.

And that favorite sweater? The next morning, I walked this beach again, but nothing. The ocean must have taken it, or so I thought. But, when I came to the parking lot, again, I felt clearly guided and approached a woman in her car to ask if she had seen a green sweater. What the heck was I doing, why would I ask her? No clue. I just trusted. Still, my mind was dumbfounded when she replied, "Does it have a zipper?" Yes, she had my sweater; a guy had given it to her after he found it on the beach. Amazing. And to top it off, I got to support her and her mother in turn in their search for a home. I love the magic, and what happens when we follow the red thread road.

***

Life speaks to us, when we are open and willing to listen; it's quite natural that intelligence is revealed in varied ways. Guidance arrives through people, animals, signs, and situations, and of course from our heart and gut.

We just covered ourselves with plenty of stuff, so we don't really hear or see. We doubt the hand of love so easily. Just because we have been conditioned by society and others that what cannot be perceived doesn't exist, does not mean it isn't true. In fact, often what we call reality, upon closer look, is a bunch of delusions. Listening to the voice of truth is a sharp sword to use to differentiate between what is real and what is make-believe; it is our surefire anchor, especially when in danger. It helped me and saved the day for others too.

***

Black leather jacket, bald head, strong muscles; the man was a picture of power and charisma. A big shot. Me, a little sweet and naïve fish in the pond. I gave him the papers and all my private information. We were talking about a million dollars and a refinance for the castle and spiritual center I owned. He asked me to sign a few papers, minor details, just for legal matters he said. I did not read the whole thing, it was written in typical endless lawyer-speak—most people don't even get through the first sentence. I figured I could trust him, because I knew friends who had invested with him and he seemed to be doing good work with their money, financing solar panels and wells for people in Africa and more. Such fronts look promising; however, it is useful to look behind the façade to see if it is the real deal or just painted cardboard. Unfortunately, I learned this later. After a knowledgeable friend vouched for him I was the little fish reeled in without looking left or right. But something felt queasy in my gut all along.

After my meeting with power guy I took a walk in the wild hills to clear my head. Something bothered me and I couldn't get what it was, like a bad smell when you cannot find its source. It was high summer in California, the grass already turned brown. I sat down on the earth, and asked for clarity. Soon after, a coyote came close to me and howled loudly. I looked into the sky; a screeching hawk circled around me. I knew in that moment, something was up. Hair stood up all over my body. A sign of truth, my body works like that. Coyote had always visited me, especially when I was being deceived. This time he walked close by me; as if to make it very clear, he looked straight into my eyes.

What in the world was he telling me? Where was deception at play once again? Right in front of my nose, and I was not seeing it. Delusion has many ways to hide what is true. I racked my brain: The mortgage guy? It can't be. My mate? Nope, clearly not. Anything or anyone else? Nothing came to mind and nobody fit the bill. So I brushed it aside to deal with later.

It seemed urgent though, because on my drive home a coyote risked his life by walking right into the street. I slammed the breaks on the windy mountain road. He strolled leisurely toward my car and stopped next to my open window. We were only inches away from each other. He looked at me silently for the longest time before moving on. These warnings were bloody serious, and now slightly nerve-wracking.

The next day the bald big shot boss of the company called me into his office for a private meeting. In a commanding voice, which left no space for discussion, he told me to invest with him all the money I was taking out from the house. He stood up, and I sat in a chair looking up at him like a little schoolgirl. He stared down at me when he spoke, an old power play I saw right through. But he'd locked the doors and made it obvious that I wasn't leaving the room until he'd gotten what he wanted. I was alone with him. My searching eyes checked the window; too high to reach, too small to climb out. When it comes to survival the mind gets basic. I'm a woman; tiny in stature compared to him, a large man. I wished I had more muscles, but it was too late now to exercise. So, I did what I could. I breathed deeply into my belly, put my feet firmly on the ground, and connected to a far greater power inside me, stronger than mere muscles.

Suddenly my fear dissolved, I rose and stood up to him. I knew not to confront him outright, since psychopaths don't do well with that. But I spoke with authority, from an inner strength. "Thanks for your offer. I will meditate on it. That's what I always do with big decisions in life. I'm sure you understand. I'll let you know tomorrow." I faced him straight on, a lioness looking through my eyes, letting him know with fierce energy, *You do not fuck with me.*

He instinctively stepped back from my fire and tried to argue. "This is a once in a lifetime opportunity, I will triple the monies within three months. Just sign now. What difference will your meditation make other than delaying one more crucial day?" Pressure and haste are the favorite tools of the devil. But I was not going to be ensnared. I firmly told him, "Open the door. Now." He did, as if commanded by a higher power. Sweat was pouring down my back. I walked out in the nick of time. Of course, coyote had been right.

Back in my car, I shook, and then spoke a prayer. "Show me the entire truth please." I knew there was more to this; it stank badly. Later I entered the White Raven, my favorite café, to get a brief reprieve. By luck or fate, the woman who worked as the bald big shot's assistant stood in front of me in line. I casually mentioned that he was my mortgage broker and asked, "You work for him. What do you know about him?" She looked panicked and kept turning around to see if anyone was listening. Then she drew me into the back dark corner of the coffee shop. Whispering in a husky voice she said, "I must not be seen or heard. If I tell you, you must not use my name. It could cost my life."

I leaned in closer to listen. When she said, "You are about to grasp the velvet glove of a vampire. Get the hell out!" the hair rose on my neck. I had fallen into one of those Hollywood thriller movies I thought I'd never watch. Only this one was for real. I was in big trouble with finances, a castle and much more at stake, if what she said was true. And would truth be enough to find a way through? I asked inwardly for more clarity; what was happening was too weird for my brain; it just didn't fit into my world. The answer to my prayer came within minutes, as my phone rang. I had not a moment to drink my delicious chai as events started unfolding in rapid speed. One of the bald big shot's workers called and said, "I want to warn you. You're a mother, I feel for you. Just minutes ago I saw some papers and it looks like he's been faking your documents and has all legal rights to your center now."

That evening I organized a meeting with the bald big shot's employees at the White Raven and we agreed to uncover the rest of the stinking mess and take him down together. The power of truth was at work in a miraculous way, revealing more and more by the hour. We would discover that he had financially wrecked over four hundred people for significant sums of money at his large black office table, and that he had a criminal record for assault and child molestation as well. He wasn't just a con artist, he was a dangerous psychopath.

Why didn't I fall into his clever trap? I was not a suspicious person, had no experience with con artists, and was a foreigner who knew little about American law and refinancing with banks. What helped me to see through his scam and saved my butt was the single blade of truth. I kept connecting to a deeper knowing, beneath the surface appearance. I trusted my intuition, which has never let me down or misled me, when I was willing to hear the voice of truth and act on it. I could have scooted around the situation out of fear, but then would he have been stopped, and would I have learned so much? Who knows, maybe this was one of love's moves and I happened to be its hands. When I have trusted the deeper song in life I have fared well. Not that it's always easy; sometimes the fire burns hot.

But the intelligence of the heart and our gut is mightier than all clever deceptions; it discerns lies from truth, and reveals what is hidden to bring forth benevolence. Despite all insanity, love's power always finds a way.

Because of this, the bald gangster was prosecuted and went to jail.

***

When I work with clients and groups I listen to this intelligence; it knows how to guide in the best way possible. Of course, just like we can't learn to drive a car by mere intuition, it is essential to have tools, skills, and expertise in place. We need to know how to play a flute, and then a refined master can allow the music of soul to pour through. I have had many remarkable results, when I stepped back and let intuition take the lead.

***

One day I was leading a professional training for a group, which presented a challenge as some members were far advanced and others complete beginners. We had people from diverse cultural and ethnic backgrounds who were between the ages of eighteen and seventy-six. I had to draw on ingenuity and attune to the wisdom field on how to bring this group into alignment and cohesion. Sure, I had a plan, but could not rely on that, as it would have never achieved what happened, when I followed the red thread that connects us all. In the end of the spiritual training, the whole group had fallen in love with each other, and each person confirmed that they had received the skills they had come for and far more. And I wasn't exhausted, but exhilarated, even though I had worked intensively with thirty people, seven full days in a row.

***

And there were times when I did not follow the red thread. I had a better idea, or plain refused to hear. You know those times, when you look back, you knew you weren't making the best choices? It happened for me in the arena of relationship, where many of us are likely to fall off the cliff.

***

He was the cool guy, a spiritual leader and gorgeous too. Our attraction was instantaneous and fiercely intense. We could not get enough of each other; like two drunks we fell, deeply inebriated. I was infatuated, believing we were meant to be soul mates for life. So I overlooked not only my instincts, but also the obvious: he had a track record of playing women and betraying them. Of course he wouldn't do that with me, especially after he had professed his undying love during a romantic dinner in a restaurant set under a starlit sky. Everything went stunningly between us and I shunted that little voice of my heart, which incessantly called out, "Wrong path, turn around," into the closet. I figured it was fear talking and I was going to take the leap all the way in anyway. Well, I crash-landed a few months later, and yes, it did hurt badly. A rough learning, it took only two more times before I got the point.

***

Years later my intuition had become my most trusted companion and reliable guide. It didn't always tell me what I wanted to hear, but spoke plain and directly truth.

***

At a time when I had literally lost everything in my life, a man I knew for a while confessed that he was in love with me. He offered me the world when I had nothing left in my own pockets. "I'll take care of you," he said. That sounded exactly like what I needed after I had gone through hell. "You can teach and write all your books and not have to work for a living. I have a beautiful home to share with you." (Indeed, it was lovely.) He was intelligent, generous, and had other good qualities. Then he said, "I would love to marry you." He followed this up with the biggest clincher: "I will buy your dream Andalusian horse and treat you as the queen you are." (I've dreamed of owning such a stallion for the past twenty years.) Oh, so very tempting.

I was stunned. A rescue boat had arrived when I was floundering in the ocean, my own boat sunk and the waves raging high. But what did my heart say? What did truth speak? I told him I needed to listen. Other voices chimed in uninvited. *I like him and he is a good man, so what's the problem? Am I nuts to not jump on his wonderful offer? What's wrong with me? For once I could have a cushy life. Am I addicted to hardship?*

This looked like the perfect road to take. But, in survival mode it's easy to make choices that aren't for the best in the end. So, I listened for days, wanting nothing else but the truth. In the end I turned down his offer; my intuition told me it wasn't the path for me to take. I said "no" without knowing the "why." I trusted the clear and simple answer from my heart. He wasn't to be my mate. Later it was confirmed why; his gifts had been tempting, but they came with a price. It would have led me astray. Too bad about my dream horse though.

Follow the red thread

We often know and sense more than we admit to ourselves. Our intuition speaks; the question is, are we listening? We hear a thousand things; our mind talking, our emotions, other people and sounds from the environment. But what do we listen to, and which voice do we act upon? If we want to know what is true and loving, one of the most important practices is to listen to the voice of our innate wisdom. There is a song, a river, and a well of knowing awaiting for us. The forgotten sound of truth resides in life and in each of us. This still small voice seems at first like a faint and distant whisper in dense fog, but becomes louder the more we give it attention. It is our intuition speaking, leading us from delusion to truth, helping us to see through mirages, guiding us through all weather conditions, situations, and landscapes toward love, basic sanity, what is beneficial, wise and for the best.

But we all have an internal radio station with voices calling us in a thousand different directions. This gets rather confusing.

One says *buy the couch*, another is vehemently against it, and yet another voice suggests a different color and shape... In the case of a couch the decision doesn't have much impact. But if we're faced with a decision regarding our health, the environment, our child, other people, the life of an animal, an organization, or a country, then our choices have greater consequence. The voice of truth assists and guides us best here.

An ongoing listening practice and small steps taken in daily life build the muscle to make wise choices in bigger matters of life. What do we listen to when it comes down to the wire? Often our rational mind is in charge, but misses the point of life. Or we act emotionally or impulsively, get paralyzed or stressed out about life decisions. Which voice are you following and acting upon? Is it the voice of truth, or the voice of assumptions, imaginations, fears, judgments, emotions, and beliefs? We may deceive ourselves, believing we act upon wise counsel, when it is covered-up fear causing us to run away from a situation. It takes training to distinguish the voice of wisdom from the many other voices blaring on our mental radio station.

The voice of intuition is found below the surface; it is in everyone, without question or doubt. It may take some digging, tuning and honing into. This voice speaks simply, directly, and guides us lovingly: "Let go." "You are held." "Take a nap." "I am with you." "Don't get into this relationship." "Leave this job." It resonates from the heart, straight and clear. Some do not hear words, but their intuition speaks through their senses, events, people, and visions, emerges as a knowing.

Not listening to or following the voice of our intuition usually leads to more suffering and creates karmic and agonizing entanglements. We become more bound, uptight, and things turn from challenging to increasingly complicated and difficult. Relationships and our life stays stuck, unhealthy behavior patterns prevent love, and we heap suffering upon already existing pain.

I have never regretted a decision when I followed my intuition. It's gotten me through hairy and dangerous situations. Like a light in the dark it has led me safely through storms, mirages in the desert, changing phenomena, deceit and danger, and brought me to clear waters, green valleys, always home to what is real, to love. The still small voice is the red thread; any diversion and forgetting aches too deep. This love is always here, for what and for whom would we betray and abandon that? Yet, so often we do, because we get confused as to what we can trust in the mire of our world.

What to trust?

Have you ever deceived or used another? Have you ever been betrayed, lied to, or been taken advantage of? Whether with a lover, friend, coworker or family member, most of us have felt a rip in the fabric of our innocence. So what can we trust in life, with others and ourselves?

How often have you asked yourself, "Is this for real?" "Does he truly mean it when he says he loves me?" "How could she tell me she loves me and then just disappear from my life?" Someone can mean it genuinely when they say, "I love you," but it doesn't mean they embody or live that love all the way. "Love can be so deceiving," I hear often from those who've been betrayed in love. Such devastating experiences may leave us confused, bitter, sarcastic, suspicious, and afraid to trust again.

When a seemingly good-hearted person hurts or cheats you, or when you hurt or cheat another, you may wrestle internally with the question, "How could they do this to me?" or "How could I have done this to them?" Some of our vasanas (conditioned tendencies) pull so strongly we may cross the line from what we know is caring and true. Being human is messy and integrity is not easy to come by. It takes strength and a sound commitment to live with honesty in a world where the false is glorified all too often.

Love does not deceive and betray, nor is love blind and naïve. But our mind makes up stories and believes an array of delusions that cloud our eyes and perceptions. We might equate certain gestures and behaviors with love, but then it turns out that the person or situation isn't what we wished it to be. We tumble into ditches, get stuck in mesmerizing spiderwebs, eat garbage and pretend it is healthy, drink poison that tastes sweet, and accept behavior that looks like love, but isn't. The more aware we are, the more clearly we see what's real. I used to be quite naïve; what is true and what is false were not always easy for me to recognize. Many deceptions had to be cleared out so I could tell what I could and could not trust. I had to encounter several shades of grey, and lift back covers to discover God—at times disguised as jerks. I had to open thick veils in myself to find my way into the light.

To see the truth can be surprising, wonderful, or extremely uncomfortable; it isn't always pretty and may go completely against what we hope or expect. Sometimes we'd rather stay in denial than face what is obvious to our gut, but veiled to our eyes. There are many cheap tours offered through delusion land.

But we find our path by trusting the truth of our own being. Sometimes we need help, another pair of eyes, an extra lamp to shed light. We are usually not all blind in the same place. A friend, a professional, can support us to clear our windows to see what is obvious before our own eyes. Maybe the person you dated stood you up from the get-go with cheap excuses, and later consistently disregarded you. Surprised? If we want the truth more than anything, it will surely be revealed. We just have to be willing to recognize our fear and denial, look behind the façade and face what's in front of our nose.

Things and people are not always as they appear. What looks like love isn't always love. And we may find love where and how we least expect it. The red thread, our still small voice and intuition, is the best guide in town and shines a light even in the most difficult situations. It connects us with the blade of truth, which cuts through the thickest deceptions and the smoothest BS. Its power is priceless; it helps us to navigate the tumultuous waters on the sea of life, shows a way through the darkest of times and leads us into a love that is true.

Love in Action

Keys to connect with our intuition:
- Meditate, let the mind-chatter pass by, and allow emotions to settle. Breathe into your body and open into spaciousness. Ask your question. Listen in a relaxed way. Drop into silence and open into the unknown. Intuitive knowing can emerge awhile later, or in the moment. Just pay attention, like a wild cat, relaxed and alert.
- We have many radio stations to choose from and many voices producing noise in our brains, making our heads spin and ache. Exhausting? Yes, of course. Tiring? Confusing? Same old shoe. Usually the "host" approach works wonders here: Acknowledge and honor each voice present in your head or in the room, but don't let just any voice run the show. This practice helps to gain space and perspective amidst the noise. None of our radio stations represent the voice of truth, no matter how loud or convincing they blare.
- What to do? Below the surface, all these voices and the noise of the world, resides the one in our heart that speaks true. The voice of love is always simple, intelligent and feels alive. It fills you and resonates in a deep way. It's sane, healthy and wise. A sense of calm, warmth and energy comes with it, even if it might be a difficult message to hear or a challenging move to make.
- Use these questions as an inquiry:
  "What is true?"

"What is most beneficial?"

"What is in alignment?"

"Is this loving, wise and for the highest best?"

"What do I know that I do not want to know?"

- And here is what we can surrender to and follow: "Thy will and way be done." Then step back, get out of the way and listen: What is the voice of truth speaking to you right now? Take one step. Act on what you know in your heart.

What helps to discern truth from delusion?

There is a fine line between delusion and reality and sometimes it can be difficult to differentiate between the two. As we all know, following either leads to a substantially different outcome. It is worthwhile to practice listening and attuning to the voice of truth and to follow the red thread in life.

- In stillness answers arise from the source itself. But for that to occur we need to be centered and relaxed in our body, to open our mind and heart. Use mindfulness and meditation practice for that.
- First acknowledge and set aside our attachments, preconceived ideas, wishes and expectations we have regarding the outcome and answer. It is crucial to discern. Make truth number one, no matter how unpleasant or surprising it can be.
- Take moments to feel into your heart, and rest here. Ask for guidance: "Please show me clearly what is for the highest best in this situation, with this person..." Open yourself wide. Listen to life. Look beneath the surface. Trust your gut and life. Check your guidance with others; if in doubt don't act yet.
- Clear the seeing lens: Become aware of your own internal landscape. Notice your fears, wishes, dreams,

and resistance, etc. Let them be there, but don't buy them as the whole truth. Then you may experience more spaciousness for what else wants to be seen. Ask for the truth to be revealed. When your own lens is clearer, you can look directly into reality without the projection screen. Dare to see what is obvious with open eyes, without interpretations and what you fear, wish, or imagine to be there.

- Get to know a person and situation. Leave mental stories and judgments behind, they won't tell you what is true. The more present and open you are, the easier information comes to you. Before you make assumptions talk with the other person, there is usually more than what we can see with our own limited vision.

- Don't expect perfection from people. No one is acting completely good or is always trustworthy, including you. People are often caught in their own knots, busy with their own story. Establish a bottom line with others and focus on building integrity within yourself.

- Conscience is useful to follow, especially when it nags from inside.

- This question is helpful to carry in your pocket: "What is in alignment with my heart?" Explore with a beginner's mind.

Trust the power of truth. Its blade cuts through all fabrications and delusions. It has a surefire knack to break the chains that bind and blind—on its own terms of course. Truth, even if uncomfortable, sets us free.

Hold onto the red thread, a lifesaving rope guiding safely through all terrains in the world, leading you home to love and what is for the highest best.

4. Igniting the Fire

Living your gift

Perhaps our life purpose has little to do with our job, the things we achieve or manifest, the healing and awakening we may experience. Maybe it has more to do with how well we love. If we can touch this one fleeting moment, this joy and pain, this one person before us, and the world that has gone a bit mad, with presence and our wild heart right now. And yes it's true, there is a precious gift that only you can live and give.

Red rock mountains, scorching dry heat, I had fasted for three days on a solo vision quest. My face was red as a tomato, burnt from the arid sun; my body ached from sleeping on bare earth and sitting in silence daily for seven hours straight on ancient Native American land. I wondered if I ever would come home with my life purpose revealed. Did I even have one? I decided not to leave until it had been revealed, no matter what, simple as that. I had plenty of water to drink with me, food was not necessary, and my sleeping bag would keep me warm in the cold desert nights of New Mexico. This beautiful place in the wild was perfect for my soul search, the panorama of stars was magnificent, coyotes howled at night and one kept visiting my camp to keep me company. I think he was curious too. Every day I went deeper in meditation, and slowly a visceral sense of intimate connectedness emerged with all that was alive. I heard the shifting of sand grains moved by the wind. It was sweet, when a little chipmunk climbed into my lap and looked up at me unafraid, as if I was his newest discovery and friend.

After five days, I wasn't hungry anymore, while countless hours had passed sitting on a rock, shaded by a shrubby tree, which had found a source of water, somewhere I could not see.

My mind became clearer with each passing moment, until no thoughts could be found. Resting in peace I was contented, even if I had no purpose other than being here. It was enough to simply abide in love. On the seventh day, deeply immersed in stillness and communion, an answer to my soul prayer arrived, a response beyond what I could have expected or ever imagined—out of nowhere the grand surprise arrived.

Above my head I heard the swishing sound of wings. I looked up into the clear sky and recognized a majestic eagle, who circled around me three times, screeching. Magic was in the air, hair stood up all over my body. I knew he had come as a messenger. And then it all unfolded so fast, I could barely catch my breath.

Veils dropped before my eyes, I emerged beyond time and space into a vast expanse, suffused with tremendous love, and was swept up into sacredness. I heard a voice rise like rolling thunder, resounding from every rock, from the sky, shaking the earth beneath. The sound was full, roaring—did I have such bad ears? I was thrown onto my knees by a mighty force, and the sheer immensity that took hold of me sent tears streaming down my face.

"Live true Love. Lead my people home." Wow, impressive, but I had no idea what these grand words meant, and had no time to ask or think. Visions as clear as daylight flooded through, none I could have conjured up: I am with different people, seeing straight into their hearts with deep love. A picture arises of leading groups in sacred circles. Another one floods in: I am sitting at an altar and teaching people. There is a castle, where people join together in meditation and celebration and nature is held with honor. The last powerful vision arrived, blowing me away. I still hold this one closely to my chest, as it is just now beginning to emerge.

I was twenty-four years old when I undertook this quest in the wilderness of New Mexico, and I have dedicated my whole life to fulfill this destiny. But I did not know what it really meant, as I had no context for it. Nor did I know what it would entail, how it would unfold and what it would require in practical terms. I just vowed to serve this calling all the way—come what may. I aligned with it and step-by-step created my life around it.

I needed to learn a whole lot, besides having a university degree and meditating. I had to grow into bigger shoes myself to be able to guide people well. So, I trained as a psychologist and became a therapist, fulfilling the vision of eyes that see into the heart. I trained as a dharma and meditation teacher and taught spiritual retreats and satsangs internationally—thus the circle of people and the altar picture from the quest had manifested. And I taught trainings for leaders, healers and teachers who make a difference in the world. Ten years after the vision quest I owned a castle (eerie how similar this was to my vision) which became a spiritual and educational center in the Santa Cruz Mountains. Here I led interfaith worship services, retreats, families, couples and women, professional trainings and did sacred activism work. It was a stunning place, surrounded by organic gardens, where we communed with nature and created a protected place for wildlife. Even owls moved in and deer gave birth in our yard. Two horses, a donkey and five cats joined our family with my then four-year-old daughter. We built a labyrinth and temple where people came from afar to meditate, pray and join in community. It was heaven on earth, and a ton of work. But so worth it to live out a deep calling from the soul and serve a mission that is in benefit to all.

Did I ever doubt the words and images from this vision quest? Sure, often I wondered if this profound experience from the desert was just fiction or some grandiose ego trip, but I kept choosing to trust anyway. I was taken on a deeper inner journey too, to grow into my purpose. It ignited a fire that grew stronger day by day and it took me to the core of the human heart. I faced obstacles and challenges on that road, the manifestation and embodiment for that calling was not delivered on a golden platter. But destiny always found its way through and carried me.

When I look back over a decade, the vision from the desert has been manifested literally in every way. It was fulfilled, amazing to realize in this moment as I write. And the last vision... well how it will take form, will be a surprise even to me. Stay tuned!

***

We often light up when we see young children playing. They just shine, without doing anything special, other than being alive. They don't worry about whether they are good enough and don't hold back in expressing themselves as they are. They have not yet been brainwashed or beaten down to question their uniqueness and light.

Are you hiding your light under a bushel, or are you shining it wherever you go? There is a fire in us that ignites the world. When we look with our eyes from planet Earth, a star appears small in the vast firmament. As we fly higher up, distant starlight becomes greater even. One shining star is mesmerizing, as you lift your eyes into the night. Draw nearer toward your north star. Turn to the gift you have in you. Deeper than the lies and shame is the diamond, your wealth of beauty, power and love. We are told from an early age that it is somewhere else outside of us, and that we need to achieve and earn what is ours all along. And we take on the coat of delusion, cover up with reason, just because everyone else does too. Yet our true soul purpose, this living flame, won't ever leave us alone. When in touch, connected with our star, we are wildly alive. As we serve our gift, we shine on this earth. The fire of life needs to be lived, just as a river needs to flow.

You have a gift so unique; in the whole universe there is not one single being found among billions who is exactly like you. Let that sink in. In all of existence there is only one who is as wondrous as you. Not a single flower in the fields of rolling hills is the same as the other red, blue blossoms dancing in the wind. The tree does not hold back to turn into an oak, a seed naturally becomes grass. It just is. Your true being, your soul essence is awaiting your permission to be realized and embodied here on earth. It only asks for your undivided *yes*. Hold back and you will get depressed. Pretend to be what you are not and you will feel fake and never quite satisfied. Try to be someone else and you miss the point of your existence here.

Much of our brain is not used, our heart's capacity for true love remains untapped, and magnificent contributions to the welfare of all beings are still marked as rare. Are you the one, courageous enough to step out of line and help in turning the tide in a world on the edge?

Imagine for a moment you could do and be anything you want. Let your view expand further than the horizon, into the land of unlimited possibilities. What would you be and do, if all is possible? How about taking the leap into what you love and are longing for in this moment now? How does it feel to step in more? Exciting; and scary maybe? What's the mind of limitation babbling? "Not possible, not you, it's just imagination not reality," or "Things must stay as they are for safety. As it always was, so it will always be? I cannot, because..." We have a long list of reasons.

Useful—in case we run out of toilet paper!

Our mission is not a fancy idea we can make up in our mind on a workday between rushed appointments. It isn't a "ready-made" thing, fitting nicely into a neatly packaged box with a pretty ribbon on top. It's not some fancy fantasy. No, it is encoded in us as a living flame. Once discovered, and ignited with our *yes*, fueled by our attentiveness and lived in action, it spreads like lightning fire across the world. Then we do not repeat history but write a new story. We become the torch that inspires hearts.

Whatever you have been yearning to live and what your soul is burning for, go for it. Actually, life is eagerly awaiting you! Because, who you are, is the gift.

Fire in the belly and heart: Discovering purpose and passion

There is a purpose each of us has been born for. We have tasted it, received glimpses of our reason for being here. What your passion truly is, only you know deep down. This fire is burning in our hearts and bellies. If we give ourselves permission, we ignite it.

To uncover your gift, ask and listen to the well of wisdom inside, here it will be revealed. Be in silence, take time out from busyness and be alone for a while, maybe go on your own spiritual quest. For knowing and inspiration to arise we need space and stillness in our lives. Do not ask for the outer form of your purpose and the how at first. This is secondary and will change at times. You are reaching further than the ceiling of the limited self, toward your being. As we open into the center of our heart, beneath the surface concepts of a clever mind, droplets and rain showers of a larger intelligence pour through. You hear a song with a message that resonates with you, or a whispering in a dream at night. You may see a sign on the street, or a clear vision pops up out of the blue. A knowing may emerge within you, an insight arises beyond the shadow of a doubt.

This question I found helpful: If I had only a month to live how would I live? Would you share love with family and friends, do nothing and just be, save the whales, or feed the homeless; meditate in a cave in the Himalayans, or create music to touch the soul or help others?

What do you love, what gives you joy and inspires you? Look at your talents and natural inclinations. One person loves to cook, another enjoys teaching, the healing arts, or being with animals; for some technology is fascinating. Herein lies one of the keys: Your treasure box of talents, grow and nurture these. Follow your natural inclinations, whether it is a business project, art, or education, and engage with it wholeheartedly, even if it isn't forever or as a hobby at first. Keep following your joy, what you love in your heart; this is the straight road for your gift unfolding in life.

Our purpose will always be of benefit. What do you want to contribute to the world, especially now?

What would you like to see in this world that does not yet exist, but you believe could? What cause is moving you to offer your talents, energy, time, and money to? Maybe you are outraged by a situation, such as the torture of animals, or poverty in your city. Involve yourself actively. What kindles your flame? The answer will light your way.

Another approach to igniting the fire and discovering one's purpose is to look at what kinds of people and actions touch you. For some it is the Dalai Lama, so they practice the dharma. For others it is a grandma, who is weird, but acts kind. Engage and learn from those who hold the torch and apply it even in the smallest way in your own life. Maybe you are already setting the world on fire and are of benefit in one way or another. You might be living your wisdom and love right in your home with your family or in your relationship and this is more than good enough. Or you might be the one who is ready to step up into a larger arena than you have ever been in before. I cheer you on!

But maybe you are in a place where you do not know what you want to live. Maybe you feel uninspired, flat as dry bread, like every day is Groundhog Day, and believe that you have nothing to offer anyway. Or that you can't do it, whatever it is you wish you could. Feeling downtrodden, discouraged or overwhelmed has taken over. Or you think, your gift is not valuable, just because it does not fit into a conventional box—no matter how much you have tried—it is still not recognized. You may not have support and feel isolated. Maybe your life is so busy with the daily grind, there is no flame burning anywhere in sight.

Encouragement from the wise ones to kindle the fire:

Wherever you are—it is OK. Come with me on a journey to a time and place before you took birth. Expand your awareness until you see the earth below you. Stand with me on higher ground, at the "La Serenata de Vida," at the golden gates where the serenade of life plays. There are great beings with you who behold you in reverence and love. They speak:

"You are a gift of life. You are valuable as you are, even if you may forget. You are always loved, no matter what will happen on your path. You are a gift, fashioned from the clay of life itself, so unique; its expression does not yet exist upon this earth. It is in your heart and always alive in you, wherever you go, whatever you do. There is a spark of love in you that will never die; if you turn, feed and live it, it will grow and touch many. It is a light that shines its special color, for without yours a color in life would be missing. This is your most priceless jewel. It is sacred. Behold it as such, for you will find the world cannot always see. It is up to you to remember your treasure, to live it wherever you are and shine it forth into the world.

Sometimes you will forget or bury it, and there will be others who will help you to remember, as you offer support for them as well, for in the density and fog of forgetfulness of this world, you need one another. Take time to listen to the deepest yearning, trust—it is yours to live. No one can take it away from you, nor can it ever be destroyed. Please know—who and what you are is important, needed and wanted on the earth, even if you hear messages that suggest otherwise. Do not believe lies. And don't fall into the trap that you have to be perfect, before you live what you've got. You will stumble and fall, that is how you learn, just keep singing your song. Let it soar—we rejoice when we hear your serenade! Live what you love, be in-spirit.

May you enjoy the ride, when it goes up and down. We always watch over you, you are never alone, no matter how difficult it may seem at times. We have faith in you. Go forth with courage and our blessings are with you always."

And here is the catch: You will first know what you are made of, when you have landed fully here on the Earth, in your body and by living your flame in the marketplace of this world. The more you root in the truth of your being and share your light, truth, your talents and heart... the more your gift will unwrap, unfold and grow. By sharing that you are of benefit to all of life.

The inner and outer purpose go hand in hand. For many the calling from inside is loud and strong: realize who you truly are, for nothing else will offer true happiness and release the bonds of suffering, but that. And there is an outer purpose to manifest our fire and love through our lives, in our work and service in the world.

Making it concrete. Down to earth and into the world

Magic is afoot, when we are in sync with our destiny.

It can be a winding road from inner realization to the manifestation here on the material plane. Light travels at lightning speed, walking on foot the same distance takes years. Don't be dismayed if things take time to unfold in their own way. Let's say you are on fire to offer your music to the world. Sure, you need to make the effort to work on cultivating your art and take the necessary practical steps to get your music out there, but we all know how it feels when we try to push the river in the direction we believe it should go. It's such a struggle. Your mind may say, "Hey, I should market this song big time and borrow some money for that." But spirit may have a different way, far more gracious, if you just put down the headphones and listen to guidance. Maybe your book got rejected and you wonder how to make it through an overcrowded market, so at least one person benefits from your creation. It's easy to lose hope, or to doubt and compare oneself with far more successful people in the field. But that will dim the light and you won't go far with that in the jungle of this world.

We do not know how it will pan out. The whole picture isn't revealed to us; so take it one day, one step at a time, and act on what arises from the spark of life in you in this moment now. I often ask, "If this was my last day on this planet, what would I love to leave behind? What would I live in this moment?" Or I ask, "Show me, my beloved, what you would have me do right now to be of service in this world." Then I step back, listen and act.

These inquiry questions open our eyes to see and our ears to hear what is true. It may lead you to share an inspiring idea with a coworker. He may have the right connection for you to bring your idea into manifestation. Or you feel moved to get flowers for an elderly lady in your neighborhood and she tells a story, which provides the answers to your questions. You live what's in your heart today without attachments and expectations... and then one thing leads to the next. You have expressed it today, a connection was formed, and tomorrow you wake up with a piece from the map. Trust, each step and act guide you on the yellow brick road.

Maybe you care about people and realize that it's time to get an education, so you can better help others. You might be passionate about painting and finally pick up a paintbrush and learn the art. Maybe your job has no room for your talents, so consider making a change. Or you are a single mother working overtime and without room for yet another project to be of service. You barely have enough to survive and need to support yourself. Just know the best offering is your presence—when you show up for your child and share your love. You are enough. And the desire to awaken and live in integrity with the dharma, the Truth, is enough too. There are many ways to live your fire today, even by seemingly small acts, such as giving a compliment to a passenger on the subway. And one day you get an invitation to speak on that stage, or you create a new business venture that makes money and brings positive change, or you meet a person in that coffee shop where you read your poetry out loud, and you two collaborate on the project of your dreams...

Follow what ignites you. Inspiration is original; it isn't the old shoe from yesterday, nor a concept or a story we have repeated in history. It cannot be forced or controlled, but arrives through a crack in our familiar view. You are on track when magic is at work, as the breath of spirit brings new life, and you are in love with what you are being and doing, you shine. What calls from your soul? Listen and act on it. Curiously engage with what is being revealed in this moment for you; follow what tastes creative, fresh and alive.

It is not so difficult to walk the yellow brick road, even if we take detours and roundabouts. You know in your heart the true flame of life.

Often it is our sacred wound, the one thing we are unable to heal, that always gets touched upon. Pay attention to it. This is an important marker; it contains your medicine to share in the world. Maybe you have experienced poverty or felt always less than others. As you tend to this suffering, a gem of your life will be revealed. Your healing journey may help others to find confidence and prosperity. (Read more about core wounds in the "Healing Wounds of Life" chapter.)

Your life's purpose is usually a mixture of who you are, what you love, your talents, your deepest wound and what gets fired up in you for a cause in the world. You, your gift is needed in a world on the edge. Bring it on and don't worry too much about the wrapping paper.

Love in Action

Inspiration to fan your fire and discover your purpose:
- What did you love to do when you were a child and what hurt you most?
- What brings you joy? Follow what ignites you. Do what you love more and more, until it fills every crevice in your house.
- Set your eyes on how your passion serves humanity and the earth at this time.
- Trust the greater flow and goodness in life to support you.
- Give one hundred percent toward fulfilling your purpose. Make a wholehearted commitment: "Yes, I am all in, even if I feel scared sometimes and doubt." Watch the magic unfold when you take this plunge. The whole universe supports you then.
- Build your life around your foundational values, such as beauty, kindness, integrity, etc. Be true to them and make a stand, even when you face rejection and adversity.
- Take time to be in silence. Listen to your inner wisdom and to the answers life offers you through people and events.
- You have all you need right now to fulfill your purpose. The power truly is in your belly and hands and your heart.
- Love, honor and share your gifts without holding back, even if they may not look perfect. Ask for help to tend to the barriers towards the fire in your soul.
- Get creative when faced with situations that look like blocks in the road.
- We need encouragement. Connect with others for support and a helping hand.

Foolproof principles to bring your gift into the world of form:
- Make sure your vision arises from your deeper knowing, from your soul and not from a mind's homespun idea or an emotional high. Your soul's calling is always in service to the highest good for all, and your talents and gifts play a big part in it. The little mind is usually only concerned for its own survival, personal gain, and short-term satisfaction.
- Commit with your whole heart to your vision and creation.
- Put the horse before the cart, not the other way round. First connect, then create.
- Let yourself feel how it would feel, if this purpose and passion of yours is already fulfilled. What do you experience?
- Ask the intelligence of life, your spark inside, to show you which steps and direction to take on a daily basis. Act on it.
- Honor your gift and do not compare it with others, or else you may throw in the towel when the going gets tough.
- Enjoy each step you are taking in the direction of manifestation. You will make mistakes and take detours. Don't judge yourself but adjust course by understanding what lesson is to be learned from this branch in the road.
- Love your business and creation. Turn selling into sharing. You will experience more joy and people will far more likely be drawn to you.
- Every day take one concrete action toward your mission. It can be simple, like playing music in an elderly home to uplift people, or it can be small, like practicing your song.

May the dire global situation move us to hold nothing back. Every day take one step toward living your star. You matter and have a greater impact than you may realize. For each star lit up makes a difference for humanity and life. Many of us stand with you and rejoice as you shine and share, unleashing love for all of us—urgently needed in these troubled times.

May we live our gift, as if it is our first and last day on this earth. To ignite the fires in benefit for all! The holy instance is now.

5. Loving You

Amore te—let me love you.

Let me kiss you awake
From your slumber.
Let me carry you
Into the soft radiance of Light
And whisper a secret,
The only one you and I
And the whole world shall know:
"You are precious as you are."

Everything else they told you,
In an insane world like this,
Was just a big fat lie
That led you,
Like so many of us,
Astray.

Let me love you all the way,
Just as you have been yearning for,
While so often others,
Feeling separate,
Have looked out for themselves, alone.
Let me tell you,
As I hold the palm of your hand,
The one truth I have found
At the core of all creation:
There is nothing but Love, here.

> May I suggest, beautiful one,
> Simply surrender
> Into THAT!

Being loved as we are feels so satisfying, sane and good, doesn't it? When you hold hands with a beloved, feeling connected and accepted you are filled with delicious warmth. Or, a friend, who just understands and doesn't try to fix you, but welcomes the embarrassing story you are sharing. Or, remember that morning, when you felt fulfilled and giddy, happy for no reason, ready to discover what wonders the day might hold? Sure, we want more of this enlivening love, much more. We want it so badly, but rarely admit our secret, ravenous hunger. You can see this thirsting for the real thing in the eyes of colleagues, a neighbor, the mailman, and looking through your own eyes in the bathroom mirror. You know the ache for unconditional love. Most folks try hard to find it somewhere, and a lot of fingers point to the moon.

Of course, each of us wants to be loved, accepted as we are, to be seen and truly heard. We know what it should look and be like. We just have to find someone to offer the elixir to us, right? In our desperate search we visit dry wells to quench our thirst, bark up the wrong trees, dig in all sorts of places for a love that finally could satisfy our craving. Maybe we will find it with the perfect partner, through fame, sex, and fortune or by improving ourselves. We try so very hard to be perfect, imagining then we'd be good enough, worthy to be accepted by the world or someone—exactly as we are.

No matter what acrobatics we have tried and all the efforts we have made to be fully loved, if we admit, it never quite worked out. We receive a touch, a glimpse, for a while—eating chocolate and rich bread, and then the person who provided so generously walks out on us. Bummer. Love happens and then it disappears again. The goods from the delivery truck aren't quite perfect, the touch has conditions attached, and we are asked to pay a hefty price for only a drop of honey.

Meanwhile, you can't get rid of the yearning—this aching on a lonely and rainy evening—to be loved as you are. Where is the fountain of honey that always flows? How do we find the oasis where we can feast to our heart's content? Sometimes we experience love so clearly and simply; at other times we feel so far away and love is just a distant word. Then loving oneself and others becomes yet another chore.

Why not let love nourish you in this moment now? By listening to music, feeling the warmth of a hand holding yours, in the breath breathing you... Remember how it felt when a friend, a partner or a parent showed you love? Or when you felt it with an angel, a saint or a stranger. Let yourself imagine this person and situation, and receive the goodness now. What do you experience? A sense of warmth, a smile maybe? Dwell in that moment of love, relish this one taste, breathe it in.

For what you desire with intensity desires you immensely.

This love is your nature and embraces the whole of you—forever and always. The well is here. Keep digging and opening to sunlight touching your beautiful face. Life holds and loves us right now, exactly as we are, even when we don't notice and have turned our backs to what we want the most.

Relating to yourself with love

This begging and bargaining with others to be loved as we are is such an exhausting game to play, but we keep trying anyway, banging our head into the same old wall over and over again. Instead interrupt the wild-goose chase by turning to the honey pot in our heart and by relating to ourselves the way we wish others would. We can give ourselves some tender loving care and be our own best friend, while noticing how we are held in a greater love, that embraces us as we are—with our upset, the resistance, the fear and exuberance—right now.

We expect other people to always behave kindly toward us, and yet in reality, how do we relate to others and ourselves? How good does it feel when we take the hammer and smash what we have created, when we criticize ourselves nonstop about all the things we did wrong? There are so many mistakes we make, that stabbing ourselves and others can keep us busy all day long. When we push and push we break down, and only end up sick in the long run. In my work I have seen more brutality in how people relate to themselves than in all wars combined! We try to be or do more, with yet another thing to improve; but contentment or peace is out of the picture then. We treat ourselves badly, as if this would help anyone. How likely is it that we will master a new language, whilst picking on ourselves for how slowly we are capturing the words? We imagine we will experience well-being and growth when we are hard, reject and beat ourselves up. It isn't fun, but a bloody business with no return other than suffering. Why not stop just for now?

It turns around for us, if we befriend ourselves. We grow and enjoy more through encouragement and by celebrating each step we take. Hey, and jump to the practice chapter for scoops of ice cream (or honey) if you are having a bad fit of self-hate and need more loving instead.

Oh, but misery-producing walls and beliefs keep ice cream and honey at bay:

When love comes, as much as we want it, most of us also reject, deny, dismiss, avoid, and defend against it. Sounds silly, but we aren't used to it, feel undeserving, barricade ourselves against it, or have a distorted view about what love is. Someone gives us a compliment; do we receive the nourishment or brush it off? When love comes it gets under our skin; when we are seen we often feel shy and want to hide away. A driver stops and waves to you to cross the street; do you notice the kindness? A friend helps us in a moment of need; do we express gratitude for the support, or take it for granted? A text shows up on your phone with a caring message; do we say, "That's nice," and forget it? Love may show up with a partner, who looks at you with sincere care; do you turn away or rejoice in this moment of connection? Just because the same person doesn't express love consistently, we say, "No thank you," we'd rather not eat the food and starve instead; complaining that we are somehow barred from the nourishment of life.

Often, it's not good enough according to our script, so we throw a gift away, because it seemed too little honey to be of value, to let in.

Yet, one drop of love truly received can satisfy—if we allow ourselves to open, to drink the elixir and eat the fruits offered by the bounty of life.

But, so often, secretly of course, we expect someone or something to fill our entire bucket to overflowing, like a beggar on the street holding out a cup with a hole in the bottom. We just can't get enough and are thirsty and hungry all the time. But, no one would admit this in a business meeting or to their new lover or the people that follow us on Facebook.

Love is here; we just have built walls against it. We may feel afraid to be let down again if we open up; for love has left us too often with the bittersweet taste of joy and pain. If we let the barriers down we feel vulnerable and can be hurt again; yes, it can be a bit scary to open and let love in. To ease the fear, we begin with one taste and one step. Would you like to try a tiny bite of ice cream or honey right now? Notice something delicious in this moment, like sunlight warming your face, feeling and reveling in this one taste of goodness.

But beliefs and stories of "I'm unlovable, not good enough, I should get more..." may stop us. We carry our favorite buckets full of beliefs, concepts that keep us out of touch with love and real life. They often begin in early childhood, passed on from generations, and we continue the legacy of misery. We hold the handle tight, as if this was our holy Bible, and the bucket of beliefs becomes our set script in life. Some think they are the most amazing person in the world, others imagine they are the dirt at the bottom, either one engages a lack of self-worth. Don't worry; most of us have this notion. "I am not worthy" is a classic belief that keeps us Western people in the suffering loop. Babies are born knowing their inherent worth and feel that they are loveable. As life moves on, the actions, comments, and attitudes of parents and other people can wear down this innate sense. We naturally expected unconditional love from our caregivers, but they may have acted toward us in conditional and unloving ways. "Why am I not unconditionally loved?" is a question that requires an answer.

We try desperately to make sense of what actually makes no sense at all. So we tell ourselves when we are little children, that it must be our own fault. Often the conclusion follows that therefore we are undeserving of love. This conviction is lodged deep down in our belly. We feel flawed. Bad. Wrong. A false sense of self or ego is created and takes the throne. We build our entire world around these mistaken beliefs; we armor ourselves and live from a sense of lack. We try to compensate, fight against it, attempt to get rid of it, act and react from it; making choices based on a lie and trying so very hard to find a way that we can finally be worthy and loved somehow.

We may join the self-improvement club to fix this. The sense of inadequacy, however, tends to stay. Improving yourself is useful, but you cannot escape the gaping hole inside by that. Just reading these sentences can make you dizzy, right? It is such an exhausting twenty-four-hour-a-day job, without any pay and no satisfying results. Meanwhile we keep aching deep inside, for we live against the truth of life. And the longing to finally be loved—just as we are—remains elusive on this hopeless road.

Those mistaken beliefs cannot be changed by the mind that created them. Emotions and sensations are connected to these, and close relationships keep pressing our buttons until they are faced. The healing and turning can happen though. Support is often needed; just as when a splinter sits deep and is infected, we need a skilled hand to help us. Once presence and love touches the boil the healing has begun. When the card house of all the false beliefs and identifications begins to tumble, it might be scary at first, yet it is truth setting life free to flow again. We rediscover that innate value is present in all beings, and nothing can add or take away from that. And our talents and essence make us unique and different in expression. For most people in the West, uncovering our worth and loving ourselves is necessary and healthy. It is a journey to let the walls crumble and allow ourselves to land home in love again. Remembering what is true leads to the fountain and new, connected way to live on this earth.

What says the truth of life?

"Like all beings, you are worthy, just as you are. Your follies and mistakes are part of being human; they cannot erase the truth at the ground of life. For, what is true can never be destroyed. You are good enough, no matter what you have achieved or how many times you've failed. You are welcomed and wanted on this earth, simply because life brought you here. You are safe and held in love's arms, even if all hell breaks loose. Like all beings you are loved, no matter what anyone ever told you, how you've been treated or what you have done. You are special, but not so exceptional as being the only one who is separate and undeserving of love. No matter how imperfect you might show up you are OK as you are in the eyes of life. The sun is shining upon everyone without exception, whether old or young, failing or succeeding, rich or poor. Love is always here, awaiting and loving you as you are right now."

May you remember these truths, despite all the made-up beliefs that insist otherwise; remember them, when you fall into the ditch or when lost, remember when you meet another who needs a hand, wandering around lost in the dark.

Loving yourself

The soul wrote a letter to us long ago: *"When you walk through this world you will forget who you are and feel lost in the desert, far from love. When the ache gets strong enough, heed it and turn, don't linger where the well is dry and mirages play—give in and let love take you home."*

We can tap into the well by becoming a good friend toward ourselves

How about taking a peek to see your beauty, your brilliance just for a second, and then a little more? How about noticing what you did well today? Linger at your honey pot, dip your fingers in and taste your own deliciousness. Don't look for perfection, but rather stir your mind toward what already is good about you. As you drop further into stillness, you experience your own luminosity. Bow to that. Yes, you have permission to fall in love with the beauty of who you are.

And how do we cultivate compassion instead of self-hate? It implies being present and embracing our experience in this moment, whether joy is welling up or agitation itches, we practice kind acceptance toward anything we experience, even the nonacceptance. To be compassionate toward our human nature, to embrace what is seemingly imperfect—warts and all—taps into the well and grows self-love. We don't have to wait, until we earn more money or brownie points for being perfect, until we have bought the house, reached enlightenment, and lost thirty pounds. Fulfillment is at your fingertips. Taste that one drop of honey, steep and linger, savor and allow it to fill you. It is a practice to love yourself for sure, and a remembering: Exactly as you are you are loved by life right now.

Self-love is often equated with egotism, or New Age indulgence. It is also mired in the confusion people feel about the message to do good unto others, to be charitable, and to give continually of oneself. While these are noble and important intentions, they can be taken out of proportion and used to downplay one's own needs and wants out of a fear of being perceived as selfish. But, sometimes loving oneself is taken to the other extreme, a "me first and you last" approach, but nothing could be further from reality than to live from such a division.

We don't have to love ourselves to be able to love others, or vice versa. Loving oneself simply means to be our own friend and to be friendly with others too. As we tap into the well of love inside, we become more selfless then, because we have no need to fill our own bottomless hole by manipulating others; or to be super independent and keep others at bay, or to hold up an image and defend against what we fear the most—abandonment and separation from love.

And we are the ones who abandon ourselves. We reject our experiences, our light, the anger, sorrow and joy. Can we offer ourselves the same care, tolerance, generosity, and kindness, as we would afford a good friend? Maybe you would talk to yourself in a kinder way, or enjoy a restful weekend, to meditate and exercise; or notice what's beautiful about you when you look in the mirror... Ask, "What do I need?" and give yourself some tender, loving care, by taking a nap or reaching out to a friend. No matter where we are on the path, or how many issues we have, we can learn to relate to ourselves in a compassionate, present and skillful way. A bath of love bubbles up from inside, as we begin to like who we are, and we get along far better with others too. Appreciating people and ourselves comes easier then.

And so, the well never runs dry, but fills us with love, producing spontaneous bursts of laughter, silliness, and outrageous happiness. And we have the juice to engage with life—and actually have fun "just being you with all your hang-ups too."

Love in Action

Scoops of ice cream and honey for everyday!

- When you are having a hard day or experience pain, offer compassion with this practice: Put one hand on your heart and one on the belly and say to yourself, *"I honor the pain. I am aware that life contains suffering. May I offer compassion and hold this pain, like it is a little child who needs my care."* If you make mistakes, this helps more than judging yourself: *"May I relate with kindness to my shortcomings and follies."* This puts you more at ease and makes you less defensive and reactive. You can apply this to others as well, especially if someone agitates you.
- Notice throughout the day how love shows up for you. Be present and let it touch you. Say this mantra, *"Thank you! More please."* Thank people who show up with kindness toward you. Thank the earth once a day for loving you enough to grow food for you. Gratitude fills up the cup!
- This is the antidote for neediness: let one drop of love in, receive in gratitude and revel in it. Ask: *"What do I really need?"* Then tend to the little one especially, who usually needs a good dose of attentiveness from you.
- Hug yourself. A lot. Smile to your body, your feelings, and your mind. A warm touch like this helps, especially when you are having a hard time or a lousy day.
- Notice what you are already doing well, see your goodness in the simplest gestures and celebrate each little success with a "Bravo." It is more fun too.

- Practice acceptance for anything you are feeling, experiencing, or doing. Accept what is arising in you, even the resistance or a hardened heart, the moment of nastiness, the anger, the recurring thought or habit. It does not mean you like it, agree, indulge, or intend to keep it.

- Good questions to ask: *How would I relate to myself as if I am spending time with my best friend? How would I talk and act, if I respect myself?* Avoid overlaying how you think other people see you; how does it help to capitulate to their idea of you? Only you can give yourself the boost of self-esteem needed.

- It is fun to appreciate yourself; write it on the mirror in the bathroom, tell it to yourself in the shower, in bed before going to sleep... that you are beautiful, that you did the best thing you could today, that you are good enough as you are... Whatever you most long to hear from others, give to yourself. Go ahead and amp it up by appreciating yourself and another at least three times every day. You might find that you are more relaxed, and instead of battle noise you will hear pearls of joy bursting forth, and will be able to relate better with everyone else too.

- Put one hand on your belly and one on your heart. Feel your hands there and say to yourself, as you would speak to a human being who is dear to you, a child, or an animal you love, *"I am here with you. I love you as you are."* Just notice and feel what happens. Do it many times, each time a little more deeply with feeling.

- Self-love isn't self-absorption. Offering generous cups of love from our well to feed others makes our well grow bigger and we are happier too.

- Say to yourself: "Thank you for being on this earth. Thank you for all the times you are kind and show up here. Thank you... (fill in your own). I cherish you." Notice what you experience.

5. Loving You

A traditional meditation practice to cultivate loving kindness:

"May I be happy and free from suffering. May I take good care of myself. May I offer kindness toward all, including myself." Speak it to yourself. In the beginning this might feel strange, but see what happens and what you experience when you apply these words as a powerful meditation for a day, a week, then some more. Sometimes it easier to access love when we remember the love we have for another person or the love they have expressed toward us. Call to mind a person you love. Notice what you experience in your heart. Wish your friend well: *"May you be happy."* Feel what happens in your heart. Then call to mind a person who has shown you love with words or an act of kindness. Feel what you experience when you remember. Then wish your benefactor, *"May you be happy and free from suffering."* Then turn toward yourself, *"May I be happy and free from suffering. May I be kind to myself."* Dwell on the feeling of warmth this practice generates.

And how to tap into love for yourself?

The easiest way is this: Call to mind a person, an animal or a place you love or appreciate. Notice how it feels right now in you. Warm? Let it expand through your body and turn that love to yourself. Sense it in your belly, your feet and drench your whole self in it. Touch the places in you that feel unwanted and unloved with breath, presence and unconditional love, without trying to change or fix it, exactly as you are right now.

The main key to your house is this: Love whatever arises and is here in you. Your feelings, whether positive or negative, your experiences and reactions, your appearance, even your nonacceptance of your wrinkles, your resistance or mistakes in life. Love this too.

And by golly, just do more of what you really love and enjoy it thoroughly. It might just be your once in a lifetime opportunity

215

to eat your favorite ice cream or dip your fingers into the honey pot. And if I could look right now into your eyes, I would only say this, "May you know that you are always loved — as you are and where you are at, no matter what is happening in your life."

True Love
Loves the whole of you.
Yes, your hang-ups and wrinkles too!
The soft radiance that shines
Through your beautiful eyes,
Your passionate kiss
And your soul's tenderness,
Your power and glory,
Dark secrets and mistakes
In this embrace
Nothing gets away!

True Love
Meets you just as you are
Here and now
In sheer grace
Beholds all of you
Never lets go
Even when you fall apart
Through the deepest wound in your heart
Surrender all the way
Into what you have been yearning for:
To be loved
Simply as you are.

Precious Friend,
There is nothing to do,

5. Loving You

True Love
Is here—
All around and
In you too.

6. A Heart Wide Open

Enter the magic door

It was such a surprise. I had been searching for this forever long and found it in a place and way least expected. Many years ago I stumbled into what wasn't written in books or what's generally taught in spirituality. Felt incredibly liberating. I laughed for hours... because it's so simple and feels true to the bone. In our deepest vulnerability there awaits hidden the priceless pearl of divinity. This fragile humanity, your broken heart is the gateway into unbounded love. Meeting unflinchingly any experience — good or bad — such leads into unshakable presence at the source. Not escaping, but turning towards what is here, touching what is aching to be tended to, compassion flowers then. For, the lotus grows from the mud and a tiny mustard seed contains the all.

Flight delayed and phone dying, I searched the walls of terminal 5D for an outlet to charge my iPhone. A friendly-looking Mexican man saw my futile attempts and waved me over. "You can take mine," he said, and then got up to offer me his seat too in the waiting area. A gentleman is a rare find these days, and I thanked him for his generosity. We began talking and soon I was taken into a story that touched my heart. He was an aide at a psychiatric hospital, a tough job indeed. He told me that he feels such joy when he enters the ward every morning at six a.m.

"What makes you so happy to deal with all this craziness and suffering?" I asked curiously. "Between you and me," he said, "it may sound weird, but it's the love I feel for the people in there. It wasn't always like that; it changed the day John got admitted. John was a little nuts... he had tried to take his life, but he wasn't mentally ill. Somehow I knew that, and I wondered how I could help this guy. Then I thought, 'What would happen, if I just showed John that someone cares about him?' So, I listened to his sad story, of how his wife had left and how his daughter died. Well, over time John trusted me. I bought a shirt and pants for him, and did other stuff to let him know that he mattered.

One day, John yelled at me, 'Why the fuck do you care about a loser like me?' I looked at him straight and spoke it as it was, 'I don't see you as a loser. What happened isn't your fault and it must have been darn tough. You were alone and no one helped. No wonder you wanted to kill yourself. So just know I care, simply as a friend.' It kinda got through to John, who broke down and sobbed for a very long time. I kept showing up for him every day, and guess what? He got better and was discharged. To this day he is grateful, 'cause that caring made him get up and live life again. And he was the guy who opened my closed heart."

This Mexican gentleman had tears in his eyes, as did I. He obviously wasn't used to crying in public spaces, and said, "I don't know why I am telling you all this."

"I am so glad you did, your beautiful story touches me," I assured him, "and thank you for what you did for John. May I include it in my book?"

He got a bit shy, but gave his *yes* to inspire others to live with an open heart in our world. That was the first time I was happy my flight was delayed.

***

Allowing our heart to open, knowing we get hurt, takes courage—especially in a world where so much hardness is, where the heart comes last and is often dismissed. But only with vulnerability is love possible.

As the petals of the lotus flower unfold in warm sunlight, a soft and tender core is revealed. Here, the jewel lies hidden, until our defenses and delusions fall away. In utter nakedness, when we are undefended, pure innocence is revealed. Here we are connected with the very breath of life and here we experience the mighty power of love, which suffuses all.

An open heart embraces tenderly and fiercely our whole world: the pain and joys, the suffering of humanity as well as your own, the magnificence of a star falling through the sky at night, and the sun rising into first morning light. It is through a wide open heart that truth shines clear and we discover love in the song of creation—in the brown eyes of a deer, in the rustling of the leaves, in the caress of a hand... And it is through heartfulness that we can love and be loved, our hunger and thirst fulfilled by drinking the nectar of life.

It's simple, but not easy to be vulnerable, allowing our hearts to open toward the whole of life, to let the quiver of a butterfly touch you and the sorrow for the loss of a dear friend pierce you all the way through.

As I look out my window at the first purple flowers emerging on the branches of an exotic tree in the courtyard, I see a hummingbird darting at lightning speed toward a branch, hovering and gently landing in its nest. I am touched by this little wonder of life, and joy tickles me.

And then I glance over to the local newspaper on my table and see the bold headline "Kids Shooting Kids at School." My heart skips a beat, my chest contracts. What's going on in our world? How have we come to this? Beneath these thoughts I feel anger, and below that a stabbing pain. I take a breath into the river of sadness and taste the salt of my tears; as I open deeper the stream turns into a sea of compassion for the suffering we create and encounter every day. A fire of renewed commitment ignites me to make a difference in the world. I feel moved into action and the chance arises unexpectedly.

***

As I entered my favorite local café, I noticed that the usually cheerful young woman behind the counter didn't look well that morning. She was pale and tense, with eyes red from weeping. I could see that she was barely holding it together. "You're hurting, hmm?" I asked. "Yeah, it's bad," she said with a shaky voice. I've met this kind of pain many times; it pierces under the skin to the bone. "Your boyfriend, I guess?"

"He left me. And my dad's in intensive care." She trembled in her pretty black blouse and white skirt. To say "I am so sorry" just isn't enough. When it hurts badly, we need a hand. So, I offered her a hug and she started sobbing into my dress, her head in my arms. Moments later she tried to pull herself together—as if tears from the heart could so easily be turned off like a bathroom faucet. I whispered in her ear, "Keep crying, it doesn't matter what anyone thinks."

Her makeup wasn't holding up; black mascara was running with her tears in a stream down her cheeks. People are so much more real when vulnerable. I took her outside to a private bench at the end of the pier, to find solace with the steady rhythm of the sea. I have sat there myself. I can't count the losses or fathom the grief I've felt there—my faithful companions on that famous wooden bench with the view of the open sea.

Once, I wanted to plant flowers there, or paint this bench turquoise or yellow, but realized soon enough, no decorations are needed when we hit bottom and become raw and bare. What is left when the heart is shattered into a thousand pieces, and no patching up will hold it together anymore? After the fury subsided and the hurt was howled out into the stormy night, I always ended up with a fine poem in my pocket and more love in my heart to share.

The young barista took the opportunity to allow her "I have to hold it together" façade to drop and feel what she felt, until nothing was left, but a relieved smile. She turned to me as we looked across the ocean and said, "You know, nothing has changed in my situation—my boyfriend is still gone and my dad is in the hospital. But I do feel so much better, not cringing and stuffed up. I can breathe again," she actually laughed now. "I sense that my dad is going to be OK, I just know. And I can deal with the loss of my friend now." I knew she was all right; the strength of her heart would carry her through the difficulties all of us face sometime in life.

***

How do we keep our hearts open amidst unspeakable horror and awe-striking wonders in this world? How do we experience grace, benevolence, amidst the waves of pain and joy, within the experiences of heaven and hell?

It takes a good dash of willingness and bravery, to soften the holding, and the way we practice control as a defense; to open unrestrained toward the wonder of a baby being born and the sorrow of being left by a partner, or grieving the death of an animal. To be receptive to a random smile on the street, the delight of the joyous play of seals in the ocean, and equally to be in touch with the suffering and the cruelty that exists, takes guts. We may ask, in a world where there is so much uncertainty, disappointment and pain,

What is the benefit of an undefended heart?

Do you want intimacy and connection? To feel alive and turn the tide in our world? As we allow our heart to soften, a sense of connection, happiness and presence is restored, and juiciness energizes our body cells. We gain access to emotional intelligence and wisdom that far surpasses the understandings of logic—essential for our own life, healthy relating and our global situation. As we let our barriers down, truth emerges and compassion fills us up. Opening our heart, daring to be vulnerable, is a pathway, leading us home to ourselves and to experience genuine connection with each other. It catapults us beyond duality, into a peace deeper than the ups and downs of the waves; right into boundless love beholding us all. Here we find the resources to face the good and the bad, the dark and the light, to rise up to make a difference in our world.

Sounds good, doesn't it? So why don't we just live fully open then? What's the problem? To make it plain: We don't want pain. We want to survive. Bottom line. We fear showing up vulnerable, because we may experience hurt, unable to control the uncertainty in life. We want the bliss, the pleasure we discover in an open heart, but we don't want pain. Never again, and so, we guard ourselves and shut down. To the degree we do is the level we experience separation from love itself.

But joy and pain just are the basic realities of life on earth

To the depth we are willing to feel and meet both is the depth we are able to be in love. If we close down to one, we shut down to the rich fabric of life. When we armor ourselves against experiencing our human vulnerability—be it gut-wrenching grief, loss, uncontrollable events, the intensity of joy and ecstasy—we close up to the world at large, to meaningful relationships, to ourselves, and love. But if we yield to feeling, stay present, soften and open through any experience, we come to discover that even in the deepest pain is a profound love; and a heart big enough to embrace the world and all of us. Daring to be vulnerable is the entry key for that. Correspondingly, suffering occurs when we avoid our power and light, and when we don't tend with kindness to what is calling out for us. Just as a child who has fallen, is hurt, or lost their way simply needs a hand when things fall apart. Often when we experience heartbreak, fear, pain or difficulty, or even a magnificent experience that goes beyond the surface and has the potential to lift us into new realms than we've ever known before, we follow the recipe that has been handed down for centuries: contract and don't feel anymore.

The mind creates the locks of our prison, with decisions such as: "Life cannot be trusted; relationships aren't safe; I am worthless; love is dangerous." We create clever strategies to protect our tender heart and hide in the fortress of a mind devoid of love. Our relationships lack intimacy and we are hunted down by fear. We build a hardened society that conforms to that, rejecting human vulnerability as being weak. As if this is the answer... yet, there is no love to share and no real happiness is found. And so we end up being out of touch with life itself and more suffering ensues. Out of our inability to meet and tend to raw pain, we live in a perpetual state of unacknowledged heartbreak.

We become afraid of life and abandon a beautiful heart that once knew love

Sounds tragic, and it is. When faces harden and eyes look empty. Even birds flutter away nervously when we walk by. The mind becomes frantic, busy making up mistaken beliefs about life, others, and ourselves in order to cope. It turns rather weird in the pursuit to keep this fragile self seemingly safe. Out of fear, fences are built, a suit of tough armor is made for protection, the window shutters are closed, so we cannot fully breathe and communicate what is true in us, and we miss the simple joy of seeing a star shining in the night.

One can paint the shell around the heart in pretty colors, looking so very pink, soft, nice and inviting. But it's only on the outside, when the heart beneath is closed and no entrance is left open anymore. Even angels get concerned and wonder how to reach us then. Seems like one is safe and fear is held at bay. Until isolation creeps in, a feeling of deadness and numbness fills the space, whilst going on the next shopping or workshop spree to take off the edge.

Maybe parties or sex will give us a sense of aliveness, a high, so we may not have to feel what's going on inside. Maybe overworking does the job? Is there a pill to cure the suffering in our soul? Or we try to transcend this mess with spiritual concepts, so we can talk our way cleverly out of what we are really experiencing deep down, when no one sees us at night. We have numerous ways to hide, run, deny, avoid, cover up and hide our shame, pain and the pot of honey inside. The longer this goes on, the greater the sense of separation grows.

Where did this train of suffering board from?

As children, we were open, innocent, and helpless. We expected the world to unconditionally love and accept us as we were. Too bad that it didn't. When the first cold slap arrived (often on the butt and as soon as we were born) we began to contract in our bodies too. The more slaps we received emotionally, physically or mentally, the more pain and fear we experienced, the deeper we disappeared inside, armoring our naked body and covering our tender heart to protect ourselves from life itself.

As teenagers or young adults, we may have fallen in love for the first time. Our innocent vulnerability emerged like a fragile blossom once again, and our reawakened passion burned like an all-consuming fire. Exuberance, vitality was bursting forth and each moment mattered as if it was our last. Do you remember it? In this magical experience we lived for a time with an open heart. Mistakenly, we may have believed our beloved to be the ultimate source of this joy, making ourselves dependent on them to provide a constant stream of pure goodness. We imagined we'd found perfect everlasting love, that we'd never know pain and loss again, and that only happiness would follow us all the days of our life. First love is sweet and can be naïve. For most the sledgehammer arrived in one way or another, crushing tender flowers that just bloomed again. When your lover rejects you. Or worse, leaves without a word and betrays you too. Or the boy you fantasized so much about only wanted sex. Or she did not understand you, even though you thought she always would. The first fight happens and something begins to hurt. It wasn't supposed to be like this we might think, but it is. And we react and pull the shutters down, yet again.

With the dissolution of our first love, some people feel devastated, like the end of life had arrived, wanting to finish it off with a jump from a cliff. Or you were the cooler sort, shrugging it off with, "She wasn't my type anyway." Friends might have comforted you, saying: "That jerk wasn't worthy of you. You deserve better than this." It may have soothed for a moment or two, but then that dagger pain returns again. You talked about it, tried to figure it out—wanting so badly to make sense of this pain, as if a mental understanding will make the grief disappear for good. But in the end it is still there, lurking around, like a monster ready to swallow you.

When you are alone in your bed and midnight has passed, you are left with another painful round of thoughts, or tears that just won't end for the soul mate, who didn't even remember your name. Others fall into a stoic silence, darkness and shame envelops them more and more, until you barely see them under the big grey coat that covers their face too. Some are the happy-go-lucky ones, who slap a good ole smile over the pain and say: "I am fine. Hey, it's a great day!" If you move in closely you taste sadness underneath the cheerful façade. Our breathing becomes shallow with all this avoidance and pretense; we walk uptight, afraid to let go into deeper waters of life.

Sure, we might not react like we did when we were younger; we only create more sophisticated defenses against unwanted feelings and experiences. When we glimpse the enormity of suffering in this world, sometimes so overwhelming, we just pull the blanket over our head; sobbing right into depression land. Some people steam with anger, beating the enemy over the head in the name of justice or religion, as if this will bring any true relief. Others pretend their trauma and suffering does not exist, disassociate into a faraway cloud, too afraid to face the depth of disconnect. We lock our gifts and daemons away and live shallow, isolated lives. What incredible knots around our heart we create as we forget the beauty, the dark and the goodness pulsating in our own being.

The very nature of the human heart is love

This jewel in the lotus flower is revealed as our hearts break open. Love gushes forth from the center of our being. But, hold back the very breath of life, shut down, and we barely survive in a flat and hardened world. Do we prefer the illusion of safety in a box too small to contain all that we are? It is a risk to open up again and step out from our prison cells, naked maybe, but untethered and liberated. If we are willing to turn toward any experience, when an earthquake hits our walls, when heartbreak arrives uninvited, and instead of putting more cement into the crack of our shaken building, we nudge toward opening, then something new emerges. What might it be? Have you ever watched a little chick breaking the shell of an egg? It had to, to be able to breathe, to live and grow.

Life pulses in everything, even in the pain and anger, and light shines through as we meet our broken heart with awareness and love. Tend to pain and to the little frightened child inside of you like a kind mother or father would do. Pain truly felt lasts for only moments, suffering a lifetime. As our walls crumble, we lose the sense of control and may fall apart. You cry until snot runs down your shirt, throw a cup, roar and sob on the floor, especially the first time around. You may tell your mate what you feel, even if it's scary to be raw and real. Allow yourself to experience fully and you will find that it isn't so bad when you yield to what is here. You are more than pain. Give a hand to that hurting child in you and feel all the way through to the other side. I promise you, you'll discover only a greater love than ever known before.

When the dam breaks, pure water flows unrestrained, quenching our deepest thirst. With clear eyes we see miracles that were always right in front of us. You experience a new intimacy with your mate you silently longed for, but never thought possible. You become naturally kinder to others and yourself. As we learn to ride the waves of pain and joy, like a surfer in the ocean, we are free to respond to this wild ride of life straight from the heart. We feel connected and discover love in all sorts of unexpected places—in the eyes of acquaintances, strangers and animals alike. Maybe you begin skipping joyfully like a child because your cup is too full to be contained. Happiness with no cause or reason has arrived, no matter what happens in life. An exquisite pearl is revealed inside a wide-open heart, and we are breathing once again freely in the rhythm of the waves of the sea.

The power of life always is victorious in the end, because it is present everywhere, in you and me. Its voice keeps rising and returning and won't be silenced, not even by death—like the sun that is shining behind the clouds, always breaking through. The nature of life, the movement of love, cannot be stopped. Just look around at how many courageous ones whose hearts have broken open, who dove into love and dared to act.

As we courageously meet beauty and horror, joy and pain, we come home, falling into love itself. Let it move and unleash you all the way—into your hands and feet, and out into the world, which so desperately needs a heart swung wide open as yours.

Love in Action

Essential Heart Practices
Heartful Awareness and Breath:
Place your hand on your heart and breathe into your heart and your chest. Notice whether your chest or your heart is contracted

or open. Let it be as it is and simply flood the area with breath. If your mind wanders bring the attention back to the heart and breath.

OK with Vulnerability:

Get familiar and intimate with all your human feelings and experiences. Don't judge or try to fix them. Rather, learn to ride each, like a surfer in the ocean. Breathe into the feeling, sense it in the body, open and soften to it; be curious and follow how it wants to flow. Allow yourself to express what you are feeling toward your friends and others. This doesn't mean you overload anyone. It can be as simple as: "Today I feel joyous," or "Right now I feel sad." Or admit, "I feel shut down and closed up." Let that be OK; just don't abandon yourself by running away from what shows up. When you find more and more ease with all your experiences, and are OK with your own vulnerability, it gives others safety and permission to be real too. Getting comfortable with discomfort grows resilience, and being authentic creates connection.

Heart Connect:

You can use this simple practice several times a day to open your heart. Remember a moment or time when you enjoyed yourself, when you felt happy or good. Allow the image to arise when you experienced this, maybe you were in nature or with a friend. Appreciate it and allow yourself to feel it now. Revel in that one taste and let it fill you throughout your whole body.

Accessing Heart Intelligence:

Let yourself relax, breathing softly into your heart, allowing all feelings to be there. Then drop your attention into the deeper space, beyond the surface waves. Ask your heart, like it is your best friend, to speak to you. Lean in and listen without any expectations, open to what wisdom might be revealed to you. Maybe what arises is an image, or words, or a felt sense. You may get clear guidance or a valuable insight for a particular situation. Maybe you feel a sense of warmth. Just abide here a little longer than usual—and honor this time with your true teacher and friend.

Walking through Heartbreak:

Don't get stuck in the stories of your mind it will repeat over and over in order to make sense of this pain in your heart. Turn instead directly toward the pain. Use your body and breath as an anchor. The anger and then the pain will move through you like waves, extremely intense at first. You will survive it; the more you stay present and lean into it and open, the easier the shell can release. Trust the flow. Ask for a hand to help you walk through this difficult experience.

Need or Neediness?

When we nudge closer under the skin with someone, our needs surface more strongly. We are usually afraid of our needs, so in reaction we squash and deny them, or act them out by demanding others to be our supplier of an endless list of wants and desires. We become needy when we don't own up to our real need. We reject the needs of others when we reject our own. The simplest way to take care of this is to acknowledge all our needs—for food, rest, being seen, respected, and so forth. Be present and attend.

I am Here With You:

Especially when you are upset, this helps. It also establishes a sense of warmth, safety and connection with others. Put one hand on your belly and the other on your heart and breathe into these areas several times. Then check in with yourself. Ask that little child inside of you, "Are you hurt, afraid or angry?" Listen to her or his voice and allow the feelings to be there. Speak to the little one, "I am here with you." You can do this with anyone; most important is that you are present with loving arms as you say those words.

Gratitude and Appreciation:

Throughout the day, focus on what you appreciate and are grateful for. It might be the food you eat, the flowers in your garden, the smile from your child... let it be simple. You can speak inwardly or out loud, "I appreciate the beauty of this lake. Thank you." Or toward another, "I appreciate your support. I am grateful." And for yourself, "I appreciate how well I did this job." Let yourself feel what you feel when you do this. Daily gratitude and appreciation opens the heart, offers joy, and fills us with warmth and love.

Be Imperfect and Play:

Give up trying for one day. Don't try to be happy, or nice, or good enough. Let yourself do things imperfectly; loosen up. Explore new things and a different way of being. Talk to a random stranger, if it feels safe, and share from your heart what spontaneously comes. Let yourself play, discover new ventures and ideas, paint or write, even if you think you can't. Without purpose, just for the sheer fun of it, like you did when you were a child. Play opens us.

Forgiveness:

We are set free, when we are willing to forgive, but this doesn't mean to condone a grievous act done by us or another person. Premature forgiving does not work; at most it is a superficial bandage, which covers an infected wound. When touched it will hurt again and again. We have to do the labor of moving through our pain, the anger, the grief, and then forgiveness emerges naturally, like nectar flowing from a flower. How do we move toward forgiveness? Read the practice in the "Healing Wounds of Life" chapter for help with this.

Speak to your Heart like a Friend:

"Thank you for your loving. Sorry for all the times I forget you. Please live freely through me. I bow to you my love." Use your own words and notice what you experience. Best speak often with your friend. That creates a good relationship.

Engaging from the Heart:

The way we engage in our world has a profound effect on our well-being and others too. A daily dose of kindness expressed grows happiness. Engage by taking practical actions to share kindness, generosity, appreciation, courage and love. Let the person in line go before you, pay for someone's meal anonymously, offer a hand or word to someone in need, give a hug, plant a tree, or speak up for justice. It can be simple, just make it a point everyday—it will turn the world around, one act at a time. Don't expect anything in return, do it for the sake of love alone. Be assured it has an impact, brings you joy and widens your heart.

Love, No Matter What
All the way through.
Meet with courage
Storms and challenges
That strengthen you.
Rise in heavenly glories
And gentle winds
That lift your soul.

Love, no matter what,
Whether you are crowned and praised
By cheering crowds
Or stoned and hanged
On this world's cross.

Love, no matter what,
Through gain and loss
In this life's play,
For Love will make you shine.
You are that blazing light
In which no shadow can exist,
And Truth just is.

Love, no matter what,
For no reason
But for the sake of Love.
Your heart is big enough!

7. Healing Wounds of Life

In the deep dark shines the brightest light

> We are all marked
> With wounds of this human life.
> Soften and open.
> It is not so bad
> To taste
> The blood of life.
> Even when it tears you apart
> In the deepest place of your heart
> Remember,
> Love heals
> What cannot be made whole
> By medicine
> Of any other kind.

Losses and sorrows—we all get to taste the blood in life, not one of us is exempt from suffering. How do we heal what cuts so deep that we could weep for days on end or scratch the infected boil nonstop? The physical wounds, like a broken leg, we can see and heal easier, but the emotional, mental, generational and spiritual wounding often runs deeper and is harder to recognize and heal. If we could see into the hearts of people, we would be shocked how covered, bruised and torn they are. If we look into our own minds we recognize internal formations, how certain thought clusters such as "People are unkind, the world is..." are false assumptions and defenses that block us from experiencing joy and boundless love. We may schlep in tow the ancient wound of betrayal passed on from generations before us.

Every culture has its own wounding. Many Native Americans, Africans, and Jewish people carry a legacy of oppression, abuse and injustice, as does the feminine. Collective and personal wounding must arise on this path of love to be tended to wisely. And, as energy is liberated through the deep labor of acknowledgement and transmutation, more life floods through. Then our nervous system needs to be reset to allow the larger and healthy flow.

But, until we heal our traumas we will continue to bleed into life and create more.

This takes the form of addiction, overworking, relational dysfunction and collective racism, genocide and wars. We cannot bypass traumas, wounding and blockages with our mind, imagination, or pretty spiritual concepts. If we do, our house will be haunted and deserted, and we will be unable to embody love in a real way. And if we practice denial, Pandora's box will open one day by surprise, for the psyche always wants to return to wholeness, and love brings even the last one home. If we do not address our hurts and internal knots they affect our entire life and the lives of others too—be assured—what you reject and try to leave behind will play out and be projected on someone or something, in one way or another. Life is the master teacher and will always bring the issues that we have left out in shadow land into the play of our relationships and in this world.

You may find yourself in the same abusive relationship pattern again, only with another person, the not-good-enough story repeating at work, and wherever you go this ache follows along. Or, you pretend to be awake, have it together, yet feel inside miserable, caught in a cycle of fear and shame... Depression has taken hold of a quarter of the American population, but a pill just won't resolve it, and we live half dead in exchange for that. We cover traumas with addictions and self-medicate, but it destroys our lives. And the cycle of racial injustice, mass murder and rape continues on from one generation to the next in the Congo, in America and all over the world.

Unresolved trauma, stemming often from early childhood abuse and our collective field, deeply affects us, our ancestors and children, and it can either diminish lives or turn into a tremendous gift for the world and ourselves—if these are acknowledged and tended to with utmost care. Shining examples give inspiration: the woman who healed her rape and became an advocate for girls; the former cocaine addict who hit rock bottom, turned his life around and now goes into the streets to save lives. We see it in people who had harrowing experiences, but who turned tears into blessing rain.

Whatever you are facing, remember this: **Love brings all home and heals what cannot be made whole by ourselves alone.** The deepest knot of separation cannot be undone by the psyche, which created it. We need sheer grace and usually a human hand to pierce through the veil to lift us home.

***

Most of my life, I walked around with a sense of feeling unloved and unworthy, a common wound festering in us Western people. Even though I started therapy at eighteen years old, doing tons of transformational growth work; was on a spiritual path; practicing meditation daily, this agonizing emotional pain was still there ten years later. And this wound played out in my world through repeated betrayal, by feeling I had no right to exist, and other such miseries relentlessly following in tow. I kept chasing a carrot on a stick, just out of reach. Do you know this one? Sometimes I got a drop of validation from one person and then this craving was back again and I would need more. I was like an addict trying to fill an empty hole.

I felt insecure and separate, and covered it in a mantle of shame. I was hopelessly hurting every day. Regardless of how much I had labored, nothing had healed this bloody wound at the core. My imprint and trauma was from day one when

I landed on this planet and it was embedded in my feminine lineage. No healing or spiritual approach did the job. Oh, I wanted it to change, desperately, for this suffering affected my life profoundly, preventing me from fulfilling what I was capable of offering the world. The view, "It's just your ego, an old story and false beliefs," did not do a thing, rather it made it worse by adding shame. No method worked, I had tried plenty. Some things were helpful on certain levels, but they never went to the core. The endless amount of working on myself did not help either with this issue, as it drove me further into a loop of despair.

Then I learned to stay present and feel it all the way, accepted the wound and lived with it; still it showed up every single day, only a little less severe. I took it as my sacred wound, the one that would take me all the way home into the truth of love. And indeed it did, in so many ways. This ache pushed me to dig deep, to find compassion, insight and connection. It enabled me to help people even in their darkest places, for I wasn't afraid of pain anymore. I knew the way through hell and was guiding lost souls from the dungeons to revive their life. I could rise to sublime heights and commune with angels, trees and hearts, enter nirvana in an instant; it wasn't difficult, I knew my way home. Sure, love kept living through me more and more and I rooted in presence, even when the world shook around me. But it didn't do a thing for the most vulnerable, the little child inside, who was seriously stuck in agonizing separation from love.

The day arrived, when my faith had crumbled to dust. I turned away from the spiritual and healing world. I was fed up. I walked in a desert, even more painful when you know where the oasis is and you refuse to go home to be filled. I had reached the end of many roads taken and was lost. Embarrassing really, after all these years to end up here. Something seriously was missing. So I went back on my knees and prayed, yet once again,

"Help! Show me a way." And even though I had surrendered many a time, this time I was so humbled, beyond exhausted, that I just gave in. In that moment of letting down, releasing the grip, I fell into immense luminous darkness, the deep feminine and the vast arms of the mother I never had. I felt held. Gentle warmth filled and surrounded me, where previously my defenses had held love at bay. Where did this come from? I was embraced in my brokenness by love in a most intimate and visceral way, like I had never felt before.

I realized I am the home, the love I had been looking for all my life. It got me in the core and I sobbed in relief from the bottom of my heart.

On the same day a person came my way and she received me; she dared to feel the pain. She did not shy away, nor try to change or fix the hurt nor compared it to some story of hers. Instead, she reached out with her human hands, and held me without words in a way that I had longed for all my life. My friend offered the missing relational piece: unconditional love by caring from one human to another. I could relax, open and felt met as I was. It was a precious moment of pure love touching the deepest wound and this is what got through, finally.

What happened on this remarkable day in answer to my prayer turned the wheel in my life. One drop of unconditional love became a bucket and now it's a river that helps others on their way.

***

Recently, I held a sweet eleven-year-old girl in my arms and stroked her soft, brown hair, while she wailed like a river that had been waiting to unleash; as she spoke what she had held back for far too long. "I just don't understand. Why do I have to learn about wars in school? Why do I have to remember the dates even, when all this suffering in the world just doesn't make any sense? Why do we torture animals? Why do some White people think they are better than Black? Don't people understand that we are all humans? Don't people know that the earth belongs to all of us and the animals too, to share? We should have lessons in school on how to create peace and learn compassion!"

Have you asked these questions too? Well, she was in the midst of it and sobbing from the bottom of her heart. What she said though came from her innocence. An innocence, which is not naïveté, one which lives in each of us, but we forget or bury it inside. Often we disconnect from this pearl of truth, this simple, yet profound knowing in our hearts — when we feel hurt, when we feel alone and lost in a world too confusing to understand. Something closes down. And then, of course we act in ways that do not make sense. How could I tell her this?

Instead, I simply held her in my arms, letting her know that I was there with her. Being embraced and met in our pain is what we need the most when we face suffering too great to bear alone. No smart advice, explanations or concepts are needed then.

After the tears had subsided, I looked into her big blue eyes and said, "I get how much it hurts. It is nonsense what we humans sometimes do, when our hearts are shut down, when we forget what is true and what really matters in life. It's infuriating, because you care, hmm?"

"Yes!" she blurted out without hesitation.

"How about we share with your teachers some of your brilliant ideas? I think they are stuck and need a helping hand." She perked up, laughed, and was inspired to bring forth change. Just like that. She simply needed to be heard, seen, met and embraced in her experience. And then she could move from tears to love and act.

***

No elaborate method, no fancy fanfare, just meeting where and how a person is, right there, with utter presence and loving arms, this does the job and is the cure for the deepest wounds in our heart.

Often we feel terribly alone in our hurt. Something painful happened and we are left, stranded somewhere out there in the cold. Being alone when hit by an arrow makes it worse. If we have someone who is present and compassionate, the pain doesn't feel as bad and you find your way through easier. Our human wounds stem from relationships and to heal them we not only need presence, love and skill, but a real person to offer us this missing experience. This is why it is essential to befriend our own human wounds, because only then can we be truly there for another, ourselves and in this shaken world.

Because one way or another, we all experience suffering. There are no "three" keys to end it in one shot. But, there is a way to relate with what is here in us and in the world. We can turn toward each other, toward the pain, the anger... to feel fully, be present, and allow ourselves to open and soften at the edge. The only way is to walk through the stages of grief, our wounds and losses in life...

On this path of love we practice being here with ourselves and with each other, even when it hurts like hell. Then a wound becomes the gateway home to our soul, to compassion and wise action in the world. For light shines forth through the cracks of our hearts and offers what was lost. If we follow curiously this pulse of aliveness, tend to the ache slowly, this natural intelligence, a way emerges from the dark, leading us into genuine love and certainly a deeper connection with all life.

And it's in our deepest wounds that we uncover love.

I underwent trauma therapy for many years and later trained in it, because I found it extremely helpful for myself and other people I guide. Spiritual practice and awakening is one part, the other is healing our human psyche in relationship to be able to engage in healthy ways in our world. All elements are needed, just like we need the water, air, earth and fire to live. Only then do we live as whole human beings, embodying love for real.

And remember, whilst we feel so often utterly alone in our hurt and suffering, a song is singing through all creation and hearts that truly love:

No matter what you are going through, I am with you.

Love in Action

Essential Pointers for Healing

Everyone is trying to resolve some wound or other. We may not have been treated in a loving way and therefore live with the sense that, "I am unworthy and people are unloving." Then we project this belief onto life and our relationships. We find evidence for it everywhere we look. The partner who doesn't show up on time is the one who proves to us yet again that we don't matter and are unloved. We try hard to feel worthy by collecting more accolades and fame, but it doesn't work, and only perpetuates needless suffering again and again. We may try to replace one of these false beliefs like "I am not good enough" with the opposite. But, exchanging one belief with another is like rearranging the furniture in your house and not addressing the moldy foundation. Working with affirmations can be helpful for the mind, but it also creates an internal war. When the emotional and somatic imprint is bypassed, healing does not occur. Those beliefs formed from an early wound need to be met on a deeper, relational level. To stop this dance of ongoing suffering, we withdraw our consent to replay the old tape and instead face, feel and embrace the ache all the way. Then beliefs will fall away and truth shines clear again.

Spiritual practice cultivates a solid connection to the most essential resource, which is awareness and lovingness. It allows us to experience that we are held in a benevolent universe and that truth and compassion live within us. We identify less with our experiences and beliefs and our practice grows the capacity to access joy, strength and nourishment, and to offer the healing medicine of unconditional love toward the wounds in this life. This causes a transmutation whereby blood is turned to wine.

Healing and transformation don't mean that we won't experience any difficulty, loss, pain or discomfort in life anymore. Rather they enable us to become resilient, not turn away, but meet what is arising courageously, and to be less reactive and defensive in life. By turning toward our wounds we gain compassion, and what we transmute heals our family lineage and future generations too. Refraining from blaming and taking full responsibility for our triggers allow us to heal and to respond wisely and freely from love to any situation that occurs. They enable us to live more and more unencumbered from our nature, rather than from the repetitive script of our hurts, or from revenge, bitterness and fear.

For this journey it is important to get to know your psyche well, which includes your mind, emotions and your body. This will help you to recognize when a wound is activated and you can tend to it easier. It helps to remember that we are not our wounds or brokenness, for who we are is far larger than that. So then we can afford to be kind toward what hurts and what calls for loving presence, which in turn grows our life and helps us to embody who we are in the world.

What to do if your Wounds arise:
Wounds are not the enemy, how we tend to them is what matters most. The medicine for our human wounds is presence, relational connection, skillful means and love.

When you are triggered the survival emergency system kicks in. The brain and the nervous system are on alarm. Then we usually freeze, fight, fawn or flee. Those mechanisms are useful to survive a shock or to run when the house is burning. Yet, we live often in a perpetual state of survival, especially in relation to our traumas. How do you turn off the alarm button when your wound is touched? Focus on basics. Notice what is physically safe in the space or room you are in. Stroke your body, this settles the nervous system. Stamp your feet, lie on the ground and sense what holds you. Use the SOS breath. First when your body is settled will the alarm bells stop ringing and you can turn to the wound.

Choose a safe environment; when we ache we need emotional security, comfort and support. Acknowledge and honor the story of what happened. For instance, *"She left me when I was most vulnerable. Everyone does that, so I won't open up again."* And consider that it might not be the whole picture, or only one side of the coin. Question what you are thinking: *"Do I know for sure what I am perceiving is true?"* Then take responsibility for what is stirred up in you: What are you experiencing? What are you feeling below the story? Maybe an ache, then acknowledge the hurt: *"Yes, pain is here and it is welcomed too."* Maybe it's a sense of abandonment, fear, or grief... turn toward it and face what is showing up for you. Do not analyze what arises. You may experience resistance. Then accept that: *"I acknowledge that I don't want to accept this pain..."* Allowing, accepting what is arising is the key. Be present, flood the sensation with breath, feel what you are feeling all the way. Know other people experience this too. Then offer this pain what it needs, for example embrace the one in you who feels worthless: *"I am here with you and I treasure you. Even in you feeling unworthy, you are worthy in my eyes."*

A kind person, therapist or friend can be of support in times of deepest grief or despair. People don't commit suicide because they have too much pain, but because they are alone in their suffering.

When your mind keeps going over and over a particular event, such as a betrayal, or you become judgmental—this points to unfelt feelings. If you move directly toward the fire of anger, the shaking and trembling of fear and the stabbing, throbbing pain in the body and offer breath and kind attentiveness, the mind will stop rehashing and judging, and the healing has begun.

Liberation—A deeper Way:
If you have engaged in healing for a while, know how to do titration well, and feel rooted in presence this might be for you. Or, jump to the other helpful ways below.

Years ago I kept bumping into the same old despair, no fixing, belief changing, healing, nothing worked to shift it at the root. Suppression or acting out wasn't the way. But, what to do instead? I often get question from others I guide. We all have a "thing" that repeats, shows up in the most inconvenient time, stares you in the face in the middle of the night. There it is. Not again. No amount of sitting with "transformed" it. Just letting it be isn't the answer either, at most it brings temporary relief. I stopped.

There in the gap between the in- and out-breath, I was shown a way. I followed the pulsing life thread right into the hot mess. Oh yes it was a wild, uncomfortable and not so easy ride. Watching the mind to go through all the acrobatics trying to escape to fully experience this wretchedness. To stay present in the body, curious, intimate, to dive into the movement of its sheer aliveness. And to fall in love, naturally, even with that. What emerged from the knot as it slowly unraveled was stunning—pure ecstasy was revealed.

If we dare to go all the way, directly experiencing, breathing, touching with presence and love, something unfurls, opens. Power arises from the anger. Love is found in the heartbreak, rapture in despair. Liberating life force is held within the contraction. And simple truth emerges at the end of the rope.

A compassionate Way, when you experience Pain:
Put one hand on your heart and one hand on your belly—this relaxes the nervous system. Then offer yourself the following words: *"I acknowledge that I am suffering in this moment."* This supports you not to fight, avoid or drown in the hurt, but rather accept what is here in this moment. Speak to yourself this basic truth of living on planet earth: *"Suffering is part of life. Others just like me are suffering from this."* You acknowledge that others are suffering as well from rejection, loss, etc. It awakens your heart by including others, you feel less alone and more connected, and open to a broader space. The next sentence is: *"May I offer kindness and compassion toward this hurt."* Notice, where you are holding the feeling in your body. Flood the sensation with your breath, breathe into the contraction directly without trying to change it. Notice what happens, follow the little bit of opening. Let yourself soften and offer compassion, just as a kind friend would do for you. Then send compassion to everyone else who is suffering with this wound. Do this for several rounds and notice what happens in you.

The Little one in us:
"I don't want to make myself small," I often hear from people. And yet, we shrink at times. Suddenly your mind goes blank, your shoes and coat feel too big. Weird, right? We experience it sometimes, get afraid, shy, and lose our seat and power. Or so it seems.

And then comes the internal fight, not to be small, instead to open your mouth and say what you really want to speak, to get out from crouching under the bed. Who wins? You only end up in a knot with that.

It just doesn't work trying to overcome or forcing to be bigger when you feel little.

It's easier to acknowledge: "Ah, here is the little kid in me showing up." That one may be very young, like three or seven or twelve years old. He, she cannot be bigger, doesn't even have to. Maybe it wants to hide behind a skirt, or stick out the tongue toward someone not so nice.

So when you find yourself shrinking five sizes or more, remember, the little one simply needs a hand from the bigger one in you. A sense: "I am here for you. I got you, sweetheart."

Not to fix or change what your kid is experiencing, but to meet this abandoned child, who is calling for a hand to hold whilst walking through the big and busy streets in this world.

Your royal Worth:
Often we feel disconnected from our royal nature. It feels vulnerable to admit and to face directly the sense of worthlessness. Most people experience this ache but rarely do they speak it out loud. We pretend with others that we don't experience this pit, the shroud of shame covers our ache. What's wrong with me that I feel this agonizing lack of worth that plays out in my life? We may go on a "fix it" rampage, yet this stinger remains. Self-improvement is OK, but it doesn't heal the pain. This deep human wound needs to be tended to with care and help. You cannot skip over it nor transcend it with some spiritual mumbo jumbo, nor with nice affirmations that promise greater self-esteem, or else you will always feel tied to the worthless chain. Our humanness feels flawed, broken maybe. We hopelessly imagine, if we change it and become perfect, we'll feel worthy, finally. Such is the relentless drive of mind... Meanwhile more misery piles up inside. Our worth is not diminished by our mistakes and handicaps, nor increased by achieving one more important thing. When you meet that raw pain of unworthiness, you discover that within it is a healthy longing to feel whole. And if we follow its pulse all the way, our innate royal nature is revealed, and our worth

is not even a question. Not a worth we gain by good and right deeds. But a worth that has been and will always be within you. Your royal nature. Always shining through the pile of conditioning and our human wounds. This diamond is already here. Linger for a while with that. What do you experience? Truth liberates...take a sip.

Simple practices if you like to drink more:

- "What would it feel like if I knew I am worthy?" Or, "How would it feel like if I walk at this moment as if I am worthy?" Use this as an open inquiry, which means to discover curiously moment to moment anew.
- Turn to the one in you who feels unworthy. Do not try to change that one, or else you make things only worse. Tend and treat that one like a loving mother, a father who sees and knows the worth in the worthless one.
- Remember when you meet others that most people grapple with the sense of unworthiness. As you become more tenderized toward that in yourself, allow compassion to flow into the world.

And if you haven't tried it, ride in the royal coach and sense how love might see you as its own.

What to do when you are triggered?
If you are triggered by someone or a situation, get curious. Refrain from reacting to the person who shot the arrow at you. We add suffering to already existing pain if we lash out or pay them back in some covert way, as tempting as it may be. It might be that nasty remark from someone that triggers fury, hurt and the feeling of worthlessness in you. Take responsibility for your trigger, use it as your pointer and opportunity: it is a call for love, attentiveness and healing. Of course you may need

to speak up to the person who shot the arrow, but do that after you have tended to the wound, as you will be less reactive then.

"May I take good care of my pain, anger..." is a very helpful attitude for your daily life to hold. Do not try to fix or change what you are experiencing or else you will be in a battle with yourself. Nor approach the hurt with a sharp knife of judgment and harshness, as it will only cause a greater rift. Don't slap an affirmation on top of it or try to fix it with some spiritual belief; it will only serve as a temporary bandage, because our wounds are lodged in the emotional and physical body. Rather, tend to any wounding with utmost care and attentiveness as a kind mother or father would do.

Speak inwardly a *Yes* to this wound, this pain, this anger. It goes against the strategies and defenses of the mind, but when you do, it will offer you relief and a way through. Let the wound express itself; pus needs to appear before the splinter can be removed. So what if it gets a bit messy, when you beat a cushion, howl, shake and let it come out? Let yourself loose, just don't dump your stuff on another person. After giving it room to move, you can then usually sense more clearly what is going on, and listen to the message this hurt, this anger has for you. Maybe it says something like this, "I am left out and have to please everyone. I stuff everything down and feel alone. I am not good enough. Nobody ever loves me..." The message is uniquely yours. Once you have heard it, be present with it, then offer acknowledgement and the healing balm.

That wounded child in us needs to be heard, validated and someone authentically being here. Again, do not try to convince the wounded one in you or another person with words like, "That isn't true, of course you are loved." This would only create more of the same, namely rejection, a feeling of not being heard and unloved. Instead approach it like this: "I get how painful this is, it is awful how nasty they treated you. I am so glad you shared this with me. I am here with you and love you as you are right now." This is a powerful way through which you help others as well. Just make sure you mean what you say.

The premise is: You want to meet the hurt one exactly where she is at and validate how she feels. Then you offer what was missing for this wounded one. For example, if someone feels like a piece of trash, then treat her as if her feelings, thoughts and her very being matter to you. Basically you give what was missing for her. It is of course far easier when you address your own wounds with the help of a therapist, skilled healer or a close friend who knows this territory, someone who can support, guide and hold you as you go through it. Like physical wounds, some wounding, depending on how deep, may take time and many rounds to heal.

But once it does, what happens is marvelous: you have more love, energy and happiness. Gems are revealed when we reclaim what has been lost in us. Fear loosens its grip and you feel freer, far more connected with yourself and all of life.

And if we have hurt someone else, it does not matter whether it was intentional or unintentional, whether they have a wound touched or not. It's always best to say, *"I am sorry. Please let me be there and understand how I have hurt you and help it to heal."* When you don't need to defend against your own wounds, image, or fear and guilt anymore, you can afford to be open and show up for another's pain. It will foster greater connection, trust and acceptance—in short—real love.

And what about forgiveness? Most do not cause harm intentionally, but act unknowingly. Some people do cause harm on purpose, like shooting another. The only way we can understand acts like these is to realize the perpetrators do not know what they are doing. On the deepest level, they have forgotten that we are interconnected, for what we do unto another is what we do unto ourselves. You don't forgive for the other person, you forgive to free yourself so you can move on with your life. Being willing to forgive doesn't mean to condone a grievous act done by us or another person.

And trying to force forgiveness does not work. We have to do the honest and sometimes difficult labor of processing our feelings, the grief, the anger, the raw pain and investigate our beliefs, first. When the tears are shed and the anger is roared, then forgiving emerges from our heart like a flower ready to bloom again. How do we move toward forgiveness? We set an intention: "I am willing to forgive," as this gives us the direction. Then we work diligently through the story of what happened, the thoughts, the experience and give room to feel all of our feelings. At some point we may say in our meditation, *"May I forgive myself. May I forgive this person."* Follow the opening and the softening, allow that to grow. Make amends, if you have harmed another. And one day you experience liberation, a heavy burden is released from your heart and the story just doesn't replay anymore.

Tending to Trauma:
Trauma means that an overwhelming painful experience occurred and you were alone without help and could not cope. In order to survive we used the fight, flight or freeze survival mechanism. We then locked the contracted energy up in our psyche and body. But when past trauma is not digested, it affects our entire life. Indications of trauma show up through varying symptoms, some which I name here are fairly common: frequent anxiety, addictions, disassociation, non-feeling, depression, uncontrollable bouts of anger, obsessive fear and thoughts, frozen or numb body, hyper-alertness and ongoing stress, repeated nightmares... The symptoms may cover up a wide range of traumatic events, such as sexual abuse, physical beating, being abandoned or emotionally neglected at a young age, etc.

If you think that trauma is at the root for you, please get help from a properly trauma trained therapist. You cannot navigate this territory alone, because you were alone when it happened way back then. If you need surgery you would go to a skilled doctor and not try to replace a hip by yourself or through a friend. Those who practice in the healing arts, please refer clients to a skilled therapist, if you suspect trauma. Modalities that are known to be effective and helpful are Hakomi Trauma Therapy, Stephen Levine's work and Trauma-based somatic experiencing.

When I work with people's traumas, I have learnt that besides a sound trauma method, it is important that I really see and feel the suffering, and at the same time behold a person's brilliance. They managed to survive, and my job is to support them to heal and thrive.

A Warning:

Spiritual or transformational practices will open you deeper. At first this will feel liberating and often blissful. As your defenses melt and energy is freed up, past traumas—yours and intergenerational—arise, in order to be integrated and healed. This healing journey cannot be overlooked or bypassed, or else a vaster split is created. Please do not endeavor to heal trauma with someone who is not skilled, as it can get worse in the wrong hands. There is a good reason why trauma therapists train extensively as this is delicate and often treacherous territory. And don't try to do it on your own as it only perpetuates the trauma cycle, nor try to bypass your human vulnerabilities. This will only backfire and you end up worse off. If you experience a strong awakening, or the Kundalini is activated in you, expect wounding to arise and seek out expert help.

The Gift:

Trauma and our wounds, if truly met and tended to, are a powerful gateway to the spirit and bestow gifts. There is tremendous wisdom and life energy in it. As we dig deep and tend to the wound, we may uncover a fragment of our soul—the innocence we believed was lost forever, the love we could not quite feel, a power and beauty that is ours to claim... Given how much trauma is stored in the psyche of each of us and repeatedly plays out in the world, what would we be able to do if healed and this power was harnessed and unleashed for love? Can you imagine?

For one drop and spark of pure love can cure a lifetime of pain and lighten up the world.

8. Turning Challenges into Victories

When your world is shaken, where to stand?

I have heard this plenty a time: "If you are on a spiritual path and awake you will float forever peacefully through this world." Nice escape and wishful thinking. You don't get a pass on life, just because you are on a spiritual road. It's about how we engage in this world and with each other. Life will throw us plenty of challenges so our capacity for living from presence, truth and love may grow. If you have signed up for the real, be prepared for the wild ride of your life. It's not a "cheesecake walk" through lofty concepts and pink clouds. More like: roll up your sleeves, get dirty, you are dunked into your humanity, this beauty, this mess right here. And your heart will break not once, not twice, but over and over again. As we stand in love, and dare to walk naked through the whole nine yards of this human experience, power is liberated and love becomes real.

The crisis and chaos in this world might just be our crucible. If we take it as such.

The wildfire was spreading faster than we could run. In the height of summer its hunger devoured everything — trees, plants and houses. Dry grass fueled rapidly growing flames and soon the fire was humongous, mushrooming like an atomic bomb, threatening all in its wake.

A loud knock. I opened the wooden door of our beautiful house with the heart-shaped window. Hurried, the police officer only said, "Mandatory evacuation, Miss. You have no more than five minutes to leave; the fire is here." Swifter than the wind I had to depart from our home, with five cats, two horses, a donkey, my daughter and all the people who were living on my land. How to gather everyone in the nick of time? And what do you take with you, when you might never see your home again? A few documents, my mala—that was it. Panic was rising and I was shaking in my boots. But this was not the time to freak-out or let fear run the show. I needed to be present to save lives. Rooting my feet firmly to the earth, breathing into my belly, anchoring in presence, I asked to be guided.

Then I was able to calmly gather our cats into the car, even though Princess, our three-legged one, scratched my arms bloody in terror. The real problem was Little Buddha though, our sweet-natured donkey, stubborn as usual, with his hooves lodged into the ground, determined to stay put where he was. No pulling on the rope moved him even an inch forward. *C'mon, Buddha, use your wisdom here!* I had no time to wrestle, but told him clearly that if he ain't coming he simply would die there. I don't know if that got through his thick head, but as if he understood me he brayed grumpily, gave in and trotted along. Meanwhile, my daughter led our horses to a larger field nearby, where trailers were parked, ready to take the animals to safe enclosures into the valley below. We had a phone list among the people who lived in the mountains and it worked; really, without community, we would have been lost. Before I kissed the ground in my final good-bye, I asked for the permaculture gardens, the temple, and our home to be protected, and gave thanks to the land for the time we had shared.

When I arrived at the airport field with a car full of frightened cats, some of the horses and animals were already loaded into trailers, most of them whinnying, bleating and plain scared. Smoke was clouding our vision, and everyone felt the urgency to flee. It looked like an apocalypse. Helicopters circled high in the sky, like tiny flies in the massive red orange globe of fire. I searched for my daughter, and saw that our white mare was tied up to a tree. But where was Magic, our brown stallion? Yemaya came to me in tears, with words tumbling out of her mouth, "Mama, Magic ran away."

Darn it. This was the last thing we needed. I gazed into the distance and saw him racing around the airport at record speed, with his gorgeous, long golden mane flying behind him. Fire trucks arrived, honking, firefighters shouted orders through the microphone. One was for me: "Get that damn horse off the runway, the helicopter needs to land. Now!" Great! Whoever had spoken this command had no idea what it meant to deal with a hot-blooded Arabian stallion, who was spooked out of his mind and bolted at every movement he saw and heard. I could never catch up to him. What to do? I had to get him—time was of the essence now—or he would shoot him. I rooted down expanded into a larger field of awareness, felt my connection with him and reached toward his being. I called him from my heart and sent a clear message across the ethers: "Magic, stop."

As if lightning struck him, he stopped in his tracks and stood completely still, gazing calmly at me from afar. Whilst I stayed in attunement with him, we walked silently toward each other, unperturbed by the noise and frantic action that surrounded us. A sense of timeless silence enveloped all who watched. When we finally met he lowered his head; I stroked his sweat-drenched neck and quietly guided him into a trailer, which usually he would not enter without a fuss. I sighed in relief when everyone was saved, heading down the mountain to the emergency shelters. The massive fire rescue team, which had arrived from all over the state, could not contain the wildfire though, it kept raging on. We prayed, meditated and asked for help. After several days they got it somewhat under control.

A week later, I drove up into the ravaged, ash-covered mountains toward our home, not knowing what I would find. I was prepared for anything, but not what I saw... I jumped for joy. The fire had literally made a circle around our land! Even the wood fence was untouched, and our castle was standing unharmed. I was in awe. That little prayer had activated grace. A greater power had been at work, saving our home and lives.

The firefighters were celebrated as heroes and the people of our community were filled with gratitude. We had experienced the best of each other by helping one another in a time of extreme need. Without everyone we could not have made it. Together we overcame an insurmountable challenge. And with raised hands we celebrated victory.

***

What to do when challenges arise and disaster strikes, or the fire is burning and you have to save lives?

We tend to react to overwhelming or shocking instances with primal survival instinct. Panicked we freeze, fight, fawn or flee. And fear increases by shallow breathing and rapid thinking as we disconnect from the body, our environment and the present moment. When we don't have enough oxygen our brain shuts down. Contracted and cut off we usually attack, jump into the defensive, tighten up and tend to make bad decisions when confronted with a difficult situation.

What to do instead when your world is turned upside down and you are frightened to the bone? Use your body and breath as an anchor; this is most effective. Stomp your feet to sense the ground below you and let your body weight drop down. (This too anchors you.) Look around your environment and focus the mind on what feels safe in the moment. This can be a tree, a picture in the room, a friend. Use the SOS breath (see the "Love in Action" section). This helps you become present. Acknowledge what you feel; it's OK. Neither stuff your feelings down nor let yourself get carried away by them. Ask in your own words for guidance, "Show me the way." Follow your senses and intuition, trust and act on them. We don't have time to sit on a meditation cushion in an emergency, but taking valuable seconds to become present and to connect, makes all the difference.

At some point we encounter those famous losses and sudden turns for the worse in life. Sounds fine on paper that challenges are part of living here on planet earth, but how do we actually travel through tumultuous and hellish times?

***

To know that my life could end today makes it quite clear what's important and what's not. And there is strength in truth, that's why my world doesn't get easily rocked. Still, it was shocking, when life took an unexpected turn and radically ripped out the floor beneath my feet. Well, more than the floorboard... Within three months I had lost the house I owned, all my money, my work and marriage, and far more than that... and I stood stranded as a single mother with nowhere to go.

I remember on the night before we had to move out, my daughter and I sat on her bed with five kittens playing in our hair, and purring cozily in our laps. I had bought us ice cream with the last money we had. My girl smiled at me, "Oh well, now we lost everything, but at least we have each other, the kitties and my wonderful bed." I grinned, "Yes, we've got each other and a whole lot of love, which is the most important thing after all. Including chocolate and kittens too. Unfortunately, honey, the bed, well uhm... I just sold that too."

At a time when I did not know what we would eat the next day, the practice which usually worked, "breathe into your belly and relax," was as far away from my mind as the earth is from the sky. Many thoughts sang in a chorus of shame. Questions like, "Why did this happen?" or "What's wrong with me? How did I create this?" "What is the meaning in this?" only made matters worse. I was resisting something I had no control over. My ex-husband had screwed up big time and left the scene. So I turned to the next best thing to find some power in this wreckage he had left behind. If I could just locate the "freak god or fate, or whatever IT was" that had allowed this to happen then I could change the course for good. You know that one?

Blame is convenient when life delivers a sledgehammer. I never found the culprit. Instead, I was burning from the inside out. The fire was ruthless and swift in my life, until only ashes were left. Like a tsunami it took everything I had built with much sweat and what I loved dearly, my home, the sanctuary and community, all the money, including my animals and more. Easy to talk about non-attachment, until you've lost what you poured your heart and labor of love into. For me, gut-wrenching grief became my daily companion, and a river of tears flowed, that could water vast desert lands. I was stripped naked, with nothing to hold onto. No strategies, beliefs or old ways worked anymore. The Titanic was sinking and no rescue boats arrived to climb into. I admit I regressed to watching fairytale movies with my daughter; at least they have happy endings.

I had no choice over what began behind my back and what had unfolded as a result of it. The only option I had was whether I would rise to the occasion or not. Whether I would resist, shut down or respond by walking through this dark period of my life with my head high in the sky and feet on the ground, to let my heart break and listen to wisdom within me, as my boat was entirely sunk and I was paddling for dear life. Why does it come in one massive wave? Everything looked bleak; my light was drowned somewhere hiding in a storage unit where an entire life was packed up in boxes. I was a forlorn human, whose life had just gone south. But I had to find a way, with no clue in sight showing me what to do. Move to Italy, sell flowers and read poetry out loud? Tempting. Instead, I kept praying: "Show me the way through."

There was no answer, but to be alone in stillness in nature, to climb to the top of the mountain and surrender with arms wide open. I uttered in deep exhaustion, "Thy will and way be fulfilled." As I stopped struggling and gave in, a surge of light, magnificent and immense, poured through my body for hours on end. It captured me whole; it's taken hold and won't let go (read more in the "Touch of Grace and Grit" chapter).

What is left when all is gone? Happiness, not of this world; and love, which never departs, even when everyone leaves town.

My fire was lit again, far more than it had ever been. Miracles happened, and life did turn around after I had kissed the dirt plenty of times. I could tell you stories all night long, if you had such a patient ear. During the years of this marathon ride of hardship, I was severely stripped and tested. It was far from easy, but I plunged into a power and depth I did not know I had, and found freedom right smack in the challenge. Liberation not from something, but being free in the midst of it all. Care arrived from kind people, and truth guided me on the narrow path—straight through hell into what can never be taken, destroyed or die.

***

Life is impermanent; this is a basic truth. One day we may own a beautiful home and luxuries of every kind, and the next, due to some unforeseen event, we lose it. We try to find security in our outer circumstances: the job, the house or relationship. But, the reality is nothing will stay the same; change is a constant of this dance on the material plane. We do not know what life will throw into our path, how the world will look when we wake up tomorrow, nor what we are made of, when we encounter a trial by fire.

There is a myth going around, if only we are perfect, enlightened enough, better, smarter, had it figured out, or could find the ultimate answer—all our difficulties would pack up and leave for good and we'd never run into a problem again. If only we could find that magic wand to wave our troubles away, preferably in one fell swoop of course.

259

Some people make a fortune off selling the latest package for salvation; others offer color-treated water as the miracle cure for being human in this world. We live in a society which has a hard time with challenges. Some proclaim that the more spiritual we are, the less trials and the more glories we will have. This is not true. Storms occur in everyone's life: earthquakes happen where I live, economies collapse in many places of the world, poverty exists, conflicts arise between people, and fear visits every person.

Great souls often encountered tremendous obstacles on their path. How they walked through them is what made them outstanding. A girl in Afghanistan with a horrific background of abuse rallied girls to make a stand to receive education, whilst facing adversity on all fronts she never gave up. Gandhi probably had more than one challenge on a daily basis. Ammachi was abused as a child. Christ was nailed on the cross. Mary Magdalene was named a pertinent sinner and whore, cast out and degraded for centuries. Martin Luther King, Jr. dealt with threats all the time. And women across the world, who paved the road to freedom for us, encountered harsh resistance from a male-dominated paradigm. Their greatness emerged because they did not give up, but did rise by walking through challenges victoriously. Their lives serve as an inspiration, alive today, even if they may have already departed long ago.

Rising to the occasion: Turning challenges into opportunities

So, trials are part of living in this world. Whether we grow the capacities to rise to the occasion or not is the primary question. We may meet obstacles like a king or queen, a spiritual warrior, who engages with a courageous heart and a creative mind infused by the power of spirit, through which we can turn even the worst situation into a victory. Challenges are the sand grains in the oyster shell that create the pearl. Our difficulties turn into opportunities, if we meet them as such.

Our problems, whether personal or on a global scale, if worked with, can bring forth a triumph for compassion, brilliance and strength... a new invention or creation. When applied in tough situations our capacity for love grows. If we are busy running from difficulties, however, fear soon drives our life. Sure, it is not easy to see the light at the end of the tunnel, to recognize the opportunity in the awfulness we may experience. It takes gumption to stay present, when the mind and society tell us to hide or run, but we are far more empowered when we face what is showing up—even if it means to feel it all and walk wide awake through a nightmare that seems to have no end.

It's empowering to seize the opportunity, to relate directly to the hardships on the road. To drop below the story and to lean into the direct experience, to feel what's there, to breathe, to touch it with presence and love. Something unravels, opens. We may discover a valuable learning, a gift, a need for healing, a softening, or a quality emerges in us we did not know we had. Often when we have no way out, pressed against a wall, an awakening dawns. Life uses anything to show the way. If we turn toward the difficulties they turn into stepping-stones on the path and boulders crumble to dust, as we touch them from a deeper power inside of us. From challenge we move toward opportunity and victory may await. Instead of asking, "Why did this happen to me? What's wrong with me?" let's turn to wisdom with an open question.

What is life calling forth in you to meet the challenge?

Maybe a conflict pushes you to cultivate understanding. Maybe a challenge urges us to make a stand for an important value we may have disregarded before; or a repetitive situation asks to take a wiser turn in life. Or quarreling over the same issue with your mate presents a call to hear what's really being said. If we deny the issue of racism playing out in our school, life will push us to grow courage and speak up.

Many of the difficulties lie within ourselves, like fear which creeps up in all sorts of places, sneaking up on you with bad timing, just when you want to fall asleep or have an important meeting in the morning. Or, after a spiritual awakening, the shadow dances more intensely than ever before, like a demon, jumping on you, when you just experienced something wonderful. Or you can't shake off the old rage that boils in your belly, even if you hold yourself together and talk about peace; you want to punch somebody out. So you snip and bark at others frequently. You believe in forgiveness, yet guilt and regret keep visiting; a story repeats like an old tape in your head. Even if you do not want it, there is an ongoing judgment commentary in your mind, about yourself, others, and life itself. We have old habits that follow us around, even if we have had awakening experiences, read every self-help book there is; as soon as you look away, it comes back up from below. And there is a good reason for it!

Conflicts with family members are a common dilemma. After you have done all this work in therapy, sat peacefully on your meditation cushion or enjoyed a beautiful day, once you visit your folks, all that peace flies out the window. Suddenly you behave like a five-year-old kid, reacting to every word spoken, stuck in the same dynamics as before. Relationships with our spouses revolve around the same painful issue for years — nothing ever changes — if only the other would. We get triggered and play our favorite patterns from long ago.

It is here that healing, integration and growth are needed, for the shadows will arise over and over again, asking to be seen and transmuted into gold. The pain we experience as a constant companion, the suffering we see at every street corner staring at us through the eyes of strangers, the anguish of a disconnected society, all can be met and tended to with presence and love. Our heart IS big enough. (For the "how" read the chapter, "Healing Wounds of Life.")

What is it that you are avoiding or are running from? A discomfort, a conflict, an unpleasant situation? Whatever it is, take a moment and consider what opportunity is presented within this. And then, when you are in the thick of it, standing on the shore of suffering and looking for a bridge across turbulent waters to the other side, there is another important question to ask.

How do I relate to challenges?

This is where our power lies, where love comes in; and this is where it gets really interesting. Usually we tend to react to bad news and don't relate to what shows up uninvited at our door. We generally get overwhelmed, withdraw, or attack. Or we use the ostrich method, putting our heads in the sand in hopes this monster will just disappear for good! How has it worked out thus far?

Instead, turn to face what is here. Resist and struggle with life as it is and you will be defeated by forces far beyond yours. A challenge isn't our enemy. Yes, it is uncomfortable and tough when plans go awry or if life takes a turn for the worse. But by directly relating to what arises in us when we encounter a difficulty we are liberated and empowered. To befriend our fear, the loss of control, and the not knowing what to do, all this gets to be here to be tended to with our breath and attentive kindness. When we practice engaging from nonresistance and curious honesty we can see more clearly which path and approach to take. We become able to engage creatively, discovering solutions that we were not able to realize before as we access intelligent presence.

Don't let a trial occupy the throne of your house and take you down. You are more than any difficulty, far more. Give the issue a seat at your table, but be aware of what else is there too. Your breath, this silent vast presence within. You may be healthy, have a friend or have clean water to drink. You will find strength in appreciating that. Especially in hard times, draw upon resources; take in nourishment every day by turning your focus toward what is beneficial in life. Even if we only notice that we have bread to eat and air to breathe, this is enough. Appreciate that, as it grows sustenance for you. Sleep, eat well, and ask for help. If you let a tragedy take over entirely, turning you into a nervous wreck, nothing is helped by that.

Love holds you, even if you shake like a leaf. Sense the ground beneath your feet. You've got what it takes to move through this. And even if you don't, others do and the earth does too.

In the eye of the hurricane we find stillness, and the further away from the center, the more we are caught in the ever rapidly spinning whirl of samsara and insanity. Prayer and meditation come in handy in times of turbulence. It can be a saving grace and anchor, when the waves rise high. Turn toward this refuge every day, rest and fill up, no matter what is going on. Feel what is holding you—the earth, the chair, your heart or a friend. This allows the nervous system to reset from survival adrenaline to a sense of safety. You can pray, "Help me to feel held." Or, "Greater power, wisdom and love... show me what is needed here." Lean in to listen and feel the still point in the midst of the storm. From here you can relate to any difficulty in a freer, calm and brilliant way.

It sounds cliché, but this too shall pass. After the winter storms have ravaged the lands bare, spring grows new life again.

As we walk through challenges we grow in love and rise like the phoenix from the ashes once again.

What's wise and the most beneficial action?

Actions taken from disconnection lead to misery. If you make your connection with source priority actions lead to brilliancy.

Moving from inner connection into outer action is always the best approach. When we have a difficult quandary, it's best at first to step back to gain a larger perspective to find the way through. You cannot resolve a problem from the level it was created, as Einstein once said. Wisdom is available when we drop below the surface, turn inward and let ourselves be guided. (For more on this see "Follow the Red Thread" chapter.)

Acknowledge the thoughts and emotions, but do not let them determine your actions. In the midst of emotional turmoil and with a mind speeding at two hundred miles-per-hour we might crash into another car on the road. We do not make good decisions when stressed. When contracted in our bodies, confused in our minds and muddled up in our emotions, we do not recognize the open door, and it seems as if we have no access to peace either anymore. We feel disconnected with no new insight available. Fresh air is missing, when all the doors and windows are shut. We do not see our way in darkness and turmoil, better to turn on the flashlight of awareness. Stop engaging further, let the situation just be for a moment, as you take space to breathe and center in your body.

Notice what you are experiencing, and give it space. Sense how you are held by the ground. Slow down, notice the space in your environment and in-between the thoughts. Or feel your appreciation for a friend or an animal... notice what you experience then, as you are slowing down, and let a drop of love fill you. Something opens when you touch the earth, listen to the waves of the sea, and the love beating in your heart. Breathe into your body; focus on aliveness. Follow the stream of life, even in the most entangled situation. It knows the way through—even in the darkest hells and most complicated situations.

Enter the unknown, here you'll find a way. In stillness, wisdom emerges, if we ask sincerely. Listen, it will show you what next step is most beneficial. When you receive an inkling, a sense, a clear image, words of knowing that come from a deeper place than delusion, act on it. The more you do this, the stronger the wisdom muscle becomes, leading often to unexpected and sometimes outstanding results. Miracles happen when we invite grace into our impossible situation. An unexpected healing occurs; a hand is offered in the gravest moment of your life; a danger is averted because you were present.

Love has the uncanny ability to bring us to our edge, and if we take the leap, more fulfillment is at our feet.

Sometimes we experience situations where we have no power to do anything other than respond from presence to the challenge. There are people like Nelson Mandela, who were unjustifiably imprisoned for many years. Did he turn bitter and grow hate? No, he came out one day wiser and more compassionate than before. He was imprisoned, but did not imprison himself. Instead he used his time of isolation to liberate himself. This could not have been an easy feat. But his victory was obvious when he stepped out of the cell toward his people.

The woman who was brutally beaten by her husband, and still carries the visible scars, gained victory by leaving him and healing the wounds. Later she established a women's center to help other women to break away from the cycle of violence. Viktor Frankl, a man who survived a Nazi concentration camp, did not go insane or kill himself after he got out from the greatest torture camp of our times, but rather grew to know the power of love, and has become an inspiration for many people around the world. This is what can happen when we turn tribulations into victories on our journey in life. Our power lies in choosing what we make of our difficulties and how we respond. Some of our greatest challenges, when fully walked through, change us for the better and turn into our greatest contributions for the world.

And how do we find courage to take a stand for love and speak truth to power, when it's challenging like hell?

Most of us run from conflict and confrontation. Some play nice and avoid, hide out in denial, others like to judge and attack. We tend to hold back our true voice, because we fear rejection. This will happen at times, no question. How to find the nerve and grit to take a stand for love anyway? How do we grow courage to face down the BS, whether it's in the form of abuse, violence, misuse of power, false prophets and perpetuated suffering? Standing up is challenging, but it's what's needed in a time such as this. Fierceness and kindness are our best allies here.

***

I was at a women's conference to speak to a large audience and facilitate groups. The founding spiritual leader was a popular, influential woman, who was idolized by her tribe. I watched quietly as she sucked the new, unsuspecting participants into her web, reeling them in through high-level manipulation games. Soon enough, capable and strong women gave their power and money away, worshipped her, believed every word this black-haired, stunning-looking woman spoke, even if it was crap with pink plastic wrapping around it. Odd, everyone clapped when she was finished speaking.

At first, it was amusing, but then I saw how she called out people and told them about their issues in front of the entire audience, without asking their permission—she nailed them to the ground. The women were too ashamed to show their hurt, some cried alone in the bathroom instead. And this teacher's ego grew bigger by the minute. It was plain to see, she fed off others' energy and unconsciously the women turned into little pleasing girls in order to be on her good side, and really, to be safe. I had to open my mouth and make a stand, even if she would hate my guts. My mind tried to convince me to walk sideways. "Don't bother, it's no use, you only will get hurt." The oppressive voice of our women's heritage is always close by. But, despite the fears, I took a breath and walked right in my high-heel black boots into the lioness' den.

First, I tried to talk with her in private about the way she hurt people, but she brushed me off. She was agitated, I already had infringed upon her territory, as I worked differently with people and did not agree with some of her teachings. She could not allow that, so she called me up to the stage and tried to do to me what she had done to others too. I looked into her eyes and thought, *Oh no, lady, not with me.* Yes, she targeted and intimidated with clever words meant to put me down and in my place. I wondered, *How do I stand nakedly in love and face her down? How do I speak from power and vulnerability at the same time?* Not easy. But, I did not attack, nor played small, instead I shared in a transparent way what I was experiencing, without blame.

She had not succeeded in the first round, so she pulled out the bigger bullets. I really wanted to run or hide then on that stage where all eyes were on me. But fire stirred inside, and instead I spoke unrestrained from a deeper power to her: "It's not OK to misuse power by putting the women down to raise yourself up. I am done with your show now." Some women thanked me afterward. It had woken them from their collective toxic cult trance. She did not like me after that, of course. The veil of illusion had been ripped; this is never pleasant and most are not liked for that.

***

But, what are we serving? The games of ego, our fear—or love? The answer to this question helps us gain courage amidst adversity and to make a stand from gut and heart. If we do, then a challenge turns into a victory for love!

Love in Action

Helpful hints when your world is rocked
"Show me the way through":
I used this simple prayer especially in tough times and I was always shown a way. With this prayer you get out of your usual way and invite in higher help. Then follow what is shown step-by-step. You'll be surprised how even in an impossible situation a way emerges out of nowhere.

SOS Breath:
Put your hands on your belly. Breathe in through your nose down into your belly, count four beats, hold the breath for four beats, and breathe out through the mouth four beats. Do this for at least three rounds. It will calm your nervous system, and offers you grounding.

Calling in help and connecting with others:
Please do yourself a favor and don't follow the voice of shame by isolating yourself. Reach out to friends, other people and the holy ones. Let them know what you are going through, that you need support. You may need a shoulder to cry on, to get wise counsel or practical help. Ask for what you need, and then be open to receive. Some people turn away or can't help, but there are others whose door is wide open for you. No one can save you from what you experience, but you do not need to go through it alone. It makes a difference, if we have at least one person to share and be with.

Taking care of yourself:
In times of shock or hardship we need to tend to our bodies to have the strength to make it through. Eat and sleep well, don't run yourself into the ground. This takes a bit of discipline, because times of intensity often drive us into a constant state of urgency. This is panic taking hold. Stop, breathe and slow down. You have the time to eat a proper meal. Go dancing or

into nature, engage in what is nourishing, it will give you the energy to deal with challenges constructively.

Surrendering challenges:
Handing over a seemingly impossible situation is often the best move we can make. Give over the challenge, lay it at the altar, "I offer this situation into love's power. Thank you for showing me a way that is for the highest good of all." Use your own words. It's not asking a God in the clouds to fix our life, it's a way of connecting to wisdom and allowing this to help and guide us.

What to do when fear drives you around:
If you feel afraid and anxious, notice where it is held in your body. Stay present in your body, as you allow yourself to feel. Flood that sensation with plenty of breath. Do not get lost in the endless stories fear likes to play with shaky conviction and intense ardor. Relate to your fear, as if you are meeting a child who is afraid. What does a little kid need, when all alone and scared? Someone bigger taking her hand, holding her and letting her know that she is safe. So you offer this by placing one hand on your belly and one hand on your heart. Speak to that little kid in you: "I am here for you." This will help. Make sure you move your body and do not follow the spinning thoughts around. Get back to ground zero by touching the earth, especially when a bomb drops into your life.

Speaking and standing up:
It's scary. It's liberating. It can be of benefit. Acknowledge your fear and do it anyway. Ask yourself: "What's bigger, more important that I am willing to stand for?" For some it is justice, for others it's love. Would you just walk by or open your mouth to protect a dog from being kicked sidewise? Will you be the one, who stands up when a girl is objectified and abused? Let fierce love move you to speak and stand for what needs your voice and action. Take small steps in the beginning, courage grows as you walk through what you fear the most, again and

again. After a while you get the hang of it and you'll enjoy to bravely stand for life, no matter what happens as a result.

Find more helpful ways in the Love in Action section of the "Wisdom for Crazy Times" chapter.

A meditation to deal with challenge:

Put your feet on the ground. Become aware of your breath and body, your environment, the sounds and sights. Notice how the earth below is holding you; let your weight drop down. Breathe into your belly, in through the nose and out through the mouth. (Use the SOS breath if you are in fear.) Allow yourself to drop down and widen into the space around you. Bring loving awareness, as you turn to the situation at hand. Say yes to the difficulty as it is right now. It does not mean you like it, it only means to disengage from the struggle. Curiously, get to know the challenge, the fear, and the turmoil. Survey the landscape of the issue with awareness; look around to see clearly what is there, without judging it as right or wrong. Just get to know the whole situation. Turn your attention to your internal landscape. Become aware of any feelings, thoughts, and body sensations that arise in you without labeling them as good or bad. Where do you contract? Where is energy held or stuck, less vital in your body? Just notice what you experience and drench it with breath. Allow all to be there without judging, trying to change it, fix it or getting lost in the mind trap of the stories we tell ourselves "about" it. Feel what you are feeling. Maybe you need to cry, to shake... let it move and rip. Stay present even when the ride gets intense, it will subside like a wave that rises and dissipates. Just for one second open into your experience. Allow, as if you have a guest at your table, who is looking for your help. Reach out and make friends by welcoming the challenge. This guest, if you listen closely, will tell you what the opportunity is for you. Be open to hear what you do not know. Relate from the wise woman or man to this feeling or situation. Give it attentiveness and ask inwardly for wisdom and guidance. Then hand the whole thing over: "I place this situation into Thy hands. Let the highest best happen. Thank you. " Be curious how love shows you a way through the challenge and leads you into a least expected victory.

Love knows the way through heaven and hell.

9. Walking the Talk

Integrity and a noble heart

Holy ones walk among us. Something happens when we stand in their presence. Maybe an awakening, a healing, a shift has occurred, even if we forget the words they said. It's the transmission that profoundly affects people's lives. Transmission is not channeled energy, it's what emerges when a person embodies the sacred, a love lived through the tough and glory. The Dalai Lama, even after his people had been brutally murdered, tortured and driven out of their home country of Tibet, is not filled with hatred toward the Chinese, but practices compassion and shows it in the way he behaves and acts. We sense the transmission, his embodied lived compassion. He admits, it's not an easy feat, even for him.

It's a triumph when conscience gains victory over convenience.

Integrity is not only a personal matter, as the way we live impacts everyone. When someone stands up in the face of adversity or when we live our values, come rain or shine, come praise or criticism, with integrity—no matter what, it's time to celebrate. It isn't about perfection or apathy, but it implies walking in the direction of love—in daily life and action. Our walk in this world is the fertile ground for our spiritual practice. Any circumstance serves to cultivate a noble heart. What do you value and stand for in life?

The path of true love is the steepest one. A student of mine recently said, "It's really annoying, more and more I am aware of how I cause suffering to others and myself. Before I was plain numb, checked out and selfish to bother. Now, when I am out of sync with my values, it hurts. I can't even lie anymore. Bummer." We laughed; so much for the joy of waking up.

She said the wrong thing and it hurt Jamie's feelings, which he expressed. Carla responded, "I am sorry, Jamie, please share with me and I will set it right. I cannot promise to never step on your toes, but I promise that I will do my best to show up when I do, to take responsibility and be there for you." She meant what she said and had shown it in action. She has integrity and was therefore a trustworthy companion.

If we want to walk with integrity, our behavior and actions need to come into alignment with our words and intentions. This is where the rubber meets the road. What we live in actuality are the fruits we leave behind. Realization and talk are the easy part. Plenty of people speak eloquently about high ideals and concepts. It's far harder to embody the dharma, to live our insights and revelations in the daily mundane, and the sacred in the streets of this world. Compassion may be important to us and a minute later we swear at the driver in front of us. Or we could send that driver a wink of kindness. However, there is no reason to hold ourselves to far-out standards or beat ourselves up each time we fall short, as we will, but rather take it as an ongoing invitation to keep doing our best, to practice with a compassionate attitude toward ourselves as well. It is simply about starting again and again, and walking in the direction of love with the words we speak and deeds we do.

I had just arrived in America and soon enough I too was drinking tea from the paper cups offered in the coffee shops. Out of convenience I joined the paper cup gang thereby adding to the mountain of trash and destroying the trees myself. I kept forgetting to bring my own mug. That paper cup was so convenient. Why take it? Convenience and habits are comfortable. The paper cup habit was easy enough to change though, once I counted the cost for our planet.

I hear people declare that they love the earth and then their next move is to take the plastic bag at the checkout counter, because it's easier than bringing one's own. Since it is far more empowering to decide how I want to show up in life and act with conviction, than complaining about everyone else, I made the change myself instead. Each time, when I forgot my bag, I carried the items from the store to the car by hand. It wasn't a punishment, but I wanted it to be uncomfortable enough as it would help me to make that shift. Then I remembered more frequently to bring my own bags instead. These are attainable, easy enough changes that make a difference. This is how conscience gains victory over convenience in real life action. At least in this case.

***

When I was a teenager growing up in Bavaria, previously the land of beer and meat, I wanted to find out where the chicken and pork on my plate were coming from. Some animals were raised on old-fashioned farms, grazed in open fields and treated in humane ways. But I found other farms, which produce for large consumption and profit, without regard for their well-being. I once entered a chicken farm owned by a schoolmate's family. In a large building without windows I saw two hundred and fifty hens housed in small cages with their beaks cut, bloody, unable to move. It looked like an animal concentration camp. And the dark building with the cows and pigs was like a horror show. They were tied up, with no room to move. They suffered. I threw up. This marked the end of meat for me. I became a vegetarian, for I could not support this torture anymore. It was a sacrifice, especially in a time and place when being a vegetarian was looked upon as completely weird. I had to make do with bread, potatoes and beans most days, and was told at least once a week by one of my well-meaning Bavarian fellows, that I would die soon. With delight I can say that I am alive and healthy, after being a vegetarian for decades now.

***

Similarly, when I found out about sweatshops where children are exploited by companies for the cheap production of clothing, carpets and other items, I made a choice, which was at first not easy to apply. I vowed to find out which of those used children for profit, to speak up to managers and to stop buying from them. After all, where you put your money is what you support. Instead, with my purchase I try to support shops that practice fair trade methods. Why? Not because I am a politically correct activist, but because these kids matter and so do the values in my heart. If I live against my own nature, suffering is ensured. It takes dedication to live with integrity and grow nobility, but it leaves a clear conscience, brings joy and better lives for all.

What inspires me most about people is not what they talk, but how they live their heart values—in the gutter or on top of a mountain, with money or without, in the storm or the sunshine, when attacked or praised, when loved or not.

It's easy to be truthful when people agree and like us. We have nothing to lose. What happens when another rejects you though? Will you turn on them, lash out and forget what you live for? Will you keep the voice of truth hidden when under threat? What do you do when standing for truth will have uncomfortable consequences for you? It's easy to open the heart and love when people are nice. What happens when others are cold, attack with harshness and you get hurt? Do you shut down and lash out too?

Please use these questions as an honest inquiry, rather than as a way to judge yourself as not good enough. Are you always truthful in your relationships? Probably not. And how do you betray and abandon yourself? What feels out of alignment with your conscience, with the dharma and the way of love? You know.

Ponder in which way you want to show up with more integrity. Like, what does it feel like when you keep your word, even when it's uncomfortable to follow through? Celebrate each time you do. For every noble step counts, even when the results are not apparent; you will feel it and others will, too. You sleep with ease. We only cultivate nobility by the way we live. And a noble heart inspires naturally. Being true to our values, even during challenging situations, expands our power and love. This is worth more than gold. Integrity is of benefit to the world and ourselves, whether recognized or not. And a noble person is trustworthy, and in my view, a blessing unto all.

Love in Action

"Help me to be true to my vow in this moment now."
If you like speak this prayer every day. I promise you it works. My heart gave it, I prayed it daily and was amazed what happened then.
Discover your "Truth" Values:
What matters most to you in life? This might be love, God, harmony, truth, presence and to live awake. What gets you worked up the most? This might be social injustice, environmental pollution, and torture of animals.
Commitment:
Make a commitment to your mission and values, dedicate your life to that and it will give you the forbearance, strength and integrity to follow through and live them in your day-to-day life.
Making choices:
Make one attainable choice to act on your values today. For example, if you value honesty, instead of gossiping behind someone's back you refrain instead. If love matters to you, think

about what you can do today that is an act of love. For example, call up your old dad and talk with him. Or stand up for social justice in a classroom where a student of color or someone who is perceived as different is being bullied.

Honesty:

Looking into the mirror to see what motivates our actions and to face the consequence of our deeds is a useful practice. It's best to apply a good dose of self-awareness so we do not get trapped in lying to ourselves and others. Again, remember not to degrade or judge yourself when you walk off the noble road, but simply face what you did, dust yourself off, and get back to the highway of truth.

Clearing your Conscience:

Where have you stepped out of integrity with your values? Just curiously inquire. Maybe you cheated on your mate or with a bill. Observe your defenses and justifications for your case and don't buy into it. Rather, keep inquiring. How do I feel about this? Maybe there is a stinger in your heart. Then you know your conscience is speaking to you. Let the truth emerge and clear your slate. To be in integrity, act on your conscience, 'fess up to your mate or you may consider paying the difference of the bill or tithing those monies instead.

Oh no, Sacrifice:

What a loaded word. But it does take sacrificing convenience to live with integrity. You promised you would show up to the meeting where people rely on you. But on that day you feel like staying in bed, for no reason other than it would feel good. Sure, you can stay in bed. It would entail sacrificing comfort to get dressed and enter the meeting room to be true to your commitment. If you do—you level up integrity.

Taking Action:

We talk about peace. What does it imply today, in this moment, to act on that? Maybe you are in a conflict-ridden situation.

What action can you take to bring about a resolve where each party feels heard, seen and met? Always use the moment-by-moment situation to act upon your values, be it in a particular conversation or encounter. It is far easier to make this a present moment endeavor, than so big and general that you only get overwhelmed and do nothing instead.

No perfection—simply walk in the direction:

Don't measure yourself against high ideals. You can strive for these, but you will always fall short and feel defeated when you don't reach your expectation. Instead of discouraging yourself, take the road of empowerment. Congratulate yourself when you acted with integrity, like you refrain from lying, and be honest in this conversation. You can commit to follow through on the one promise you made today. You can leave that paper cup untouched and drink from a mug today. And tomorrow?

You decide each day anew, until the road of integrity becomes your favorite highway and your walk naturally reflects your talk.

III. For Us

1. Heart of Relating

Lover and Beloved are eternally seeking to unite, until they realize that they are one in love, forever and always.

We forget that the one we are relating with is the one we are, just in a different form. Is the form lesser then the eternal? No, for divine is formless in human form. And holy is the dance of relating, the one with the one, always pointing back to the one. So we relate between human and divine, form and formless, dancing between the shores of forgetting and remembering with the eternal song: love is the only one here. It's easy to recognize this, but to live that truth in relationships, is not.

Most traditional religions prescribe to undertake the spiritual journey solo. Enlightenment alone on a mountaintop is the classic way. However, there is a rapid-fire way to awaken and to embodiment if we engage relationships as a spiritual path. Mary Magdalene and Yeshua walked the path of sacred union and lived a great love story with each other. But why were their marriage and advanced teachings cut out from the bible and masses of the Cathars murdered for living that way? Essentially, those rebels defied the patriarchal power structure, which was ruling the people already back then. An equal relationship between a man and woman didn't fit the old control script. Nor, did an empowered woman who was a teacher in her own right. But deeper than that, it undermined the religions teachings, for they united human and divine, sexuality and spirituality, masculine and feminine, showing that each is crucial for the embodiment of soul here on earth. And their mere existence together rocked the boat of the creation story and original sin. We won't go further into exploring this sad split that occurred thousands of years ago and continues on today.

But rather, let's widen our perspective and grow capacities to relate with all of life as a path of the heart, to turn the tide in our lives, relationships and this world.

***

I vividly recall the soft mornings as if they were yesterday's dawn, even now twenty-five years since my stay in Plum Village in Southern France, as we walked mindfully and slowly in silence through fields of sunflowers together with Thich Nhat Hahn, a throng of children and a handful of people. He wasn't famous then and our contact was close up, when I lived for several months in the monastery with the monks, nuns and some fellow practitioners of mindfulness. The living quarters were simple as was life.

It was an abode of peace, just stepping into the meditation or eating hall brought deep relaxation and stillness of mind. Every hour the bell rang and we would stop what we were doing or speaking, to breathe mindfully for several rounds: "Present moment," with the in-breath, and with the out-breath: "Wonderful moment." No matter how important it was what you had to say or do, the subject lost its pressure and importance, and more spaciousness, ease and peace was available and felt. This hourly mindful breathing practice significantly impacted our way of relating for the better.

Once a week a whole day was designated to tend to our relationships. Can you imagine what that would do for a country and ourselves? In the meditation hall monks and nuns shared with each other, practicing deep listening and speaking, and also resolved conflicts skillfully together. It was inspiring to experience. I saw how humans can get along together, not only on the surface, but how every interaction contributed to understanding, happiness and helped ease suffering.

***

When I lived in the Findhorn Foundation in Scotland we practiced communicating consciously with everything and everyone. We listened to the voice of plants and people; and even houses, cars and computers had their own names. We explored new avenues for relating with each other, whether individually or with eight hundred people in a room, experimenting with what worked and what did not. It isn't easy to live in community with people from around the world, ranging in age, background, spiritual and cultural orientation, with varied professions and languages. Making decisions was at times annoyingly lengthy endeavor, until we found a mutually empowering way that worked. The intention was on learning to live love, to support awakening and collaboration. This created a resonant field, where plants and humans grew to greater heights (in the early days, giant cabbages brought fame to the community) and a way of living that contributes to harmony on earth. Today, after sixty years, Findhorn serves as an inspiring model and is an educational center for people around the world.

For many people, relating is far easier with plants and animals than with our fellow humans (for magical stories, read the "Loving Wild Earth" chapter). Our psyche is complex, we carry a whole bunch of baggage around, which has created a long string of misery, spreading over centuries. No doubt, cultural and family conditioning influences our relationships. Some of our inheritance is healthy; but other old hand-me-downs of destructive relating need to be questioned and end. That requires learning the sacred art of healthy relating.

But schools do not teach the basics of that even though we need these skills desperately to survive and thrive. Of their own volition more and more people are finding new forms of communicating. This movement is birthing forth a world many are only dreaming about. I have been steeped in this dynamic quest and gladly affirm it is spreading far and wide.

Because globalization and turmoil in our world pushes us to collaborate together, so we can rise to the occasion to tackle the issues we are facing. But "together" remains a fancy idea, if we do not know how to build a bridge across divided countries, languages, views and lives. Wars start at home and in the world, because we feel separate from one another and do not know how to relate. We may have profound insight into the essential nature of our innate interconnectedness, but how we relate in daily life with the shopkeeper, the trees and our families is what turns the cycle of suffering in our world.

Remember when you felt connected with your mate or child? Or you experienced mutual understanding that didn't need words? It is satisfying and nourishing, like being at home with each other. It's relating from resonance, the "we" space, the experience beyond "other" or "me." A place where our personal differences, wants, desires and struggles are included, but where we feel connected to the deeper river of life, flowing in between and uniting us in the now.

We are the beloved One expressing itself in a myriad of forms. Always in relationship—with the water we drink and the food we eat, the wind and sea, coworkers, ourselves, the dog sitting beside you, and the touch of a hand holding yours.

How are you relating?

Is life a struggle or an adventure? Do you feel intimate when you stroke your cat or dog? Are you present or in some far off land in your mind when you talk with a friend? It happens for all of us at times. Are our relationships an economic trade— who gives what and how much? Often that's the case. Is your way of relating an attempt to change your spouse so you can feel finally loved? Do we live our relationships based on fear, ignorance and conditioning, or are we moving step-by-step toward connection? Relationships have the potential to be rich fields of love, war zones, desert lands or jungles. Often they are a dance "in-between." Let's nudge closer toward love.

Relationships of any kind provide the fuel to awaken; it's a fire of equal challenge and opportunity. If we take it as such.

Love is that fire, drawing the lover and beloved in one flame together. In the burning it brings all our issues to the forefront, it cleans house, especially through our relationships. And it wakes up the gifts you did not know you had in the dance with another. So how do we dance then in a sacred way?

What does it take then to open the door to authentically connect and communicate heart-to-heart? How do welcome human awkwardness and infinite divinity with each other? Seems like a paradox. How do we deal with conflicts and find mutual understanding and intimacy—not in the avoidance, but right smack in the midst of it?

With equal intensity we are drawn to each other and run away at the same time. Relating with humans can be scary, painful, joyous, beautiful and all shades in-between. Face-to-face with another we encounter our deepest longings, hurts, fears, beauty and strength. How do we relate with all of it?

We need a radically new foundation for relating
One that helps us to truly connect—across the divides, dysfunctions and differences in the world. As we learn the necessary skills to engage in beneficial ways our relationships grow healthy, providing a gateway into who we really are, into connection and collaboration to benefit our world together.

How then do we enter this "we" space of resonance? Even devoting a moment to being present with your child, spouse or coworker makes a shift. Ask yourself: *What matters in my conversation with you the most? That I win the argument or that we connect?* Just by shining the light of awareness you have a choice to shift the course of a conversation. Or explore what is alive between you and your friend right now and speak that. Lean into stillness, deeper than opinions. Discover what happens in your relationship when the baby screams night after night. How do you grow closer with your partner and not drift apart then?

Relationships need attention, nutrients that feed our gardens instead of poisoning the soil, and skills for relating for connection to grow. Nobody expects a beginner to safely drive a car, without first learning the "how to." Yet, we expect we should know how to relate with others or parent a child without sound reeducation. Even when people spend years on the meditation cushion, which certainly provides the necessary insight and compassion, this does not teach them how to relate with people in the streets of this world.

Because, let's be honest, none of us has the sailing of relationships perfectly down

Most of us have experienced bumps, scratches and sunken boats in our interpersonal relationships. Like the guy she betrayed. The person you barked at, because he snapped at you first. The fights late at night, the blame and the mounting misunderstandings. This sense of defeat and a yearning for things to be different in a relationship that went down the drain. Some people have become experts by notoriously drilling holes into relationship boats and wonder, why in the world are they always sinking? Some just have a knack for stirring up friction and conflict with their fellow human beings. But building a bridge across the chasm of the divide, between "the other" and "me," requires more than a "should" and good will. It takes skill to communicate with compassion and clarity.

Others know enough to sail smoothly, when the sun shines bright and the weather is balmy. You enjoy a lovely afternoon tea with a pleasant conversation together on the boat, as long as no wave disrupts the cozy nest. Many people cannot deal with the emotional ripples, conflicts or disagreements and rather stay in the bay or in the shallow waters of friendship.

And then there is the other kind of person, who gets right into the muck, whose impulse to throw a bomb of anger is easily to hand, than pausing to face the turmoil inside and responding from a healthier place. But healing harm done in relationship takes so much more energy and time, than breaking trust with swift punch into a tender heart.

There are the dramatic, passionate people who seek out the tumultuous waters in the sea, but are incapable of sailing the boat through. They get swallowed up in the rising tide or find themselves smashed against the cliffs at the end of the night. They might be the kind of leader who takes risks with their team, but who doesn't have the tools to navigate the challenges that always arise between people. Because, when a storm is raging, people often start blaming and beating up everyone else on board instead of working together as a team. And the fearful relationship sailors will escape to the cabins below and never arrive on deck to engage. They withdraw instead. And some desert the boat altogether to sail forever alone, for they don't like storms nor intimacy and have given up on human company altogether.

And yet, the invitation for sacred relating remains

To listen into the silence between the words in an argument. To sense what your heart reveals and to speak that truth regardless of how another might react. To observe your judgments, opinions and emotions toward another and not react, but pause, take a breath instead. To visit the world of a stranger with curiosity. To view each person we meet as a messenger from beyond. Or one who calls out for love, or who appears as a challenger, thereby inadvertently supporting you to harness the powers you may have locked up inside of you.

The invitation from life remains steady even in turbulent waters: to become aware of the ocean that carries your relationship, how love flows between you regardless of what happens in your encounter, to stay true to that. Notice how life itself is relating with you in this moment now. As you shift your awareness toward your relationship with life or love itself, or with the universal mother or father, what do you experience? How is your relationship with the divine? Maybe strained, distant, or a longing is aching below the surface. Often our consciousness plays out this soul relationship in our daily life and in relating with another so we may awaken and come home.

And given how many people we are at this time, it's crucial to realize: Yes, we are all together on this great ship called "our planet," our future depends on that we show up on deck and relate in ways that are of benefit. It's more fun and an entire new world opens up for us when we do.

For instance, the relationship that endured hardship and two people came out from the sea more strongly connected. Or a conflict is resolved and you depart in peace. The coworker, who becomes your friend after you shared with him heart-to-heart. As you snuggle into the arms of your beloved and express your vulnerability, you feel connected. And you get to experience daily a way of relating with life itself, that is enlivening for you and everyone you engage with.

It is possible. You are the steward of this ship and it is entirely up to you how you show up in relation to who and what is here. How we relate to someone who feels angry, sad or happy reflects how we relate to that in ourselves. And there are people like you, who are willing to engage from presence and love, thereby turning of the tide in our world. Some information and practices in this section you might already know, some might be new for you to try on in your own relationships. As always, take what works for you—and welcome on board!

Love in Action

The four key questions and discoveries:
1. Who is relating?

Who is showing up in the relationship? Who is leading your boat? Is it the child in you, the grown-up, the angry or needy part, the one who wants to win at any cost and be right...? Don't make it wrong, just notice. Are you showing up from a centered place, taking good care of all the parts in you? Are you present when you communicate with another or did your mind wander off to a faraway land when your friend shared a sad story with you? Are you available for connection, allowing yourself to be seen and inviting the other to get to know you too? The quality of the relationship is determined by who shows up and what you offer. You may not know the dish another brings to the table, but when you give your best, the possibility for shared joy, connection, more fun in working together and greater love is available. Of course—it takes two to dance and create together.

2. Who are you relating to?

This is a useful question to ask, for it helps us to get to know another person's world. It requires us to see and hear, without our own projections, assumptions, or expectation glasses we tend to wear. Reacting to one's own mirage is no fun and leads nowhere in the end, other than into a tangled up knot and becoming the narcissist you never wanted to be. Asking the question, "Who are you, what world do you live in?" and stating, "I want to get to know you," opens doors to another. Be curious to discover the world of another. Be receptive to a different world than your own and refrain from judging and comparing. Rather, open your mind to discover, "Who is the other person, what is he/she really saying, what are they experiencing that is different from me?"

When you recognize who you are relating to, you also recognize where another person is at. A three-year-old child needs a different way of communicating than an adult; an elderly person might need to be related to at a slower pace; someone in obvious pain does not need to hear a lecture, but a hand around his shoulder might be more appropriate. An abuser is easier recognized under the charming cover when you are attentive. And the mischievous smile on your friend's face may invite you to play with abandon.

3. What is here and alive between us?
This question leads you into presence with each other. Ask it as an open inquiry. Do not try to answer it with your mind, but discover fresh, each time, and know that with each person it will be different. This is the first question: What am I experiencing in this relationship in this moment? Then ask this: What are we experiencing? What is happening between us now? The more attentiveness you bring to the "we" space the more it reveals riches far beyond your comprehension. The key is to be present, even to the moment you have checked out, by admitting it. Staying close to the direct experience in the present moment and transparency is the key here.

4. What is true and important?
This is an interesting question. If you follow this inquiry curiously it leads you right back to the basic thread that connects to the heart and what is truly important at the end of the day. This question invites a fresh answer to be discovered in each meeting. It helps to stop the mind train in the tracks. Maybe you like to argue and what's seemingly important for you is to be right. But, when you ask this question to interrupt the cycle of non-relating, *"Is this true? What is really important in this moment for me in this relationship? What is the deeper truth here between us?"* then a new way opens up. It can lead your

marriage into deeper waters. It may mean that you share what truly matters to you, to speak honestly and lovingly. Or you might understand your friend and a bridge is formed, where there was a wall before. You might be willing to take a risk by being more transparent, because intimacy with your spouse is important for you. It leads into a "we" where each person's well-being matters, providing a space for both of us to evolve and flourish, rather than oppressing, controlling, manipulating and trying to change another to fit into our predetermined mold so we can finally feel safe.

These approaches open us into a field beyond the usual, "You are wrong and I am right." When we both matter, without losing our individuality, we discover a new dance, one so unique as never danced before. We mutually awaken and join in a feast of love where each is fed. This is not a pipe dream. It is practiced and lived by more and more people on our human relation ship. Just look around and join, c'mon, to sail with us.

May we relate anew again and again, for the sake of our ancestors, children, our relations and all life on earth. It makes a difference.

2. Connecting for Real

Ingenious ways to relate

The deepest need of every human is to be truly accepted, heard, seen and welcomed home.

I arrived in Europe, after having lived abroad for over twenty years. As I walked the cobblestone streets of Barcelona, I noticed how many cafés were filled with locals drinking coffee or tea with friends. I wondered if this was a holiday? No, this is normal, I remembered. People stood on street corners, gesticulating and talking with each other. I had been so used to driving in cars and being busy with work in America that I had entirely forgotten how different other cultures are. You make no appointment, but knock on your neighbor's door to see if your friend is home. Relationships have a higher priority than success or money. What impact does that have on people? Less isolation, depression and violence are a few of the many advantages, when we live more connected lives.

When I stayed in Greece to complete the final chapters of my book, the elderly gentleman Giannis, from whom I had rented a house, invited me to join him for one of his delicious home-cooked meals, a traditional wedding, and helped me out by driving me to the local market in his beat-up car, even if I had not asked for it. We spoke a hodgepodge of English-Italian-Spanish-Greek languages and had such fun. Connecting heart-to-heart, I became part of his family and a large network of friends.

***

What's the magic that helps us to experience real connection with each other? This sense when you are at ease with a person, accepted. You experience aliveness, understanding, a flash of brilliance, and a tingling warmth in your heart as you sit together on a bench beside a river. When defenses are down and you hear, see and meet one other — *beyond the field of right and wrong,* as Rumi so eloquently writes — deeper than the judgments and assumptions, yes, there is a river beckoning us to dive in and swim together.

This is both a new and ancient way of relating, which connects us with the larger web of life. Few are experts; some are more or less skilled than others. Yet, we can grow our capacities to relate in a real, present and heart-to-heart way. In the "Connected or Living Dead?" chapter you find many practices; and in this chapter we delve more deeply into relating with any person we meet along the road of love.

***

In Nepal, in a remote Himalayan village, a little girl with a happy smile walked barefoot toward me, folded her hands, looked at me with her big brown eyes and said sincerely, "Namaste," which translated means, "I bow to God in you." I felt touched and bowed as well. In Germany the greeting is "Gruess Gott" (I greet God). These salutations, which exist in diverse cultures and languages, are meant to remind us of the true essence in each other. Often, they are spoken habitually, without feeling that indeed we are greeting the Buddha on the road. But, "See the light in one another" offers a connection cord. Yet, how do you recognize the essence in strangers, in people that agitate you or those who judge you? Sure, there are others in whom you find delight, it's obvious and you enjoy being together. "May I see the light in you" can be our silent intention and prayer, when we engage with one another. Try it out for one day and observe what you experience with people and in yourself.

For, what you pay attention to, is where energy flows. And your energy and emotions are what speak miles in relationships. Whether people sense it consciously or not, everyone feels energy to a greater or lesser degree. You might be exhausted, drained and sad; then it's no use to pretend otherwise, as you transmit that to people in any case. It's better to be authentic, or else you are sending mixed signals into the field and the recipient will only get confused. If you say, "I feel happy," but you are grieving, your partner will receive an incongruent message and the connection isn't real nor alive.

***

Anna and Carl sat tensed up, opposite and distant from each other. They could not feel the love, nor see the light; while they fought over who should take the baby and whose turn it was to do the laundry that week. Their faces contorted and the argument escalated, as they reached a bigger issue: "You never help and you don't love our family." Carl was furious, how could Anna say such an outrageous thing, when he worked so hard? Anna had spoken from hurt and desperation. You know those arguments, which turn worse with every word you utter. It was time to stop them on the familiar road of misery. I interjected, "Stop for a moment. When you leave the office you can continue, but you did not hire me to let you walk the same old road. Want to approach this differently?" And then I asked each to state what they were feeling right now, without blame or shame.

"I feel hurt," Anna said.

"I am angry," Carl mumbled.

I responded, "Take a breath into your body. Sense into what you are experiencing."

The storm settled a bit. I asked them to look at each other for a second, which isn't easy, when you feel angry and hurt. And I invited both to let themselves be seen and heard.

Anna spoke first. "Carl, I hear and see how furious and upset you feel."

Carl felt acknowledged and softened a little when he turned to Anna and replied, "I get how much it hurts you."

She burst into tears, but also was willing to be present for Carl. Those two knew already how to dance well together, so I guided them a little deeper and closer, as their hands tentatively reached out to one another.

Anna spoke chokingly, "I want to hear your view, Carl, but sometimes I feel so alone in our relationship and the hurt takes over. And all I see and hear is attack. Then I fight like a cat."

Carl nodded, "Yes, I understand, that happens for me too. But instead of tears I see red and then I go after you. You know the bull that I can be." They laughed.

Authenticity, vulnerability and skilled communication had led them together again. Once they felt connected, the issues with the baby and the laundry were easy to resolve. They found a solution that worked for both of them.

***

Always make connection more important than the task or issue at hand. First connect, than act—let that be your motto for any relationship, whether at work or at home. And then the problem can be resolved in ways that you could never have imagined. Connection opens doors.

But what about those times when you do not feel connected nor see the light? When you can't stand your mate, when you are furious with your friend, when the world is turned upside down and you feel isolated, alone? Or when your partner is in the throes of depression or anger and is shut down. How do you reach across the chasm then?

We don't want connection that is based on a model of perfection. This isn't love. Let's throw this false spiritual notion—of always being positive, always feeling light, always being happy—overboard. Instead, let's meet with each other how we are right now. If you are sad, I acknowledge that and maybe we sit for a while with your river of tears.

Let's not turn our backs so fast from what is uncomfortable, but instead turn toward what is calling out for our love.

We don't need to fix, lecture or change each other. That only creates distance. Sometimes just meeting your old friend on that bench at the river and contacting the loneliness, being alone together, sparks connection alive. It grows through acceptance of how we are, built through meeting unflinchingly who and what is here, exactly as it is right now.

***

She was happy and he was upset. How do you connect with seemingly opposites poles of the emotional color scheme?

He acknowledged her, "You are beaming big time, really happy, hmm...?"

"Yes, I could fly to the moon, I got such good news! I received a promotion!" she burst forth enthusiastically.

"I am so happy for you, Shirley," he said, and meant it.

"And you, Andrew, you sound upset, what's up with you?"

He mumbled: "I am bummed out with my life, nothing seems to work out for me."

She refrained from giving him advice or trying to pull him toward happiness. Instead she joined him for a moment in his bleak world: "It's tough that you have gotten so many rejections for your proposals. Man, I can only imagine how painful that is and how you begin to doubt yourself and want to give up. Do you want to have a coffee and share a bit more with me?"

He perked up his head a bit; he felt seen, met and accepted. The two experienced connection beyond duality, making a bridge across the grand color scheme of life.

***

It isn't so difficult to dance in intimacy, but it does take a different approach than the usual kind. Our ground is truth: we are already connected in the river of life. Even if you don't like each other, even if you depart in anger, still the connection is there, it cannot be destroyed.

We often cover it up, just like love, we may deny, dismiss and forget it, but beneath all of the conditioning our hearts are beating as one; they do know. Our practice is remembering that and using skillful means that allow connection to shine forth, even amidst the storms and challenges of life. When we do, our relationships take a different course: you experience genuine love with each other, no matter if the waves rise high or low, whether you feel blue or bright; you are in touch with the essence—the bond that eternally unites.

Love in Action

The main House Keys for Connecting
The Key of Curiosity:
A healthy dose of curiosity opens doors for relating and leaves judgment in the dust. Apply a curious mind to discover the different landscape of your friend. He might experience fear and see ghosts from out of the dark and rocky landscape of his past. Don't try to change your friend but be inquisitive: "How is this for you? What are you experiencing?" Don't make comparisons,

such as, "I experienced this dark time too." Don't try to fix it: "Oh, but there is so much light." These approaches never work, but serve only to alienate. Rather get to know what is going on within him or her, without making it wrong or right.

Apply the attitude, "I want to get to know your world, which is different than my own." Discover the world of your partner, friend, child or coworker. Find out what it is like to be them and how a particular situation is for them, as if you are exploring a different country. Inquire into their world, how they feel and what they think. Apply fascination and curiosity to find out what their life is like. For example, do they have children, an ailing grandparent they are taking care of, or how do they really feel tonight? Find out what this stranger loves and what they are afraid of. Of course you do not ask questions like you are sniffing into their life and then use the information against them. Talk more in a casual way, such as, "I have children, two and four years old. There is always a lot of chaos, when I come home. And you, do you have any kids or grandparents living with you?" Make a nonthreatening statement by revealing a little about yourself and then invite the other person into the conversation by asking something related about themselves. It is important that you don't make the conversation solely about you. You are leading into connection, by making yourself available, but then turn the conversation to the other person. You might be curious about how they feel about their job, what this person does for a hobby, what challenges they might be facing in their life. Be personal and engage, but without crossing boundaries or interviewing people.

It's a dance. And curiosity and fascination help us to truly see, hear and meet each other.

The Key of Heart and Emotional Intelligence:
We grow connection through the heart. Emotional intelligence allows us to feel empathy, the main ingredient for any relationship. To cultivate emotional intelligence it is vital that

you are in touch with your own feelings and can be at ease with any of them, be it joy, anger, fear or delight. (For more on navigating the landscape of feelings read the chapter, "This Human House.") Then you won't need to resist the emotions of another and are available in relationships. Presence helps us to be there and Lovingness, the ability to accept and embrace, allows connection between people to unfold naturally. (Read more on loving embrace in the "Foundation Stones" chapter.)

Allow yourself to feel empathy when you engage with another person. Sometimes your heart is closed; you are guarded, and you do not have to fake it. Admitting to yourself where you are at, without judging, helps. And being transparent with your partner fosters intimacy and connection, like saying: "I feel my heart is so closed up. I feel numb. I want to open again, but have no clue how to right now." If you offer acceptance toward what you experience you may notice a softening inside. Then no faking is necessary.

And you can go straight toward the sunlight. You can look at the person and see something you like about them, their eyes or smile, or remember one behavior, attribute or quality that you appreciate about this person. Notice how you feel. With some people we experience strong barriers, and here you can use a simple silent mantra, "May you have happiness. May you be free from suffering." This allows you to feel a tad of human empathy and warmth. You can also generate empathy when you put yourself into that person's shoes, to feel how they're suffering, to consider that this person had a hard day and that's why she might be grumpy.

When you heart opens even a tiny bit, you will feel more connected and in turn the other person will feel safer with you. You might have already come upon this, that when your heart is open you naturally can establish a connection, even with a difficult person. It does not mean you need to like the other person or take them out for a meal. It simply means you connect human to human. Emotional intelligence is the best asset for relating, but we have to cultivate it. And keep leaning into our heart; it knows how to connect no matter how difficult the person or situation is.

The Key of Presence:
Your presence is the basis for connection. Most people just want someone who truly is here with them. We want to be met. When you are present you understand and see others, without trying to change, fix or judge them. You disconnect when you are stuck in your internal story or rummaging in your thoughts. Then you do not even register that there is another here with you. If we are not present we are basically not relating. However, when you pay attention, as if this is the most important moment and meeting, then you will connect in ways that are fresh and enlivening.

Being able to be present of course requires that you become aware when you depart from the connection, to admit, and come back to this moment, into what is happening right now. It means that you are aware of your own world (your feelings, thoughts and sensations), that you are aware of the other person and what is happening between you at the same time. We have to cultivate our capacity for that. Mindfulness practice comes in handy. (For more see the "Foundation Stones" chapter.) Embodiment practices and emotional work help to show up grounded and present; and therefore we experience true connection together.

The Key of Acknowledgement:
We want to be seen and heard. When another person shares, do not wander off thinking about what you will say next. Do not give advice or interrupt. Listen for a few minutes attentively. Then acknowledge what the other person shared with you. You might say, "I hear that you had a hard day." Validating another

person's experience grows understanding and connection. Even if the person has an opposing opinion and you don't agree, practice validating their view. This creates a bridge across different worlds. It allows the person to feel seen and heard. This also helps to resolve misunderstanding.

The Keys of Authenticity, Transparency and Vulnerability:
These open the doors to each other's hearts. "I don't feel like connecting with you. I feel tired and exhausted from work." Even if this sentence is honest and states clearly where you are at, it also slams the door on the other person. You could say instead, "I know you were looking forward to connecting tonight, to share a meal together. I don't want to disappoint you, but I am so tired from work that I won't be of much use tonight. Can we meet tomorrow?" Show up in a real way with another, as you are. Sometimes you feel afraid or sad, admit that. Sometimes you feel happy, share what is happening for you in the moment. If you can't do something or it's a "no" for you, speak that without too many explanations. Authenticity does not mean you have to reveal the most intimate secrets in your life. It just means you are in touch with your present experience and share it. "How do you feel in this moment, my love? Would you like to join me on a walk? I have been missing you and would love to connect, if you like." Vulnerability also opens the door for another person to feel safe with you. It's a risk to be real, but it bonds us. (See more about transparency, authenticity and vulnerability in the chapter "Vulnerability—Friend or Foe?".)

The Key of Appreciation:
We tend to forget this beautiful key that unlocks the heart. This is why I have included it in so many chapters of this book. Genuine appreciation makes people feel safe, seen and more connected. For example, you could say, "I appreciate your dedication to our project

and your unique ideas." Or, "I cherish the creativity you bring to this work." Look at what people are doing well, not perfectly, and point that out. You grow more inspired, alive and confident people when you actively appreciate, rather than criticize them.

A great approach is to point out what connects you and what you appreciate about your relationship: "I appreciate that we have worked a long time side by side with each other and have moved through major challenges together. We have grown big time as a team." Make it a daily practice in any relationship to appreciate what connects you both.

The Key of Resonance Communication:
Learning the language that connects nourishes and can turn the wheel in any relationship. Adjust your way of communicating and watch the flower of your relationships blossom before your very eyes. It may feel unfamiliar to validate others and to talk in ways that establish mutual resonance, but you can learn it like any foreign language. Some of this will come easily and some you may have to practice over and over until it turns into your mother tongue. Practice the communication skills presented in the next chapter.

The Key of Tolerance:
Long-lasting friendships carry a special quality of two people knowing and accepting each other's uniqueness, gifts and imperfections. Too often I hear: "She did not agree with me so I did not want to meet her again." Or: "We had a fight and then we never talked with each other again." Or: "He is often late, so I don't hang out with him anymore." I have some friendships that have weathered the seasons; we may not see each other a lot, but I know I can call on my friend in the middle of the night if the shit hits the fan in my life. A close friend of mine has some annoying behaviors (she probably thinks the same of me) like behaving controlling and picky, but I have learned to accept her

as she is nevertheless. In the past I tried to change her, but now I just smile when she barks her commands. We even laugh at it together now. I let her be and love her, just as she is. Sure, there are behaviors that should not be tolerated in a friendship, such as lying, abusiveness or betrayal. But to cultivate tolerance for people's oddness helps create lasting bonds that weather any changes in life. Such a friendship is worth more than gold.

How do we generate a Field of Safety?

People need to feel emotionally safe to open up. If a sense of safety is established in relationship, connection blossoms easily. But, you can't convince anyone to feel safe and trust just doesn't grow overnight. Offer instead to be a safe refuge. Generate a field in which it is palpable that you accept people, as they are. What does that mean? Refrain from judging and making assumptions about others. Be real yourself. Be curious about people's views, experiences, feelings and thoughts. Validate another's experience. Get to know them as a human being, someone who is different from you and who is not responsible for fulfilling your needs and wants. Have clear boundaries; for example, nonviolence in speech at work. That can mean a confidentiality rule, the no gossip rule, no swearing at each other and so on. Clear boundaries of respect help both to feel safe. Let yourself be seen and known by revealing and being human yourself. Acknowledge and appreciate people, they will feel safer when you mean it. Remember underneath the façade is often a child asking: "Is it safe to be with you?" And the answer: "I am here with you" is the safe ground for connection to flourish.

Common Dilemmas:

If you get lost in others:

Become present to your environment and yourself, breathe into your belly and your feet. Bring your energy back to you.

Notice the support from the chair or couch. Center in yourself. Only when you are here do you relate with others.

If you are stuck in your own small world:
Become aware what else is here and who is with you. You are more than your personal story. Follow your direct experience to open internal doors, get curious, pay attention to the life force. Then drop deeper—whether through prayer or meditation—to stillness, to the love, to the beauty.

If you get lost in emotional overwhelm or contract with certain emotions:
Become aware of one specific emotion and where you experience it the strongest in your body. Stay present and give it breath. Allow it room to move and soften. Ground to the earth with your body (movement and/or nature helps) and notice that you are held. If you are in a conversation with a friend speak out loud what you are presently experiencing. Just refrain from explaining and trying to make the experience go away. Speaking what is presently happening, even if uncomfortable, releases the tension and shame, and the conflicts fly out the window then.

If you are frequently stuck in the mind:
Use mindfulness practices and connect with your body. Then turn toward your feelings and allow yourself to feel. Don't buy into judgments, or all the stories from the mind. Watch the mind, but don't let it run you, for it does not know the way of love. Ask yourself: *And what else is here? And who else is here but me?*

Basic Reminders to Connect:
For some of you it is easy to form connections and for some it is a challenge, and many of us are in-between. No matter where you stand, remember:

2. Connecting for Real

- Connect first with a person and their world.
- Let your heart soften.
- Show up present and authentic.
- Inquire with friendly curiosity into the other person's world.
- Validate and acknowledge what you hear.
- Share openly about yourself as much as it feels appropriate.
- Express yourself transparently with vulnerability.
- Point out and appreciate what connects you both.

Make connection number one and all else will follow in tow.

3. Who is Relating to Who?

Mirror, mirror on the wall, who do I see—me or you?

Recently I visited a land in which people had wealth and appeared conscious and seemingly spiritual. As exciting as it was to mingle among them, I sensed unease below the shimmering glitter. People did not relate so much with each other, but were involved with their personal show and talking about themselves nonstop. Most of them tried hard to impress another, to stand out as more special, conscious and accomplished. It wasn't any different than other social settings where people asserted themselves as more successful, richer, more influential. Notice the "more." The façade looks different in each group, but the underlying message and insecurity is the same: *Am I accepted and good enough?*

Social scenes can be marvelous fields of exploration. Come, walk with me into the party and let me introduce you to some of the characters at play:

In the center of the grand reception hall we have "Mr. Attention Grabber" talking to "Miss Worthless." She listens intently to the bragging, he gets the attention fix he needs for the day and she feels a little less bad, because he looks at her as if she matters—for once. This lasts only minutes though, but any morsel will do for her.

When "Mrs. Special" enters the scene "Miss Worthless" runs off and disappears out of sight. Meanwhile, "Mrs. Special" and "Mr. Attention Grabber" fight over the remaining space; the energy picks up rapidly between them and adds to the exciting hype. The attention grabber goes on to suck energy like a vampire, hoping that he might feel somehow important, that he matters and is good enough. It's a tough competition, because "Mrs. Special" wants the same. Who will get the most airtime to fill up their empty hole inside?

Ah, now look at that. Just in time, "Sir Cool" enters the party, and with his calm the heated space becomes a little colder, so all heads turn to him. He has the advantage of being taller than everyone, which makes it easy to notice him. But, before he can use more of his cool presence to impress, people turn fast toward the opening of the large entrance door of the mansion.

Excitement ignites the room. Who is she? With style, flair and flowing hair, in comes a grandiose and influential woman, dressed stunningly in a tight blue shimmering dress, for everyone to notice of course. "Mrs. Special" and "Mr. Attention Grabber" fall to the wayside, as everyone flocks like children to "Ma'am Grandiose." They want to get a crumb of attention, in hopes that a piece of glitter will rub off on them; those who don't have as much charm and success. Maybe she could provide the lift to a higher ground of social standing? The "oh so important" woman gets the juice from everyone, but when I look into her eyes, they ask the same question as all the others: *Am I loved and accepted?* Heavily painted with mascara, her sparkle is on the outside, but these eyes have a look of deadness inside.

Meanwhile, "Mrs. Care" smiles and offers sweet treats, quietly looking after everyone. She is the selfless one who feeds each guest dutifully. She is liked, but people forget about her when she is not around. She is exhausted all the time, and although her care is genuine in part, she tends to others' needs as a way to be accepted by everyone.

***

It sounds funny, doesn't it? The games and roles we play—to be loved, seen and accepted. And it is tragic too. Nobody in this all-too-common party is naturally who they are and it becomes the play of the hour for everyone on the dance floor. Who will get the most attention and love?

And what's your interesting garment you hide under? We create an identity, a role, to experience belonging and acceptance, which we believe will give us what we want and need. We cover our insecurities and relate from a sense of unworthiness and unlovedness, and nobody feels OK or accepted as they are. And we reinforce this behavior with each other. Bring some loving awareness to the matter; it helps to break this mesmerizing collective and agonizing personal trance. What would happen if you stepped off the game board, threw caution to the wind, stopped faking it and forgot the rules of pretense?

Taking a closer look into the mirror of projections

Yes, we want to be seen, trying so very hard. But who is seeing? We tend to project our own fantasies, mirages, expectations, assumptions, judgments, fears and wounds onto another person, as if they are our favorite mirror on the wall. Our lens is generally covered with the thick slime of projections. Did you ever attend a conversation, when your "better half" goes off the deep end, attacking you as if she or he was talking to someone else in the room? And you scratched your head in confusion and wondered: *What is he talking about?* Or your spouse reacts to you as if you are the father who left her; or the previous partner who betrayed her, suddenly becomes you—even though betrayal is not one of your characteristics. Projections feel weird and confusing, but they are powerful, and sadly, so very common.

Who do you project onto your partner, boss, or your friend? What do you see in your child and react to?

Who do you wish to see in your spouse, but who seems to not be there? You know the story of wanting someone to be different than they are. This never works out. We tend to have endless expectations that another is supposed to fulfill. For example, your spouse is the chosen one who will finally make you feel loved for good, the one to fill the hole that has ached since birth. It is hard to breathe under this mountain of expectations.

Actually, we don't relate at all, when our projections run the show. What we project impacts others and our own behavior. If you see your mate only as a little boy (even though he might behave like a child sometimes) you turn into a mother; he becomes more of a boy and your lovemaking has seen the end of its days. Or you may see the best in your child, and he or she will most likely grow into that even more. If we relate to people like nobody is ever good enough, most will feel diminished in our presence. When we have intense conflicts with others, we tend to bring a lot of people into our communication—usually a long line of people who have hurt us in the past.

If you find yourself stuck in the hall of mirrors, take a breath, step back and pause. Consider that what you see is not the reality of this one person standing before you, who is not your mother, father or ex-lover. Own up to your trigger and projection first. Then get curious to discover who this person is. Ask: "Who are you really? Let me get to know you." This helps to disidentify, to gain perspective and to resolve the difficulty at hand with more ease.

When we get to know another, we discover again and again: people are human, each valuable with a divine spark, even if covered up. We see more clearly by being aware of our own junk on the lens. The projection might still be there, but it does not take over the entire windshield. Being honest foremost with ourselves, allows us to see beyond the goo-covered glasses. And therefore we are able to relate with each other. Seeing another without projections, fresh and anew is a wonderful practice for love to grow in any relationship.

Who is showing up in relationship?

We relate to others like a child, an adult, an enemy, a friend— it is our choice. Are you showing up to your forty-year-old spouse as a five-year-old girl who wants her daddy to take care of her? Who is showing up in a conflict: a mature adult or a terrified, traumatized individual who is attacking the other as their enemy? It's often a mix. And again, there is no right or wrong. But when we stay unconscious that we play roles it manifests in many weird ways in our relationships. Bring awareness to those areas. This frees us to then choose where we locate ourselves and relate from. We can relate from our power as a grown-up at work, or relate with the nurturing of a mother to a little child...

We gain free range when we become conscious. And enjoy connection, because we discover each other for real, not as mirrors or imaginary characters of our own make-believe world.

If you like, recall a person whose opinion and view means a lot to you, someone who respects you, holds you in high esteem, someone who understands you. Notice how you feel in this moment as you are remembering this person. You might feel warm, at ease. When related to without projections we feel received as we are and love is just here, without twisting, trying and working so hard. It's a relief and connection grows.

Offer this gift to one another

Stay on the edge where aliveness surges from the depth. Breathe as fear and excitement cautiously begin to dance. In this place between knowing and unknown, between crumbling and birthing worlds, here my friend we meet and touch hands.

Look with fresh eyes, as if you are meeting the other person for the first time. (Actually you are because no one is ever the same as yesterday.) Engage with warmhearted curiosity; get to know the world of your friend, as if you are entering an unknown land. Listen from behind your heart. And be yourself and see what might happen along the way.

There are wonders to be found as we meet in aliveness, freshness and authenticity. Love then flows unrestrained between us, because nothing is in the way. That's what love naturally does, all the time, between each of us. It just might look differently than we imagine, for every encounter has its own unique flavor; if we are willing to feel all the feels and lean in, to touch what's true, to see who is here with you and engage. Then we literally dance together—with all of our stumbling and gloriousness—right into love's embrace.

And what about these masks? We use them just to play as children do, but put them away when we want to meet God with each another.

Love in Action

1. Ask this question inwardly when you encounter another: *Who are you?* Apply curiosity and a sense of discovery concerning this territory you know nothing about (or only a little).

2. Apply looking with fresh, curious eyes even toward your partner whom you have been with for a very long time. Nobody is the same today as yesterday.

3. When you take full responsibility for your experience and present state of affairs, it opens up the space to relate. Own up to your judgments, needs, expectations, assumptions—admit to the cover on your lens. Acknowledge you have them like everyone else. If you like to be brave, share more vulnerably and be transparent with another.

4. Take your own assumptions about others lightly, knowing there is always more than the eyes behold. Ask yourself: "Is it really true what I am perceiving? What else is here?"

5. Refrain from comparing your story and experience with another. No two individuals' lives and stories are the same; all have pearls and sorrows of a different kind.

6. Follow the aliveness in connection with each other. Be in the body and employ all your senses. Feel your heart

pulse and what is alive between you and another in this moment now.

7. "I see the light in you" is a way of seeing others that connects you to God, to Spirit, the Dharma, and the truth in all. Apply this attitude for several days toward anybody you encounter and notice what happens in your relationships. And remember, seeing the light in another doesn't mean denying and ignoring the personality and the shadow:)

Have fun with the masquerade but don't forget who you are.

4. Being in the Flow

Receiving and giving love abundantly

Breathing in and breathing out, rain is falling upon parched soil and is absorbed; plants and grains grow, feeding people and creatures alike. The circle of receiving and giving has no end or beginning, what is natural is whole and alive.

We are swimming in an abundant sea of love. But, everyone is thirsty for drops, even though pure water is all around. Seems like a paradox. Love is as natural as the air we breathe and the ground we walk on. It is here to be lived and shared; our life depends on it. As we eat from the feast of life and contribute to the health of its soil, we are in the flow. When we receive the natural goodness that is here, we are fulfilled. As you generously give, others are fed through you as well. How is the river of inflow and outflow in your life and in your relationships? Do you receive openly, when love is given to you? Do you give love as much as you would like to?

She entered my office in tears, sobbing as if the world was coming to an end. For her it did. "My relationship just ended. We tried so hard, but neither of us felt loved. What's wrong with me?" Nothing was wrong with either of them, but those two had a hard time receiving and giving love. I had seen their suffering dance together and wasn't surprised that they went their separate ways. It did not need to go that way, but it would have required work for both. Our blocks in giving and receiving show up especially in relationships. We want to be loved, but keep nourishment out when a gift, a compliment or kind word arrives at our door. We long for closer connection, instead we hold back from sharing with another. To be available for love requires us to meet the barriers in us and unclog the river.

We want true love, yet who is giving it? And who is receiving?

Often we find that a gift is given with conditions, and, whether spoken or not, you sense the expectation to offer something in return. You wish to express appreciation, instead you say nothing because you are afraid to look silly. Joe pays for Sally's meal, but expects to meet her in bed afterwards. Amanda offers affection in order to get a commitment from her new guy. And on and on it goes. We bargain and keep score with love. Giving becomes an exchange, like a business deal, control and manipulation follow on its heels. This is about getting to be honest. If you feel drained, what have you been trying to get? Let's not judge, but bring awareness to these areas to liberate patterns, which prevent the free flow of love.

We want to feel nourished, but whatever is given is never right or perfect enough. The hand that offers is dismissed and the compliment is disregarded too. We long to be received and accepted, but shut down to such a degree that no one can enter our lonely world. One person is seen as the ultimate source of giving us all we want, but we revert to blame and judgment when our chosen object doesn't deliver the meal as we ordered it. We act needy and clingy, but the real need never gets addressed. We might feel entitled, as if life or the other owes us, so we demand love with a tight fist of self-righteousness. Or we wander as beggars in the land of love, our cup always empty, left out from all the good we feel we do not deserve. Some are like misers, holding onto what they have, and becoming smaller every day by not sharing, as if love could be possessed or would grow that way.

We have established customs to block the flow of the river, learned early to create clever contracts in giving and receiving. Unfortunately, these barriers, if unaddressed, prevent love and connection with others, ourselves, and the entire universe. But, we are so much bigger than our blocks; we can include and touch them with loving awareness—those places in us that are afraid, in pain and mistrusting, or in resistance to the flow. As we touch with unconditional regard what is holding so tight, the river is freed and may flood across the prairies, watering the thirsty plants of our relationships.

It may be wild and surprising when the mighty flow takes you. Giving and receiving love asks us to take risks, to step beyond the comfort zone; to be vulnerable and courageous, to grow and engage wholeheartedly, to risk being rejected and hurt, and simply put—to look like a fool. These risks are worthwhile to take though, if we want to fully live and love. It also means to learn skills to expand our capacity to swim in that river together. Then we experience an intimacy where everything is allowed to be here—the hate, the upset, the joy. We drop into sharing with each other what is so utterly, wildly true and alive—an ever-flourishing circle of love, where there is no more receiving and giving, nor you or I, but one flow.

Receiving a full Cup

I am sitting with delicious food and friends at the table, offering thanks to what is given by life and the labor of many hands. Slowly I taste the flavor of the delicate sprouts, lightly steamed spinach, pine nuts and feta cheese, pasta made by my daughter with juicy Mediterranean sauce. The more I engage my senses, the more I taste, the more I am filled. Sensual is this feast of ours. As I chew the organic veggies, sweetness and a slight bitterness delight my tongue. Eating is intimate and turns to lovemaking with food. I linger before swallowing; one bite alone is ecstatic now. As food fills my tummy, I feel satisfaction all around. I have received and feel nourished by life with every bite. How different is this experience from other meals, when I ate without being aware of what I was eating. I gulped food down in a hurry. No matter how good and healthy the food was, there was no satisfaction. The body was fed, the rest of me not. And I kept feeling hungry no matter how much I stuffed down. Do you know this experience?

A present is given to you. How do you receive what is offered? Do you wave it away? Do you reject it even? Do you pick on what is not perfect in the wrapping? Or do you nod with a polite thank-you and leave it unopened in a corner for later. Maybe you get busy figuring out what to give in return. Or you grab the gift, wanting more and more without ever fully digesting? Maybe you allow yourself to fully receive without resistance, with open hands and gratitude, letting your heart be touched and filled up by the gift another offers you. Life is always giving to us, if we are available to receive.

Jonathan spoke his truth at a spiritual retreat I was teaching. "I've been sitting on a meditation cushion for years. I have given everything to this path, and yet I feel dry like an old cracker. I know every concept under the sun and still I don't feel the love. It's like I am left out from a feast I am supposed to join. I just can't find the door in." Most of us have hidden dams against receiving love. We feel forgotten, neglected and left out from the abundance of life. It's excruciating, this sense of separation.

I too had much to learn about receiving, because I felt unworthy of love. I am sure you have your own story. And being receptive feels vulnerable and tender. It challenges internal beliefs such as, "I'm bad, unworthy, therefore I do not deserve..." Pay attention to what particular blockages and fear you carry around, lean toward your direct experience and tend to these thoughts and emotions.

Many have experienced abuse; to receive love can take then a little more work. If you were violated or raped, then even the most tender touch may evoke terror. It takes patience to heal what was harmed, when we were young and helpless. Or, we might confuse poison with love and wonder why we get sick. So used to eating what's toxic, we go for it over and over again, until we throw up. If you cannot say "no" to the bad apple—the cruelty, abuse, lies, nastiness or the garbage covered with sugar coating—get help to recognize what is beneficial for you. If we have been harmed severely, it feels unfamiliar to receive what is healthy. Sometimes we resist love more than anything else, simply because it is unknown and doesn't fit into our script.

How good does it feel to you, though, when you speak an appreciation and it's not received by another? It's like your love has no landing place, as if you gave water to a thirsty fellow who just won't drink. How different it is, when your water is tasted and a person's thirst is quenched. It feeds you too. And if you want to widen your receiving capacity start with one drop, one taste. Too much at once may feel overwhelming, but exploring how one touch of warmth feels, is possible.

One taste at a time is the way. Use this mantra: *In this one taste of love I dwell.*

Remember in as much detail as you can, when you experienced a moment of love given to you. Let yourself feel it again in every way. Taste the sense of aliveness, the goodness, even the tiniest flicker. Say to yourself: *This one taste of love I cherish.* Revel and bask in it, receive this nourishment that arises from within. Let your body cells be drenched in it. What might it be like to take in a fuller deeper breath, allowing this experience to fill you up right now?

Life is feeding life; the river of love is moving, desiring to fill your cup to overflow. May you open your hands to the abundance that is already here. Sip one drop from the water of life that is here now, rejoice and feast, then shower it upon the land and each other. As we open to receive, we have more to give as well. By that we are living in love.

Giving for Real

This question, "Do you love me as I am?" is asked by almost everyone we meet on the street. Most are too shy to say it out loud though. Who then is offering an answer?

A longing is aching through our voices and eyes, for someone to say, "This moment is entirely for you. I am present, receiving you—just as you are. No story about me is standing in the way. My mind is still and open. What benefits you has priority. I meet you exactly where you are at, and offer my love freely, without trying to gain even the tiniest crumb from you." Yes, to give unconditionally takes quite a bit.

Turning toward love is a choice and to give entails action. You take initiative when you bake the bread and feed your guests. Real giving has no expectation for a return; it has no strings attached. It has no reward other than love's own. If we give genuinely, we feel more alive and we become a bigger space for love to move through us. One man said that it makes him happy, when he is at a restaurant and he sees someone who is looking downtrodden, sitting alone at the table, he pays for their meal anonymously.

Giving is not about ourselves, but another. Your friend likes strawberries. You might prefer pineapples. Of course you would not buy the pineapple for your friend, but the delicious red berries instead. Giving always has to do with attuning to the likes, needs, and longings of another, to step into their shoes. You offer an expression of love in whatever way is beneficial for your beloved. This means we let go of our own agenda and what we imagine is best for another.

This question comes in handy, *"What is beneficial for you? What do you love?"* Ask outright, if unsure.

Sometimes giving flows easily and spontaneously, and at other times it requires us to stretch, to make an effort. Your kid is whining for you, but you would like nothing better than to disappear to a peaceful island in the Caribbean. Instead, you choose to turn around and pay attention to her. You have earned barely enough, still you choose to tithe with people who have even less. Your partner is in a crisis, so you show up, even if it is past one o'clock in the morning. It might mean stepping beyond your comfort zone, to reach out when you are feeling shy and engage in a conversation to help another feel safe. Where could you stretch a notch to give more of yourself without expectation of gain?

Some people are experts in stretching and caregiving to the point of losing themselves and breaking down, forgetting that they too exist. If you are running on empty you are serving no one in the end. Learn to say "no" to another's demands. This too is an act of giving, especially, if we stop harm by that. And spend some time on the receiving part of this chapter, if this sounds like you.

Marty told me, "I want my wife to give back to me before I give more to her. I want an equal exchange. I made her dinners every night for a week; I think it's her turn to give as much as I have given to her. But I notice how I am stuck in the tit-for-tat game and don't feel any joy or love at all anymore."

Ask, "Am I giving in order to get something?" This could be approval, a sense of worthiness, praise, being liked, etc. Just notice, without judging, when you are in engaging in "love business," trying to get by giving. If I give you affection, you do the laundry for me. We all do this to a certain degree. The basis of the separate sense of self, the "me bubble" tries "to get something outside" to ensure its survival. It usually comes with a bill in the end, called dissatisfaction and disappointment. It serves to bring awareness to our hidden deals and agendas we make in the name of so-called giving. No thriving or expansion is possible through that, however, because it's not real love.

When you truly give you are the river, which leaves no traces, no karma, stickiness, nor demands with the gift. Love gives, simply because the river flows, it never sends us an invoice in the end. But authentic giving takes courage, your offering might not be wanted, received or reciprocated, someone makes fun of you, or worse—turns your gift against you. Yet, if you don't bring your love out, it stays like honey trapped in a comb—

being of no use to anyone, not even to you. The honey dries up, becomes hard and you do too. The question is: what do you want to live? Let your living be the answer.

And c'mon, don't hold back your love. As they say: the more you give it, the more you have. Express love creatively, fresh, in a thousand and one ways. Give unto life itself, do it for love's own sake. People on their deathbed don't worry about how much money they made. What they often ask is: "Have I loved well?" May you have fun to live this "yes" today!

Circle of Well-Being

As we receive and give love, we experience that the circle is whole. There is no giver or receiver anymore. When you give you receive, as you are receiving you are giving. This is a natural flow, with a sense of resonance, ease and upliftment for each. Intimacy emerges and well-being is enhanced for all. You are in the river together; growing in love. Then love only becomes bigger and there is more space in our togetherness to include everything, even the difficulties. Mutual support, enhancing each other's qualities, talents and lives gives joy. It is a spiral upward as we rise in love with each other.

Enjoy, for there is no end as the river is carrying you both into the infinite sea of love.

Love in Action

1. Growing capacity to receive a full cup.
One Taste: Take one experience, like eating or looking at a sunset and say this mantra: *This one taste of love I cherish.* Repeat many times during your day and notice what happens.
Gratitude: Being thankful for what is given is an attitude toward all creation. By feeling gratitude we receive what is given and take nothing for granted.

Receiving Nectar: If you receive a compliment or an appreciation from another, feel, let it sink in and savor it and thank the person.

Enjoy cake: Don't worry when the cake, meaning the nourishment, will be gone, whether it will come again in this form, or if it is OK to eat at all. Most likely love will not arrive in the same way, it will be in a different form, and such is the reality of the changing nature of life. Meanwhile eat the cake— and enjoy every bite thoroughly, as if it is the only one of its kind. It is. Today your mate brings flowers, tomorrow not. Should you not receive the flowers because he did not give those gifts previously or won't continue to do so? Smell them; take them in as a gift from life to you.

Craving/getting versus receiving: Trying to get is a struggle and makes you tense. It is exhausting work. While searching for dry bread, the food on the table is getting cold. We often do not eat the good that is provided. We are like a hungry ghost, whose belly is swollen from starvation, our mouth wide open to swallow anything up, yet our throat is closed tightly and no food will ever go in. The hands grab and greedily take more and more, yet the ghost is never satisfied, eternally starving, nothing is ever enough. If you have even a mild case of this, tend to this, or else it does prevent you from receiving the love that is available here and now.

Responsibility for your needs: Take ownership and responsibility for what you need. Do not expect the other to guess. Ask directly for what you want and need, without manipulation. Leave it free for the other to choose and respond, whether with a "yes" or a "no." (Refer to the "Connected or Living Dead?" chapter and the "Resonance Communication for Every Season" chapter, about expressing needs.) Neediness comes from disowned and unacknowledged needs. Find creative ways to meet your needs, if no one is there to help you. Once you have embraced your needs then you are ready to receive.

From codependency to maturity: Another person is not the source and is not on the planet to fulfill our entire need for love. If your cup is empty it is your responsibility to take care of it. Do not keep drinking from the wells of others, without tending to your own. No one is born to remedy that void in you. No person is the ultimate source of love, but each is free to share what he or she wants with us. Fill from the well in your heart, from the source; receive from life in all the ways love shows up for you.

Looking for the treasure: This is fun to do. Take a walk, whether in a city or in nature, and look for simple treasures of love. Feel the warmth of sunlight, a kind word from a stranger, a sign, a picture that makes you smile; breathe it in, receive life and let it touch and fill you up.

See and revel in what is good: See the cup as half full instead of half empty. Nothing is perfect. If you weigh everything as not good enough, you end up hungry all the time. When kindness is given to you, don't get stuck on the imperfect wrapper, look for the goodness, even if it is a tiny bit. Let this nourish you and simply leave the rest.

If it smells bad, don't eat it: You do not need to eat crumbs, trash or poisons. Not all that pretends to be love is the real bread. Just because someone offers a bad apple doesn't mean you need to eat it. Go for what makes you feel well and healthy. Learn to differentiate.

Different styles: Do not expect others to give love in the same way you do. Learn the diverse love languages. See how another expresses their love and be curious how it feels when you receive it. Your friend gives plenty of hugs; maybe you are not a hugger. It is her way to show love, you have another way. Communicate about this.

What are your nourishment barriers?
Explore and find out. The issue of worthiness is important to look into for most people. The inflow is certainly decreased,

when we insist that we are not deserving of love. You cannot change this belief overnight, but you can shine awareness on it and embrace the one in you who feels ashamed.

Engage with what feeds you: Usually these are simple things: taking a bath, walking in nature, spending quality time with a friend. Enjoy doing more of what you really take pleasure in and love.

Celebrating: Celebrate each taste, step, good and gesture of real love that comes your way. By that you are allowing in grace, you digest better and therefore you grow more of it (you could call it maximum leverage) and raise your energy into the natural flow of love.

Receiving from life: Life itself is the giver and taker. A baby is born, a man dies. One day you have a lot of money, another day you haven't even one penny. Here is the ultimate receptivity:

"Thank you, life, for all that is given and all that is taken. Let me be an open vessel to receive what is true and real. Thy will be done..." This level of surrender ends all quarrels we tend to have with life (spirit, truth... use your own words), and opens us to receive directly from the greatness of life what is of the highest benefit for us.

2. Growing capacity to give for real

Appreciation: Frequently express genuine appreciation for qualities and deeds done by the other. (For more details see the chapters, "A Heart Wide Open" and "Resonance Communication for Every Season.")

Taking loving action anyway: You don't want to change those stinky diapers one more time, but you do it anyway. You may not like your neighbor, but give a hand anyway. You are steaming with anger, but relate with respect to your coworker. You feel tired, but help your friend to move anyway. I'm sure you can think of plenty of examples yourself. If not, start adding to this list to go the extra mile. (And if you do that too much then cut back.)

How can I be of benefit to you? Find out the likes and needs of the other. Ask the question more often, *"How can I help, what can I do to support you?"* Don't make assumptions; instead ask the other person. Then act on what you discover.

Take initiative: State what you want to create: "I would like to have more fun with you." Offer a suggestion such as, "Would you like to play volleyball together?" Include the question: "What would be fun for you?" And then take action.

Extend your hand: Get out from your own shell, reach out to another and move toward connection. Even, if you are nervous — do it anyway. You have nothing to lose, except false pride and a sense of isolation. Care in action: "Looks like you are having a hard day. Do you want to talk about it? I am glad to be here for you." Or, "You just moved here, let me introduce you to our neighbors." Or, "I'd love to invite you for dinner tomorrow. Will you come?"

Take action: What can you contribute? Look for what is needed. Make a choice and even if it takes effort — put it into action. Send money to the cause you care about. Make the call to your family member that you have been putting off. Take the time to be with your mate and create something beautiful. Surprise others; giving can be creative and fun!

Act in real time: Don't wait for a better time to express your love. Don't wait for the other to make the first move to resolve a conflict. Don't ask for permission, but act on what is in your heart. Buy those flowers; speak these words of love that have been sitting on the tip of your tongue for a long time. Give what you have today, for tomorrow indeed may never come.

What is truly beneficial? No single answer, method or gift fits for all. Ask this question frequently: "What is beneficial?" and see what opens up. Engage from a place of curiosity.

This is a new plant, what does it need to blossom? If we use manure, which feeds the potato plants well, even with our best intentions, a delicate flower would shrivel up from. One type of medicine is good for one person, but another person might become sicker. One person could benefit from a hug; another benefits more from a kick in the butt.

Some people give, yet their own life has turned into a wasteland, by trying to rescue one more drug addict or lost one. Is it truly beneficial to pour life energy into someone, who isn't yet ready to make a change and sucks your vitality, like a vampire leaching free blood? Maybe a boundary and a firm "no" is in some cases more helpful, if it comes from love. Let's not confuse unconditional giving with having no boundaries, acting codependent, or being the doormat—seeking to find our worth or to be loved under the disguise of care.

Showing up: Often the best gift we can offer another is to be present with an open heart, to fully show up for a friend, a person, and a situation. You do not need to have the answers, offer advice or fix anything. You can just be there. All else will become clear. If you have a conflict with another be the first one to reach out and show up to resolve it.

What and who does it serve? This is a useful question to ask at work, in a group, in life. What to give and which direction to move in will become clear to you, as you connect with the higher intelligence in your heart. Let love lead and show you the way.

"Show me what you want me to give. Show me how to be helpful." A daily prayer to the Universe, to God, to the light inside of you can guide you and exponentially expand your capacity to give authentically. Listen to guidance and follow through.

Giving as an act of Devotion: Let your giving be an offering to your God, the Goddess, to life, to the spirit. Offer your actions daily unto the altar of love. In that way you are freed of attachment and your actions are sanctified, rippling out into the world far and wide in benefit of all.

Merge with the ocean of love, let it sweep you up with no shore in sight. And you will have life more abundantly.

5. Vulnerability—Friend or Foe?

What scares and connect us

Sure, there are plenty of qualities to cultivate for healthy, loving and authentic relating. Vulnerability, integrity, awareness, responsibility, care... the list goes on and on. Nobody has all of these attributes, obviously. What do you bring to the table? How do you want to show up in your relationships?

The most important is our loving presence, for the wings of awareness and lovingness lift any relationship to higher and fuller ground (for a review read the "Foundation Stones" chapter). I am focusing here on three basic staples you will need in all your relationships: vulnerability, transparency, and authenticity. Let's begin with the least liked, most feared and yet most essential for relating.

Yesterday, a new friend shared with me how he values vulnerability and authenticity in people, but also how challenging it is for him live that in relationships; and how often he was rejected, when he showed so-called signs of weakness: tears, tenderness of heart, and his joy and awkward weirdness.

Yes, vulnerability is often seen as our foe, feared like a monster in a closet. How often do I hear, "Yikes, this is scary. Let's not go there..." Just when you opened up to another, you got stabbed in that tender place. Really, why do it again? When you showed grief or anger, you might have been told to get over it. And sobbing in a public place, such as a bank or office, is a no-no. Who decided this?

For the mind, vulnerability is the giant fat spider to be avoided at any cost: "You are weak, when vulnerable. You are too sensitive and can be wounded, when you show your feelings and heart. Button up, run, and hide. Or defend yourself and attack the enemy out there. Make life predictable and control it with all your might; be in charge so you will never ever get hurt again."

Many spiritual paths feed into this avoidance dance by turning transcendence into a God, but when stuff happens and you are in a ditch, that one is nowhere to be found. In order to rise above into a "higher self" we degrade our humanness, dragging it into the dirt—and therefore each other. Some get stuck in a war against themselves and others, trying to improve and fix themselves, and peace is eternally out of sight. All because we want to escape the present moment and avoid being undefended. Sure, it does take a good dose of courage to show up real in our world.

But why bother with our human vulnerability, when it's sometimes such a messy business in relationships? When it means to move in closer to uncomfortable feelings, the anger, shame, tenderness and passion, to be present with all—and to top it off—letting yourself be seen by others in all your glory and imperfections too.

Let's put this straight: **without being vulnerable you cannot experience real love.** There you have it.

We pretend that being human is the bad secret in town, as if no one ever feels insecure, fearful, unworthy, and not good enough—except you alone of course. As if sheer exuberance is reserved only for children, and tears are for wimps and girls. We get overwhelmed, and often can't deal with the impermanence in life and our human fragility. Just the thought that we can't stop death and that our bodies will fall apart one day, freaks people out. So, we try our best to control what cannot be controlled in life, we pretend we are fine and build those famous walls against each other and life. And then we wonder where love is?

Let's turn the other way around

Vulnerability, the ability to feel, be present and show it, is our highway into connection with each other and into the vast truth of who you are. It's the eye of the needle thing. The holy nous (Gnostic). Your naked vulnerability is the gateway into your greatness, the mystery, as well as the key to experiencing intimacy with others. I discovered that when I felt emotionally tender and raw, but relaxed and softened in the midst of this, a door opened. Suddenly, I felt so alive, strong and such love surging through me. I felt free and relating became far easier and enjoyable then.

"Become like children," Jesus said. This doesn't mean to regress, to be childish and naïve. It implies openness and innocence. Easily accessible, when you haven't been hurt in that soft spot inside. But, as we explored in the chapter "A Heart Wide Open," because we all have experienced pain, this is why we tend to it with kind attentiveness. I cannot promise you that you will never experience the ache of betrayal or loss when you open, nor will I tell you some new age myth that you are invincible and that no one can hurt you. From an ultimate perspective it is true that our vast nature can never be destroyed or harmed. However, if you live in a human body, you are certainly affected—just as a friendly welcome warms you, a rejection stings. The kind of vulnerability I am speaking of is not to walk around like a child in dependency, crumbling from the effects of how others relate to you. But to make friends with our vulnerability and become mature to show up with that. And what has that to do with relating then?

Susan asked her friend if he had a moment to be there for her. She was not sure if he would give her unwanted advice as she had previously experienced with others. But she reached out anyway. She needed support, shaken by difficult news she had received. Susan allowed him to see her, crying and angry steaming, she shared what was going on. Just what the doctor ordered, he didn't try to fix her, was present and offered to hold her in his big bear arms. It relieved her and brought them closer together too.

***

Joe, who had participated in one of my fire of connection retreats, dated a woman and told me how he was growing courage by being real with his new lady when they went for a first walk in Golden Gate Park. Instead of putting up his usual superman façade, he told her that he had felt a bit nervous about meeting her, as he wasn't sure she'd like him. It was freeing to him to simply share what was vulnerable, yet authentic to him. He did not need an answer from her, but was surprisingly OK. He also said to her that he had really wanted to take her out, but he couldn't decide which restaurant, because he didn't know what she liked to eat. So, laughingly he asked: "And what food do you like, my lady?" It broke the ice, and she laughingly replied, "I would love to go out with you to a vegetarian restaurant! And I am so glad you are real with me, because honestly I have been nervous and tongue-tied too." Just having the freedom and safety to express how it was for her, the tightness left her body. He had taken the first step and as a side effect created safety for both of them. They connected, and as far as I know, are in a relationship now.

***

But what do you do in challenging situations, during those times when we tend to shut down? How do you walk into those situations with your vulnerability, when all our thoughts scream inside to press the emergency button— to hide, run and shut down?

***

Jane, a student whom I guided through this bumpy adventure, had rented a cabin for a decent amount of money, far in the wilderness. The owner of the land lived there, too, and some of his buddies. It looked like a fine find. Soon, Jane discovered, though, that the refrigerator was not working and it ruined her food. The toilet stopped flushing. Gas was leaking and almost killed her in her sleep. Once the rains arrived, the holes in the roof were perfect for taking a shower under. A heater never came, even when it got freezing cold. No matter how many times she asked that these things be fixed, she was given the same promises without any follow through. To top it off he kept making sexual advances and knocking on her window at night. She was hoping he would change, especially because he talked much about honoring women, spirituality and integrity. But he did not act on that.

After a while too long, Jane knew she had to confront him. He was a big man, a classic narcissist and psychopath in New Age garb, and a tough businessman with an arsenal of guns beside his bed, along with a Kwan Yin statue—symbol of compassion—on his altar. Interesting combo. To all the many people that came to the communal land, he presented himself as an evolved spiritual man. But he had a killer rage stored up under the charm, ready to explode. As a woman, her safety was in question—if she pissed him off, she was alone on the mountain with this guy. She could tell him what a jerk he is, or not say anything and just disappear... She admitted how afraid she was to speak up, feeling like a little five-year-old girl, wanting to hide or run. But, with help and encouragement she decided it was time. She took a deep breath, and rooted into the earth, gave a hand to fear and allowed her heart to soften. With every step as she walked up the mountain to meet him, strong life energy flooded through her, because she vowed: *I will speak up for my own sake and all women, to break those thick chains of silence and fear.* It gave her courage to include her sisters too.

His attention span to hear others was extremely short. So she spoke directly from her gut, without a trace of nastiness or sugarcoating, just truth: "It's scary and absolutely not alright when you grab me. The living conditions are not OK. I feel angry and hurt that you made promises, which you did not keep. I am done. I want my money back now and I am moving out today." He was speechless for once. It was a surprise that he returned her money and apologized. And before he could change his mind she packed her things and left the Wild West with the false spiritual show. Vulnerability and authenticity had become her best friends and allies now.

***

Not so easy to show up real, to stop pretending what we are not. The con artist plays the trump cards in a false game, luring people into his snare of deceit. Now, most of us do not veer to this extreme, but we all pretend in certain ways, afraid to be seen. If I share my personal stories in this book, you could judge me. Maybe you will, but I would rather be authentic than fake it in a book on love. Of course, I considered just writing the pretty parts and leaving out the defeats and embarrassments. It took courage to write these stories as they truly are—beautiful, wondrous and some horrible, difficult too.

What do we fear, under the masks? Faking is costing us connection and meaningful relationships. And we sadly abandon ourselves.

Beneath the layers of hiding we are afraid to be discovered with all of what we are. Who wants to be seen, when in the ditch? A polite smile with a crisp "thank-you, I am fine" is the norm to cover up with. If you are honest, you might wish for a hand, someone you can tell what's really going on for you. But, if you are hiding, who can give you this hand? Some people are masters in pretending that their mere existence and experiences are insubstantial. They may say, "Oh it doesn't matter, that's just nothing," meanwhile yearning to be recognized and seen. There are those who stand out with a form of pretense that offers plenty of kudos in society—a grandiosity that hides insecurity. What if someone sees through? It may feel uncomfortable and unfamiliar. What if you blow your own cover and leave the makeup for a day and reveal yourself with all the beauty and misery? We often feel ashamed, condemning ourselves as not good enough. Yet, how refreshing it is when you encounter a person who is real with you. Haven't you felt safer in their presence and encouraged to let the curtain down as well? When there is room for you to be as you are and for the other too—you meet. What a relief.

Authenticity takes a dash of courage, as it implies honesty with others, saying what you mean and meaning what you say. You are hiding nothing, even if it isn't pretty. If you don't have a job, you do not brag about a fabricated fancy career so you look good when you engage with other business people. You refrain from lying in order to be accepted. If you feel shy while engaging with a person, you just admit it. Authenticity is being you, human without pretense, blame or apology. This builds strength and confidence. If you do not like to be touched by a certain person, you say no without longwinded excuses. If you feel sad or happy it shows on your face, without explanation. You are not busy in the cover-up department; if you make a mistake you admit it, even if it is uncomfortable. Being authentic does not mean that we have to show everyone the color of our underwear, or advertise every feeling, thought or neurotic tendency. It means foremost to be honest and OK with ourselves.

And it doesn't mean we practice brutal honesty and forget compassion.

***

A lovely gentleman kept making advances and repeatedly invited me to go out with him. I found myself unable to tell him that I wasn't interested in him. You know this experience: when you give gentle signals, but the receiver doesn't pick up on them and you are tiptoeing around in order to not offend someone? I was uncomfortable and did not know what to do. When he knocked on my door again I wanted to pretend that I was not home. But instead I opened the door and sat down with him at the table. Over a cup of black tea I told him how I appreciated him, which was true. And I said, "I am not going out with you because I do not want to be in an intimate relationship with you. It isn't right in my heart and there is nothing wrong with you."

I made sure to check in with him and asked, "What are you experiencing when I tell you this? I want to know, because I care." He replied, "I feel sad. And I am relieved you are honest with me, that you care enough to check in with me." Of course he was disappointed, but I had not rejected him as a person and so he felt respected; and after a while we became friends.

***

But what happens, when another reacts with defensiveness and attacks you instead? Do you pull up your guard, shoot the guns, or turn into a doormat? How do you relate and not get caught in the reaction trap? As always, to break the reaction chain, slow down. Pause. Notice your breath and body sensations first. Give presence and acknowledgement to your feelings. And then respond in a way that feels authentic, empathic in the present moment.

In this situation I probably would have said: "I hear that you feel upset. I understand that it is not easy to receive this news." Let there be space for the other person to breathe and respond. Maybe they will settle down, maybe not. If they go on with attacks, it's time to pack your bags and leave with a clear slate. (More on conflict and the messy relationship realm in the "Resonance Communication for Every Season" chapter.)

No matter what occurs, show up as a real human being in relationships

But, why risk rejection, judgment, hurt or discomfort? Through vulnerability, authenticity and transparency we step beyond the game of fear and thereby discover strength, connection and love. It's a way toward liberation. You are available to be loved for who you really are and you come to accept others as well, as they are. If people like you only for the show, what happens in the evening when you walk home? You are alone. What use is it to be accepted for a mere façade? Then you have to run away each time someone comes too close, so he does not see you beyond the mask you wear. How long can we keep it up without becoming an unhappy pretzel? Being real draws people who are authentic and grows trust and emotional safety among each other. Once again—more love and fun goes around. And the interesting thing is that the more vulnerable and authentic you are in relating, the more acceptance toward yourself and others is happening. Connecting then flows naturally, because we do not need to resist our humanity, and get to enjoy each other.

Vulnerability and authenticity are such loyal friends; they never lie to you nor leave and betray you. Yes, sometimes those companions can be uncomfortable to be with and they won't let you escape into delusion land. It's a practice to stay true, regardless of what another person does or says. But, if your deepest commitment is to truth you will have the strength, clarity and empathy to show up with integrity. Let this always be your primary relationship, above and beyond all else.

Being transparent, authentic and vulnerable is anchored in the truth of what is presently happening in you and with each other. This is a "we" based relationship, which includes you, the other person, the connection and that which carries your ship—Love.

It seems like a lot to navigate. Let's make this simple.

Love in Action

1. Return over and over to what is happening in the present moment. Keep turning toward vulnerability, authenticity and transparency. And let love have the final word.

2. Notice how you feel and acknowledge that. Notice what your experience in relating is right now. Take full ownership, without placing blame or shame. Drop the wording, "You made me feel..." or "It's because of you that I am upset," instead say, "I feel upset." Stay close to your own experience and expand into the vast space around you that is you as well.

3. Remember, the other person may experience something entirely different than you. Include that so you can relate in the "we" space with each other.

4. Communicate what you experience and what is happening in the present tense without judging, trying to fix or explain anything, or to be right. For example: "I notice there is tension between us. Do you experience this too right now?"

   "I feel afraid and experience resistance in this moment. My body is so tense and I feel at a loss about what to do. And how are you?" Or: "I am so in love with you, I just want to be alone and snuggle with you right now. Would you like that?"

5. Be curious and discover how your conversation wants to unfold from here.

Expanding your courage to be real:

What are you trying to hide, even from your friends? Maybe it is loneliness, insecurity, shame, fear, habits, your longing, dreams, your hopes... Take a risk, and the next time you meet your friend, share that. For example, "I am excited to see you. I feel afraid to be judged, when I tell you how lonely I feel these

days. But I want to be real with you because you matter to me."
Notice what happens in your relationship then.

*Take a risk friend, reveal yourself and play with us for real in this one
wild field of love.*

6. Bread and Chocolate

Healthy ingredients for happy relating

Love is cooking in this kitchen. Bread is offered for daily sustenance, filling the tummy and soul, if it is real and healthy. Chocolate gives deliciousness with a taste of lusciousness. A feast awaits you at the table of relating. Come and enter, friend.

I'm hosting one of many gatherings in my center. The living room is spacious, with room to dance and move. Where is everybody then? As usual, they're crammed in the kitchen, where the food is, intimacy and connection always seems to occur. Twenty people are sitting around the table. I don't know how everyone does it, but spirits are high and the conversation's lively, without any artificial stimulants. Did the chocolate cake in people's bellies create such exuberance? Perhaps the pasta did the trick; its disappearance apparent by a large empty bowl.

My kitchen is buzzing and vibrant as a beehive; people are laughing. Have you noticed that relationships quite often spark in kitchens, where nourishment is found? The delicious smells draw people like a magnet, unless you've burnt your cookies. (I often did, much to the dismay of my daughter, who in response to my disasters became the best cookie baker I've ever known.)

Some kitchens are inviting; others are not so welcoming. What makes the difference, if we don't consider the architecture? I have feasted in the tiniest kitchens and felt at home, and I've visited the fanciest kitchens where I felt cold in body and soul. I still remember a family of five in Ireland, who had only two rooms in their farmhouse—a bedroom and a kitchen to share. There were four chairs so one child sat on someone's lap while a basic breakfast was served. What made it so good that I did not want to leave their kitchen? The warmth this family exuded, the care they put into the food. With utmost sincerity they

340

offered me one of the precious eggs from their hen. Each egg was treasured, three a day could not feed the family. By sharing this meal I felt honored as their guest.

Do you have bread and chocolate at home for your partner and friends?

"Is your kitchen a welcoming place?" I asked a friend, to which he replied: "What in the world are you talking about? What have kitchens, bread, and chocolate to do with relationships and love?" Well, everything really (I would include chili too). Take this as a metaphor. What ingredients do you have in your kitchen, that grow healthy relationships? Bread, chocolate, spices, flour, greens? Do you live on and share mainly shrink-wrapped, frozen, canned or fast foods? Is there food rotting at the bottom of your refrigerator?

What nourishment do you offer to your relationships? Is your basket filled with delicious apples of kindness, or is one moldy apple of nastiness hiding among them? Or do you walk with an empty basket, taking only from others, like the blue jay I'm watching from my window, who swoops down to steal the egg from the nest of the little dove? Some people delight in sharing the exquisite wine of genuine love; others offer the cheapest version of themselves. What do you put on the kitchen table for your guests? We all have goodness in us, and we can learn to bring forth our best without perfection.

It's useful to inquire honestly how we show up in our relationships and take stock of the ingredients we use in our kitchens. We may discover jars that need filling and containers that need to be emptied. Like baking bread, it requires labor to provide what has substance for the way we relate.

Our supercharged, consumer-oriented culture promotes cheap sex, fast food, instant intimacy, and quick results, without using our heart or our hands. No wonder people experience emptiness—nothing satisfies, and hunger growls for what is real. Superficial relationships are like fast food; if we don't invest time and energy we're left with an empty belly and soul. A homemade meal, made from scratch and with love, gives the message, "I value you, myself and our relationship." The quality of a relationship is determined by how we show up and what we give to it. When we offer resources, skills, care and labor, we grow love.

Being able to offer real bread is a basic necessity for any relationship. The natural texture and healthy grains contain a filling richness; unlike Wonder Bread, which—if squeezed—turns into a small ball and tastes like plastic in the mouth. Wholesome bread is like the ground we stand on, it is attained through integrity and commitment. Do you offer the substance of consideration and care toward your relationships, even when inconvenient? Or do you behave as less than you are, displaying a wrapper without content? Nobility isn't found in expensive silver forks or a delectable fancy meal. A noble heart shows through even in the attentive way we prepare a meal as simple as rice and beans.

Of course we may crave something sweet and delicious. Chocolate is the ingredient of my heart. It always turns me on. I like the raw, rich dark, organic chocolate sweetened with coconut crystals or honey. What are your favorite treats? It tells me what makes your mouth water and the flavors of love you enjoy.

Chilies represent the fire of passion; fiery when they touch the tongue. They must be delicately handled. Too much intensity burns up relationships like a wildfire leaving nothing in its wake. But without passion you have no flame to cook what feeds more than the body and inspires the soul.

There are plenty of spices for tastes, seasons and reasons to choose from. Each person has a different cooking style and the usual dish they make in relationships. But it might be fun to amp up our creativity in this area. Some people tend to cook very plainly, with salt and pepper only. You might want to explore adding spices for varied flavors; love isn't so bland, and relationships have rich tastes. Let your senses take hold of you and guide your choices. And what kind of spice would bring forth the sensual nature of your mate or yourself? Explore adding a new ingredient from your repertoire. Certain chefs overcook their meals, so keep things fresher. Maybe you tend to over-spice the food; then what is it like to allow the straightforward taste of vegetables to take precedence? How about getting into that avoided issue and conflict no one wants to talk about? What might it be to show up more authentic with another, to speak what you have always wanted to say?

A water bottle with purity of intent is another basic ingredient to place on the table of relationships. The simple intent to show up with love is enough. It helps to be honest about what we want, even the desires and hidden intentions we might not want to admit to ourselves.

Yet, truth and clarity allow our relationships to grow.

You might add flowers to your salad, and a tad of vanilla in your dessert, to celebrate beauty and sensuality in your relationships. If you wish to keep it simple, by all means do, just add love and attentiveness—magic ingredients when preparing the food in relating. And a song or prayer infuses your feast with luscious blessedness.

Quantity is not as important as quality. Loving one person is the work of a lifetime. Loving our partner, a child, friends, humanity, all are equally valuable. May our kitchen table be welcoming to all and may our food be an offering of true quality and nourishment. Mixed with a dash of exuberant joy. By the way, bread and chocolate are always good to carry with you and share in company.

General Cooking Tips:

Few of us are experts in the field of interpersonal relationships and parenting. If you want to improve your cooking skills for relationships, continue to educate yourself. Cookbooks on the matter come in handy, as do relationship and parenting courses. With practice the apprentice becomes a master, one who can truly create a five-course dinner and dance flamenco afterward.

Scrumptious meals can be created by cooking together. Too many cooks do not spoil the joy of a tasty meal as each contributes with their talents and gifts. If we apply curiosity and are willing to learn, we expand our usual repertoire. It can be boring to always fry eggs for lunch, to relate the same way by using our old familiar recipes. Branching out, discovering new ways of relating, and taking risks is a wonderful adventure into kitchens where you've never ventured before. What kinds of chocolate or bread, what new tastes might be awaiting you? What new meals might you be able to provide once you expand your list of kitchen ingredients?

Wafting aromas of rich and delicious smells from a restaurant kitchen draw travellers without elaborate advertisement or a big show. Our healthy instincts and bellies tell us when we taste real food. Sometimes we have to reawaken our senses and relearn what is good and beneficial to eat and serve. Just eat more of what is nourishing, become familiar with what is truly satiating in daily relating. May you offer this magic to all you meet in your life's kitchen, with real bread and chocolate (and chili too).

Bon Appetite. Happy cooking and relating!

Love in Action
A general checklist for your relationship kitchen

Use this overview to stock up on healthy foods, and to clean out rancid toxins in old jars.

1. Basic ingredients for healthy relationships
Always have bread, chocolate, fresh water and greens on hand. Replenish and fill up jars and cubbies for happy relating with the following items:

Express love bountifully: Fill up a whole cupboard with varied potions, condiments and tastes. Express yourself in a thousand and one creative ways.

Presence: Being truly here with another person is a gift and a basic ingredient where actual relating happens.

Realness: When I am authentic with you, you don't need to figure me out. I do not play strange games with you, and you can be yourself as well. Don't fake it, keep your relating real.

Politeness: Once I heard the comment, "If people could just be polite we would have no war." It might be so; let's begin in our own home.

Appreciation: Make a big jar full of cookies and chocolate. Hand out for free and lavishly. (For practice, see the next chapter, "Watering the Flowers Not the Weeds.")

Acceptance: I accept you as you are. This is the basic bread to bake for everyday.

Thank-you: Make a major jar of it and express gratitude frequently for the little and big things another gives or does.

How are you? Inquire about the other with genuine interest and listen attentively. This builds connection.

I am sorry: I admit that I made a mistake; I apologize with sincerity; I am willing to set it right.

Responsibility: I take one hundred percent responsibility for my behavior and attitudes.

Listening: Real listening is an art to learn and a great gift to offer. (See Chapter 8 in Part III on communication.)

Accountability: Keep your word and follow through. This grows trust. If you have to change things, check in with the other person first.

Consideration: How is this for you? How my actions and behaviors affect you is important, because you matter as much as I do.

Celebrating: Each drop of goodness is worthy to be acknowledged and to be celebrated.

Encouragement: You can do it. I believe in you. You did this well already.

Openness: I am open to your world and engage you with my heart.

Curiosity: An attitude of discovery to get to know the other.

Vulnerability: I share from my heart; when hurt I speak it without defense and attack. I allow myself to be seen as I am, including being tender. When you are vulnerable, I am gentle with you.

Commitment: I commit to a relationship. I keep my word, I follow through in action, I deal with the consequences of my choices.

Seeing the goodness: Noticing what is good about another person, even with the smallest sign.

Sincerity and integrity: I put my heart in all my actions, and do my best to walk true, even if I stumble at times.

Honesty: A crucial ingredient for basic bread.

Care: I care about your well-being as a fellow human being.

Share: I give from my resources of time, food, love and cake freely. I receive gifts graciously from others too.

Spontaneous acts of beauty and kindness: Find creative ways to beautify your environment and your relationships, and spread acts of kindness like flowers.

Enjoyment: Not doing "busy" but simply being together nourishes relationships. Enjoying each other's company can be easy. Revel in each other's presence; nothing needs to be perfect for us to savor maybe our last moment we have together.

Humor and fun: Playing together fosters joy and helps us to take ourselves more lightly. Laughter and happiness lifts the clouds and brings a ray of light right onto the table of love!

Fill up jars with heaps of the above ingredients. Use abundantly. Refresh daily. Snack on those ingredients yourself as much as you want or long for. No danger of getting sick on these, especially when you share.

2. Poisons jars to empty

It's useful to do a regular spring-cleaning of hidden or obvious habits we have established over time. Some ingredients in our kitchen not only create bad smells and tastes, but are toxic in relationships.

Violence: Toxic and destructive in every way.

Deceit and Betrayal: These two usually walk hand in hand. Both kill trust in relationships.

Me, myself and I: This stance creates a lonely and self-centered world called sucker-doom or vampire land.

You are my all: I use you as my drug of choice and the god I worship. Until you fall from the pedestal when you won't provide what I expect. Then I treat you like dirt on the bottom of my shoe.

Judgments: We all make them. Problem is, you are usually wrong. Why? Because judgments stem from fear. They serve as a wall between you and the other. They are a defense against intimacy and connection. Look what's hiding behind them.

Control: An unfortunately familiar way of non-relating.

Defensiveness and attack: Common backyard poison. Highly addictive; never offers a good solution or a healthy connection.

Refusal to take responsibility: Dumping emotional garbage and projecting on another backfires. Best to get one's own trash can.

Withdrawal: Silent punishment frequently used as an emotional escape from relationship.

Lies and fakeness: Charming and playing games with another might get us what we want in the short run, but it leaves an empty, nauseating taste. And it bounces back to us sooner or later. Be assured.

Using for advantage: Treating people like objects for the purpose of advancing one's career, getting money, sex, etc. is a sure path to isolation.

Trying to change and fix: Always the other person of course. Give it up. It never works, and no one will feel loved anyways.

Dripping niceness: The overly sweet and pink covering of fear. Better to admit when scared or angry.

Criticism: Even though we might be experts at this, use sparingly, if ever. It undermines another's self-esteem. Constructive feedback is different.

Rejecting and degrading: Can be underhanded and is harmful.

Threats, force and manipulation: Trying to get what we want at the cost of the relationship, another and love. If used, we lose.

Resentment: Infects all our relations. Non-forgiveness harms you the most.

Blame: I keep you at a distance with labels. I'm afraid of intimacy and connection. Blame says: It's all your fault and you are bad.

Fault and "what you did wrong" approach: A very tedious job without any advantages. Causes frequent headaches and fights.

Avoidance: Conflicts and misunderstandings happen. Just deal with them straight instead of bailing out.

I am better and you are lesser: Or the other way round. Both feel equally rotten and increase lack of self-worth on both sides.

I am right and you are wrong: Same as above.

Passive aggressiveness and revenge: If angry be direct. Revenge does not lead to long-term satisfaction; we pay for it triplicate in the end.

Gossip: Stabbing others with a knife in the back. Don't stoop that low.

Perfection trip: Nobody, including you, is ever good enough. Constant nagging and struggle is assured.

Sweating the small stuff and pettiness: Produces nonstop unhappiness and causes uptightness. Keeping tabs of who did what, and giving only as much as was given to you, is such a sad way of living.

You know which jars above need to be emptied in your kitchen, which foods have gone bad, and which ingredients are poisonous. Clear your kitchen of toxic materials. It makes everyone feel better, including you. The more we fill our kitchen jars with healthy ingredients the more we experience joy and well-being. We become wonderful cooks in the land of love and enjoy the feast of nourishing relationships. I know, relating is a two-way street. But you make yourself available when you clear your end of it and provide a healthy meal.

7. Watering the Flowers Not the Weeds

The ole critic and its entourage don't live here anymore

Valentine's Day is a big deal in the US and I had an idea. Many people could do with a dose of love, especially on a day when feeling left out, forgotten, unappreciated or unseen can be even more accentuated. With some friends I made little note cards. On each we wrote a statement such as, "You are important and precious."

I walked to the grocery store, and hid some of these cards between the flour and cookies, since this is where people often venture when they need a taste of sweetness in their lives. I stopped by the coffee shop, slipped a note between the croissants, quietly watched. Soon a young girl pulled on the sleeve of her mother, who looked rather sad and exhausted, and called out, "Mom, there's a note for you that says, 'You are special and beautiful.'" Her mother smiled and the clouds of worry left her face. I continued to watch as people found the handwritten notes, and saw how their spirits were uplifted.

I had prepared one large note on green construction paper for those who probably wouldn't get any Valentine's Day card. I placed it on a shabby redwood table in a public area in my town, put an empty beer bottle on top, and waited behind the corner to see what would happen.

Sure enough, three homeless men soon showed up, advancing toward their usual afternoon spot in the sun. One, a long-bearded man in a worn grey coat, lifted the colored card and read out loud: "You matter. I believe in you." *Cool,* said his companion. One wiped his eyes. Each took the hand-painted card and read it again and again, as though it were a priceless gift.

All the smiles on strangers' faces, reacting to these simple but heartfelt notes, made it for us the best Valentine's Day ever.

***

Now, I didn't grow up with this tradition. And I certainly didn't grow up learning about the joy that people get from expressions of appreciation. In fact, in Germany (where I was raised) the ingredients we most commonly blended into our relationships were criticism and judgment—to be applied as often and as much as possible. That formula has since spread; you can get it for free pretty much anywhere. We were taught that these attitudes would help us grow, make our children and partners change, and create a better world for all. But it never did, and the desired results never appeared. Quite the opposite: the nauseating blend left everyone worse off. If ingredients in the food make us sick, why would we continue to use them? If we pour poison on a plant what's the wonder, when it shrivels up and even dies?

Long-standing habits tend to stick around, even if the outcome consistently produces suffering. This is where facing reality becomes our friend: criticism and judgment never offer the results we want in our relationships.

Let's look at what happens to our partners, friends and coworkers when we pull out the ole critic. When, say, we repeat like a parental parrot, "You never do the dishes—you are *so* lazy!" Since, of course, that's never inspired a partner or child to do more, we try repeating it more often and more loudly. Believe me, I've tried this. With my child. The outcome? My daughter started avoiding not only the kitchen sink, but me, as well. I got the message after a while.

After all, how do *you* feel when someone talks in that way at you? And how does your body feel when you speak in the cold and uptight tone in which we usually launch judgment? I'd bet that unhappiness expands, a frown crinkles on the face, the desire to attack and defend rises, and maybe tears flow.

Have any of us *ever* performed at our best...

... when a teacher was handing out a daily dose of this harsh formula and told you, whether in words or actions, that you just didn't get it, that you just didn't have it in you? As a child this can make you feel like a failure. You drag your heels on the way to class, find that you have trouble waiting until school is over, and dream about some other time and place. It might be that sport just isn't your area of strength. But when we are subjected to constant critical remarks, our performance grows even worse. We do not learn under such conditions, but become contracted and the brain cannot think, due to basic lack of oxygen. The result? We scrape by at best.

This old-fashioned recipe of pointing out what's wrong—of picking, nagging and criticizing to get rid of unwanted behavior—parallels the way we tend to approach weeds: attack, poison, kill them. Apply this to relationships. Has this formula ever worked to build peace at home or increased the experience of happiness? Actually, has anyone changed for the better? The reality is: this approach leaves only miserable humans and failed relations in its wake.

We have the nourishment for healthy relationships available. Some ingredients we may acquire through learning, while others are innate qualities already within us. Relationships are like gardens with flowers and weeds. We can call the weeds the unhealthy ways we relate that cause suffering. "He never comes home on time for dinner and he just doesn't understand me. She always wears the worst perfume in town. My kid always leaves dirty clothes everywhere and puts boogers under the chair. He is such a slob. She is too emotional." (Note the "always" and "never" and the degrading labels.) We have long lists of types of weeds that range from just plain annoying to not acceptable, to those to be entirely eradicated. Out come the clippers, the weed whacker and the toxins that kill them—once and for all. Only thing is, the herbicides leave the ground poisoned and drained of nutrients. The individual plant might die, but the weeds come back anyway. Let's put the old toxins away in our relationship gardens and learn new ways. It's more enjoyable, and ultimately, far less work.

Healthy relating is like organic gardening

What kinds of plants live in your relationship gardens? What personality type is your mate, friend, or coworker? Inward and quiet? Socially active? A culture follower or nature lover? It helps to recognize what kind of person we are relating with, because then we are able to understand which nutrients this plant needs, and where and how it grows best. A social butterfly won't do too well living far off in the wilderness, even with the most wonderful mate. A child who likes adventures needs a stimulating environment, while a quiet one can easily be overwhelmed with too much input and activity. A soft and gentle person won't respond well when you get too forceful; he or she will most likely withdraw. We do not water or fertilize a flower the same way as a tree, we don't plant a cactus in rich soil, nor do we place vegetables in sand. Get to know a person; he or she is certainly different than you.

And which flowers do you wish to grow in your relationships? Maybe qualities such as intimacy, caring, understanding and a sense of responsibility. Behaviors such as helping to wash the dishes or cleaning up? Let the focus be on what needs strengthening. Then the inquiry would be like this: What can I do to grow intimacy in my marriage? How can I bring forth more understanding between us? Pay attention to the qualities that are *already* present in the relationship, like shared fun, lively communication, or interest in each other's well-being. Water them by acknowledging and appreciating. This way, you support what you wish to grow.

What is already here and alive in your garden? One way to find out is to ask: what would you miss if this person wasn't in your life? Maybe your mate isn't the best at cleaning the bathroom, but expresses his affection by bringing you flowers or fixing your car. Perhaps your friend cooks delicious meals for you when you visit, or your child infuses the house with exuberance, or your coworker often brings you coffee and cares enough to ask how you are—and means it. Look for all the ways your partner is already expressing love in their own way, even in tiny amounts. It can be a revelation after years of living together. Instead of taking things for granted, pay attention and celebrate what is here. Appreciation fills the garden with a special glow, after all, we never know how long a gorgeous flower blossom will stay with us.

What do you wish to grow more of with your friend, child or spouse? Acknowledge what your friend or partner gives you that you would like to see blossom yet more. Maybe you want the other person to be more considerate of your needs. Of course ask for what you want, but also acknowledge when your mate actively considers you. I call this approach noticing the glass as half full (even if it's a drop, use what is there to grow more). For instance, even if it's difficult for your child to learn to make her bed in the mornings, at the times when your boy or girl does remember, point it out and express your approval. Most likely they will do it more often. Watch what happens in your relationship garden when nourished with doses of encouragement and appreciation.

Focus on strengthening and feeding plants and people with organic fertilizer, watering them neither too much nor too little. Some will need more sunlight and special care than others. If we tend to the needs of each particular person or relationship though, it will flower. This does not mean we deny the presence of weeds. But when we don't feed and water the weeds, they won't grow as tall or take up as much space. We acknowledge the weeds as part of our garden without letting them overtake it. They have their place in life.

The friend who talks a lot, as annoying as that can be, might be the easiest person for others to connect with. The person who prefers solitude over parties is perhaps able to understand another in a deeper way. The student, whose academic performance is low, might be the one who soars artistically. What is considered by some as a useless trait can be recognized as an important quality by others. If nurtured, a unique characteristic could become the most beneficial plant in the garden.

Watering the flowers rather than the weeds means that we offer more positive regard to the qualities of others and focus on valuing what is already good and healthy in our relationships. Weeds such as inappropriate or destructive behavior can then be addressed more easily, without mowing over the entire person or eradicating the whole relationship—even if we decide to take a separate path in life.

As always, both plants and people grow better in the presence of love. It is as essential as the soil, the rain and the sun. May we tend well to our gardens, enjoy and celebrate what is already alive and full between us, and grow together in love.

With all this fun, Mr. Judge and the ole critic might just pack their bags and leave town.

Love in Action

Daily feeding and watering of relationships

Presence: The best and strongest fertilizer for our garden is to be present with another. This is easier said than done. Please go to the "Connecting for Real" chapter to explore this rich field further.

Appreciation: Appreciating is a way of seeing, an ability to find goodness right here. The simple practice of giving voice to appreciation easily brings forth wonders, and increases the level of well-being in relationships. Most important is that you are genuine. We can express appreciation of both qualities and actions. "I appreciate your beauty." "I appreciate that you gave me a hand with this car issue." Don't wait to offer appreciation until another performs perfectly according to your opinion—that day will never come. The garden blooms in the summer, in winter it has its own beauty; it would be useless to lament that the tree bears no fruit during the colder season.

Acknowledgement: Acknowledging how the world of another person is, without trying to change or label it, increases connection and understanding. "Sounds like you've had a hard day... I hear how important it is to you, that we all travel to meet your parents for Christmas..." This doesn't imply that you agree, you simply acknowledge how things are in the other person's world; what they are experiencing. If this is done without judgment, you'll often notice the other person exhibiting a sense of relief as they feel understood, seen and therefore met. Practice daily.

Gratitude: Receiving and giving "thank-you" fills us up. Every day we can easily find numerous reasons for thanking people. For someone carrying our bags, opening a door, making a meal or preparing a table. You can spend the whole day with "thank-you" on your lips. Be fed by taking in what's good, and others will feel nourished too.

Boundary: Sometimes we need to set a clear boundary, especially if another person tramples through our garden without much consideration. A "no" toward what is toxic and destructive is crucial. Boundaries foster respect. However, there is a distinct difference between setting a healthy boundary and a hardened barrier that comes from a closed heart.

Requests: "I have a request. Would you please pick up your socks, they are creating an awful odor throughout the house?" Requests include respect and do not carry criticism for another person. Never attack the person, but address the behavior!

Celebration: Celebrate each flower that blossoms, each little seedling that makes it into the light. Celebrate each time you discover what is alive and precious in your relationships. Flowers do not last forever, we might as well rejoice whilst they are in bloom.

Read the next chapter "Resonance Communication for Every Season" on how to deal with weeds and to nourish the flowers.

Enjoy growing healthy and happy plants in all of your relationships!

8. Resonance Communication for Every Season

A language that connects

Sixteen-year-old Piedro already speaks four languages and his Italian family, crowding the little cottage in the green hills of Tuscany, communicates in a mix of Italian and English with me. I have to laugh. Everyone, from the grandmother, to papa and mama, uncle and aunt, are talking with a good dose of emotion all at once. What a lively buzz fills the living room. But, how do you understand a word in this chaos? It doesn't matter really, so much warmth and aliveness exudes from this group and it fills the soul. And when they argue with gesticulating hands and raised voices, it's loud, but not scary. Like the music suddenly turned into staccato reaching final crescendo and then it's peaceful again. Throughout the entire performance they stayed connected with each other. No one disappeared, even when it got heated and intense.

***

The language of heart and dynamic presence, encoded in all living beings, carries the thread of intelligence that connects us. From an early age, while listening intently to animals and plants during my adventures in nature, I discovered this. I learned to communicate with unseen beings in stillness. Wide open in body, mind and heart the song of love flowed and I heard words of truth that made all the difference in my life. I realized that these same principles work for communicating with people. And I took every single training I could get my hands on to learn and refine the skills to communicate with diverse people in a connected way.

You know this feeling, when you share and your friend gives you her full attention, as if every word you speak matters to her? A sense of satisfaction arises, when you get your point across to your boss. Or when you listen so deeply to your mate that you hear the song of his soul. And what a relief, when you have resolved a long-standing conflict, because you found a way to communicate with and not against your partner.

We communicate nonstop, through the body, mind, emotions, energy and our soul. Our repertoire to be in resonance is rather limited though. We may use our mind to say the words, but emotionally we are disconnected from them. Someone says, "I love you," and doesn't feel a thing. You sense the emptiness. Or your body is a knotted ball of tension, when you reach with soothing words to your frightened child. That little one feels it and cannot relax. Or you say the right words, which are meant to come across as friendly, but inwardly your fury is boiling. What do you think is heard? What our energy, bodies and emotions speak always infuses each word. That is why we need to engage all of our instruments and align them so we can communicate in a connected way. Then we can play in harmony, creating music of the stars together.

May our word become flesh and our flesh become word

The sound of pleasure purring in my lap is from a long-haired black street cat; the circle of communication is easy and satiation fills us, as our bodies speak by touch. The sprouting birch tree's leaves are stroked by gentle summer winds, and caressing a woman's face as she walks by. What is the song of the wind speaking to you? And what are you sounding out into life right now? Have your lips uttered in the wee morning hours the melody of love or did they begin the day with a trail of endless worry and misery? The voice of mystery, truth, a deeper knowing is revealed through and around us every moment; touch, movement, images and words speak it if our ears can hear. These are the colors and seasons of light, woven into the fabric of time and space.

Before the word there was light and shining darkness—pure energy from which poetry, song, books and communication emerged. The fine craft of language is a tool. In the hands of a master it transmits the vibrant resonance of our living presence— uplifting, awakening, igniting and connecting us. We commune to bridge worlds or we use the word to destroy what has taken form. One word has the power to crush or enlighten us.

Most of the time, however, we don't communicate, but interpret what has been said based on our background, experiences and cultural conditioning. And then we wonder why we can't find a way to each other. But people of every creed and color are longing to be heard, seen and truly met. Resonance communication makes this possible. It is a language that connects us, flying on the wings of love and presence, to carry our innermost message across the worlds.

It takes a bit of relearning, since most of us have grown accustomed to a way of non-communicating, which leads to suffering and mounting misunderstanding. It's like playing the violin upside down and blowing the trumpet in all the wrong ways. It hurts more than the ears, when we do not know how to play our instrument in the grand orchestra of life. So often we use language as a way to manipulate, attack, defend, cover up, exclude, belittle, shame, degrade, lie, pretend, exploit, deny, fight, hide—all the many unconscious forms of so-called "normal" communication that divide and inflict harm, which block the sound of truth.

Especially now, in the age of globalization, we need constructive communication tools that create bridges across diverse worlds. We are dealing with complex issues, because our lives have become more intertwined, like interreligious and interracial marriages, merged families and changed structures of relationships. The level of isolation and the obvious need for more compassion in our world is acute. In a time such as this—when the Internet connects virtually every country and person, when employees from diverse cultures work together in one company, when international politics and economies affect us locally—we urgently need a form of communication that works from the inside out.

Our relationships depend on excellent communication skills, which we can apply for all seasons, not just on a sunny day, when we are having a nice dinner and agree with each other. Present, dynamic and heartfelt communication makes the difference—even when you experience challenges at work with your coworkers and boss, when we encounter a heated summer or icy winter in our intimate relationship, when we need to perform as a team during a major crisis, or deal with international or home-based conflicts. A language that connects always works.

Focusing our way of communicating on what is essential helps to truly hear one another, to speak authentically, to deal with conflicts constructively, to awaken together, to express love freely and enjoy life together. Communicating skillfully supports you to bridge the gap between different worlds, to work effectively in a team, to access greater intelligence together, so we can find ingenious solutions to the most pressing issues of our times.

Resonant communication leads us beyond projection and reaction into the blossoming of intimacy and communion. It's the language of embodied love.

Love in Action

Language skills to refine your communication instruments: Be forewarned, this is a long practice portion. I recommend that you take it in smaller doses and apply these in your interactions right away. In that way it's not just a practice, but becomes part of your relating foundation.

Principles for resonance communication:

Use the practices for loving presence from the chapter "Foundation Stones" as your basis. Acknowledge the chatter of mind and put any issues aside for later. Focus on what is alive, present, as well as the stillness, deeper than words. Let your heart soften; feel into the love here and now. Open with curiosity toward the other person's world. Listen with your whole being. This isn't about you. Refrain from giving advice, lecturing or comparing the other's story with your own. Focus on hearing the words, the content, the emotions, and the body... and then dive deeper. What is being spoken within and below all the words and content? What is essential? See the person behind the words and open wide to hear their unique song. The same principle applies to hearing your own wisdom, to understanding an animal, a plant or the holy ones whispering into your sweet ear.

Use discrimination and check in:

All too often we mix our own projections, hurts, imaginations, what we want and what we don't want to hear. Notice and then stop for a moment. Self-awareness is the key. Check in with yourself and ask, "What is my story, trigger or imagination, and what is actually being said?" If you are unsure always check in with the speaker, and ask, "Do I understand this correctly? Is this what you meant?"

Go for connection:

When you talk, make connecting with the other person number one. Put that before any content, information or issues. Why? Because connection is the foundation, without it your content won't land and the issues won't be resolved. Helpful opening words include greeting a person by looking them in the eyes and asking, "How are you today?" or stating, "Thank you for coming to the meeting." The next sentence should be a contact statement. (Please read on for these.) Give space for others to speak if you usually deliver monologues. If you are a more quiet type and usually withhold, risk by speaking more. A conversation is a dance, and if it isn't, nobody will feel fulfilled.

- The Golden Keys

The first golden key:
I repeat this on purpose: always connect with yourself and the other person, before you deliver any information, content or advice. If you do not connect with the person and you are not present, whatever content you wish to convey will not be heard and is frequently misunderstood.

Depending on the situation or the person, you can use both verbal and nonverbal communication to connect. With a friend, a gentle touch, a hug and the question, "How are you?" often initiates contact. With a coworker you might want to look him in the eyes, smile, be present, and say something like, "It's good to see you this morning." Let it be simple, genuine and from the heart.

Remember you want to address the person in the suit, not the suit.

The second golden key:
In every conversation and confrontation, know that someone will always be asking: *Are you listening to me? Did you hear what I have to say? Do I matter to you?* I bet you know these underground questions, murmuring within yourself when you talk with another. And like you, every person wants to be heard, seen and loved, no matter what the conversation is about. We just don't admit it out loud. We build a bridge by hearing, seeing and acknowledging people. Remember, the most important thing you can do for another human being is to validate their existence. And how do you communicate that?

Validate their experience. For example, "I hear how difficult and frustrating this job is for you if you do not have the support you need." Validation does not mean you agree with or even like what they are saying. But it does mean that you respect how they feel and think—how they experience life, even if it is different than in your world.

The third golden key:
Deep listening is the solution to many conflicts. Most of us do not listen well; we think we do but when it comes right down to it, our minds get busy with: *What am I going to say when this person has finished talking?* What's your worst listening habit? Is it interrupting, planning out what you're going to say, getting distracted—like checking e-mail or your phone—or something else? If you are engaging in these habits, bring awareness and stop yourself frequently. Take a breath, and intentionally, even if it feels awkward, simply pause without saying anything. You are resetting yourself to be able to shift. Then engage again in the conversation. Without being present, there is no one home and you are not relating. If you are here, and listen into the world of another, and come into resonance with the river that connects both of you, you might be surprised at what is revealed. You begin to see and hear life itself.

Get to know the world of another with fascination and curiosity, without judgment, interpretations, projections, should or should not, right or wrong. *I wonder how your world looks like?* The thirteenth-century poet Rumi said, "Out beyond ideas of wrongdoing and right-doing, there is a field. I will meet you there." Listen to a person, as if you are travelling into a foreign country you want to explore. You might say, "Please tell me more about how you experience this situation." Inquire and open your mind and heart to a world that is maybe vastly different than your own. It can be a lot of fun and quite fascinating to discover another person's wonders and dark valleys. Be brave, go on an adventure.

- Tune your Instrument into Resonance

The effect:
Have you noticed that the same sentence or word spoken can have a very different effect? It is the energy and the feeling that is transmitted through the words you speak, which have the most impact. When you speak "I love you" and your words are spoken from love they come alive, they touch, and move as a living testament to your beloved. When you feel angry and force nice words, it won't work. First admit to your partner that you experience anger. Then your words aren't muddled with an undertone that will put anyone off. Notice how your communication comes across to the other. Are your words received? If not, do not continue to talk at the person, but pause. You can say, "I notice that what I share isn't reaching you. Is your mind somewhere else?" Or, if you experience tension in the conversation you can always check in by saying, "I wonder what is going on between us right now?"

Does your message carry anger, even if you framed your sentence in a non-blaming way? The emotion will come across to the one who receives the delivery. The words might be kind, but if the energy contains fury this is felt. Mixed messages like these usually create confusion and misunderstandings, a sense of being out of sync, like something doesn't sit right, doesn't match up. We sense, unless we are closed down, the energy behind what is communicated. The more we can be coherent and the more our instruments are aligned, the easier we connect.

The instrument of mind:
In our culture we are used to letting the mind do the talking. So we become talking heads. Seems safer that way, except we

neither feel alive, nor do we love and relate. Notice when you are mainly using your mind to communicate. How do you experience your relationship and the other person then? Shift, include and play the other instruments you got.

The body instrument:
Practice speaking without words; let the body express what you want to say through movement and gestures. Engage with your body when you speak with people. Notice what wisdom wants to be communicated through the body. Your shoulders rise up, your breath is shallow and your face feels stiff. Fear and discomfort in the body translates into a strained conversation. Breathe, connect first and then open your mouth to speak. Our bodies are wise, they send us clear signals that a situation or person isn't quite as it seems. Listen to your body, let it speak and move more freely.

The instrument of emotion:
As we explored in other chapters, emotional intelligence plays a vital role in the language of connection. Empathy is primary for healthy relationships. Our capacity to feel and to express, without blame, shame and attack is what fosters connection with each other. To express: "I feel sad" not "you make me feel sad" is just one way to help ourselves. (Please read more about emotional intelligence in the "Connecting for Real" and "This Human House" chapters.)

The instrument of energy:
Become aware of energy and how it affects your way of relating. Notice the energy in a landscape at first. It might be tranquil in the green hills of Tuscany or it might be a buzzing energy in the city of New York. Then use the metaphor of a landscape for yourself. How is the energy right now? Peaceful, turbulent,

silent or erratic? Then attune to the landscape of another person with an open mind; what do you experience? It is important that we neither interpret nor project onto another what we imagine. Here discrimination, honesty and self-awareness come in handy. We communicate a lot through our energy. For example: I was happy, my energy felt light and so, when I talked with my father about a challenging family issue, I could communicate my point of view without attack and easily include his standpoint too. We both felt uplifted by the end of our conversation. Previously, when I had approached the issue with a pressured energy that spoke miles—"I have to get through to you"—I only created walls between us.

Heart, presence and spirit:

The ability to listen into the field of resonance, the spirit, to your heart, while being in conversation with another person, takes some practicing. When you are in touch with your essence, your communication will rise to higher ground, because it is illumined by grace. You know what to say and when, as you are connected to the deeper life song singing through you. Often when I sit with clients I listen into what spirit has to say. I tune into another person and my heart communicates what is essential, what wants to be spoken and heard. Connect, listen and then speak. This is when the magic happens with people.

When we engage all our faculties and align them with our loving presence, it is felt in our heart and gut, formed into words by our minds, and is expressed through our body, the mouth, the eyes... then the orchestra plays in unison, in resonance with all of life.

Own your experience:

Speak in "I" statements: "What I experienced when we went shopping was..." This is a nonthreatening way to communicate and leaves room for the other to have a different view and

367

experience. "I" statements make your conversation personal and lead to connection. Don't hide behind generalizations: "What you experienced when you went shopping is..." and avoid speaking for others: "What we experienced when we went shopping is..."

Where are you coming from?

Use a good dose of self-reflection in communication. Sometimes we feel like a little boy or girl and we use a child's language, such as, "You always do this and you never do that. You are mean..." When this happens just acknowledge it: "I guess my five-year-old child in me is upset." If you are talking with someone less intimate you can notice and then remember that you are an adult and ask yourself, *What is my intention in this communication?* This will help you to shift to your grown-up self.

If you think you are right and the other person is wrong, then the other person will feel that and will most likely be on the defensive. If you want to blame the other, either own up to it by using transparency (for example you say, "I want to blame you") or you refrain entirely from blaming by turning your mind toward a more constructive way of communicating. The approach, "I am right and you are wrong," or "It's all your fault," or "You *made* me feel or do it," never works. The outcome is separation in one way or another then.

- Communication to truly hear, see, accept and meet
The Magic Words:

I hear you
I see you
I am with you
I care about you or I love you
What I appreciate about you... (a quality or deed)

I request or need...
How is this for you?
What are you feeling or experiencing?

Contact Statements:
Contacting the person behind what has been said is an art and a surefire approach to connection. If your friend shares a long-winded story that puts you to sleep, look for the person who is telling the story. How does your friend feel while she is telling the story, what is her body telling you? It is important to remember that it is not your job to figure out what is going on for her, or to analyze her, or to assume anything. But instead your job is to be curious: *Who is the storyteller? How is the storyteller doing while telling the story?* Check in with your friend: "As you are telling me the story I notice how your body crouches and that your voice becomes rather quiet. Something is hard for you, hmm?" Remember you address the storyteller and the present moment. If the other person doesn't state that they are sad for example, but you sense it clearly from their facial expressions and the way they tell the story, then make a contact statement with a question mark. For example, "Feeling sad, hmm?" Contact statements are a powerful way for direct, fresh and alive communication and they always lead into connection.

The Five Gates for Speaking
- Is it true?
- Is it kind?
- Is it alive?
- Is it essential?
- Is this the right moment?

What is essential for you to say, what's on your heart? We feel drained, if we do not speak what's true, but enlivened and inspired if we share what matters most to us. Sometimes we talk on and on; we put too much fluff around the truth. Hardly anyone will get what you are really trying to say. Talking at another person is a classic one-way communication, a dead-end road. It misses the point and the other. Let there be space in your speaking, pause and make connection with the other and listen as well. Risk speaking from your vulnerability and your soul, fresh and uncensored. This is the way home into sacred communion.

Inquiry Questions for Speaking:
What wants to be spoken?
How does love want to speak through me now?
What leads us toward greater connection?
Remember: Let life and what is of essence speak through you.

The Five Gates for Listening
- Curiosity
- Discovery
- I want to get to know you
- What is alive?
- What is fresh?

Often we do not hear the other, because we are busy preparing the next thing to say, trying to defend or attack, or worrying about whether the other person likes us or not. We also compare, for example, what she shares about her ill dog reminds me about the time my dog was sick... and so we are back in our own little world and think we understand another. Far from that. Listening means to step beyond self-concern into another's experience and world. Only if we walk in the shoes of another, for at least a mile and truly hear them, do we gain some understanding.

Inquiry Questions for Listening:
What is the deeper song beyond the words that this person is sharing with me? What is spoken through these words that is essential for me to hear?

What am I not hearing that wants to be heard?

Remember: Life is speaking to you, if you are listening.

Reflective Listening Response:
This is one of the nonviolent communication tools developed by Marshall Rosenberg, which prevents misunderstandings and makes people feel heard. Reflective listening means you mirror back what you heard the other person say. It doesn't need to be the exact words, but you speak the gist of it. It will save you much trouble and unnecessary heartache in relationships and it will strengthen the connection. You will be surprised how often we hear half of what is said or we muddle it in our heads, so it means something different than what the speaker said.

"What I hear you say is..."

For example: "What I heard you say is, that you want to travel abroad and that you would love for me to take care of your dog for two weeks." You also include the feeling state of the other if he showed it: "I can hear that you feel sad to leave."

Check in: *"Did I hear this correctly or is there something else you wish me to hear?"*

- Step into Resonance Together

Communicate direct experience:
This is a profound approach, which leads directly toward connection and awakening. Begin with, "What I am experiencing right now is..." Here you include sensations, feelings, mind states and what is occurring for you in the moment. You can also begin with, "What I am aware of is..." Stay present and be curious about what is arising in the moment. Communicate

that. This allows the other person to see your world in an undefended way and feel connected with you. Then give room for the other to share what they are experiencing. Go back and forth a few times. Then, you can take it to the next level: "What I am experiencing while being with you right now is..." Hear the other person too. Then drop even deeper: "What are we experiencing right now?" and "What is happening between us right now?"

Again, this is an inquiry and discovery question, an invitation to notice what is arising between two or more people in the moment. Use curiosity and a nonjudgmental attitude and know this can take you into a surprisingly deep connection with another. This way is powerful and takes some practice and presencing.

A three-step communication formula for awake relating:
Speak what is happening in the moment without judgment: "I notice that you are touching my body."

Check if it's true to avoid assumptions and interpretations: "Is it true that you are attracted to me?"

Make a statement about where you are at: "I am happy to be your friend, and I do not want to explore any other relationship with you."

You can apply this formula to most communications. It's simple, it's easy and it works. This will save you a lot of misunderstandings, worries and troubles so common in communicating with people.

Communicating in the present: What is alive now?
What is alive about the story you want to tell? What is the flavor of your story? Maybe it feels sad. Then allow the sadness to speak through your voice, your tears, your body and words. If I admit the sadness that is present and stay close to that, then my communication is clear and not sticky.

When we talk from what is alive now, not from yesterday or fifty years ago, then our words express freshness even though we have used the same words and told the story a hundred times or more. For example, "I remember how we used to hitchhike together. Just the mere thought of us meeting again brings a smile to me right now." Don't deliver chewed gum with all sorts of hair and paper attached, but give a fresh one. Now this takes some awareness and practice of course, but so worth it because we experience a whole new level of relating, feeling even more alive, nourished and connected.

- The five A's for Resonant Communication

Awareness: Allows us to be present. "I am aware that I feel pressured to get the job done." (Read more in the "Foundation Stones" chapter.)

Acknowledgement: Validating another person and their reality is a key for connected communication. Honor what is and how it is, without fixing or employing the should not's. For example, "I hear that you feel upset with me," instead of saying, "Why would you feel upset with me?" Acknowledgement doesn't mean you agree with that person's view, it just means that you honor their experience.

Appreciation: Appreciate qualities of another, such as, "You are beautiful." Appreciate actions of another: "I am grateful that you fixed my flat tire." You can be more specific and luscious. Discover the thousand and one ways of appreciating on a daily basis and I guarantee not only you, but also others around you, will be uplifted. And best of all: It is fun! Do not forget to appreciate yourself too! (For more, see the chapter, "Watering the Flowers Not the Weeds.")

Affection: Express affection plentifully through nonverbal communication, by touch and acts. Never hold back expressing your affection verbally; it makes a positive difference for your relationships when you speak love out loud.

Acceptance: Even though you think the other person knows it or feels it, it is always better to actually say, "I accept you, just as you are." Or, "I am here for you whatever you might need to share." Or, "Your feelings are welcomed with me." Of course only say these if you mean it.

- The Do's and Don'ts

1. Your business is not to change and fix the other, but to hear and get to know another person's world and to share your world.

2. Communicate in real time: don't let any difficulties fester and do not wait to express your love.

3. Speak what you feel without blame and shame. Don't blame: "You are insensitive, controlling... You make me feel bad." Take 100% responsibility for your experience and feelings: "I feel angry... I experience fear... I am happy to be with you..."

4. Do not use manipulative language or expect another to read your mind about what you want and need. Say what you need and want directly; deliver with compassion and without coercion or hiding behind vague sentences or questions. Make clear, simple statements that reveal what is true for you. For example, "I want to be with you. Do you want to be together tonight?" Or, "I would love to go out for dinner. Would you like to come with me?" Or, "I need help. Do you have some time later today or not?"

5. Do not threaten, dismiss or disempower people, but rather make it safe for people to be direct with you. Speak your request in a way that allows the other person the freedom to respond with a "yes" or "no." For example, "Would you be willing to walk the dog?" Or, "I request that you help with the chores at home."

6. Do not criticize and judge. Speak what you would like to see more of and appreciate what is already there. "I

appreciate that you completed the project with excellence and enthusiasm. I'd like to see these qualities also expressed in other areas of your work."

7. Get off the reaction train. Refrain from attack and defensive speaking. If you do it, admit it. For example, "How dare you say this? After all I have done for you..." This is an attack that can be turned toward connection: "I feel hurt when I hear what you say. I need to take a moment first before I can reply." Or, "I notice how I want to defend myself, but what I really want is for us to connect and understand each other."

8. If you want to tell another person what bothers you or if you request a change, do not attack the person; solely refer to the specific behavior. For example: If your child does not wash the dishes properly, do not say, "You are always so sloppy." But rather say, "When you do not wash the dishes well, I have to wash them again. And I don't want to have more work." Then make a constructive request for what you want, such as, "Could you pay more attention to washing the dishes properly please?"

9. Do not gossip negatively about another behind their back nor shame them publicly. Approach the person directly and privately. If you need support ask for a third person, who does not take sides, to be present. Do not stay silent when you notice abuse. Speak up and out.

- All the What's

Avoid the "why" questions if you want to connect. "Why" questions are like closed doors, they only lead into a wall. "Why are you doing this?" Or, "Why do you not help more?" leads usually to defensiveness and/or "I don't know" answers.

Instead, use curiosity, open-ended questions, inquiry and statements that foster clarity, nonjudgmental discovery and understanding. For example, *"What would you like me to understand? What hurts you? What is your experience? What brings you joy? What do you mean by this...?"*

What happens for me in this moment is... What is arising, is triggered, touched in me is... What I enjoy... what I am aware of...

My world
What I need/want
What would help me
What I want to create is
What I hear you say is
What I experience is

Your world
What I appreciate about you is
What do you need, want, and wish for?
What can I do for you?
What would help you?

Our world
What we can do together
What would help us?
What are we experiencing in this moment?
What is alive in our relationship?
What is good between us?
What needs tending to in our relationship?
What would be most beneficial for our project or relationship?

We-Connecting language:
Some countries are more "we" centered than others. This becomes apparent in the way we use language. Healthy communication, however, is "we" oriented, it implies that both people matter in the conversation.

Inclusive language: The great "And"

This little word "and" connects not just sentences. "You like sports and I like hiking, what can we do together that we would both enjoy?" Or in an argument, "Your view is that immigrants should not be allowed in this country and mine is that they should be allowed. I am curious about your view and I would also like you to hear what my thoughts about this are." You acknowledge both worlds and unite them in one sentence. For instance, "I understand that you feel alone and I feel happy to be together in this moment with you." Or, "Your need is to go for a walk and mine is to take a nap. What are we going to do about that so that we both get our needs met?"

Inquiry:

"What are we creating here? What is happening in this group? What is the purpose of our communication? What are you aware of about the dynamics in this relationship? What would help our situation and family?" Or, "What is for the highest best for us to do?"

The word "and" as well as "we" includes you, me and far more. The moment we are fully aware that another person is here, that essence is greater than the "little me," we begin to communicate with each other. If it is all about oneself or only about the other, it is a one-way dead-end street and relating is actually not happening.

Boundaries:

For most people it is difficult to set boundaries. The usual approaches are: Set no boundaries at all, be nice, let yourself be walked over, say nothing so you won't be rejected and have no conflict. Familiar? You end up feeling resentful and disrespected and will dislike the other person very soon, and of course yourself too.

The other unhelpful way goes like this: Speak your truth without regard to the other person. Create a harsh wall of "no." This is fear rearing up, ready to attack.

Setting a boundary is best done with clear and simple communication, such as, "I don't want to share my car with you, even though I know how well you drive." Or, "I will not work longer hours without proper compensation. Can you do that or not?" Or, "You are not allowed to stay at the party later than ten o'clock, even though I understand how much you want to party till after midnight."

Conflicts and challenges:
You may want to escape, or at least avoid conflicts at any cost. Or you might be a master in covering over, not talking about this constant tension between your mate and you, or pretend the conflict doesn't exist, hoping it will go away one day by itself. But how have these approaches worked out thus far?

Instead we can normalize misunderstandings, which occur even between the best of friends. We can use any conflict as a gateway home, to connect and learn. At the root of every conflict is a call for love. Go toward that and use communication tools to navigate challenges with others skillfully. It certainly is helpful when the other person also has the capacities, but even if not, you get quite far by applying these tools yourself and cleaning up your side of the street at least.

- Basics for Conflict Resolution:
Acknowledge conflict and state intention: Sounds obvious, but this often isn't done. Without blame or judgment simply state to the person you have a challenge with this: "We have a conflict. I would like to resolve it with you." Or, "I experience a challenge with you. I would like to talk about this with you and find a way together."

Address any conflict in real time: If you let conflicts smolder for too long they fester. They do not disappear over time but will get worse. Instead, let the other person know that you would like to sit down together to resolve the matter, the sooner the better.

No text and e-mail. Meet person to person: If you have a challenge that needs to be addressed, set up a meeting on the phone or in person, where you can hear each other's voice and best see each other's face. Never share your thoughts and feelings regarding a conflict in an e-mail or text. Why? Because people don't get the emotional content and only read the words, which more often than not will be misinterpreted. And then you end up in a mess.

No blame: It takes internal discipline to refrain from blaming during arguments and conflicts. That ole language goes like this, "You made me feel angry... you never do this and always do that... you are so stupid." This kind of talk is solely pointing fingers without being vulnerable and taking responsibility. You may have your own version of defensive speaking. Check with yourself honestly by asking, *Do I want to blame the other person?* As self-righteous as we might feel about it, that it's their fault that things turned bad, we have a part to play in this. Nor put all blame on yourself. By refraining from blaming you do not add more suffering to already existing pain.

Take responsibility: Instead of shaming take responsibility for your side of the yard. For example, "When your son cut down the tree in my garden I felt very upset. It wasn't OK that he did that. And when you did not call him out on it I felt really angry with you. Now I have cooled off some and want to talk with you about it." Taking responsibility means you own up to what you experience and what you feel.

Cool off: If you are worked up and see red, you won't be able to communicate well and will only make matters worse. Literally take a time-out during a heated argument, saying, "I need to take half an hour to cool off. Is it alright with you if we meet in half an hour to talk about this?" Take a run or a shower, punch a cushion, and don't speak those words of anger. You might regret it otherwise.

Sacred pause: Two people agree to take a pause for a minute to just breathe, refraining from speaking and focusing on the breath instead. Move your body, let the energy move, make sounds instead of words. A simple pause like this enables the parties to take a different route in their communication.

Slow down full speed: When you encounter conflict, slow everything down. Emotions run high when there is disagreement, tension, etc. When we feel threatened we speed up, and then either attack, defend or freeze in our communication. When the stress button is pushed we absolutely cannot hear the other, nor speak from a centered place. We create more misunderstandings instead. The key is to slow down the breath and conversation on purpose to interrupt the vicious cycle of stress.

Power over and under: Authority issues plague almost everyone. If you communicate as the top dog, the know-it-all, the one who has to control others at all costs, know that people may do what you want but they will resist, rebel and fear you. On the other hand, if you downplay your position by communicating in submissive, unclear ways such as: "I am sorry if I say this in ways you may not like... Is this OK with you all..." you will not be respected. Speaking from an inner authority can foster connection: "I hear your view on this matter and understand that you feel strongly about it. I have a different perspective that I want to add to our discussion."

Reflective listening—rather tedious but so worth it: Even if it feels really hard to do, this provides the ground from which to resolve any conflict. (See above how to do this.) You have to be patient and diligent, especially if there is a conflict, and remember that when you speak first and do your best to really hear and acknowledge another (this doesn't mean agreeing), the conflict can be resolved. Even if the other person doesn't offer you the same courtesy, you walk away more at ease with yourself. Ideally, however, two people care enough and are willing to do the dirty work of unraveling the knots together.

Do not attack the personhood, but address the specific behavior: This is crucial when you want to resolve a conflict or you are dealing with a challenging situation or behavior. (Please see above under "Don'ts.")

Feedback sandwich:

Address the person in a constructive way, such as using the feedback sandwich:

1. One appreciation: "You work very hard and give your best. I appreciate that about you."
2. One specific behavior that you would like the person to improve or a piece that needs correcting: "I want you to pay more attention when you are invoicing our clients. Go over it several times before you send out the e-mail please." Always phrase it in a constructive way, such as stating what you want to see and refraining from pointing out what you don't want.
3. End with one appreciation or encouragement: "I know you are a fast learner and I am sure you can handle this. If you need any help, do let me know."

- Other Practical Ways for Stormy Seasons:

1. Establish a daily meditation practice and center yourself at least twice during your workday.
2. When challenges roll in: Practice grounding first, and listening, rather than reacting.
3. Use the information and practices in the "Turning Challenges into Victories" chapter on how to relate to discomfort.

4. Get real with people; be personal, as this establishes safe ground. Share with them how you feel, something about your life. Get to know the person, what they are struggling with. Hear their hopes and fears. The more real you are, the more likely it is that you can weather any storm.

5. Do not sweat the small stuff, otherwise you will be constantly worked up.

6. Use light humor, not laughing about another or downplaying an issue, but look at yourself with more lightheartedness and find what is funny in your reactiveness or the storm that is whirling around your abode.

And what about the sunny seasons?

Bask, savor and nourish the good. Communicate more frequently what is presently nourishing between you. Simple ways, for example: "I enjoy seeing our kids getting along right now." Or, "I am reveling in this beautiful moment we get to share with each other." Or, "Thank-you for coming today, you are such a help to me." Or, "I am thankful that we had those years of friendship and all that we have gone through together. I hope we have many more years to enjoy." Express what is good between you and your friend or coworker and share gratitude in your communication. It feeds your relationships with any person and during any season.

In our fast-paced technological world we succumb frequently to using short "sledgehammer" language. We have less time for lengthier conversations, for cherishing talks on a leisurely walk or over an afternoon cup of tea. However, just because we are required to express ourselves more briefly in many areas of our life, does not mean that we need to lose the richness and sophistication of language in the process. Instead, as we refine and grow our skills in communicating, the impact is deeper connection and flowering. As we learn to speak and listen to the essence we grow the field of resonance and love together. In a world where we can communicate instantly with people, let's make connecting for real a priority.

And if all of our instruments for communication become finely tuned, we are able to play together in resonance, a symphony that encompasses both challenging and glorious seasons. This does create the music of the stars and changes our world—one word and one communication at a time.

Abide in your true nature and allow the words to emerge fresh from the source into flesh. You may be surprised what you'll commune in resonance with all of life.

IV. For All

1. Loving Wild Earth

Communion with nature and living in kinship with life

There were five of us: my daughter, two friends, the captain and myself. We journeyed far into the open sea off the coast of Hawaii on a tiny sailboat, searching for the gentle giants. Our captain had been diagnosed with incurable cancer, but now was completely healed. His face lit up as he shared how swimming with dolphins and whales had cured him of an assured death sentence given to him during his last hospital visit years ago. A broad smile crossed his brown, weather-wrinkled face as he spoke of how he became friends with the dolphins, whales, turtles and even sharks. Inspired, he shared with us his intimate experience of a love flowing through all of creation that had given him new life and purpose. After his own healing he'd dedicated himself to connecting people with these intelligent animals, to inspire us to care and learn to live in harmony with the earth.

The four of us sailed in silence; our captain seemed to be listening, intuitively sensing where we would meet his friends. Suddenly, not far away, we saw spouts! Joy welled up in me, as a humpback whale pod of several mothers and their calves circled us, spouting when they rose for air. They came close to our tiny boat, rocking us in the deep sea. They were enormous; one unfortunate move could shatter our boat to pieces. But these gentle whales stayed with us for several hours, ever careful not to throw us overboard. I was awestruck being so near to them. One mother came to the side of our boat only a few feet away from where I sat. I reached with my whole body to touch her; my hand felt her skin covered with thick barnacles. I had to hold myself back not to climb onto her and ride with this magnificent whale into the horizon. Instead...

She surprised me, rising up, her eye looked directly into mine.

Our meeting was intensely intimate, I felt myself pulled into her. The whole earth was in her look, piercing my being to a far greater depth, than ever known before. The eye of this mighty whale carried stillness from the deepest place in the sea and ancient wisdom from the earth resounded through her song. It was otherworldly and profound. Sacredness moved me to tears, a connection so deep and true filled my body with the realization, that we are one with the earth and every living creature here.

Her eyes and melody carried a message: *"Help us. Carry our song forth into a world that has forgotten the beauty of the earth and how to live in kinship with us. Look with the eyes of the deep sea to remember our connection. Let your light shine bright and ignite the people to honor and love all of life."*

Everyone on the boat was stunned into silence; tears flowed like floodwaters, opening us to a greater love residing in every living being. Forever etched into my soul, I will never forget the eye and song of the whale.

***

When I've touched the dolphin's silken skin, or the fur of my horse; when I smell the sweet scent of jasmine blossoming in spring; taste crystal clear water from a mountain stream; watch a tiny seedling grow into a head of lettuce I share with friends; or hear the sound of waves lulling me to sleep at night; with all my senses engaged I experience a profound connection with all creation. I am part of the great web of life; a pulse is coursing through the banquet of manifold expressions and beauty. The earth is a living body upon which we tread. With every step she rises up to meet our feet. Have you felt this wonder?

Nature is constantly in relationship with us—when taking a shower it might not be as obvious as standing beneath a roaring waterfall. Yet, all the elements of her are living in our bodies too. How then do you relate with the river, your own body and the dark brown ground that not only holds, but feeds us too?

Since ancient times people have related to the living earth as sacred. Even science now acknowledges her to be a "living organism with its own intelligence." Without her water, air and food we cannot live. We completely depend on her sustenance, and are given it for free. She doesn't say "pay me for each breath you take, each bite you eat, each drop you drink." The soil we stand on and grow food from doesn't stop giving, unless we deplete it of nutrients.

Whether we like it or not, rain falls, lightning strikes, the moon waxes and wanes. The movements of nature have their own rhythms and ways, which we cannot control.

For far too long now, humans have used nature as a disposable commodity and treated the earth as an object to be dominated and controlled, exploited and conquered. Through this mindset and subsequent actions, much has been destroyed. Indigenous people and those who possess wisdom know a basic truth: What we do to the earth, we do to ourselves. By polluting our resources—soil, water, air—we poison ourselves and deprive future generations. The law of cause and effect is fairly easy to understand.

Now many people are waking from the spell of ignorance, realizing that we are nature, intrinsically interconnected with all species and the web of life. How can we live in attunement with the natural laws? What might a loving, intelligent relationship with the earth look like?

The ancient Ones, keepers of the earth wisdom, urge us to treat the earth as sacred, to relate with her and learn from her, to communicate with the animals and plants, to become stewards of nature and life itself. For those who walked before us, this also meant to be willing to give more than we take and offer gratitude for the sustenance we receive.

It requires effort, intelligence and care from you and me to relate wisely with the earth. We have to find solutions together and live differently, because the threat of climate change is immanent and resources are coming to an end. I wonder what Jane Goodall, one of our environment activist elders, was whispering into Greta Thunberg's ears, who is moving mountains as the inspiring leader of our younger generation. When they met at the European Convention, I imagine she said something like this: "You are so brave! Don't let them get you down. We are together in this." Never doubt that your voice and actions have an impact. They do, even if you can't always see it straight up. There is a revolution unleashing from all corners of the world and probably it's brewing in a house and heart right next to you.

We got it in us to turn this ship from total destruction, to foster ways of thriving together and enjoying the paradise this earth really is. It is here and the time is now.

***

The waves on the sea in California's Monterey Bay were calm on this sunny January day. The sky was cloudless, perfectly clear, and the air smelled fresh and crisp. A path of golden sunlight guided our boat. I was celebrating my birthday with a group of friends. Suddenly one shouted, "There, look!" as dolphins leaped out of the sea near our boat, beckoning us to play with an infectious joy; I began to laugh and giggle like a child. A little further out we saw the spouts of several majestic whales. The hand of a friend touched mine as we shared this exquisite moment in rapture of the sublime.

There were darker days; not so long ago whales were massacred until the sea was blood red. Not so long ago slaughter ships hunted them down without mercy. They were driven close to extinction. Only a few survived.

Now people come from far and wide to ride boats in this protected bay—a marine wildlife sanctuary—to enjoy and learn about these magnificent creatures. What happened? More and more people became aware and began to care. People fought tirelessly, even risked their lives, to protect whales, the dolphins, and the ocean. In time the situation changed. A movement that began with a handful of people acting from love for the earth created far more than one marine wildlife sanctuary. The protection of the oceans and our last remaining wildernesses around the world is happening globally now. People, young and old, are making a positive difference by standing up for nature with their hands and hearts. Thank you for doing your part. It matters, for the planet, for each animal, and for each of us.

Communicating with Nature

Can you imagine how life on earth would be if we learnt to communicate with plants and animals already as children in school? How would we treat nature then, if we understood her and spoke her language?

A whole world beckons, a natural way of relating with animals and plants, which paves a healthy way to live upon this earth. Our souls know the universal language of creation. Animals and plants talk with us, if we attune. When our intention is pure, connected, open in our hearts and still in our minds, we discover that we commune easily with her. Being in the wilderness, away from the noise and buzz of cities, we may be able to engage more intimately with the wild ones, returning to a deeper sense of the sacred in life.

In some indigenous cultures, communicating with animals and plants is normal. Often, when I am alone in the wilderness, animals come close to me. I feel at one with them and communication just happens then. It is not supernatural, but simple. How could it not be so, since we are the same life, just in different forms? I had to unlearn and relearn this though, since I was not brought up with this way of communing. I spent much time alone in nature, deeply listening, to be able to hear how and what a tree or a bird might speak.

Each of us has some kind of connection with animals and plants, even if latent. If you have a dog or a cat, aren't there moments when you understand your companion, without any words spoken? If you care for them well with food, right care and affection—they tend to engage with you more intimately. For some people their pet is their closest companion; they tell stories about their relationship and the love they receive from their friend. My cat used to sleep on my lap when I was meditating every morning. She recognized instantly when I was present and communicated clearly then, getting her point across with perfect timing, telling me what she needed from me (more petting or food usually), or what I most needed to hear. "Just enjoy life," she'd often say. She was a queen in her manners and domain until she died in my arms at the stout age of eighteen.

Intelligence is inherent in each living being, whether a cat, an ant, an elephant, a leaf of grass, or an acorn that knows how to grow into an oak tree.

Communicating with Plants

Plants talk with us; if we attune to them we hear and sense. If you listen with an open mind and heart to a houseplant that is not doing well and you've tried every method you know, your plant will tell you what she needs to thrive. Besides practical information, plants offer profound wisdom. Standing beneath a redwood tree you may experience its strength and peace in your body. If you relax at a river and listen to the sound of flowing water you may hear the wisdom of creation. Or your own plants might surprise you, just as the deva (a Sanskrit name for the

"Shining Ones," the intelligent spirit inherent in each plant) of the red rose bush did one lovely spring morning at my front door:

"There is no separation between us. You too are part of this creation. You breathe and live with us. What you do affects us too. As long as you believe yourselves to be separate from the living earth, so long will you destroy through ignorance. But when you awaken to our oneness, our work together will be a blessing for this earth."

As we become present to love, we enter into a magical communion with all of life, far beyond what we may have thought possible. The herb garden deva in Findhorn speaks to this:

"Sense your connection with us and we commune with you. All plants are filled with the spirit of life; realize we are one with you. But so often humans walk with closed eyes through this world of wonder, and you forget that we are alive. You forget where you come from and where you are going. We cannot forget who we are, but fulfill our destiny. Humans have unending possibilities, you have free will to choose which way you live. Do not get distracted in the world of illusions and appearances, for you will only suffer. Rather, turn to the essence of life, to the beauty within us all and work with us in collaboration. Together we have the power to bring forth heaven on earth."

***

Once, in California after a long hike I sat down, leaning on an ancient redwood tree in a shaded forest. Too tired to think, I became still and tuned into my new friend. Immediately, I heard the redwood tree deva speak to me:

"Lean into me, lean into peace. Rest into stillness and feel my roots grounding you into the earth. Feel how you are held and nourished.

Humanity has cut itself off from the roots of life, from nature, but without roots, humans are lost, deprived and become sick. If a tree has weak roots a storm will take it down. If roots are cut, no life force can flow and death is certain. The way of nature shows the way life is. Turn against or ignore its laws and humans will perish. It is simple."

I am curious to find out more from this wise friend: "Do you feel pain when people cut forests down?" I inquire. *"We are interconnected. When a tree is felled its spirit departs and it always affects the whole."* I feel a bit silly but ask anyway, "How does it feel?" My friend speaks: *"It feels like a limb has been cut off when one of us falls."*

Sad really what we do to our kin. Another question arises with an obvious answer, but I want to know it from the redwood tree directly. "Is it different, when people cut down a tree with respect and replant one of your kind?"

With endless patience (well, after 2,000 years of standing there, patience is a trademark for sure) the answer comes: *"Anything done in respect, in harmony with the greater whole, anything done in love does not cause suffering. Then it's more like a leaf that falls from a tree. Natural. Humanity has much to learn and much wisdom to gain."*

OK, nice, most of us know this by now, but I want to dig a little deeper: "Could you tell me what is going on with us humans that we destroy, abuse and make such a mess of this planet?"

"It is a long story, but to put it simply: Unlike us, humans are given free choice to live in separation from the spirit of life or in alignment. Suffering is caused by living in separation."

"Why do we have such a choice, when we apparently create such suffering on this planet? It doesn't seem that we deserve such faith, I mean look around at what we are doing to the forests, the waters, the animals, our people..." I trail off and lose connection. I take a breath, re-center and my mind drops into silence. I feel the soft bark against my back and let my fingers trail along its strong roots. This redwood is just beautiful. I listen again and hear:

"You have the intelligence and the power of the divine in you; if you align fully far greater things can be created through your hands than ever seen before. When humans are connected a love and brilliance is unleashed that creates worlds, which is always of benefit to all beings."

Hmm, we have the power to create. Yes, my redwood friend can't just walk off and start a revolution on the streets in New York. "So you are all banking on our potential?"

"We are banking on the truth that resides in all of you. We help you to connect and live in alignment. From this connection you create in harmony with life, which helps and benefits us all to evolve and thrive."

Well, thanks for having so much faith and putting up with us, I think. I feel a bit embarrassed for our human tribe. But the redwood tree assured me.

"There is no lower or higher species. There is just the pure intelligence of life flowing through all of creation. Every being is an expression of the Spirit, just in a different form. All speak the same original language of creation and it is written in the heart of each human. When you learn to communicate with us, you open up to your own nature and the connection with all life. Naturally, you create what is beneficial."

"What do you recommend to us in this perilous time?"

"Be with us, rest a little and be nourished. Open your hearts, listen to us in silence and learn to become a steward of the earth. You are nature. Respecting and loving us in your deeds is honoring what is sacred, what is life, what is you."

"Thank you." I bow to my newfound friend. A soft wind swishes through the branches and caresses my face.

***

What if we learn to commune with the trees, the rivers, the mountains... and create together? What is possible if we talk with the land when we make decisions that affect the gardens, farms, land and resources of the earth? And what would a world look like where we collaborate with nature? When I look further I see, indeed, this is not a fairytale, not my imagination, but life expressed at its fullest, purest, and most brilliant. It is a clear calling from creation, showing a way for us—toward a life, where unnecessary suffering ends and love flows abundantly.

Communicating with the Land

I travelled many times to one of my favorite islands on the west coast of Scotland, Iona (the name "Iona" means "the Dove," also known rightly as the heart of Europe). To the outer eyes this little island looks rather plain; wooly sheep graze across green hills, a few farmhouses are spread out between here and there, an old stone monastery reminds of a time long passed.

But the inner eyes see more. This is a cathedral of nature. The soul recognizes the ancient sacredness of the land, the purity and peace in the air is felt by many pilgrims who visit Iona.

I climbed Dun I, a little mountain from which to view the island and the endless sea crashing toward the shore. At the top is the fountain of youth—a well—long revered by the Druids. Today, the water still flows from the crevice of a rock. It is one of many altars on this special island, where nature was worshipped as goddess and god, honored as a holy fire of life. I heard the song of this old island through my heart and feet; listening into the relentless Scottish winds, the voice of the land spoke to me:

"This is holy land, be welcome, friend. The gates into the mystery open for the one whose heart and intent is pure. Tread with care, for many beings reside here."

I turned to the large stone Celtic cross standing amidst the ruins of a graveyard. This cross has a circle in the middle, and where the vertical and horizontal lines intersect, heaven and earth meet. It symbolizes the never-ending circle of life. As I attuned and looked from within, a rich world opened up, more layers of wisdom were revealed. Each day I walked into the hills, long-forgotten secrets emerged. I sensed the blood that had been shed on the land, and the grievances left behind. I heard the voices of beings that had resided there before, and those who are still the guardians of this land. Not everyone will discover these hidden altars across the land, for these are the gates into a mysterious world one must first be prepared for in order to enter. I felt the Ley lines, a powerful vortex and the pulse of life beating through the veins of this earth, and faeries and angels were close by...

In stillness this land communicates living truth that fills the thirsty soul. Veils part and eyes see true. At home in the sacredness of life, so near with a beloved friend, in whose arms we are deeply held.

***

The endearment "Anam Cara" (meaning "dear soul friend" in Gaelic) is used on the island for people, and for a land related with as a true friend.

We can live and behave as friends with creation. Living in harmony with nature isn't complicated, the universal thread pulses in us. Will we stop the destruction train, protect instead what is precious, and learn to live with instead of against the magnificence of creation? Well, once again it's up to each of us.

Communicating with Animals

I have had plenty of intimate encounters with wild animals and I share some stories throughout the book and in this chapter. May they awaken in you what is wild, alive and free. May they inspire you to connect and communicate with animals, to protect and love them. Because, what we connect with, we will care about.

Stories of Magical Encounters with the Wild

Robbers in the Kitchen

It's pitch black dark when I return home with shopping bags and my daughter in hand. As we approach the main wooden door of our house, we hear a noisy commotion coming from inside. No lights are on; no one else is living with us in our countryside estate, except our five cats, two horses and a donkey. *Who's there?* I wonder. Robbers, taking advantage of the night? It's spooky. What to do? Call the police? It would take awhile until they arrive on these winding mountain roads. So, I decide to take matters into my own hands and prepare for battle. For good measure I grab the big broom with the thick wooden stick that leans against the wall of our little castle. This will have to do to knock a robber over the head. As I turn the golden knob to the entrance, suddenly all falls silent. I tell my little girl to wait outside, as Mama will take care of any danger. The few steps to reach the light switch inside seem like a forever journey. And then light illumines the entrance hall and our open kitchen.

I gasp at what I see and burst out in relieved laughter. What a sight—four raccoons in a row staring at me. The mother with her three young ones, whose faces are adorable, have put up camp in our kitchen for a family outing and aren't going to give it up. Behind her I glimpse the mess that they have created on their move-in day. My flower-painted fruit bowl is shattered in pieces—apples, pears and half-eaten bananas decorate the floor. The cabinet doors are pulled opened— flour, rice, millet, and bread spilled out on the kitchen floor. The cats' water bowls are thrown over; raccoons wash their tiny hands after a feast. At least they are neat in one way.

I like to share food with those in need, but this is over the top. Time to set a boundary. I tell the mother in a stern voice to pack up her young and get the heck out of our house. "No," she growls at me, "We stay." And that was that, or so she imagined. She has audacity, a way for her to survive and fill four bellies easily. I understand the challenges of single motherhood and sole provider. Yet, I have to send her out with firmness. "Oh no, you won't live here. This is my kitchen and you came uninvited, eating my food and creating a whole pile of mess." I do not feel generous; it's late at night and I have reached my limit.

I glance at the back door, which is ajar and ask her how she was able to open it. Smugly she answers: "Climbed the trellises and pushed handle with paw. Easy." I reply, "OK, the same way you came in, walk out. It's even easier, 'cause now the door is open for you." She turns, ignores me and strolls with her gang back into the kitchen to finish up some of our home-baked organic bread. Well, the kitchen is her territory now and she isn't going to leave without a fight. When words don't work, action just might send the message clearer. I take my broom and go after her to push her out. But she isn't the slightest impressed by my size or weapon, rather she tries to attack and chase *me* out. Her kits try to help their mother, growling fiercely at me with bare teeth.

Raccoons can be feisty and dangerous, they fight ferociously. I try in vain to shush them with my soft weapon, but one bites into the broom and another goes for my leg. Four against one isn't a fair deal and I back away, which appears to the gang a guaranteed victory. It would certainly give her more free delicious meals, if she wins this battle. I know she will fight for this sumptuous kitchen with her teeth and to the bone; and my presence and the ole broom are too lame for the gang of thieves.

What now? I can't give up and leave them, even for a free overnight stay in our house, no matter how much I love animals. My daughter has walked into the house tentatively, and watches the whole time in delight; but even at eight years old she realizes our predicament. Yemaya calls over to me, saying, "Mama, maybe Princess can help. She is here."

Princess is our tiny three-legged cat whom we had saved from death in a shelter, since nobody wanted to have her. She isn't cuddly and hops weirdly on three legs. But she has a particular quality we soon discover. Her pretty face peeks around the corner to see what the ruckus is all about. I do not want her to come too close to this wild bunch, because raccoons can kill cats. But our usually shy cat shows no signs of fear. Before I can stop her she turns into a fierce, determined and deadly protectress. With a confidence and feistiness I have never seen in her before, she hisses, growls and then shoots at them full speed with outstretched claws. The raccoon mother literally turns on the spot and runs for her life from the tiny cat, who appears like a ferocious lioness. The robber gang escapes without any further ado through the open door, chased through the length of our yard by a hobbling and courageous cat. Princess returns with her head held high. I swear she's walking taller and more dignified since then. I lift her into my lap and say, "Princess, you are amazing." She looks at me with pride, as if she knows. "You did not know I had it in me." No, I didn't. And as for the robbers, they are never seen again.

Meeting a Wild Bobcat

I walk on a path through an open and wild area on the California coast with my eleven-year-old daughter. She too has a good connection with the animals. As we stroll along hand in hand, we see the high grass moving and stop in silent mutual understanding; present, watching, sensing. What is moving between the grass blades under the bright midday sun? Whoever it is clearly comes closer toward us; soon it is so near we can see the back of a large brown-furred animal. As we watch, quiet with anticipation, out of the grass and onto the trail emerges a most beautiful, gracious bobcat. I motion to my daughter to

22

slowly sit down. I too touch the ground and wait, as the cat leisurely strolls toward us.

She approaches, looking straight at us, and only an arm's length away, she lies down before us. She isn't injured or ill, but healthy, strong and at ease. I'm thrilled to meet this wild creature so intimately, but hold my excitement at bay, not wanting to scare her off. She calmly looks at us, catlike; completely relaxed and alert, she stretches out, as if for a nap. A most beautiful, unusual friendship circle has formed among us. We give her our full attention and she communicates to us; telling us how to be at ease and walk through life with natural grace.

When our communion is complete, my daughter and I silently thank and bless her. The bobcat gives us one more look, as if to say good-bye in her own way, then gets up and strolls away. We wait a few moments, watching her in awe, before we leave as well. I will never forget her face, the captivating grace she exuded. What a way to walk through life like that!

Face to Face with a Mountain Lioness and her Cub

Our adventure that day isn't over. After encountering the bobcat we meet two other wild cats. A little further down the trail we recognize a mountain lion mother with her young cub walking toward us on the path. At first I rub my eyes; the sight I am seeing seems otherworldly. Quickly I realize that I am not dreaming, that I should feel fear and run, but my daughter and I keep walking forward hand in hand. We cannot turn away, as if a tremendous force is magnetically pulling us toward the golden lioness and her cub, who are stately strolling toward us.

Suddenly, at the same moment, the four of us stop. We are woken by surprise when we realize we are facing each other only from about thirty feet away. My daughter is mesmerized; so am I. At lightning speed I check with my body senses: Is there any danger from the mountain lion? (That would be too late now anyway.) I sense none from this proud and magnificent animal, who is standing in open sunlight with golden shimmering fur. Her lean muscles vibrate with strength, ready to pounce if need be. But she relaxes in our presence. As if in silent knowing, she is recognizing me as a mother. Both of us are leading our young. She isn't hungry apparently. We watch and sense each other, just looking at one another with an open curiosity. The meeting is profoundly intense, and surprisingly relaxed.

My daughter is at ease, so I quietly whisper that she communicate with the cub. The dignified lioness and I have a "mother to mother" talk. She teaches me much in these remarkable minutes, during which time stands still. She shows me what living from true power really is. My daughter seems to make friends with the cub, as if this is the most normal thing to do. She does not put her experience into words, but receives gifts from the cub in her own quiet way, and I think this furry young lion bundle feels my girl's love too. Then our meeting comes to a natural ending. But the bond we formed continues on in the wild beating of our hearts.

We bow as the wild cats turn and slowly walk away. A magnificent sight to behold, we both will never forget.

Running with Wild Mustang Horses

After riding into Canyon De Chinle, a revered place on the Navajo reservation, I guide my group of retreatants to meditate on Spider Rock. This tall red rock megalith is, according to the Navajo, a mighty vortex where heaven and earth meet, and where Spider Woman weaves creation. I am deeply moved by the sheer beauty, purity and sacredness of this wild canyon where 5,000-year-old caves of the indigenous ancestors still exist untouched. A calling leads me further into the valley, to a place where these ancient ones walked. As I listen into the wild, I hear the neighing of wild horses nearby. Following the pull with soft footsteps on the earth, I come around the majestic red rock and I am welcomed into a lush green valley where a river flows and a large herd of wild mustangs graze.

What a beautiful sight to behold. I stop in awe. The herd with mares and foals do not run away as they usually would when humans enter into their territory and energetic field. Have they even noticed me? Wild horses, like all untamed animals, are highly alert and can sense what is going on even at a far distance. Yet, I had wandered right into their circle and they do not seem to be perturbed, nor do they stampede away. I sit down among thistles and green grass and ask the herd inwardly if I can stay for awhile with them.

Exactly at that moment the black stallion raises his head and looks straight at me with his gorgeous dark eyes. In silence our eyes meet, and the pulse of life between us is powerfully felt. As if giving his consent, he lowers his head and continues to graze peacefully, ever alert to watch out for his well-fed mares.

Meanwhile, I enjoy watching the young foals whose curiosity about this new horse (myself) has brought them nearer. Unafraid, they are bucking and playing now right next to me. Frolicking with natural exuberance they nuzzle each other; the brown and white youngster is chasing another one-year-old. A snort, then a kick, lets the tiniest foal know she is too young for their rough play. The mother mare neighs for her baby foal, who readily trots to her side. (I suspect she would rather suckle mother's milk anyway, than be bitten by these rascals.)

I raise my eyes to the clear blue sky; above, a red-tailed hawk is circling us and screeches. What has he found, what might he see below? I will never know; but maybe he was sending a warning, because suddenly the whole herd gallops off. Without stopping or turning back, they are running across the green valley further into the wild canyon, where mysteries are still alive and untouched by humankind.

What a sense of freedom and connectedness fills me, what a joy it was to be with them. My heart is bursting, as I yearn to run with one of the few remaining mustang herds alive on this earth. Let us not kill and tame every creature, but protect what is wild and free—Life.

Love in Action

A meditation to connect with plants and animals:
Connect with your breath, feel your body and anchor deeply into the earth. Become aware of your "inner house"—sensations, emotions, thoughts—without getting lost in these. Just notice your environment: sounds, smells and sights, without getting attached to anything. Allow your awareness to expand into a wider field. Touch your heart and let yourself feel your love for animals or plants. Then open to a particular animal or plant, sense its energy, and ask for any communication this being has for you. Let your mind rest in the backseat; allow yourself to be curious about what you do not know. Discover. This beginner's mind and heart is the basis for relating. Listen. Sometimes you will receive words, an image, or a sense as a response from the animal or plant. If nothing comes, just be in silent communion. It will strengthen your connection. You can also express what you wish to communicate and soon enough you are involved in an often surprising and revealing conversation. Offer your gratitude at the end of each encounter with a plant or animal friend.

A daily practice to nourish:
Expressing appreciation for your plant or animal goes a long way. Not only do they feel it, they are nourished by it. Just like us. I lived in Findhorn, a community that became world famous for its communication with plants and the astounding results they achieved through working with devas, the spirits of plants. Findhorn gardens produced humongous cabbages and other vegetables in barren sand... Miracles occur when we relate with plants as living, intelligent beings. We always talked with and appreciated the plants, just as you would a good friend.

Practical basics for living on the earth:
If we love nature, it translates into our actions. Here are some suggestions that you might find useful:

1. It helps the planet and our health when we buy organic food, use our feet (and bikes). Abstain from using toxins and poisons in your home and garden. Living as green and sustainable as possible is necessary for all of life at this point in time. Detailed information about what more we can do is nowadays widely available.

2. We are guests on planet earth. Treating the natural world with care, respect and kindness can become our innate behavior. Expressing gratitude for the food on our table increases a sense of connection with the natural world for children and adults alike.

3. We support and vote for what we purchase with our money. Many beauty products have been tested on animals, who are tortured in the process of manufacturing them. Buy shampoo and face creams that are labeled "not tested on animals." Purchase clothing made from organic cotton and products that do not harm the earth and its inhabitants. Every dollar makes a difference.

4. Consider becoming a vegetarian. Or buy meat from grass-fed and humanely-raised animals, who are allowed to move freely in the fields. It's the kinder way. Hormones and other substances used to make animals grow faster, bigger, produce more milk, etc. is bad for your health, and theirs. Educate yourself by reading books and doing research available on the Internet on this important matter.

5. For houseplants and animals: make sure you give your companions what they really need. I have met well-intentioned people, who love their pets and plants, but don't know the basics and thereby unintentionally cause them suffering. Love means to educate oneself to provide well for the needs of an

animal or plant. And sharing affection with our friends brings forth much joy for each.

6. If you are an activist for the earth, do not drown in the suffering you encounter. People will not change by force and anger. Keep your heart open, for that is your power and your connection to the earth. She will show you ways to be of help. Educating and helping people to connect with the beauty of our earth can turn minds and hearts.

7. When you wish to enter into a temple of nature always ask for permission. Don't take anything away from a sacred place, nor leave anything behind, except perhaps an offering of fruit. The less we disturb any natural habitat, and the less we take, the more likely it will survive and thrive.

8. A word of caution: If you want to get to know wild animals better and commune with them, begin with deer, birds, and squirrels. Don't try to interact with a wild cat, bear or snake unless you have plenty of experience. Begin by listening to them at a safe distance.

9. Please do not touch or go after wild animals. For example, dolphins have become tourist attractions and their sleeping, feeding and breeding areas are being heavily disturbed.

10. Speak up against animal abuse and hunting in the wilderness. We have very few remaining wildlife and they need our protection. Animal abuse is unfortunately common; the more of us that speak up and act, the more this sad story changes.

11. And then, from time to time let yourself fall unto the earth, breathe the wet soil, drink from a spring with cupped hands, touch the bark of a redwood tree, just rest and merge in nature's lap. She will fill you up until your cup runneth over.

May we enjoy all creatures and plants, not as objects to be used or owned, but as unique and precious gifts of life. May we remember our innate connection with every step we take upon the earth, and offer our love through the way we act today.

The nature communication practice:

Entry: If you walk into a wild area or sacred place, please always ask for permission to enter. This is the house of nature—behave like a guest in a temple. Fruit or flower offerings will be received by the spirits of the land. This creates a stronger relationship too.

Meditation: Find a spot in nature with a tree or a plant. Become aware of your breath, your body, emotions and mind. Let the mind drop into the background, allow your body to relax, soften and open in your heart. Engage your senses, listen to any sounds in nature, see the colors and movements in your environment and tune into the energy. Use the meditation above.

Connect with the plant or the land: Turn to the plant, touch, feel, smell, see the whole being. Appreciate the plant. It helps you to feel love. State your intention and/or question. Open yourself to the invisible energy/being/intelligence. Merge. Listen from a place of not knowing, with curiosity and openness. Receive the message and communication via words or images, felt sense, or knowing. Send your message via words, images, feeling, and energy from the heart. **Stay present, still, relaxed and in lovingness.** Communicate back and forth or just listen. Enjoy it!!! **To end the conversation:** Always thank the plants/ land or animal.

If we align ourselves with the wisdom of earth, if we learn to listen and then act, we bring forth beauty, healing and harmony in our own gardens and the planet.

2. Women Rising

A new era begins

I am the dark and the light one, I am the colors of life and I am the mother of all. With loving arms I sweep through the lands and hearts to take my children home. I weep the tears with those lost and grieving. Your outrage is my fire. I rejoice in the blossoming of the first flowers and burst into pearls of laughter with you. I feed all my children without exception. I run wild as the lioness through the mountains and valleys. I am gentle, fierce; untethered in my power I love my own. I am the feminine seen in all the faces of those who travel this earth. I breathe the breath of life through you, I am alive in your belly and whisper and roar as your voice. I say unto you now: For the sake of all beings awaken from your slumber and rise!

A volcano is erupting, the rumblings of which are heard by those whose hearts and ears are open. A monumental change is sweeping across our planet. The feminine is unleashing as an unstoppable force, its momentum is building, taking hold of those who are ready to change the course in a world on the edge. Like a tidal wave, women are rising around the globe, in a magnitude as never seen before.

She is standing at the bow, courageously turning the ship for the sake of all. This tide is rising every day, as our voices speak out on behalf of our ancestors, the children, animals and the earth, for human rights, for girls and women and the well-being of our people. The roads were blocked and every street was filled with people of all colors and nations standing up together for women and girls in every major city in 2017, marking the biggest march in American history.

Women are waking and rising for the sacred in all of life. Girls are stepping forward, not waiting for the grown-ups, boldly creating a new legacy. The feminine is on fire now. She is leading into a new dawn for humanity and our earth. Women begin to empower each other, to reclaim lost dignity, value and sovereignty. We are stepping into our power so long oppressed, our voice kept small far too long, our beauty—in all shapes she walks. We come bearing our inherent connectedness with the source and ancient wisdom, so needed for these times, but which had been suppressed and doubted—in fear. Even, if we are shaking in our boots and high heels, masses of women, whether in the huts of Africa, in the furthest reaches in India, here in California—literally everywhere—women gather and rise.

Women are changing the world. Malala Yousafzai was fourteen years old when she was shot by the Taliban for advocating for girls to have the right to education. She survived and received the Nobel Peace Prize in 2014 for her outstanding work, which reaches far beyond Afghanistan and Pakistan where her mission originally began.

Dedicated to the wholeness of life, many work tirelessly toward shifting patriarchal structures that have dominated the world for centuries, and which has led us to this dangerous and precarious situation on the planet. For ages, spirituality and religion have pointed toward transcendence, the formless, emptiness, heaven, and a distant god ruling, but disregarded the feminine. Thereby it left out our relatedness, immanence and interdependence, the honoring of the sacred in form— found in the smallest pebble, in the silent growth of majestic trees, in your body and the face of humanity. (Read more on the feminine in the "Foundation Stones" chapter.) Old structures, based on greed and hunger for power, autonomy, competition and control—divorced from the feminine and separated from life—have led us to where we are today. The earth is ravaged, poisoned and polluted.

In many places of the world girls still have less value than boys and do not receive education, thereby being trapped in a cycle of poverty, forced into child marriage, sex slavery and sweatshops. To this day, women with the same qualifications and skills receive less pay than a man in the United States. The number of single mothers who live below the poverty line is staggering. Mothers are often considered as worth less than a high-earning CEO, who goes home after the work is done. Yet, hers is a twenty-four-hour job with no pay and no recognition.

We burnt the witches and fear feminine power even today. Women are still raped as a weapon of war. In the Western world alone, one out of four girls is molested or raped before reaching adulthood. Every second girl in the United States is on a diet before she turns twenty, hating her body, because beauty is defined by male and sex-oriented media. The sacredness of the feminine, the woman as a human divine being, has been violated, degraded, used, dismissed, devalued, oppressed, treated like a disposable object and destroyed. And we as women have perpetuated it too.

How we have treated the feminine parallels what we have done to the earth. This is how we have related to life itself far too long.

But this era is ending now. The turning is happening with each one of us standing at the bow. Yes, she is roaring, rising from the deep dark and birthing forth a new way—or is it an ancient one that we have always known deep down, emerging from the very heart of life itself? Like any real change it always begins inside. Women need to reconnect with the power of life, the Shakti, our wisdom and legacy, to heal the wounds of the past centuries and cultivate the courage to walk courageously into the unknown to birth forth a new dawn.

She is taking the lead in a world, which has fallen out of alignment with the very heartbeat of life.

She was hidden, but the curtain has fallen and she is lifting on wings of grace to center stage. The black Madonna, Kali, Sophia, Mary Magdalene—and many other faces of the divine feminine—are being delivered from forgotten and degraded altars and temples into the streets and the public eye.

A huge revival is taking place; men and women hunger for "Her"

The presence of Tara is particularly relevant today. For centuries, Tara has been revered in the East, representing universal compassion and enlightened activity in the Hindu and the Buddhist traditions. She enables living beings to cross from the ocean of samsara to the shore of peace. Her ancient story speaks for the feminine: It is said that eons ago, she was born a king's daughter in Asia. She was a deeply devout and empathetic princess, highly advanced spiritually and had developed great merit and accomplishments. The monks told her that they would pray for her to be born again as a man, so she could attain full enlightenment and spread the dharma teachings. She responded boldly with a vow: in order to liberate all beings, henceforth she would only return in female form until all beings had awakened. She stood up for the feminine and lights the way for many today.

And there is another great one who is rising from the dark. Mary Magdalena, who mysteriously and powerfully ushers her women home.

***

It was storming and rainy, when I arrived in the old Cathar land in France to take shelter in a tiny chapel on top of a hill. The wooden door creaked and only a few candles were lit. Dim light softly illuminated the exquisite statues and paintings of women saints and Mary Magdalene. One man was sitting bowed in the wooden pew, praying. Silence, thick stillness enveloped the air. I joined in meditation, feeling her. An hour later the man turned around and introduced himself to me. We talked about our connection to the Magdalene, and it felt auspicious when he invited me to come to a secret cave, also called the womb and birthing cave. It was a three-hour journey away, somewhere in the mountains and hard to find. It's the kind of place you must feel called to and have a guide, a hidden power place not a spiritual tourist attraction. All hair rose in recognition. "Yes," I said excitedly. Was I mad? I shouldn't go with a stranger and a guy I don't know, I already had learnt that as a child. But something in me knew that this was right and he was safe.

After a long drive and hike, I shivered as I faced the entrance, which was beyond anything I had ever seen. She beckoned me to enter through the entrance of the enormous yoni-shaped rocks and slide down on my butt into the sacred womb cave. It was in this depth of darkness where she revealed herself, the way of the feminine, so different than we have been taught.

***

She veils herself, covering her naked soul. Not only to hide for fear of violence or in submission to oppression, but for another reason—a deeper one. You see, you can't just rip her veils apart and march in there. You will never find her, for she will not show herself that way. You have to prepare yourself, to discover her and touch each layer with reverence, sincere adoration and love. Only then will the petals of the flower unfold and she may grant permission to enter this holy cave, so you may receive what is hidden in plain sight. She may offer you the grail, for which they have been searching since ancient times. And let you sip from the exquisite red wine, the intoxicating nectar of everlasting life, which restores the weary, heals the broken, wakes the dead and utterly enlivens your heart, belly into your very bones.

Maybe that is what salvation really means: to come truly alive. I realized there and then:

Enlivenment this is the feminine way

Matter is sacred and your pain, joy and hand are Her. She calls us to surrender in radical union between divine and human, and live a way that honors all life as Her.

I assure you, you will not meet her by transcending this form and world, by disappearing detached into a faraway sky, but by immersing into the luminous dark unknown. Even, if you must crawl on all fours into the cave. And then, in her inmost sanctuary she will strip you bare of all you imagined yourself to be, reveal your worst fears and all the clever ways you denied, silenced and pushed her away. Sheer rage, grief and terror may emerge as her untamed power rises from the wet, musky ground below and takes hold of you. Oh yes, we are as frightened of the feminine as we are of love itself.

Why are we so shaken by creation's power?

For centuries we burnt her at the stake, repressed her wisdom and wildness, tied her in shackles for the imagined crime of being Eve, the evil one. We desecrated the earth for a God, we believed, is beyond form and what is so human in us. And then we poured asphalt over her breathing, living body too. Even the common spiritual path treaded today is often taught in a conceptual, whitewashed way, thereby denying her very existence—so vibrantly alive here on earth, in relationships and beating in your heart right now. We yearn for her, to experience this pulsing thread of aliveness, this intimate oneness with all beings, in our bodies, at the kitchen sink whilst washing dishes, and as we meet each other in a coffee shop.

She is here, siempre. She will not be quieted and disappear, she keeps showing her face in the mirror and your friend's embrace. She breaks through cement, just as the ocean takes over land. The truth returns again and again; no matter how much we want to control, she has her own way. Gentle as a dove she caresses you and with a feather light kiss dissolves your sturdy walls of defense into a flood of tears. You hear her deafening, fierce lioness roar into a world that raped her: This shall not pass! Veiled, she walks the streets and wakens people from slumber. She uplifts the fallen ones, gathers the lost and outcast. And she rises up for you, our earth and all that is sacred, igniting us to show up for the great turning. For, through her power we can turn even the most horrific situations around and help in these times when our survival is hanging by a mere thread. You may have seen and heard her more frequently of late on the streets or feel her rumbling in your own belly and heart.

2,000 years later, Mary Magdalene, after being cast aside as a whore and the lesser one, after being degraded, is popular now. Why? She has experienced every single wound of the feminine and did not back down, but walked barefoot through it all. In her power, sensuality, humanity and true love, she is a fiery torch for us to show the way, and embodies the tower of strength.

***

For three days I sat in her dark womb-cave alone. She pulled me deep, down and in. For this is the way of her. I became so vulnerable, raw and wept, for the children, the animals... and laid bare the suffering in my soul. I laughed until my belly hurt. In rapture I danced wildly, taken by her. Until I was utterly emptied, stood naked in the shining darkness, face to face with Her. That's when an immense transmission unleashed and surged through me from the ground up, rising like a snake

2. Women Rising

through my spine. Words can't tell, I felt one in every way. She gave me the original teachings of the ancient feminine lineage and made it clear, that the teachings based on a male model do not help women. I experienced liberation through the deep feminine way, by merging with the primal life force, the Shakti, rising from below, through the spine and body, illuminating every part upon reaching the crown.

***

The yearning for her is answered, as we allow the dams and shackles to break, to weep all our tears and laugh all of our laughter. Just like the women experienced who I guide to the holy cave. On their knees they surrendered to her to embrace what's lost, to let this pure life power surge through the womb and ignite them. They were taken home into the fire of true love.

She beckons that we recognize this truth—she is made manifest through our bodies and luminous faces, the trees, rivers... and she has incarnated as your voice, hands and feet. As you stroke your cat, dog, another body, you are touching her. Let her take the lead in your life. She will take you and raise you into who you really are. She will give you courage to stand up and act in benefit to all in your labor of love. She is here, honor her and when she calls—follow her. She will show you a greater love than you may have ever known before.

I have called you since before time. The hour is dawning, my beloved. Step into the unknown, I will meet you here and raise you up. Come unto me and I behold as you weep, laugh and dance. I take you into my embrace all the way—as my only one. Fly on wings of grace, my love. Come home. And let me rise through you to bring forth a new dawn for humanity and this earth.

***

415

Yes, the deep feminine way means to go down and in, and to merge with this untamed life, a force that has been feared and oppressed for so long. To reclaim and embody it. And this power strips us into raw vulnerability; like when we give birth, and through that juicy fire we are enlivened. It is that life force, also called Shakti, which lives as and through all forms and matter — vibrantly alive in everything — intimately, radically, unabashed and unencumbered living truth.

She renders sacred the broken, forgotten, calling all her lost children home. And it is that wild power, once liberated within us, that turns lives and rises the tide in our world, when we allow it to move us all the way and unite.

This movement is not a fight against men, nor is it about establishing a new matriarchy. It is not about a lonesome heroine journey, but women collaborating with each other, walking hand in hand in cooperation, not in competition. Nor is it about women becoming hardened and forcing our way, although some have taken on this coat to reach the ladder of success in a male-dominated business world. Nor has Sleeping Beauty time to wait for Prince Charming to rescue her, for she is waking by the kiss of life and a greater calling, in which she has an important part to play. And it does not mean that women are better than men, for we all have the same worth in the eyes of creation. A paradigm shift is happening far more encompassing. Women are called to step forward with their voices and gifts. Men are needed to support women and the causes that are in benefit to life. We are urged to bring the feminine principle to the forefront, unto center stage and bow to Her.

Can you imagine if women could walk safely through any town, knowing rape was a thing of long-time past? What if women were heard in business dealings, on the street and at home? For some this is a reality; keep in mind, for many women around the world it is not. What if you could trust your sister to have your back, instead of fearing that she might stab you from behind or betray you, which is the dark side among women? What would it take instead of competing with other women to collaborate and empower each to create allegiance and support? And how would you feel if you did not doubt yourself and suppress your own life force and voice anymore?

How would our lives be if women and men build a bridge across the divisions, heal the wounds between the feminine and masculine and create a thriving world together? It's not utopia, this reality is sprouting already. And for this turning the feminine needs to take the lead now.

The "#MeToo" movement and events like "One Billion Rising" to end violence against women and girls, which occurred in two hundred countries around the world in 2018, was inspiring. A strong sign of a new time emerging — the tide has reached the masses now. We are uprooting the causes of suffering, to honor what is sacred and work together toward the flourishing of all life. We stand for an embodied spirituality and a responsible way of living. We rise together hand in hand for real love! A revolution is unleashing. Many already have answered the call — and more are joining every single day. C'mon, get on your horse and ride with us — this one is for LIFE and YOU!

Love in Action

Enjoy these feminine embodiment practices that I also teach more in-depth within my "SHE RISES — The Deep Feminine Way" immersions and retreats for women. (For more on the feminine and helpful practices please read the "Foundation Stones" chapter on Loving Embrace.)

Free from oppression:
Face the fears that would keep you small and tell you that it's dangerous to speak your truth and to take your seat. Practice speaking what is true for you, even if it's difficult, imperfect or might upset someone. Express your fears, vulnerabilities and strengths

through sound and then through words. When you open to the life force and to your deepest wisdom, terror will arise. Expect that, because women have been killed and tortured for it for centuries. The memory of the witch burnings and other atrocities lives in your cells and bones. Ask for the support of others who are familiar with this and take someone's hand, like a guide or teacher or therapist, to walk through the gates of fear, freeing yourself from the shackles and burdens of our shared past history and legacy.

Your softness is your strength:
Soften your hardness and toughness and all the ways you tried to protect yourself in a harsh world. Let the armor down. Your strength does not lie in your defense, but in the power, which is found in your most tender vulnerability.

Feel all your feels, they are your best friends and allies. Allow your emotions to move freely and fully without trying to diminish, to make a drama or to cut off any emotions.

Even if you think you are empowered, like a mother keep touching the places inside of you that feel vulnerable or are still tied up and afraid.

Make friends with your body and redefine beauty for yourself. What if natural beauty includes your so-called imperfect parts—the fat tummy, the hair that you wish to be different, the pimples that keep reappearing and the lines that show no matter what creams you use to make them disappear? And who labeled them imperfect in the first place? What if all this is part of your beauty and uniqueness?

Explore your feminine nature:
What do you really want to speak? Let your voice come out. Let her rip, let her roar, let her whisper, let her soar.

What is your womb and belly wanting you to hear and to express? Listen and lean in.

How does your body want to move in this moment now? Let it move wildly or softly, exactly how it wants to.

Connect with your feelings regularly: What do you feel in this moment? Feel all the way, it won't kill you, but it will set your life force free to flow.

Let the most feared, primal life energy for women come forth in you. Invite Kali, who is the fierce, red Hindu Goddess with skulls around her neck, who unleashes the pure and wild Shakti power, which we need in our world to be able to make a stand, to speak a NO to abuse and injustice, and to protect the vulnerable.

Rejoice in your sensuality. Pay attention to all your senses, immerse yourself in each. Taste a spoonful of honey slowly and deliberately with all your sense engaged. Allow the nourishment from life to fill you. Invite Lakshmi, the goddess of abundance, to your table, let her show you how to enjoy the bounty of life. Dance in nature, swim naked under the moonlight in a lake, taste a strawberry as if the goddess herself is feeding you the most delicious nectar of life.

Honor and respect yourself:
If you have a "pleaser" personality and always take care of others, explore what pleases you, to care for yourself. Yes, you may not be liked for it at first, but if you let fear run your life you will not like yourself in the end.

If you have hardened yourself, afraid of your vulnerability, your softness, explore letting your battle armor down with a friend. So you can breathe and feel the feminine power alive within you. So you enjoy genuine, intimate relationships.

If your strategy to survive is self-centeredness, explore what it is like to see and treat everyone as important as you are. For the natural way of the feminine is to live in interconnectedness, to honor all of life.

If you use independence to make it in the world, ask for support and let others be there for you. Explore what it's like to receive help.

Striving and the new age trap:

Our Western society is driven by "have more, be more, do more..." This can translate into an endless self-improvement trap, whereby you never come to rest and be nourished. It goes against the feminine way. Lay down the striving for a day and notice what happens in you. It may be uncomfortable at first, but then you might just enjoy simply being you and taking in the nourishment here for you.

New Age, just as all religions and approaches, has a shadow side. The shadow of the New Age Movement affects women in particular. The message is: Rise above your darkness, cast away your uncomfortable feelings and be the best most positive person you can be. Cutting off the dark and transcending the murky waters does not work. It creates a greater split and it'll come haunting you at night. Do not forget in the dark is the gift, if you dare to face and embrace it.

Sensuality:

Go slower in this fast-paced world of ours. For example, deliberately slow down when washing the dishes. Feel the water pouring into your hands, sense it with your whole body. When you slow down, open to all your senses, letting yourself experience intimately what you are doing, the flower of your femininity will open to the first rays of sunlight. Enjoy your senses, let that chocolate melt slowly on your tongue and taste all the nuances. Merge and melt into the one taste. Dwell in the one taste of love. Your senses guide you home.

How we speak to ourselves:

Language is a powerful tool and we can use it to uplift or degrade ourselves. Women have a long-standing history of belittling themselves with words such as, "I am too fat, I am not beautiful. I am sorry that I am taking up space..." You know the way you degrade yourself. Do not judge that you are doing it, because most of it is inherited, but rather bring loving attention to your "self-talk" and remember that you too are worthy, a valuable human being. You don't have to become the goddess to deserve love.

Connected to the earth:

Women need to connect with nature, to walk in the fields of flowers, to shower in a summer rain and to bathe their bodies in sunlight. When disconnected from nature our female nature dries up; we become ungrounded and get stuck in a racing mind. It's really not a "hippie thing" to hug a tree, it's lifesaving for us to connect with the source of life in a visceral way. Go daily into nature, even lying down on a patch of grass will do.

Cherish your relationships:

Women thrive in relationships. If you listen closely you will find that women talk the most about relationships, whether about her mate or how she gets along with her girlfriend, her family and her children. It's because we are naturally wired for connection and relationships. If you get caught up in busyness and your relationships come last, you suffer, for you live against your nature. Make it a point to meet with a friend at least once a week: for a walk, a chat, simply to go out and be together. It will nourish you.

Facing the dark side of women:

A long time ago women learnt to compete with each other for a strong man in order to survive. But the times have changed, we do not depend on a man to protect us, we can be strong together. Learn new ways to collaborate with other women, empower them instead of seeing them as a threat. Another survival strategy for women is to talk behind each other's back, to gossip and stab each other from behind or shame another woman in the public eye. This fear-based behavior, the suppressed rage, needs to be consciously dealt with. If you have a problem with a woman talk with her directly. Women betray each other, even by sleeping with a married man. Please honor your sister by refraining from such hurtful behaviors or confront a friend who engages in such acts that hurt all of us. Women tend to worship men and put them before their female friends. Old wiring. Regard women friends with the same importance as we give a man. We still have to learn to support a woman who is doing good works and has the guts to stand on the public stage, even if we have to confront envy, as she has to endure far greater challenges than any man in the same position. In short, we cannot afford to continue with our destructive past time patterns. We have to shed light on them and let them go. For we need to stand together now, if we want to turn the ship and thrive together in this world.

Women unite:

Women's groups exist all over the world. Join one or create a circle of spiritual and human support even if only with one or two other women. It is important that you do not walk alone and can share in a safe harbor together.

Turn to Her:

Make it a daily habit to tune in, to meditate and connect with Her. Listen to her voice in your womb and heart. Allow the power to rise, even through the terror, surrender to her wisdom, and wild force. She is gentle and she is strong, and she rises from the deep dark. Get to know her intimately, be assured, she wants all of you. And act on the guidance, the felt sense, the stirring of love to move you in life.

Follow Her beckoning all the way home. Roar, cry, dance and laugh... revel in this aliveness unabashedly. Drop deep and rise up, my love— for life, no matter what! You are not alone; we are with you this time! And may you receive the blessing she bestows upon you in this moment now.

3. Welcome Humanity

Making a difference in the world

A collective crisis needs a collective solution. We do not know how to individually solve the urgent issues in our world, but together we can, for each has been given a thread to weave into the tapestry of humanity. We have woven plentiful stories, like children we have played with creation. Now our mere survival depends on the kind of story we will create together. What story will our children experience and tell?

Glorious. Bloody. Humanity. Centuries interwoven with times of peace and war, terror inflicted and happiness shared, threads of beauty shine through, and toxins are spilled upon the carpet of life. The color of insanity is close by, horrible and beneficial deeds stand out; the greatness of the human spirit and strokes of historic genius follow us throughout the ages; we are born and die over and over again. The fabric of humanity is a mighty one, an epic played out that continues to this day. The story is alive in our cells and bones.

A kaleidoscope of humanity flocks together where I live. On my morning walk along the beach, I am greeted by people from Asia, Europe and Africa; rich and poor people, and everyone in between. White, brown and black faces smile at me; others are in a serious mood. Some families build sandcastles together happily; surfers boldly catch the next wave; athletes, in a different shape than those who have partied all night long, run strong. Lovers walk arm in arm into the sunrise, drawing close for a passionate kiss. Homeless people, who sleep under the bridge, search in the sand for lost pennies to buy a meal, and a screaming woman on drugs is arrested by the police. Yesterday the kind black man, who sold lemonade on the beach, was killed in a violent shooting nearby. He was innocent.

On the other side of the world, a terrified mother, whose husband was murdered, tries desperately to protect her children from the crashing bombs. In Afghanistan, a soldier is hiding in the bushes; he isn't yet numb and trembles time and time again, when ordered to shoot his fellow humans down. In a distant city a brutal mob raids through the streets, taking everything valuable they can get their hands on—including the women they rape.

In Bali, as the morning sun is rising over the paddy fields, families venture to the little altars at the roadsides to offer sweet prayers and flowers. Children walk hand in hand to school; artists are painting in the luscious rice fields; dancers gather for the next religious celebration. At the same time, a shopkeeper opens his store in Italy, greeting the day with a loud shout and a song that his neighbors join in singing. Somewhere, a baby is born, just as another leaves this world. All human expressions are found right before our eyes; with all the suffering, insanity, and terror existing alongside beauty, peace and joy.

Where does love come in for our beautiful, bloody humanity?

***

I am sitting in a long line of chairs, waiting. A Tibetan monk and Christian nun are placed in the row before me. A little girl, who sits beside me, about five years old from Japan, is squeezing a bouquet of flowers with her little hands. Behind me is a businessman in a formal black suit, seated close to a punk, whose arms are fully tattooed. I am not sure how the police officer feels when he finds himself beside a hippie in dreadlocks and ripped clothes—but here we are all joined together in a peaceful ashram nestled in the hills of San Ramon in California, eagerly awaiting a hug from a great saint.

What does a simple hug do that draws the masses like flocks of birds to a fountain? Her embrace answers a deep longing and prayer that people across the world carry in their hearts: to be embraced as they are and to discover true love.

Ammachi, a spiritual leader and recognized humanitarian, has meanwhile embraced over forty million people across the world. More and more people flock to this Indian woman who grew up in poverty and with abuse, but has been handing out unconditional love ever since she was a young girl. People are hungry and thirsty for a drop of this—an embrace in true love.

Several people in the line are crying, some because of their suffering, others because their hearts are opening the closer they move toward her. She is dressed in a simple white Indian sari, and after hours of hugging thousands of people, her shirt is stained with humanity's tears, snot, lipstick and sweat. On days like these she keeps going—twenty-four hours at a time—without taking a bathroom break or eating anything.

She offers the water and bread of life as she hugs and then serves Indian food for each of us personally. Through her organization, "Embracing the World," houses are built for the poorest of the poor, schools are established across India, care for nature is practiced wherever she touches ground, free hospitals offer outstanding health care, women are empowered to build their own businesses—all through these chocolate brown hands of a woman, who is a living embodiment of love and reminds us, that we are too.

I marvel as she holds a tall, proud man, drawing him into her lap, and he breaks down in sobs. Later he shares with me how his heart had long been shut down. His focus in life had been on making money and achieving success, and he had hurt many people while climbing to the "top" of the corporate ladder. He admitted that he had become empty inside and had forgotten love. With one hug, Amma touched his hardened heart open. He was grateful, and probably walked away a changed man.

Amma (the Hindi word for "mother") known worldwide as the "hugging saint," does not ask anyone to follow her, she simply serves humanity with her hugs and acts, like a river of love that never ceases to flow. She invites people to open their hearts, to let the honey pour forth into a world that needs people who live from love. Ammachi, like many great teachers, says, "It is our dharma (duty) to help ease suffering and pain."

***

Could love be a solution to our current dilemma?

Never before in history have the issues we are facing affected humanity so greatly as today. Regardless of race, color, ethnicity or education, we are realizing that we are in this together, even if we are sailing in different boats. Environmental pollution, overpopulation, impact everyone, no matter where we live. An urgent SOS call is resounding across the world, from one person to another, to find global solutions together.

We might show some care toward ourselves and extend our love to our own family. This is a very good beginning, but the Nazis loved their families too. We may expand our "care circumference" to include friends, coworkers, our community and the country we live in. But for the turning we need to extend love into the wider world and include our shared humanity by welcoming different religions, ethnicity and cultures. May the well-being of all children matter to us as much as our own child. What happens to the people in Africa, as cropland is deteriorating and the desert is expanding, is as important as our friends' problems. The recognition that we are one human family, even if we have yet to learn how to act as one, is essential for our survival. To expand our hearts by including all sentient beings, leaving out no one and nothing, is the practice then.

We know this. Even the guy I met in Ireland who slept with a gun next to his bed says he only wants peace with his fellow men. What stops us?

The long-standing notion of "me" and the "others over there" creates separation. We are different in our personalities: some people appear as wolves in sheepskin; some as radiant angels; others behave like jerks; and then there is the sweet one who can't hurt a fly. Holy saints and rambunctious thieves board the same train in this world. Some people prefer traditional lives; others live in-between extremes and on the edge. The rich tech geek, who owns a fancy villa with servants, certainly has a different life than the person who sleeps on the street with a sheet of cloth wrapped around his waist.

However, below the apparent differences, we are connected; we are the same in our core, at one with humankind. Every person wants to be free of suffering and yearns to be happy. In our heart we all want to love and be loved. Every human in this world needs shelter, water and food to survive. People across the world have dreams and longings, become frightened when in danger, and experience moments of joy and pain. It is the dance of the duality in us. And in each of us abides the jewel of intelligence, beauty and compassion beyond duality. The red thread of life unites us, no matter how buried it might be. This we share. We are the One in its many expressions.

In the eyes of love each of us has inherent worth, deserving respect. We all matter in the grand picture of life; each is precious in the garden of creation. When we forget this basic truth we create separation based on our varied expressions, as if a tree is greater or lesser than a flower. Nature does not discriminate like this; rather each has a place of belonging as part of the whole.

We stand up for our countries. What about our shared humanity?

We tend to fear what's different from us, and try to make everyone be and look the same; it seems less threatening to our fragile self-image. We might stay in our exclusive white circles, it seems safer that way. And so we do not know how life is for people of another race and social standing. We avoid seeing the violence acted out daily against black people. We perpetuate untold suffering through silence and established privilege. Native Americans are still to this day treated as a lesser people. We took their lands in America and committed genocide, under the disguise that they are "not human, but bastards." We must not forget, the indigenous people welcomed the invaders to their table to share bread together.

We divide what is originally united, by looking at some people with disdain and at others with admiration. We may treat some as better and others lesser, depending on our judgment of who is deserving of respect and who is not. We create artificial fences to keep out what does not fit into our own little made-up world, but forget that the one who is looking into our eyes is one of our kind, just with a different color and shape. The barriers get built and wars are fought from this sense of separation, missing out on what is real and our basic human connection.

This hurts us all.

"What we do unto another we do onto ourselves" is the truth. What I do to you affects me, whether for better or for worse. The effects might not be immediately felt or visible, yet remember when you screamed at a friend or your child, how badly it felt. If our heart is not closed we feel the results of our behavior. When in touch with conscience, we will take responsibility for mistaken actions—without question. And happiness shared by one lifts another. Whatever we do has a ripple effect on all of humanity, whether we see an immediate impact or not.

What does it take to act on this truth? How do we embrace the whole of humanity, the glories and the beauty, as well as the follies, horrors and suffering? We have tremendous potential to express creativity, intelligence, sanity; and we each have the potential for cruelty in us as well. Good and bad seeds. So it matters what we water, what we choose to grow and live.

Presence and facing the shadow is the water for our soul seeds. It awakens love for our shared humanity and we may realize: indeed, we are the world.

If every aspect of our human race is within us, how then do we love the "whole enchilada" and act to be of benefit? How do we tend to intergenerational traumas that continue to play out en masse on the world stage? How do we contribute to the flourishing of humanity, bringing forth its greatest potential, where the sky has no limit for expressions of magnificence? It takes all of us and begins with you. (See the meditation in the "Love in Action" section below. Or read the "Loving You" and "This Human House" chapters.)

Where does it end, all the ways humans have continued to perpetuate suffering by inflicting it on others? It changes with you and me.

What would it be like to shift into a closer connection with humanity, living with a "we" rather than a "me" on our lips, in our hearts and acts? What does that look like in our daily life? Your partner wants a holiday and you are concerned about money. You can have a fight and see who wins. Or, honor the needs of both and dance in a fresh, creative way.

If you make your connection number one and the issue number two, you discover a way that works for both of you.

How would it feel to embrace all of our people?

The Jews, Muslims, Christians, Buddhists, atheists, environmentally and socially conscious or unconscious people? To be courageous and meet the whole spectrum of humanity, our own and another's, with all the horror and genius? See no stranger—get to know another's world, so different than our own. This is a spiritual practice, one that takes us beyond mere concepts and brings dignity to our walk. It's easy when we meet the pretty sides of people. And it is challenging to offer respect for another when we encounter the face of hardness and cruelty. For instance, when I found out that close to our home young girls are sex trafficked and used by grown men. We must not put a pink blanket over those acts and cover our eyes with an airy-fairy love light. But, we remember their basic humanness, even when they have forgotten it themselves—apparent by their abusive deeds. And from this connectedness, it's far easier to stand strong and speak up.

For, love does not mean to gloss over, deny or condone atrocious acts. When a teenage boy in our neighborhood was shot by a gang, the whole community was hurting, as we joined together to grieve his death and held the men accountable who committed this horrific crime. When the masses gathered on the streets of India to stop the rapes of women and girls, many of us on the other side of the world celebrated the beginning of a desperately needed change.

We do not have to like certain behaviors or even another's personality; nor does love entail niceness. But it is through love's power that we are able to stand fierce for what is true and just, while keeping the heart open, seeing another as a human being—even one who is buried in ignorance and behaves like an "ass."

***

One of my neighbors was a tough guy, angry most of the time, a lonely and unhappy man, who alienated people on our street and sowed anger wherever he went. Unfortunately, we shared a well on our adjoining properties. Because I hosted many people at my center he often turned the water off on me. So I was forced to deal with him. He screamed, threatened… his face turned red whilst spitting rage. At first I was intimidated and tried to be a good girl and please him. But, the more I shrank, the bigger he blew up. Then I got angry, too, so we fought, but that did not help. And I still had no water. As uncomfortable as it was to engage with him, I was challenged to step through his dramatic displays, into my center to find human connection. I reached into myself for some warmth and clarity that would cut through this insanity. By that, I felt his heart and could relate to him. Then I was friendly but fiercely firm, despite his threatening power game. At the end of our encounters he usually was calm and would invite me for tea. I had the slight suspicion that he kept turning off the water so I would visit him once a week for a chat, as he had no one to talk with. This sense of isolation and alienation so rampant in America can drive people nuts.

***

People aren't monsters, although they certainly can behave that way. What to do when you meet one like that? It comes down to an internal commitment we make with ourselves. It's a spiritual practice not to retaliate and perpetuate painful cycles for ourselves and others; instead to offer respect to any human we meet, no matter what. How do you do that in a bank? Look the clerk in the eyes and notice what connects you in this moment. Maybe the banker behaves like you are an object; don't treat him likewise, instead ask how his/her day is going. I've heard plenty of human stories breaking through the cement blocks in a bank.

Befriend the all too common human failures, successes, wonderfulness, foolishness and insecurities we all have. Stand up for justice, despite the discomfort that we encounter, especially when we are confronted with the dark side of humanity. And daily discover anew to live as if we belong together, with all the differences included.

We are connected by a thread far greater and stronger than the bonds of blood and creed. Love is that red thread. Here we meet.

Making a Difference

Her body shivered as she returned from ocean to land. Towels were quickly wrapped around her by caring hands. This sixteen-year-old girl swam with ten friends for a mile in ice-cold water in the Pacific Ocean in California. She was buzzing with excitement and shouted, "Yes! We made it! We raised the money for Lizzy!" This was a benefit swim for a young girl from their school with cancer, a girl these inspired teenagers had taken under their wing. Later she told me, "You know it just feels great to support Lizzy. I never thought I could swim the mile, but thinking that I am doing it for her gave me all the fire I needed to finish the race." Indeed, serving a greater cause gives strength.

***

Days before Winter Solstice many years ago we still had no tree. My daughter and I went to the Christmas tree lot; there we found a few leftover, crappy-looking trees leaning against a fence. It usually was a happy adventure for us to search for a live Christmas tree, one that, after the festivities were over, we would plant in nature. Both of us loved to decorate the tree with homemade ornaments, apples and red candles, as is the tradition in Germany. When those twenty candles were lit on Christmas Eve, they illuminated the room so beautifully and brought forth a magic that made my daughter's eyes glow each year again and again. It was one of the family rituals that held special meaning for us.

Yet, this year we could not find a living tree in a pot. I don't buy a cut one just to have for ten days and then throw it away. After all, the evergreen tree represents life. My daughter and I looked forlorn in that big empty lot on a cold afternoon. "What are we going to do, honey?" I mumbled in disappointment. Suddenly a grin appeared on her face as she said, "Mom, the spirit of Christmas is really about giving love. How about we do something different this year? With the money we have we could buy a goat for a family in Africa. Then those kids have milk to drink, they can sell the cheese, and then they can buy clothes." She became excited, "Can we do that?" I was thrilled. We ran home and sent our donation. A small act, but you know what she said to me on Christmas Eve? "This was even better than having our own Christmas tree. It made me real happy, Mama." Me too.

***

Spiritual awakening is lopsided, if it doesn't lead to engaging and taking action in the world. But, sometimes we think that the only way to make a difference is by doing something grand, and then we discount those smaller acts, or do nothing instead. Yet, one act from love has an impact, even if it does not make it into the hall of fame. We have talents and hearts and hands, through which we make a difference. Opportunities are found, if we look around.

I keep meeting people who grab hold of these moments as they move through the currents of time. I met a porter in New York who makes it a point to give each person who walks through the door a smile and a word of acknowledgement. Some notice and receive his gift and for a moment their spark is lit. The guy on our street, who looks rather disheveled, has a kind word for everyone who passes by, despite his own hardships and that some treat him like a worn rag. This may seem trivial, but acts from unconditional love leave a mark for those who receive and give it. Maybe they are far more important than we realize...

Sadly we sometimes dismiss the goodness others express, the beauty among us, the love that flows between us. We may take it for granted and do not appreciate what folks do, those who work tirelessly for a better world. Or we doubt that we have anything valuable to offer to another person and this world. Some work hard to make a difference and become plain worn-out. We do not need to save the world. Nor follow a "should" or do good deeds in an attempt to escape our own suffering or to prove we are a good enough. Our actions won't cause the effect we might hope for and love is on the sidelines if our own attachments are too strong.

Mirabelle sobbed when she heard of the shootings in a school, "Does anything ever change with us?" Sometimes we can get distraught about the messy state of affairs. It can be overwhelming to face the seeming endless suffering around us, trying to understand insanity with the question: "Why?" It's easy to become hopeless, when we hear so much news on TV of yet another crime or war. And when we hate the other bad guy over there, even in the name of justice, we just create more harm and the outcome is usually not beneficial for anyone. Or we hang our heads, not caring about anybody else but ourselves, maybe we even hide in a narcissistic spirituality that not only misses the mark, but a heart. Some disappear into a pink cloud, deny the shadow side of humans, and ignore the effects of their actions with defense and naïveté. Some try to rise above the human suffering with fancy concepts that feel empty and cold, or worse, they numb out and do not care, as if nothing and no one matters anymore.

Or, we turn toward humanity and respond from presence and love

You do not need to resolve all the suffering in the world. Remember when wiping one tear has made a difference—for your child or friend. We don't have to end all hunger, but one child fed is one more not going to sleep with a growling belly. It's a waste of time to wait until you are rich, so just give one coin for a greater cause than your own. We do not need to end all wars, but to stop violence with a fierce "no" makes a difference to the boy who is beaten up by bullies at his school. You do not have to point to all the troubles in our world; one creation of beauty inspires the one who walks into your life. Nor do we have to serve to exhaustion, for one step taken in service of love, always leaves a mark.

To tend to family and our relationships is of equal importance as working toward peace in the world. You don't have to clean up all the trash, but one plastic bag not taken at the checkout counter sets an example for the next customer and may save a turtle from drowning in the plastic sea. We do not need to be famous to have an impact, just shine your light without holding back. You do not need to lift up all the fallen people, but your presence and words of encouragement might help another. Nor do we have to have a thousand hands to help out. Giving a hand to the one who sits beside us or reaching out to someone who is on the edge already makes a world of difference. It starts simple, beginning right here in this moment with you.

There is much need and trouble in our world, it can be overwhelming and infuriating, but our hearts know what to give and what not to. Lean in and listen. To discover how we can best make a positive difference we have to make a bridge into an unknown world, to release our judgments and assumptions and be curious about: "How is the world of *You*?" To step beyond our own familiar worldview and what we imagine is beneficial for another.

***

Recently I heard a funny story that illuminates this:

An Italian charitable organization set up a project in a village in Africa; with the best intentions they tried to end starvation. They wanted to teach the African villagers how to create their own vegetable gardens, so in turn the people could feed themselves. The idea sounds good, right? But to their surprise, the villagers did not help to dig and plant the gardens. The volunteers planted the seedlings anyway, imagining that once these juicy Italian tomatoes were ripe, the people would get such a delicious taste, that they would be inspired enough to grow gardens themselves. The charity put in money, time and energy and excited volunteers; proudly thinking they were teaching the people an important thing.

Until one day, when the crop was just ready to be harvested. Helplessly they had to watch as the Hippos paid a visit to the pretty gardens and indulged their afternoon feast with the ripened Italian red tomatoes. Within the hour the gardens were trampled down and the crop was gone. The villagers had known about wildlife in the area and that is why no one had participated in this well-intended project, which had missed the point entirely. The charity learned from this failure, changed its ways, and has become very successful, because they now listen to the wisdom of the local people and work together with them.

***

We do not always know what the course of wise action is and what is helpful for another, so we need to look deeply, ask and listen with an open mind to the land and the people we desire to care for. The attitude of "I know better than you" or "I know it all" or "One method fits all" is not a useful approach and usually backfires. We discover what truly serves when we let their wisdom reveal what's beneficial for them. Use the tools of curiosity and inquiry. Then we can work together, each offering what they can bring to the shared meal. This is a far more empowering and effective approach.

And our innate wisdom knows what to offer and how to help, if we open to it, listen and act.

Maybe your teenager needs tough love, a boundary, that lets him know you won't let him wreck his life with drugs. A little one may need to be held when she has a tantrum so that she can release what is pent-up inside, instead of giving her a "time-out" once again. Your wife might need more attention from you, just letting her share without trying to fix the situation. Someone needs money to help them through a crisis, but rather than throwing coins into a tin, their self-esteem might increase when given a job to earn their keep. There are kids who live in dumpsters who don't need fancy toys, but if you fund a school that provides education, they will have a future. Even just a pair of shoes would already make a difference for those bloody feet.

When a call rings true in your heart, answer and take a step right where you are. Your gifts are waiting to be shared, and in so doing your own life becomes more fulfilling, rich and inspiring too.

If a cause ignites you, be it human rights, ecological activism, or social justice, by all means engage with what you've got. Join a group, give your time, money, energy, whatever you have to offer and whatever is right for you—get involved. Maybe what calls for your love isn't established as an organization? Even if no one has yet seen what you have recognized, simply start with one action, for one step leads to another. And if a revolution or a movement emerges from that—great, let's celebrate. If no one notices that you have given others a hand and you do not receive a deserved thank-you, don't give up. Know you have etched a mark in the world. If you give of yourself wholeheartedly, it is more than enough, even if the results are not always obvious. You may already be engaged in a project and have made an impact on humankind in a small or a big way. Just know that what you have done from your heart matters and has value. Thank-you on behalf of everyone. Every act of love has an impact often far greater than we realize.

Behold with honor your dream for humanity and the gift that only you can give. It is here for you to live, and may come true on a larger scale, when least expected, as you walk in growing presence and love—wherever you are and in whatever you do. Begin with you, in your home and in your community and then love your way further into this world. True change comes from the inside out, from one heart to another, from the grassroots it grows. Movements of positive change most often begin in kitchens and living rooms, when we are together with people who ignite the fires of love.

***

I stood on the ridge of the Apache reservation with a wise elder. The old days were long gone when they could roam freely in the wild with their tepees and traditions intact. Genocide and ongoing ill treatment through the white people and their government, the dry lands that they were forced to live upon, had left serious wounds in their psyche and a breakdown of their own culture. As the elder of her tribe she was seriously concerned for her people. Alcoholism had taken its toll and the suicide rate among their young was extremely high. But most Native American tribes and reservations receive no support; they are still the outcasts of society.

We talked for a long while into the setting sun. She was at a loss of what could be done to bring relief to this hopeless situation and asked me for help. We prayed together and she offered me a rare white eagle feather as a gift. In that moment an idea sparked. I had a friend who had time on her hands and she was good in organizing group events, so I contacted her to see if she wanted to get involved. Soon enough the three of us hatched a plan. We created an exchange program for the Apache teenagers with the European teenagers through the Findhorn Foundation.

And we saw how the native kids returned far more empowered, inspired and stronger than when they had left on their journey across the sea. They had been admired, respected and included by the European teenagers. The Native American kids found their way back to their roots, valuing their heritage and vowing to make a difference for their tribe. The suicide rates dropped. And the European kids experienced what it means to live in poverty, seeing firsthand injustice against a minority group perpetuated, and experiencing a tribe that cares and lives in simple ways. Both teenage groups learnt to build bridges across diverse cultures and began to heal the wounds of generations. The program was a success.

It began small, with a sharing from the heart, a prayer for help and a white eagle feather to show the way.

Love in Action

Small beginnings with great impact

This is how the following grassroots organizations grew from seed to tree:

Together Women Rise: Marsha and her women friends dined in a potluck style at a kitchen table together. They decided to donate the money they saved from not going out to a restaurant, to empower girls and women who live in extreme poverty in a developing country. One meal shared together became a foundation. At each dining-in evening the women gather and educate themselves about specific situations in developing countries such as India and Africa. Each month they choose a specific and well-researched grassroots project to fund. After six years Dining for Women has grown to seventy chapters across America, which have donated 3.3 million dollars, making a far-reaching impact in people's lives, one dining-in gathering at a time.

Pencils of Promise: This "for purpose" organization started small, too: with one little boy in India who wished for a pencil and a young man from America who was moved to act. He bought this seven-year-old boy a pencil and saw how happy it made the little fellow. And then... within several years, he had several schools in impoverished countries with more and more kids achieving literacy. Now these recipients read and write and contribute to the world in a way that would have been impossible without an education. This integrity organization, with its unique approach (combining both business and humanitarianism), has now grown into a global movement that affects many people's lives.

Sold—Human Trafficking: Jeffrey D. Brown travelled to Nepal and saw firsthand the sex trafficking of girls there. Young girls bought from uneducated, poor families under false pretense by pimps, who sell them to brothels in India. This business with girls aged between six and fourteen years old is tragically common around the world. Jeffrey dedicated his life to help the girls, to educate the families and to spread awareness. As an American film and television director, he created the film *Sold*, which has been screened meanwhile in major cities in America and Canada. He spends all his time, effort, energy, skill and money to raise awareness, to educate impoverished families and to build safe houses for the girls they rescue from the brothels and to offer trauma work to help them heal from such a horrific crime.

Ishara House: I have been supporting Ishara House since its humble beginning, now a thriving home in the Democratic Republic of the Congo for orphaned and vulnerable children. Clare's project began small and her strong commitment is inspiring. (Read more about how it all started in the "Voices of People and Saints" chapter.) The Congo has four million orphans—due to an extremely long ongoing war, poverty, malnutrition and disease. Most of the conflict in this country exists because of the fight for control over its vast mineral resources, of which the local people do not receive any benefit. Instead they suffer the consequences. Ishara House makes a dent in the sea of suffering and has welcomed forty children now. Little Ishara, the first child rescued, is now happily thriving in a safe and nurturing home.

Simple steps:

- What is your internal and external border of your love circumference for humanity? Which color, race, or culture do you leave out? Which part of humanity do you abhor, reject, judge or resist? Be honest with yourself. Which one do you have no care for? Which one do you feel drawn to and find easy to like? Notice what is evoked in you. Then reflect on that all these people are part of you, your world. What happens in your heart as you expand?
- Consider the basic human connection we share in every encounter today. Notice what happens in you and how you interact.
- What is a difference you can make in someone's life today? It could be as simple as a word of encouragement, a hand in support, or a listening ear. Make your action simple and concrete even if it means you have to go out of your way.
- What worthy cause is calling for you? Engage and involve yourself in ways you are able.
- Random acts of kindness are fun. Be creative and don't expect a return.
- Get to know one person a month who is different than you, in color, status, background or lifestyle. Be curious.

A guided meditation journey through the garden of humanity:
Sit with me for a while in the garden of humanity. Join on a bench nearby and let's look together to see what two eyes alone might not be able to recognize. With each breath, let your heart soften. Most of us are closed up, because we are afraid of being hurt. Isn't it in your tender heart too? And do you feel the longing for love in the eyes of

your fellow humans, often hidden behind the masks? Where do you sense it in your own body?

Yes, anger flares up in people and you too; and ignorance usually makes a bloody mess. Simply allow acceptance toward your own present experience—be it comfortable or uncomfortable—to envelop you. At times you might be scratching your head in confusion about others and yourself, so let's not figure out all the complications of different pathologies right now. Just stay with me for a while; let's go for a walk among our human friends. I understand, some do not seem like friends and have behaved in cruel and insane ways. Do you remember when you stumbled and messed up? And you may recognize the pain in other people's eyes and the tinge of sadness in your own heart. Speak silently, **"May I have compassion for others and myself."**

Stop for a moment, don't hurry away so fast from here, allow yourself to feel what is arising for you. Hold the pain with tenderness and refrain from trying to fix it, avoid it, run away or dump it on the next fellow over there. Offer breath, awareness and loving toward the ache. You might offer this presence to the friend who lies crumpled up in bed, all alone and finding it difficult to deal with sorrow. Compassion emerges as we embrace pain. Put your hand on your heart and turn toward the pain of humanity inside and all around. Speak silently, **"May I offer compassion toward human suffering."**

And as we continue to walk in the garden of humanity, now look over there, kids are playing happily! Shall we join in the laughter until our bellies ache, and roll with the children in the sand? Let's be so silly they will think we have gone mad! All we are doing is sharing joy, just because. People are drawn to us, as they too want some of the infectious fun that is bubbling up between us now. We need to laugh more often than not. What has this to do with embracing humanity you ask? Everything! How is your heart feeling right now? Speak to yourself, **"May I be happy and joyous. May you have joy. May we rejoice in life."**

*Do you see the person who is climbing the highest tree to reach for the stars? People who invented a car that drives using water; those who save the lives of violated children; those who are shining a light that ignites yours. Allow the wonder of the human spirit to fill you. Widen, by what you see and feel as we meet humanity. And take a peek behind the veils toward the one who painted the sunset in such glorious colors that could make even the sun jealous. That one who smiles and cries through every single face. Notice what you experience—be it numbness, joy, pain—and turn to others, who too experience this. What does it feel to welcome your own humanity and thereby the whole of humankind for a moment or two? Close the meditation by wishing for each person in the world, without exception, this, "**May we all be happy, may we be free of suffering.**"*

A Buddhist Prayer
May I be free of suffering. May I be happy.
May I experience joy and compassion.
May you be free of suffering. May you be happy.
May I offer compassion toward the pain.
May I grow joy for all.
May all beings everywhere be free of suffering.
May all beings in all realms be happy.

4. Service Rocks the World

Sacred activism and the great turning

Tears are flowing today. Glaciers are melting faster than ever, the Amazon is burning up by the minute, black people are beaten on the street, and children are used in brothels... You know what I am speaking about. When the Titanic hit the iceberg and began sinking, they pretended all was fine. When Hitler took the Jews into the gas chambers, they looked the other way. Who are they today? In each of us is denial, a defense to survive overwhelming situations. But some stay stuck in it and it destroys us. Spirituality divorced from life on earth is a bypass. And ignorance isn't bliss, it is our downfall. Yet, not all is lost and bleak. A great turning is emerging and life itself is rising up through many of us. A roar, fierce and wild, "Wake Up!" is shaking us. Not very polite... I guess "the great mother" has just had enough. Time to ring the bells, go to the streets, whatever love compels us to—don't hold back—live it now, my friends. Sleepy time is nice, but when the tidal wave arrives— the consequences of our actions—better to show up to give a hand. The time is now and it is up to each of us. For the love of all beings and all of our sakes, rise up.

Spirituality has often been used as a bypass to not take action in our world. But to become a bliss-addicted, disengaged couch potato is not what spirituality is about. On the other hand, activists without a practice of the heart and rooted in the nature of impermanence are fueled by anger whilst fighting against injustice. They end up exhausted, bitter. There is a different way. In sacred activism we root in the wealth of love, cultivate compassion and ignite passion to take liberating action *for* a worthy cause in our world.

My most serious question to people is: *What do you stand for? What is your life for?* Inquire openly, go deep, and be honest with yourself. And when the knowing from your soul emerges, act on it in the most immediate and simple way.

Sacred activism means rooting in what is sacred and taking wise action for change. We drop down into our being and from here we let the force of love move us. We meditate to rest and gain nourishment, insight and strength so we can stand up in the world, even when the whole tsunami of human conditioning hits us in the face. It's not a comfortable road if you sincerely want to awaken and make a difference in the world. Will you stand for love, even if you get killed for it? Sit with this inquiry question, for it will unleash you to be of actual service here on earth and to rise during these tumultuous times.

***

Once upon a time wild buffalo herds stampeded across the wild open prairies; a magnificent sight to behold, mighty animals not only in body, but in spirit as well. For the Native Americans the buffalo was the embodiment of sacrifice, providing flesh for food, skin for clothes and fur for a warm bed during cold winter months. Hunting was done in respect and prayers of gratitude were spoken with tobacco offerings in recognition of the gift this animal had given to sustain the life of the tribe. The indigenous people honored the truth that all beings are serving each other, each with a place and part to play on the grand wheel of life.

Most spiritual traditions point out the importance of service, as it is the natural way of life. Without it nothing and no one would flourish. Mothers serve by birthing and feeding a child, plants provide us with food and medicine, rivers and rains serve animals and humans alike, the song of creation flows on as we receive and give of ourselves.

I am writing at the California coast, one of the most stunning natural areas, as my eyes gaze across the ocean to Whale Rock: an ancient sacred site of the Native people, now protected as a nature sanctuary. Folks worked hard to preserve this land and it took many years of free labor to assure it would be safeguarded. The immense rock is shaped like a whale with a blowhole through which water spouts when the waves are high. It is one of my favorite spots to pray, offer ceremony and meditate; where many people come to sit and drink in the peace and the connection with all life. During the winter you can see the Humpback whales on the way to warmer waters, singing ancient wisdom that the Buddha and all true awakened teachers have shown: All beings are interdependent, each serving the one life we are part of.

Only by serving the wheel of life do we survive and thrive. We know this. Without nourishing a baby with milk and attention it would die. Someone offered it to you, so you can live today. I look at a bird's nest in the oak tree and the mother flies busily to and fro feeding her young with worms. The guy next door to my home leaves his house at six in the morning to do construction work, he does not like the labor per se, but he does it to provide food and shelter for his three children who depend on him.

"Me, myself and I," is a common road taken in our world, especially in cultures where independence is highly valued. Yet, taken to the extreme, this is a solo journey into isolation, disconnection and separation. Living for oneself alone is out of harmony with the truth of life and therefore causes suffering all around. Then love has no room, the heart and life just contract in a small, self-absorbed world and unhappiness mounts.

Service does not mean to give oneself up and behave like one has no worth, as often is a mistaken notion especially among women, nor is it about trying to earn brownie points by being a "do-gooder." It means to include the well-being of others and ourselves, to find our place and gift and offer it in service to the web of life. When we serve what is greater than ourselves — without conditions attached — we in turn become greater and happier as a result. Our innate qualities such as compassion, courage and understanding will grow. Abilities we did not know we had emerge. We step into living our true nature, and to top it off we have a beneficial impact on others and the world. A treasure is revealed when we walk right through difficulties, happiness follows suit, love flows naturally because the vessel is open. You wake with a "yes" upon your lips in the morning and feel a satiating sense of belonging by being part of the larger web of life. You are indeed.

***

I walked around like a sleep-deprived zombie. Due to "milk brain" I forgot everything from where I left my car and what I wanted to buy in the grocery store; and my clothes were usually stained from the throw-up and slobber of my sweet baby.

But I was in love with this glorious, helpless bundle, like a love-drunk I would do anything for her, even if I could barely remember what time of day it was and that I was wearing two different kinds of shoes. I carried her for nine months in my womb and then for nine months on my back, until my spine gave in. I wanted to make sure she received the holding and contact babies need. I could not get enough of watching in delight how she grew, and how she discovered the world with exuberance through her with big blue eyes. It made my discomforts seem insignificant. Taking parenting as a spiritual practice opened the door to a love I had never known before.

I wasn't prepared, however, to give up what also mattered to me in my late twenties — a project that I had successfully created — to travel to Guatemala and plant trees for peace with the locals and an international youth group and train them in spiritual leadership and stewardship practices. I was determined to lead the journey, all was set to go. I would just take my newborn baby along. Hey, why not? I was thoroughly mistaken. I had no idea what it meant to serve a wee little one, twenty-four/seven. It sounded so easy to breastfeed and change diapers; what was the big deal anyway?

Reality was different than imagined. I was lucky to take a five-minute shower once a day, and I lived in a state of continuous exhaustion. Maybe I would have been able to plant one tree in this land, stained with the blood of the indigenous people, but to lead a whole program with a newborn was out of the question. I was upset; I felt like I wasn't fulfilling my calling, that I wasn't doing anything important or of value, other than taking care of a child. I was a young mother, this had not been my plan and now I was stuck. I wondered if my life had just ended with motherhood. Yes. "My" life as I had known it had ended with her birth and my plans crumbled to dust. I had wanted to be of service, but my way, not like this. Until I was humbled to realize that raising this beautiful girl was teaching me about true love and offered me a perfect opportunity to be of service. It was a thorough training for eighteen years and continues on.

***

Parenting is a long road of service, and not easy. If approached as a spiritual path, it's the highway into true love.

When being of service as a parent, we must learn to respond to what is needed: such as holding our child when he or she is scared, dropping plans in an instant—even when it is inconvenient—and attending to our child first. When you serve more than your own self, you grow an internal discipline not to let your anger out on someone more vulnerable than you, even though you might feel like exploding, when your best dishes are shattered and the bathroom is flooded yet once again. You learn to set healthy boundaries, even when you get a full-blown tantrum in reaction, because love is more important to you than convenience and comfort. Or, your teenager may hate you if you draw a line (don't worry, this too will pass). You might work overtime in a job that isn't to your liking to provide for those who depend on you. And often there is no one to cheer you on, or to appreciate what you give. The journey of conscious parenthood is a tough training in unconditional love. If you have been there or still are, I bow to you.

But, you do not have to become a parent to be of service in the world.

There are a thousand ways to kneel and kiss the ground, to do what your soul calls for

It can be to dedicate your energy and resources to a certain cause: such as finding ingenious ways to end pollution; to create technology to help humanity; to make music that evokes beauty; or to bring peace where there is war. It may mean taking good care of your sick friend. Maybe you serve people who are less fortunate than you. Or, you awaken your passion and take a stand for justice.

Service is often the least liked word

It sounds like heavy effort, sacrifice and losing yourself in endless caregiving or saving lives or projects. Often it is accompanied with a "should." No wonder this word isn't attractive. But there is a difference between service with a little "s" and a big "S." Serving from our little personalities is a strain and takes a toll on our health and well-being. When you make your cause, your child or someone else, more important than life itself, you will feel no joy over time. It becomes a drag to get up in the mornings for the job you hate. Being there for others gives no energy, but drains you. You become resentful, when your service is not acknowledged and paid back.

However, when you serve from the big "S," which means your dedication is to serve life, the truth and love itself, you are lifted. Essentially, you offer and surrender your life unto the very life that is breathing and living you. One and the same. It's devotion. This way includes your own well-being too; it inspires and gives you energy.

Ask in the mornings upon waking, "Show me how I can be of service, how can I be truly helpful?" Turn to your inmost being, to Spirit, to guide you. The answer might be to take a day off to rest so you can fill your own cup. Or, to take food to the homeless nearby. Maybe the answer is to slow down and meditate in silence. Or, you are guided to tithe your monies monthly. When serving the big "S," you feel less attached to the outcome of your actions, as you lay the fruits of your labors as an offering onto the altar of love. You are in the flow of life, by letting Spirit guide you regarding who, what and how to serve. Service to love (or God, the dharma—use whatever name resonates most for you) is one of the most powerful intentions you can make: it offers you happiness without a cause; it will challenge you to grow your capacities; it ignites a fire of passion in you; and it leads you to take wise action in benefit to all, even when it is uncomfortable.

Mary was furious and crying at the same time, when she spoke of the latest disasters from USA policies that cause even more suffering immigrants and the environment. "We are already on the brink, why keep sinking the Titanic even further? Most of my young friends feel overwhelmed and infuriated in the face of this suffering created by narcissistic greedy sharks that are in power. The earth is already plundered, why destroy the rest? Because of those idiots we won't have a world in which we even have the basics to survive and thrive." She is right and it is natural to feel outraged and saddened when ignorance wrecks lives. If we know what is at stake and if we care, just like Mary, we will feel all this and more.

How can we be of service when faced with the magnitude of problems on our planet and so little time left?

Get frantically busy, run or hide, too overwhelmed to do a thing? Or, to say, "It's just a dream or delusion anyway," and float away? How do we respond from our true nature and not react from fear? Sacred activism is not for the fainthearted but for those who dare to love deeply, passionately. Spiritual warriors are rising in this time, and more and more people are waking and taking the lead to turn the wheel.

We are in the time of the great unraveling and turning as prophesied by the Hopis, the Tibetans and others. This time has been foretold long ago, as one of the most extreme ones—when lies are worshipped as truth, when the earth is ravaged and greed has taken over across the lands and hearts. It is said that in a time when our mere survival is hanging on a thread, great female and male warriors will rise. They will wield the weapons of truth and compassion. They will walk fearlessly into the darkest of the dark and dismantle false structures to bring a new dawning for humanity. They will awaken the people to turn the tide in our world.

Are you one of those brave ones who dares to show up? Yes, we are on the edge and where it will go depends on each of us. How do we serve when faced with such bleakness; how do we find power and not drown or numb out? As sacred activists we need the weapons of great compassion and clear awareness to be able to cut through delusion and to dismantle systems that cause harm. (You can read more on this in "Foundation Stones.") We must have a sound spiritual practice to take refuge in, guidance and a community to be sustained by during such a time, so we don't burn out or get consumed by despair.

We need fierce love in the face of adversity, a love that can say, "This shall not pass." To do so, our worst foe becomes our best ally: anger. Neither squash your rage, nor act it out on anyone. It contains life-giving energy for action, once you learn to harness it. Be present with it, feel it fully and allow it to move through your body. It will free you up and give you power to make a stand and to act. Of course we need the tenderness of an open heart, so we are rooted in compassion and have access to greater intelligence to guide the way. Our minds become brilliant when dedicated to serving the truth. That is how we navigate through treacherous territories with grace. Most of all we do need each other for support, inspiration and guidance. We don't walk alone, but take each other's hands and serve life together. A far greater force and joy is available then. Let the Spirit guide us—that which helps us to feel that we are loved and carried by life no matter what hell breaks loose—and allow the greater power to move us in service to life itself. This might just turn our sinking ship around, or at the least it will help us to rise in love together.

Ultimately service with the big "S" is love in action. It is a deep bowing before the sacred mystery and to simply serve life itself, no matter what happens, not knowing what you are called to do and what the outcome is. It may not look grand; there might be no glory and fame, no ribbons or trophies to decorate a room with. But you will stand with a great heart in a life fulfilled. A life of love lived spreads through generations, touching people and creatures far beyond the horizon of what we see; across the web of life your devotion and selfless acts flow. If we could see beyond the veils of time and space, we would be amazed what one life lived in service actually does in benefit to all.

Love in Action

Use this inquiry practice:
"What do I stand for? What is my life for?" Let the answers of your mind pass by, drop below and allow the voice of your being to emerge.

Ask daily:
"Show me how I can be of service." Watch for signs and what appears during your day. Maybe you meet a person on the train and you offer words of comfort. Or, you find a stray kitten and take it home. Maybe in a discussion with a friend your next step of action becomes clear. Maybe during an evening meditation your purpose on earth is revealed to you.

Gather your talents and gifts to be of service:
Look at what you are naturally inclined to do and what comes easy for you. This might be music or writing or leading. Grow your talents. Offer them to a higher cause, in service to life and love itself. (Read more about this in "Igniting the Fire.")

If stuck in self-absorption:
Again, without judging, just notice that you have contracted and been busy circling around yourself. Give it breath and acknowledgement. Pay attention to what you feel and drench the fear with warm attentiveness. Hold the small self in compassion. But do not let it lead your life. Pay attention to what else is here. And what you wish to serve.

Ask yourself, "What am I living for?"
This inquiry question can lift you to higher ground and free you from the shackles that bind. It will give you courage and strength to take bold steps in life.

You matter too:
Taking good care of yourself is essential. No one is served if you burn out. Fill your cup, eat good food, take a nap, play with friends, meditate and go into nature. If your cup is full it overflows and serves others too.

Service isn't about you:
"What and whom am I serving?" Ask this question when you are showing up to be of service. For example, you are leading a group. Don't do what you think you want or imagine is the right method. Look at the group deeply and ask, "What is most

beneficial to do in this situation?" Or, you can ask this when you are in a situation that requires your help, "What is needed and important here?" Even if the task isn't what you most like to do—you do it anyway. Do not make service about you, about looking good and being liked, nor about your personal preferences. Or else you miss the point.

A spiritual warrior practice:

This is a spiritual practice to harness power, clarity, truth and bravery from the energy called anger. Turn from the story to meet directly your fury. Feel it and stay present. Notice where the sensation is most alive in your body. It often is found in your belly or solar plexus. Breathe with the anger; let it move through your body. You might feel strong sensations, burning, just stay present and allow it to move. Express the energy through movement, like beat a cushion. Let the anger express itself through your voice and sound. Don't try to force it, nor diminish the power. Let it move and drench it with breath, presence and your repeated Yes. As this energy is liberated you will feel intense power surging through your body. Don't collapse, stay with its fierceness, as if a lioness or lion is waking up in you. Once you feel this raw power then let words come from the deeper truth. Let yourself be surprised, these words might not be familiar to you. It is life itself speaking through you. Maybe she roars: enough. The line is here. Just feel this, allow this, and hear and bow to this. And then rest into this life-giving power from source itself. At some point it will move you into action naturally. You will know what to say or do in the world and you will have the strength and wisdom to carry it out. This power has nothing to do with control, nor with hate or vengeance or any story the mind may play.

It cuts through the BS and delusion; it shoots an arrow of truth and hits the mark. It frees you to take inspired and wise action in the world and your life.

What moves you deeply?

It does not have to be what you perceive as a greater cause. Maybe your heart is crying for people who are hungry, for those who are vulnerable and have no one to defend their rights, or you are simply moved by music. Follow that opening in your heart; follow that thread and calling, for it is your soul beckoning you to a greater life, in service to all.

Sacred activism:

This implies to realize our interconnectedness and to live in kinship with all life. We honor, protect and care for what is precious in all of life. We act from connection. How do we create change? Being present and wholehearted leads us into connection. Inner connection combined with skillful means supports us to take inspired, wise and powerful action. This creates impactful change in the world.

Use a daily prayer for all beings:

"May all beings be free from suffering. May all beings be happy. May all have food to eat and a place to rest at night. May I have compassion and live in benefit to all." (Buddhist Prayer)

Or chant the ancient Hindu Prayer for peace: *"Lokah Samastha Sukhino Bahvantu."* And bless the land and people with your love wherever you go.

I dedicate the merit of this book to the benefit of you, all sentient beings and unto the feet of love.

Epilogue

Thank you for reading this book. I hope it sparked your flame, touched your heart, lifted you and gave you skills to make a difference. Who you are, your awakening, healing and embodiment, and engagement, and what you live matter in this time of the great turning. For your own sake and all beings. I am glad you are here, part of this epic movement — to unleash love in a world on the edge!

And if you want to learn more deeply from this beautiful, integrated spiritual path I teach, or attend a retreat or training, feel free to contact us here: nicolaamadora.com.

One sunny or stormy day our paths may cross, and until then may your life be bountifully blessed!

My love is with you, Nicola Amadora

Acknowledgements

The kindness and generosity of many hearts and hands have given birth to this book. I have deep appreciation for the great teachers who showed me the way of love. I learnt from them in person and they left an irreversible mark on my life. Such as my beloved Mary Magdalene Lady, Ammachi, The Dalai Lama, Thich Nhat Hahn, Pir Vilayat Khan, Tom Yellowtale, Sai Baba, my wise old Shaman Lady who doesn't want to be named, Tsultrim Allione, Mother Teresa, the Yoginis in the Himalayas, and others like Anandamayi Ma, Yogananda, Bruno Groening, and Yeshua who already left their bodies behind to grace us from near and afar.

I honor my less known teachers of love, who have touched me in significant or ordinary ways. I met them on my walk through this world, bus drivers, shopkeepers, children, neighbors, friends and foe alike. I am grateful for my daughter Yemaya, being a mother to you taught me more about living love than anything else.

I treasure my wild animal friends, Freddie the dolphin in Scotland, the wild mountain lion mama with her cub, the anaconda snake in the Amazon, the grizzly bear who shared his blueberries with me, the wild horses, Magic and Ganesha my horses, Jenny the Humpback Whale, Little Buddha our donkey, my cats and all the many creatures who showed me intimately the power of connection and how to live in communion with all of life.

I offer my heartfelt thanks to dear ones and friends who supported this book. Because of your encouragement and active help I kept going. I bow to you: Clare C., Lisa L., Marlies C., Joy T., Elizabeth P., Pedro C., Lori S., Kelley S., Kelli S., Esther C., Philip L., Barbara S., Sergio B., Lisa G., Lindy J., Cece McN.,

Alice L., Laura P., Rachel S., Charlene N., Christie C., David G., Jorge, Annie B., and my blessed angel Michael R.

I am grateful to my wonderful and diligent editor Magdalena Montage. It was such a joy to work with you. Thank you to the additional editing hands of my precious assistant Marlene Wolf, Ilya Munn, Doug Childers, and the editors of JH publishing.

I owe my deep gratitude to all my clients and students, and my global sangha. This book would not exist without you.

For your support and believing in me I am forever thankful, Dad. You always encouraged me to write books. And here it is!

Appendix

A Handy List of Recommended Spiritual, Environmental and Social Change Organizations

Spiritual Organizations:

Spirit Rock https://www.spiritrock.org/
A Buddhist insight meditation center founded by Jack Kornfield, providing practitioners with teachings to manifest wisdom and compassion in all aspects of their lives.

Association for Spiritual Integrity https://www.spiritual-integrity.org/
The ASI is an evolving force in spiritual ethical education so that there is greater integrity and professionalism within the modern spiritual landscape.

Ammachi https://amma.org/
Amma teaches love and embraces people of all walks into her arms. The organization has established "Embracing the World®" as a global network of local and regional charitable organizations and projects, currently active in more than 40 countries around the world.

Bruno Groening Circle of Friends https://www.bruno-groening.org/en
A worldwide network for help and healing on the spiritual path through the teaching of Bruno Groening. Free of charge, medically verifiable and nondenominational.

Ananda Foundation https://www.ananda.it/en/
Based on the teachings of Paramahansa Yogananda offering meditation and yoga education. Communities are established in the USA and Europe.

Findhorn Foundation https://www.findhorn.org
A charitable trust, spiritual educational center and NGO recognized ecovillage. One of the oldest and largest spiritual

communities. Everyday life is guided by the inner voice of spirit, they work in co-creation with the intelligence of nature and take inspired action towards their vision of a better world.

Environmental Action Organizations:

Pachamama Alliance https://www.pachamama.org/
Empowers indigenous people of the Amazon rainforest to preserve their lands and culture, and educates to bring forth a thriving, just and sustainable world.

One Tree Planted https://onetreeplanted.org/
An environmental charity dedicated to making it easier for individuals and businesses to give back to the environment, create a healthier climate, protect biodiversity and help reforestation efforts around the world. All by planting trees!

Earth Guardians https://www.earthguardians.org/
They inspire and train diverse youth to be effective leaders in the environmental, climate and social justice movements. Through art, music, storytelling, civic engagement, and legal action, they are creating impactful solutions to some of the most critical issues we face as a global community.

Women's Earth Alliance https://womensearthalliance.org/
WEA equips women with the skills and tools they need to protect our Earth and strengthen communities from the inside out.

Jane Goodall Institute https://www.janegoodall.org/
They are a global community conservation organization that advances the vision and work of Dr. Jane Goodall. By protecting chimpanzees and inspiring people to conserve the natural world we all share, they improve the lives of people, animals and the environment.

Greenpeace International https://www.greenpeace.org/international/
A global movement fighting actively for climate justice, protection of the oceans, sustainable food, renewable energy and more.

Dolphin Spirit https://dolphinspirit.org/
Protecting wild dolphins and whales. Fighting for release of captured dolphins, orcas and whales.
Heirs to the Ocean https://h2oo.org/
Youth in action to change the ocean and water crisis.

Social Justice Organizations:
Amnesty International https://www.amnesty.org/en/
Is a global movement of more than 7 million people who take injustice personally. They are campaigning for a world where human rights are enjoyed by all.
Together Women Rise (formerly Dining For Women) https://togetherwomenrise.org
Is a global giving circle dedicated to eradicating poverty among women and girls in the developing world. Together Women Rise funds grassroots organizations that empower women and girls and promote gender equity.
Shared Hope https://sharedhope.org
A venue and voice for survivors of sex trafficking.
City of Joy https://www.cityofjoycongo.org
A transformational leadership community for women survivors of violence, located in the Congo (DRC). City of Joy heals women from their past trauma through therapy and life skills programming while providing them with the essential ingredients needed to move forward in life, love and community.
Heifer International https://www.heifer.org
Works in 21 countries around the world alongside local farmers and business owners. Supporting farmers and communities to envision their futures, providing training to improve the quantity and quality of the goods they produce, and connections to market to increase sales and incomes.
Bumi Sehat https://bumisehat.org
By caring for the smallest citizens of Earth—babies at birth—they are building peace: one mother, one child, one family at

a time. Their mission is to improve the quality of life and to encourage peace.

Limitless Horizon ixil https://limitlesshorizonsixil.org

Creating opportunities for the indigenous youth, women, and families of Chajul, Guatemala, to develop the academic and professional skills needed to effect change in their lives and community.

BIPOC https://www.thebipocproject.org/

The BIPOC Project aims to build authentic and lasting solidarity among Black, Indigenous and People of Color (BIPOC), in order to undo Native invisibility, anti-Blackness, dismantle white supremacy and advance racial justice.

About the Author

Nicola Amadora, PhD, offers a refreshingly real and embodied way of spirituality to unleash love for the great turning in our lives and this world. For three decades she has been guiding thousands of people as a Spiritual Teacher, Psychologist, and Speaker worldwide. She is the founder of Living Connection and the Deep Feminine Way, and is the author of *Nothing but Love*, truth poetry from the heart. When she isn't teaching, she loves to write and ride horses in the wild. If you want to know about Nicola's labor of love or host her, contact her team at nicolaamadora.com.

O-BOOKS

SPIRITUALITY

O is a symbol of the world, of oneness and unity; this eye represents knowledge and insight. We publish titles on general spirituality and living a spiritual life. We aim to inform and help you on your own journey in this life.

If you have enjoyed this book, why not tell other readers by posting a review on your preferred book site?

Recent bestsellers from O-Books are:

Heart of Tantric Sex
Diana Richardson
Revealing Eastern secrets of deep love and intimacy to Western couples.
Paperback: 978-1-90381-637-0 ebook: 978-1-84694-637-0

Crystal Prescriptions
The A-Z guide to over 1,200 symptoms and their healing crystals
Judy Hall
The first in the popular series of eight books, this handy little guide is packed as tight as a pill-bottle with crystal remedies for ailments.
Paperback: 978-1-90504-740-6 ebook: 978-1-84694-629-5

Take Me To Truth
Undoing the Ego
Nouk Sanchez, Tomas Vieira
The best-selling step-by-step book on shedding the Ego, using the
teachings of *A Course In Miracles*.
Paperback: 978-1-84694-050-7 ebook: 978-1-84694-654-7

The 7 Myths about Love...Actually!
The Journey from your HEAD to the HEART of your SOUL
Mike George
Smashes all the myths about LOVE.
Paperback: 978-1-84694-288-4 ebook: 978-1-84694-682-0

The Holy Spirit's Interpretation of the New Testament
A Course in Understanding and Acceptance
Regina Dawn Akers
Following on from the strength of *A Course In Miracles*, NTI
teaches us how to experience the love and oneness of God.
Paperback: 978-1-84694-085-9 ebook: 978-1-78099-083-5

The Message of A Course In Miracles
A translation of the Text in plain language
Elizabeth A. Cronkhite
A translation of *A Course In Miracles* into plain, everyday
language for anyone seeking inner peace. The companion
volume, *Practicing A Course In Miracles*, offers practical lessons
and mentoring.
Paperback: 978-1-84694-319-5 ebook: 978-1-84694-642-4

Your Simple Path
Find Happiness in every step
Ian Tucker
A guide to helping us reconnect with what is really important in
our lives.
Paperback: 978-1-78279-349-6 ebook: 978-1-78279-348-9

365 Days of Wisdom
Daily Messages To Inspire You Through The Year
Dadi Janki
Daily messages which cool the mind, warm the heart and guide
you along your journey.
Paperback: 978-1-84694-863-3 ebook: 978-1-84694-864-0

Body of Wisdom
Women's Spiritual Power and How it Serves
Hilary Hart
Bringing together the dreams and experiences of women across
the world with today's most visionary spiritual teachers.
Paperback: 978-1-78099-696-7 ebook: 978-1-78099-695-0

Dying to Be Free
From Enforced Secrecy to Near Death to True Transformation
Hannah Robinson
After an unexpected accident and near-death experience, Hannah
Robinson found herself radically transforming her life, while a
remarkable new insight altered her relationship with her father, a
practising Catholic priest.
Paperback: 978-1-78535-254-6 ebook: 978-1-78535-255-3

The Ecology of the Soul
A Manual of Peace, Power and Personal Growth for Real People
in the Real World
Aidan Walker
Balance your own inner Ecology of the Soul to regain your
natural state of peace, power and wellbeing.
Paperback: 978-1-78279-850-7 ebook: 978-1-78279-849-1

Not I, Not other than I
The Life and Teachings of Russel Williams
Steve Taylor, Russel Williams
The miraculous life and inspiring teachings of one of the World's
greatest living Sages.
Paperback: 978-1-78279-729-6 ebook: 978-1-78279-728-9

On the Other Side of Love
A woman's unconventional journey towards wisdom
Muriel Maufroy
When life has lost all meaning, what do you do?
Paperback: 978-1-78535-281-2 ebook: 978-1-78535-282-9

Practicing A Course In Miracles
A translation of the Workbook in plain language, with
mentor's notes
Elizabeth A. Cronkhite
The practical second and third volumes of The Plain-Language
A Course In Miracles.
Paperback: 978-1-84694-403-1 ebook: 978-1-78099-072-9

Quantum Bliss
The Quantum Mechanics of Happiness, Abundance, and Health
George S. Mentz
Quantum Bliss is the breakthrough summary of success and
spirituality secrets that customers have been waiting for.
Paperback: 978-1-78535-203-4 ebook: 978-1-78535-204-1

The Upside Down Mountain
Mags MacKean
A must-read for anyone weary of chasing success and happiness
– one woman's inspirational journey swapping the uphill slog for
the downhill slope.
Paperback: 978-1-78535-171-6 ebook: 978-1-78535-172-3

Your Personal Tuning Fork
The Endocrine System
Deborah Bates
Discover your body's health secret, the endocrine system, and
'twang' your way to sustainable health!
Paperback: 978-1-84694-503-8 ebook: 978-1-78099-697-4

Readers of ebooks can buy or view any of these bestsellers by
clicking on the live link in the title. Most titles are published
in paperback and as an ebook. Paperbacks are available in
traditional bookshops. Both print and ebook formats are
available online.
Find more titles and sign up to our readers' newsletter at
http://www.johnhuntpublishing.com/mind-body-spirit
Follow us on Facebook at https://www.facebook.com/OBooks/
and Twitter at https://twitter.com/obooks